# חמש מגלות

# THE FIVE MEGILLOTH

SONG OF SONGS
RUTH
LAMENTATIONS
ECCLESIASTES
ESTHER

SONCINO BOOKS OF THE BIBLE
EDITOR: REV. DR. A. COHEN, M.A., Ph.D., D.H.L.

# The Five Megilloth

HEBREW TEXT & ENGLISH TRANSLATION
WITH INTRODUCTIONS AND
COMMENTARY

*Edited by*
THE REV. DR. A. COHEN, M.A., Ph.D., D.H.L.

SONG OF SONGS
RUTH
LAMENTATIONS
ECCLESIASTES
ESTHER

THE SONCINO PRESS
LONDON · JERUSALEM · NEW YORK

FIRST EDITION 1946
SECOND IMPRESSION 1952
THIRD IMPRESSION 1959
FOURTH IMPRESSION 1961
FIFTH IMPRESSION 1965
SIXTH IMPRESSION 1966
SEVENTH IMPRESSION 1967
EIGHTH IMPRESSION 1968
NINTH IMPRESSION 1970
TENTH IMPRESSION 1971
ELEVENTH IMPRESSION 1974
TWELFTH IMPRESSION 1975

*PUBLISHERS' NOTE*

*Thanks are due to the Jewish Publication Society of America for permission to use their very beautiful English text of the Scriptures.*

*All rights reserved including the right to reproduce this book or parts thereof in any form*

PRINTED IN GREAT BRITAIN BY
THE WHITEFRIARS PRESS LTD
LONDON AND TONBRIDGE

## FOREWORD BY THE GENERAL EDITOR

THIS is the third volume of THE SONCINO BOOKS OF THE BIBLE and contains the Five Scrolls, *Song of Songs*, *Ruth*, *Lamentations*, *Ecclesiastes* and *Esther*. These small compositions illustrate the varied character of the literary style and theme, in poetry and prose, of the Scriptural writers.

The series is distinctive in the following respects:

(*i*) Each volume contains the Hebrew text and English translation together with the commentary. (*ii*) The exposition is designed primarily for the ordinary reader of the Bible rather than for the student, and aims at providing this class of reader with requisite direction for the understanding and appreciation of the Biblical Book. (*iii*) The commentary is invariably based upon the received Hebrew text. When this presents difficulties, the most probable translation and interpretation are suggested, without resort to textual emendation. (*iv*) It offers a *Jewish* commentary. Without neglecting the valuable work of Christian expositors, it takes into account the exegesis of the Talmudical Rabbis as well as of the leading Jewish commentators.

All Biblical references are cited according to chapter and verse as in the Hebrew Bible. It is unfortunate that, unlike the American-Jewish translation, the English Authorized and Revised Versions, although made direct from the Hebrew text, did not conform to its chapter divisions. An undesirable complication was thereby introduced into Bible study. In the Hebrew the longer headings of the Psalms are counted as a separate verse; consequently Ps. xxxiv. 12, e.g., corresponds to verse 11 in A.V. and R.V. It is also necessary to take into account a marginal note like that found against 1 Kings iv. 21, 'ch. v. 1 in Heb.', so that the Hebrew 1 Kings v. 14 tallies with iv. 34 in the English.

It is hoped that this Commentary, though more particularly planned for the needs of Jews, will prove helpful to all who desire a fuller knowledge of the Bible, irrespective of their creed.

A. COHEN

## CONTENTS

# שיר השירים

# THE SONG OF SONGS

INTRODUCTION AND COMMENTARY

*by*

RABBI DR. S. M. LEHRMAN, M.A., Ph.D.

# INTRODUCTION

### AUTHORSHIP

TRADITION assigns to king Solomon the authorship of this Book, as well as of Proverbs and Ecclesiastes. According to one Rabbi in the Midrash, Song of Songs was composed in his youth, 'for it is the way of the world that when a man is young he composes songs of love. As he advances in years, he likes to couch his wisdom in maxims and aphorisms, and it is only when he becomes an old man that he speaks of the vanity of things.' Support for this traditional view of royal authorship is found in 1 Kings v. 11f. where it is stated, *And he* (Solomon) *was wiser than all men . . . he spoke three thousand proverbs and his songs were a thousand and five.* Moreover, apart from the opening verse which specifically claims Solomon as the author, there are several other references to the king in this Book (cf. i. 5, iii. 7, 9, 11, viii. 11, 12).

Objection has been raised to this claim on several grounds. Firstly, that it was customary in ancient times to attach a famous name to an anonymous work in the hope that it would have greater authority. Secondly, evidence of style and language points to an age later than the Kingship in Israel; in fact, to the Hasmonean times when many Greek words had been naturalized into Hebrew. On this account, scholars like Grätz, followed in our time by Klausner, attributed the Book to the period of the Second Temple, in the reign of Antiochus III. Such a view, however, has no solid foundation. The shortened form of the relative pronoun, e.g. which occurs often in this Book (cf. i. 6, 12, ii. 7, iii. 1, iv. 1) is also found in the earliest Biblical Books (cf. Gen. vi. 3; Judges v. 7, vi. 17, vii. 12, viii. 26, etc.).

A more serious objection against the traditional view is that the Book does not constitute a single whole. The various sections succeed one another without logical sequence, giving the appearance of a patchwork of incongruous fragments. This led the German poet and scholar Herder to treat the Book as a string of independent lyrics, a kind of anthology of rustic love-poems current in northern Palestine and entirely dissociated with Solomon and his court. Yet the Book does possess a unity—of ardent love, abundance of imagery, vivacity of movement, pleading tones and warm passion. Equally groundless is the objection that the Book is devoid of any explicit reference pointing to the fact that the authorship is Israelite, and also that there is no mention therein either of the God or Faith of Israel. It bears traces of composition in the North of Palestine, where life was less religious than in Judah. Besides, there was no call to parade religion in a Book which tells of human lovers.

### THE NARRATIVE

Despite problems of authorship and interpretation, the story is briefly told. It describes the trials of a beautiful peasant maiden from Shunem, or Shulem, who was employed by her mother and brothers as a shepherdess to their flock of goats. She had fallen in love with a shepherd of the same village, but the brothers did not look with approval on the union. They, accordingly, transferred her services from the pasture to the vineyards, in the hope that there her meetings with her lover would not be possible. One day, as she was tending the vines, she was seen by the servants of king Solomon, when he chanced to pass the village on his way to his summer resort in Lebanon. Impressed by her beauty, they try to persuade her to accompany them. She refuses and is finally led away as a captive to the king's chambers. No sooner does the king behold her, when he, too, falls violently in love with her. He sings her beauty and uses all his endeavours to induce her to abandon her shepherd for the love and wealth he can shower upon her. The ladies of the court also join in trying to dislodge her love for her humble swain. Her heart, however, belongs to him and she remains steadfast.

During her stay in the palace, she yearns for her lover and is tantalized by the taunts of the ladies of the court that he has rejected her. In her agitated state of mind she speaks to him as if he were in her presence, and even dreams that he has come to rescue her and escort her back to her mother's home. Awaking from her dream, she rushes out of her chamber to seek him in the streets where she is roughly treated by the watchmen of the city, who misjudge her character.

When the king is finally convinced of the constancy of her love for the shepherd, he dismisses her from his presence and allows her to return home. She is now joined by her lover and, leaning on his arm, approaches Shunem where a warm welcome awaits her. They come upon the scenes so dear to them, and she recounts the vicissitudes through which she had lately passed. The story ends on a triumphant note. Not only could her love not be extinguished by the temptations offered by the king, but she also assures her brothers that their solicitude for her virtue was unwarranted. She has proved that love is capable of heroic endurance. The tale she tells to their assembled friends makes a strong protest against the luxury and vice of the court, and pays testimony to the beauty and dignity of pure love and fidelity.

### ITS CHARACTERISTICS

Such is the story in its barest outline; details are described in the following pages, from which it will be seen that the contents may be grouped into various divisions. Though the number of these sections varies with the whim of many a commentator, these are usually given as five. The first is from i. 1 to ii. 7; the second from ii. 8 to iii. 5; the third from iii. 6 to v. 1; the fourth from v. 2 to vi. 3; and the fifth from vi. 4 to viii. 7. The epilogue consists of the last seven verses (viii. 8-14). Budde, e.g. who accepts Wetzstein's theory that the Book is a collection of songs sung at wedding celebrations, divides the contents into twenty-three parts consisting of choruses and snatches of songs which were once popular. The strongest refutation of such a theory is that the nobility of thought and sublimity of expression that permeate every utterance of the lovers were not characteristic of the masses who abandoned themselves to riot and sensuousness at marriage-feasts in Syria and other lands of the East.

A close study of the Book will reveal why it has become, next to the Psalms, the most popular and beloved section of the Bible. Yet no two Books could be more different; for whereas that ascribed to David holds up the mirror to every faithful heart, that ascribed to his illustrious son, seemingly, has no direct connection with religion. Nevertheless the love between a man and a maid, which it so vividly depicts, is so holy and beautiful, that the magic of its words can only be described as heavenly. In fact, Rabbi Akiba declared that if the other Books of the Bible are holy, the Song of Songs is 'holy of holies' (Megillah 7a). As if this were not praise enough, this greatest of Jewish sages added that 'the whole world attained its supreme value only on the day when the Song of Songs was given to Israel' (Yadaim iii. 5).

### ITS INTERPRETATION

From early times it was felt that this story possessed an allegorical interpretation; otherwise the inclusion of a secular love-tale in the Biblical canon could hardly be justified. The Midrash and Targum, followed by the mediæval Jewish commentators, understood the Book as depicting the spiritual marriage between God and Israel after the Revelation at Sinai. Hosea ii. 4, 21, Isaiah lxii. 5, Jeremiah ii. 2 and Ezekiel xvi. 8 spoke of the relationship between Israel and God in terms of that between a bride and her groom, and often in the Bible the faithlessness of Israel was denounced in the language of marital infidelity. Philo, the Jewish philosopher of Alexandria, had interpreted the whole of Scripture in an allegorical vein, and it is worthy of note that even a rational thinker like Maimonides cited many verses of the Song of Songs giving them an homiletical meaning.

This allegorical interpretation was forcefully upheld by the Rabbis, one Talmudic passage even asserting that 'he who recites any of the verses as a wine-song at a feast brings evil into the world' (Sanh. 101*a*). According to the Targum, the first half of the poem was a symbolical picture of the history of Israel before the captivity, and the second half presented a prophetic view of the subsequent fortunes of the nation. It must be confessed, however, that this forced mystical interpretation, though it gives many a varied nuance to a Biblical story, mars to a great extent the fine poetic character of the Book. Interesting is the remark of Samuel ibn Tibbon (d. 1230) that he had heard from his father that the Song of Songs was merely a love poem, a view with which he disagreed, contending that it must be interpreted allegorically.

This reading of the Book was upheld by Rashi and Ibn Ezra in the brief introductions to their commentaries, supporting their contention that it was the practice of the prophets to speak thus of God's love for His people. It was this esoteric significance of the Book that saved it at the Rabbinical synod at Jabneh in the early part of the second century, when it was threatened with exclusion from the Biblical canon. Perhaps the reason why both Philo and the New Testament never refer to the Song of Songs may be due to the fact that it was so excluded until Rabbi Akiba rescued it by the assurance quoted above. It was only natural that the early Christians should also have regarded the Book as a mystical allegory of God and the Church. When Bishop Theodore of Mopsuestia (360-429 C.E.) ventured to give it a literal interpretation, his work was banned by a Church council in 553.

In recent years, the pendulum has swung back to a more literal reading of the story, not excluding, however, the moral to which it points. In 1776, the German poet, Goethe, translated the Book and expressed his unbounded admiration at the beauty of the imagery. In this admiration he was joined by another of his countrymen, Herder. He it was who, as already mentioned, first advanced the hypothesis that the Book is a collection of love-songs during the week of festivities held in connection with a wedding celebration. Wetzstein lent support to Herder's theory by describing the *vasf* celebrations in Syria, where the villagers assembled in gay mood, setting up the threshing-floor as a throne on which the newly-married pair took their seats as 'king and queen.' Songs were then sung in praise of their physical charms, and dances held in which the couple participated. In accordance with this hypothesis, the *king* of the Book is the bridegroom and the *daughters of Jerusalem* the village maidens attending the bride; the dialogues describing the charms of each being excerpts of current folk-songs. But plausible as this interpretation has appeared to many, it is unthinkable that Rabbi Akiba would have taken so bold a stand to save a collection of rustic folk-songs which, though dramatic in form, would appear to have no logical sequence. It is true that we have evidence in the Talmud (Keth. 16b) that wedding festivities were characterized by lavish praises of the bride; but from the Song of Songs it is evident that here sang a poet of the highest rank whose charm of style will be looked for in vain in the collections of Eastern folk-songs. Equally groundless is the theory of the Church Father, Origen (third century), praised by Jerome, that the Book describes an *epithalamium* sung at the marriage of king Solomon with the daughter of one of the Pharaohs.

Summing-up the evidence on each side, it is not easy to discover any justification for the Rabbinical explanation that the Book represents successive events in the history of Israel, a view so much favoured by the Midrash and Rashi. Modern scholarship has abandoned, to a large extent, this allegorical interpretation in favour of simple literalness. Yet the mystical view, according to which the poem sets forth spiritual ideals, has pleas ranged in its favour that demand some consideration. The fact that it is read on Passover in the Synagogue and in the home, by many after the Seder service, and that many others read it before the advent of the Sabbath, indicates how strong was the tendency to interpret it in a spiritual sense.

## THE MORAL

The main moral of the Book is that love, besides being the strongest emotion in the human heart, can also be the holiest. God has given the gift of love to sweeten the toil of the labourer, as in the case of Jacob to whom the fourteen years in which he toiled for Rachel appeared *but a few days, for the love he had to her* (Gen. xxix. 20). Love transfigures and hallows, but it is a boon that requires zealously to be guarded and sheltered from abuse. This Book pictures love as a reward enjoyed only by the pure and simple, a joy not experienced by the pleasure-seeking monarch and the indolent ladies of the court. It is a joy reserved for the loyal and the constant, and is denied to the sensual and dissolute.

This moral doubtless preserved a Book otherwise devoid of religious character, in which the name of God does not appear unless it is included in the word *shalhebeth-yah* (viii. 6). Some have found offence in its freeness of expression, but it is debatable whether there may not be a deeper purity in the frank recognition of such subjects and straightforward language about them than in the veiled circumlocutions we find in modern literature. The Book is not for children, but for men and women who should welcome delicate matters openly stated rather than uncleanly imagined. Besides, manners change with the passage of time, and what may seem to moderns coarse and sensuous was considered natural and pure in an earlier period.

The best moral of the story, however, is that the Book portrays the guardianship of God over His people and the loyalty which Israel has displayed throughout the ages towards his faith. Like the Shulammite in the story, Israel has also been forcibly taken from his homeland. Many suitors clamoured for Israel's hand—Rome, the Church, Islam, who called with siren voices that he exchange his God for another, but the reply has always been that *many waters cannot quench the love* for his ancestral faith. Like the Shulammite, Israel suffered because of his refusal to be unfaithful, but in the end love and fidelity always emerge triumphant. *Amor omnia vincit.*

## THE SETTING

The scene is one of the royal tents, probably at Jerusalem, in which the Shulammite and the ladies of the court are gathered, with Solomon putting in an occasional appearance. The peasant girl, ardently in love with a shepherd, from whom she had been parted to be unwillingly dragged before the king, yearns to be reunited with him, prizing him above all the luxuries the court can offer her. She has just been introduced to the royal court, but feels out of place amidst all the splendour. The *daughters of Jerusalem* seek to divert her affection from the shepherd to the royal admirer, but to no avail. She scorns their temptation and cries out longingly for her lover to come to her rescue. On receiving a mocking answer from the women, she becomes even more rapturous over him and disdains the king's attempt to win her love.

# THE SONG OF SONGS

## 1 CHAPTER I א

1 THE song of songs, which is Solomon's.

2 Let him kiss me with the kisses of his mouth—
For thy love is better than wine.

3 Thine ointments have a goodly fragrance;
Thy name is as ointment poured forth;
Therefore do the maidens love thee.

1 *שִׁיר הַשִּׁירִים אֲשֶׁר לִשְׁלֹמֹה׃
2 יִשָּׁקֵנִי מִנְּשִׁיקוֹת פִּיהוּ כִּי־
טוֹבִים דֹּדֶיךָ מִיָּיִן׃
3 לְרֵיחַ שְׁמָנֶיךָ טוֹבִים שֶׁמֶן
תּוּרַק שְׁמֶךָ עַל־כֵּן עֲלָמוֹת
אֲהֵבוּךָ׃

* v. 1. ש׳ רבתי

1. *the song of songs.* The repetition of the noun in the genitive expresses the superlative; e.g. *most holy* (Exod. xxix. 37, lit. 'holy of holies'). This is 'the choicest' of the songs composed by Solomon (cf. 1 Kings v. 12). The Rabbis interpreted the phrase as 'a double song,' in which extensive use is made of the device of parallelism. Rabbi Simon said, 'It is double and reduplicated, containing Israel's praise of God and God's praise of holiness, and reduplicated in its beauty and holiness' (Midrash).

*which is Solomon's.* The *lamed* prefixed to Solomon's name denotes authorship, as in *mizmor leDavid*, 'A Psalm of David.' Though the authorship of the Book has been disputed (see Introduction), yet the powerful and fluent style points to the time of Solomon.

2. *let him kiss me.* Either spoken by the Shulammite of her absent lover, or by the *daughters of Jerusalem* of Solomon; probably the former. Some translate, 'Oh that he would kiss me!' So intense is her passion, that she changes from the second to the third person almost in the same breath: *let him kiss me* followed by *thy love.* Those who contend that this verse was spoken by the ladies of the court hold that their purpose was to excite her admiration for the king. Perhaps one of them utters the first words and the others follow with verse 3.

*for thy love is better than wine. Dodim* (love) also means caresses and manifestations of love. It is a Hebrew idiom to call every banquet of pleasure and joy by the name of *wine* (cf. Esther vii. 2; Isa. xxiv. 9). Allegorical interpretation refers it to the giving of the Torah and God's speaking directly to Israel.

3. *thine ointments have a goodly fragrance.* Or, 'for fragrance thine ointment is good.' The Midrash applies the verse to Abraham who spread the knowledge of the true God as perfume diffuses its scent.

*thy name is as ointment poured forth.* He is esteemed by those who know him. The verb is fem. in form, the subject masc., but grammatical accuracy is overlooked by the maiden in her ardour. She addresses her absent lover sometimes as if he were near her and sometimes as if he were far away.

*therefore do the maidens love thee.* It is natural for a lovesick girl to imagine that everybody is in love with the object of her own affection.

4 Draw me, we will run after thee;
The king hath brought me into his chambers;
We will be glad and rejoice in thee,
We will find thy love more fragrant than wine!
Sincerely do they love thee.

4 מָשְׁכֵנִי אַחֲרֶיךָ נָּרוּצָה הֱבִיאַנִי
הַמֶּלֶךְ חֲדָרָיו נָגִילָה וְנִשְׂמְחָה
בָּךְ נַזְכִּירָה דֹדֶיךָ מִיַּיִן
מֵישָׁרִים אֲהֵבוּךָ׃

5 'I am black, but comely,
O ye daughters of Jerusalem,
As the tents of Kedar,
As the curtains of Solomon.

5 שְׁחוֹרָה אֲנִי וְנָאוָה בְּנוֹת
יְרוּשָׁלִָם כְּאָהֳלֵי קֵדָר
כִּירִיעוֹת שְׁלֹמֹה׃

6 Look not upon me, that I am swarthy,
That the sun hath tanned me;
My mother's sons were incensed against me,
They made me keeper of the vineyards;
But mine own vineyard have I not kept.'

6 אַל־תִּרְאוּנִי שֶׁאֲנִי שְׁחַרְחֹרֶת
שֶׁשְּׁזָפַתְנִי הַשָּׁמֶשׁ בְּנֵי אִמִּי
נִחֲרוּ־בִי שָׂמֻנִי נֹטֵרָה אֶת־
הַכְּרָמִים כַּרְמִי שֶׁלִּי לֹא
נָטָרְתִּי׃

4. *draw me, we will run after thee.* The Shulammite muses, mentally addressing her beloved one, beseeching him to take her away.

*the king . . . chambers.* A reference to her being taken by force from her home. Ibn Ezra interprets: 'Were even the king to bring me into his private apartment, still I would rejoice and be glad in thee.' Others explain *we will be glad,* etc. as the answer given by the women who preferred the company of Solomon.

*we will find.* lit. 'we will commemorate'; perhaps the best rendering is 'we will declare.'

*sincerely do they love thee. Sincerely* is connected with the Hebrew word for 'upright'; hence the explanation, 'not only do we, the maidens, but also the upright love thee' (Rashi, Rashbam).

5. *I am black, but comely.* The Shulammite replies to the scornful remarks of the court ladies. Her swarthy colour is not natural but due to the harsh treatment of her brothers by exposing her to the sun. The Midrash makes the homiletical comment: 'The Jew is black with anxiety during the week, but comely on the Sabbath.' The Hebrew for *black* denotes a ruddy hue from sunburning. Gaining courage, she makes a proud retort to the pale, pampered women of the court. The verse can also be understood as a soliloquy; her suffering may have been due to her beauty.

*as the tents of Kedar.* With poetic exaggeration she compares herself to the black tents inhabited by the people of Kedar, a tribe of nomads descended from Ishmael (Gen. xxv. 13; cf. Ps. cxx. 5). Some modern commentators regard this verse as proof that the scene depicts a royal tent pitched in a favourite summer resort of Solomon, *black* alluding to the tents of Kedar and *comely* to the curtains of Solomon. They who maintain that the Book is an *epithalamium* composed for the marriage of Solomon with an Egyptian princess will find it hard to reconcile this verse with their theory. Egyptian princesses are naturally dark and not just temporarily scorched by the sun. Moreover, why should an Egyptian princess look after other people's vineyards?

6. *look not upon me, that I am swarthy.* Better, 'do not look upon me scornfully that I am swarthy, since the sun hath tanned me; the swarthiness is superficial and when it passes I will be found to be fairer than you'.

*my mother's sons were incensed against me.* Her father was probably dead; her

7 Tell me, O thou whom my soul loveth,
Where thou feedest, where thou makest thy flock to rest at noon;
For why should I be as one that veileth herself
Beside the flocks of thy companions?

7 הַגִּידָה לִּי שֶׁאָהֲבָה נַפְשִׁי אֵיכָה
תִרְעֶה אֵיכָה תַּרְבִּיץ
בַּצָּהֳרָיִם שַׁלָּמָה אֶהְיֶה
כְּעֹטְיָה עַל עֶדְרֵי חֲבֵרֶיךָ׃

8 If thou know not, O thou fairest among women,
Go thy way forth by the footsteps of the flock
And feed thy kids, beside the shepherds' tents.

8 אִם־לֹא תֵדְעִי לָךְ הַיָּפָה
בַּנָּשִׁים צְאִי־לָךְ בְּעִקְבֵי
הַצֹּאן וּרְעִי אֶת־גְּדִיֹּתַיִךְ עַל
מִשְׁכְּנוֹת הָרֹעִים׃

9 I have compared thee, O my love,
To a steed in Pharaoh's chariots.

9 לְסֻסָתִי בְּרִכְבֵי פַרְעֹה
דִּמִּיתִיךְ רַעְיָתִי׃

brothers kept careful guard over her, making her work in the vineyards to prevent her meeting her beloved in the fields. Those who assert that the Book contains fragments of a professional singer's repertoire have difficulty in explaining the reference.

*mine own vineyard have I not kept.* Some read into the words a regret that she had neglected her appearance; but how can *mine own vineyard* mean 'my face'? And how explain the words which precede? The allusion may be to the carelessness that has brought her to her present danger. Ibn Ezra renders: 'My brothers were so angry and so severe with me, that they made me keep their vineyards, a task I had never done before even to my own.'

7. *tell me . . . feedest.* She addresses her absent lover. Where can she find him? Being modest, she says *at noon*, not like the wanton ladies of the court who seek their lovers at night. The fierce sun at noon compels people in hot countries to desist from labour and recline in some cool part of the house (cf. 2 Sam. iv. 5). Shepherds then lead their flocks under shady trees near a stream (Ps. xxiii. 2).

*as one that veileth herself.* lit. 'as one covered up'; either referring to the practice of a harlot (Gen. xxxviii. 15) or a leper (Lev. xiii. 45).

8. The women answer her sarcastically that she had better leave the pleasures of the court, since she spurns them, and return to her duties as a shepherdess. Addressing her mockingly as the *fairest among women*, they tell her to go and find her lover.

9. *O my love.* Probably it is Solomon who speaks. Seeing his love despised, he determines to try once again to win her.

*a steed in Pharaoh's chariots.* Solomon was the first to introduce the horse and chariot as a regular part of the equipment of Israel's army. The beauty of the Egyptian horse suggested a comparison which is strange to the western mind but frequent in Arabic poetry.

**10** Thy cheeks are comely with circlets,
Thy neck with beads.

10 נָאווּ לְחָיַיִךְ בַּתֹּרִים צַוָּארֵךְ בַּחֲרוּזִים׃

**11** We will make thee circlets of gold
With studs of silver.

11 תּוֹרֵי זָהָב נַעֲשֶׂה־לָּךְ עִם נְקֻדּוֹת הַכָּסֶף׃

**12** While the king sat at his table,
My spikenard sent forth its fragrance.

12 עַד־שֶׁהַמֶּלֶךְ בִּמְסִבּוֹ נִרְדִּי נָתַן רֵיחוֹ׃

**13** My beloved is unto me as a bag of myrrh,
That lieth betwixt my breasts.

13 צְרוֹר הַמֹּר ׀ דּוֹדִי לִי בֵּין שָׁדַי יָלִין׃

**14** My beloved is unto me as a cluster of henna
In the vineyards of En-gedi.

14 אֶשְׁכֹּל הַכֹּפֶר ׀ דּוֹדִי לִי בְּכַרְמֵי עֵין גֶּדִי׃

**15** Behold, thou art fair, my love; behold, thou art fair;
Thine eyes are as doves.

15 הִנָּךְ יָפָה רַעְיָתִי הִנָּךְ יָפָה עֵינַיִךְ יוֹנִים׃

**10.** *thy cheeks are comely.* Equals 'how comely are thy cheeks!' The king resorts to flattery to entice her. 'Thou art, indeed, beautiful even in humble ornaments; how much more beautiful wilt thou appear in the jewels I am ready to shower upon thee!'

**11.** *circlets of gold.* These costly adornments will be exchanged for the modest beads she is then wearing.

*studs of silver.* The king offers her strings of beads made of precious metals or stones, to hang down over her cheeks in layers, as was the fashion in the Orient.

**12.** *table. Mesibbah* is a divan, lit. 'a round table.' The cognate verb is used for partaking of a meal in a reclining fashion, as was the custom among the nobles.

*my spikenard sent forth its fragrance.* Even while the king is speaking, her thoughts wander to her shepherd, her *bag of myrrh* (verse 13). The king is nothing to her in comparison. For spices used as a means to incite love, cf. Isa. iii. 24.

**13.** *that lieth betwixt my breasts.* Sh implies that her love is constant and en shrined in her heart. It is always wit her, asleep or awake, and the extent of th fragrance of that love reaches the kin even when he is at the royal tab surrounded by a variety of charm an beauty. Also the thought of her love refreshes her heart as perfume would d

**14.** *a cluster of henna.* It grows i clusters of small whitish flowers and i found to-day at En-gedi, the modern Ain Jidy, whose steep rocks are frequented b wild goats.

**15.** *thine eyes are as doves.* Solomo continues her praise, while she sti thinks of her lover. The point of com parison is the innocence and purity c the dove. The king pleads, 'Not possess attraction; it is thou who art mos beautiful.' According to Rabbinic teach ing, a bride who has beautiful eye possesses a beautiful personality; the are an index to her character.

16 Behold, thou art fair, my beloved, yea, pleasant;
Also our couch is leafy.

16 הִנְּךָ֨ יָפֶ֤ה דוֹדִי֙ אַ֣ף נָעִ֔ים אַף־
עַרְשֵׂ֖נוּ רַעֲנָנָֽה׃

17 The beams of our houses are cedars,
And our panels are cypresses.

17 קֹר֤וֹת בָּתֵּ֙ינוּ֙ אֲרָזִ֔ים רָהִיטֵ֖נוּ*
בְּרוֹתִֽים׃

v. 17. רהיטנו ק׳

## 2 CHAPTER II ב

1 I am a rose of Sharon,
A lily of the valleys.

1 אֲנִי֙ חֲבַצֶּ֣לֶת הַשָּׁר֔וֹן שֽׁוֹשַׁנַּ֖ת
הָעֲמָקִֽים׃

2 As a lily among thorns,
So is my love among the daughters.

2 כְּשׁוֹשַׁנָּה֙ בֵּ֣ין הַחוֹחִ֔ים כֵּ֥ן
רַעְיָתִ֖י בֵּ֥ין הַבָּנֽוֹת׃

16. *our couch is leafy.* Ignoring Solomon's flattery, she mentally addresses her absent lover. Thinking of the field in which their love was first aroused, she says, 'Lovely is our couch of flowers and bed of green compared with the royal divans of this court.'

17. *the beams of our houses are cedars.* Not that cedars were used to build their humble cottage, but simply an allusion to the cedar trees under which they found rest and shelter during the heat of the day. The plural *houses* is significant: 'we have not *one* palace but many in the forest glades.'

*our panels are cypresses.* The word for *panels* is not found elsewhere and the meaning is suggested by the context. In later Hebrew, it is the word used for 'furniture.'

## CHAPTER II

1. *I am a rose of Sharon.* The maiden continues, describing herself as a humble meadow flower. She feels out-of-place in such luxurious surroundings. 'As for me' (*ani*), she modestly protests, 'my beauty is not remarkable, for I am just one of the flowers of the plain.' The word *chabatseleth* occurs again only in Isa. xxxv. 1. The LXX and Vulgate understand it as 'lily,' the Targum and Saadia as 'narcissus,' Ibn Ezra and Kimchi as 'rose.' The narcissus is plentiful in Palestine and beloved by the natives. *Sharon* refers probably to the coastal district from Cæsarea to Joppa.

*a lily of the valleys.* A flower commonly found. From v. 13 it would appear to be of the red variety since it alludes to the colour of the lips. Rabbi Eliezer said, 'The righteous are to be compared to the lily of the valley which goes on blooming, not to the lily of the mountain which soon withers' (Midrash).

2. *as a lily among thorns.* Taking advantage of her modesty, Solomon pays her a delicate compliment: 'True thou art only a lily, but a lily surrounded by thorns (i.e. the women of Jerusalem); compared to them thou art beautiful indeed.'

3 As an apple-tree among the trees of the wood,
So is my beloved among the sons.
Under its shadow I delighted to sit,
And its fruit was sweet to my taste.

4 He hath brought me to the banqueting-house,
And his banner over me is love.

5 'Stay ye me with dainties, refresh me with apples;
For I am love-sick.'

6 Let his left hand be under my head,
And his right hand embrace me.

3 כְּתַפּוּחַ בַּעֲצֵי הַיַּעַר כֵּן דּוֹדִי
בֵּין הַבָּנִים בְּצִלּוֹ חִמַּדְתִּי
וְיָשַׁבְתִּי וּפִרְיוֹ מָתוֹק לְחִכִּי׃
4 הֱבִיאַנִי אֶל־בֵּית הַיָּיִן וְדִגְלוֹ
עָלַי אַהֲבָה׃
5 סַמְּכוּנִי בָּאֲשִׁישׁוֹת רַפְּדוּנִי
בַּתַּפּוּחִים כִּי־חוֹלַת אַהֲבָה
אָנִי׃
6 שְׂמֹאלוֹ תַּחַת לְרֹאשִׁי וִימִינוֹ
תְּחַבְּקֵנִי׃

v. 4. קמץ בז״ק

3. *as an apple-tree.* Ignoring the king's compliment, she praises her lover. Compared to other men, the royal suitor included, he is like the apple-tree, sweet and fragrant. He stands out among them like the apple-tree amidst fruitless trees. She continues, 'I delight to repose beneath the apple-tree because of its delicious fruit.'

*under its shadow I delighted to sit.* Sforno, following the Midrash, allegorizes the passage as referring to the Revelation at Sinai. In its literal significance, she expresses her joy at being in his company beneath its shade.

4. *and his banner over me is love.* 'I follow the banner of love which my friend bears before me as soldiers follow the military standard and never desert it' (Gesenius). According to the Midrash the *banqueting-house* represents Sinai and the *banner* the Torah.

5. *stay ye me with dainties. Ashishoth* is a kind of raisin-cake (Hosea iii. 1), probably prepared by roasting on the fire (*esh*). A.V. 'flagons of wine' is derived from Ibn Ezra and other Jewish commentators. Some conjecture that the word is the name of a scent. Her longing has reduced her to a state of physical weakness and she needs stimulants.

*refresh me with apples.* Others translate: 'Spread the good scent of apples around me.' *Raphad* has the meaning 'to spread' (see on iii. 10). The Midrash remarks that *dainties* allude to the *Halachoth* (legal lore) and *apples* to the *Haggadah* (non-legal doctrine) which sustain the faith of the Jew.

*for I am love-sick.* From hope deferred. The LXX translates 'wounded by love,' reading the Hebrew as *challelath.* The Midrashic comment is very stimulating: 'For my sickness is due to my love. Suffering has made Israel love God all the more. Jewish suffering originates in the love which the Jew has for God. Hence, although I am sick (i.e. sinful), I am still beloved of Him.' As long as a man is well, he eats whatever is set before him; when he is sick, his craving is for dainties.

6. *let his left hand . . . head.* Or, 'O that his left hand were under my head.' She feels the need of his support in her hour of trial, when attempts were made to alienate her affections. The verse is repeated in viii. 3.

7 'I adjure you, O daughters of Jerusalem,
By the gazelles, and by the hinds of the field,
That ye awaken not, nor stir up love,
Until it please.'

7 הִשְׁבַּעְתִּי אֶתְכֶם בְּנוֹת
יְרוּשָׁלִַם בִּצְבָאוֹת אוֹ בְּאַיְלוֹת
הַשָּׂדֶה אִם־תָּעִירוּ ׀ וְאִם־
תְּעוֹרְרוּ אֶת־הָאַהֲבָה עַד
שֶׁתֶּחְפָּץ׃

8 Hark! my beloved! behold, he cometh,
Leaping upon the mountains, skipping upon the hills.

8 קוֹל דּוֹדִי הִנֵּה־זֶה בָּא מְדַלֵּג
עַל־הֶהָרִים מְקַפֵּץ עַל־
הַגְּבָעוֹת׃

9 My beloved is like a gazelle or a young hart;
Behold, he standeth behind our wall,
He looketh in through the windows,
He peereth through the lattice.

9 דּוֹמֶה דוֹדִי לִצְבִי אוֹ לְעֹפֶר
הָאַיָּלִים הִנֵּה־זֶה עוֹמֵד אַחַר
כָּתְלֵנוּ מַשְׁגִּיחַ מִן־הַחַלֹּנוֹת
מֵצִיץ מִן־הַחֲרַכִּים׃

7. *I adjure you.* Having avowed her loyalty to her beloved, she pleads that they desist from trying to turn her affections towards another.

*by the gazelles . . . field.* Gazelles are common in South Lebanon and are held in high admiration. Being graceful, they are a symbol of feminine beauty. It is natural for shepherds to take an oath by familiar objects around them.

*that ye awaken not . . . please.* A kind of refrain marking the close of a section (cf. iii. 5, viii. 4). True love, she admonishes the women of the court, needs no arousing from without. It should be as free and as unfettered as the gazelles and hinds.

8-14. Here begins a new section ending at iii. 5. The first scene concluded with the failure of the king and his court ladies to persuade the peasant girl to be disloyal to her lover. The scene is no longer Jerusalem but a royal residence in the country, probably in the north of Palestine from which the lovers hail. Again the speakers are the Shulammite and the daughters of Jerusalem. This section is devoted to an account of how, one Spring morning, her shepherd came and invited her to join him in the field. To prevent this meeting, her brothers transferred her work to the vineyards from which she had been taken by force to the royal court. She finds consolation in the certainty that her lover would seek her. His approach is traced until he reaches the wall of the building in which she is confined. Peering through the lattice-window, he fails to see her and pleads for the sound of her voice. In reply she sings to him selections of a vineyard song (verse 15). In the next verse she addresses him in rapturous language and then, fearing for his safety, exhorts him to depart until *the shadows flee away* and they can meet again. 'This section is among the most perfect love verses in the world. They are reminiscent of the lines of Tennyson, "And all my heart went out to meet his coming, ere he came"' (Harper).

8. *hark! my beloved!* For *kol* (lit. 'voice'), in this sense of *hark*, cf. Gen. iv. 10; Isa. xl. 3. In her imagination she actually hears his footsteps although he is still in the distance, where she sees him hastening over the hills with the speed of a swift-footed gazelle. She must be alluding to her shepherd, since the language would not be used of a king.

9. *he peereth through the lattice.* The Midrash mystically applies the words to the *Shechinah* peering through the outstretched hand of the priest when blessing the people. The Hebrew verb for

10 My beloved spoke, and said unto me:
'Rise up, my love, my fair one, and come away.
11 For, lo, the winter is past,
The rain is over and gone;
12 The flowers appear on the earth;
The time of singing is come,
And the voice of the turtle is heard in our land;
13 The fig-tree putteth forth her green figs,
And the vines in blossom give forth their fragrance.
Arise, my love, my fair one, and come away.

10 עָנָה דוֹדִי וְאָמַר לִי קוּמִי לָךְ
רַעְיָתִי יָפָתִי וּלְכִי־לָךְ׃
11 כִּי־הִנֵּה הַסְּתָו עָבָר הַגֶּשֶׁם
חָלַף הָלַךְ לוֹ׃
12 הַנִּצָּנִים נִרְאוּ בָאָרֶץ עֵת
הַזָּמִיר הִגִּיעַ וְקוֹל הַתּוֹר
נִשְׁמַע בְּאַרְצֵנוּ׃
13 הַתְּאֵנָה חָנְטָה פַגֶּיהָ וְהַגְּפָנִים
סְמָדַר נָתְנוּ רֵיחַ קוּמִי לָכִי
רַעְיָתִי יָפָתִי וּלְכִי־לָךְ׃

v. 11. הסתיו ק׳ v. 13. לך ק׳

*peereth* signifies 'to sparkle' and perhaps suggests that she thinks of her rescuer as so close that she can see the ardent gleam in his eyes.

**10.** *my beloved spoke.* She now vividly imagines her lover calling her to join him.

**11.** *the winter is past. Sethav* occurs only here and probably denotes the cloudy season which ends with the rains in March and April.

**12.** *the flowers appear.* Nature, as it were, is calling the young lovers together. The Spring flowers in Palestine present a wonderful sight.

*the time of singing.* The LXX, Targum and Rashbam render: 'the time for pruning (the vines)'; cf. Lev. xxv. 3. Others maintain that *zamir* is the name of a migratory bird that utters song on its return in Spring. The Midrash refers the verse to Moses and Aaron (the flowers) whose coming to Pharaoh resulted in Israel's singing *Az Yashir* (Exod. xv) at the Red Sea after the winter of oppression in Egypt.

*the voice of the turtle.* The turtle is not a singing-bird but a bird of passage (cf. Jer. viii. 7). Its voice announces the coming of Spring.

**13.** *putteth forth.* The literal sense of the verb is 'sweetens with spice,' which is also used for the act of embalming with spices.

*green figs.* Hebrew *paggeha;* ripe figs are called *te'enim*, and those that ripen early *bikkurah.* Figs ripen at various times, usually from August onwards. Some remain unripe on the tree until the following Spring. The *green figs* are slightly darker in colour; and the verb *chanat*, which is related to the reddish brown wheat (*chittah*), suggests the translation, 'the fig-tree maketh red-ripe her winter-figs.'

*the vines in blossom.* Noted for their sweet fragrance. *Semadar*, a word of unknown origin and occuring only here, is interpreted by the Rabbis as 'tender grapes when they first appear.' A few weeks later they become *boserim*, and when fully ripe are called *anabim.* 'When the blossom falls away and the grapes are visible, that is the stage of *semadar*' (Rashi).

14 O my dove, that art in the clefts of the rock, in the covert of the cliff,
Let me see thy countenance, let me hear thy voice;
For sweet is thy voice, and thy countenance is comely.'

14 יוֹנָתִי בְּחַגְוֵי הַסֶּלַע בְּסֵתֶר
הַמַּדְרֵגָה הַרְאִינִי אֶת־
מַרְאַיִךְ הַשְׁמִיעִנִי אֶת־קוֹלֵךְ
כִּי־קוֹלֵךְ עָרֵב וּמַרְאֵיךְ
נָאוֶה׃

15 'Take us the foxes, the little foxes, that spoil the vineyards;
For our vineyards are in blossom.'

15 אֶחֱזוּ־לָנוּ שֻׁעָלִים שֻׁעָלִים
קְטַנִּים מְחַבְּלִים כְּרָמִים
וּכְרָמֵינוּ סְמָדַר׃

16 My beloved is mine, and I am his,
That feedeth among the lilies.

16 דּוֹדִי לִי וַאֲנִי לוֹ הָרֹעֶה
בַּשּׁוֹשַׁנִּים׃

17 Until the day breathe, and the shadows flee away,
Turn, my beloved, and be thou like a gazelle or a young hart
Upon the mountains of spices.

17 עַד שֶׁיָּפוּחַ הַיּוֹם וְנָסוּ הַצְּלָלִים
סֹב דְּמֵה־לְךָ דוֹדִי לִצְבִי אוֹ
לְעֹפֶר הָאַיָּלִים עַל־הָרֵי
בָתֶר׃

v. 14. יתיר י׳ v. 15. נ״א פתח בס״ף

14. *in the clefts of the rock.* Kimchi renders: 'On top of the rocks.' Doves nest in clefts of rocks which they are reluctant to leave when frightened. The shepherd lover, impatient at her delay to join him, urges her to leave her hiding-place.

15. *take us the foxes.* This verse, together with verse 14, may be excerpts of a folk-song sung at harvest time. She sings it in answer to his plea for the sound of her voice.

*the little foxes.* Perhaps she is referring to her danger at court. Comparing herself to a vineyard, she calls upon him to save her from *the foxes* who seek to destroy her true happiness.

*in blossom.* The word *semadar*, used by him in verse 13, is repeated by her as an indication that she had heard him calling her from the other side of the wall.

16. *my beloved is mine.* Turning to the women, she makes this passionate confession as though to imply, 'My brothers succeeded in separating us, but we are for ever united in our love.'

17. *until the day breathe.* lit. 'until the day blow,' i.e. the evening breeze rises. Alarmed for his safety, she implores him to leave her for the present.

*and the shadows flee away.* The separation is to be only until sunset when she will expect him.

*upon the mountains of spices.* This translation follows Grätz. The final word *bather* means 'division, separation,' and may refer to the intervening mountains which the shepherd had to cross in order to reach her. The word 'division' is aptly used of mountains that appear to be cleft. Other explanations proposed are that it is a proper noun, 'the mountains of Bether' (A.V., R.V.), or the name of an aromatic plant.

1 By night on my bed I sought him whom my soul loveth;
I sought him, but I found him not.

2 'I will rise now, and go about the city,
In the streets and in the broad ways,
I will seek him whom my soul loveth.'
I sought him, but I found him not.

3 The watchmen that go about the city found me:
'Saw ye him whom my soul loveth?'

4 Scarce had I passed from them,
When I found him whom my soul loveth:
I held him, and would not let him go,
Until I had brought him into my mother's house,
And into the chamber of her that conceived me.

1 עַל־מִשְׁכָּבִי בַּלֵּילוֹת בִּקַּשְׁתִּי
אֵת שֶׁאָהֲבָה נַפְשִׁי בִּקַּשְׁתִּיו
וְלֹא מְצָאתִיו׃
2 אָקוּמָה נָּא וַאֲסוֹבְבָה בָעִיר
בַּשְּׁוָקִים וּבָרְחֹבוֹת אֲבַקְשָׁה
אֵת שֶׁאָהֲבָה נַפְשִׁי בִּקַּשְׁתִּיו
וְלֹא מְצָאתִיו׃
3 מְצָאוּנִי הַשֹּׁמְרִים הַסֹּבְבִים
בָּעִיר אֵת שֶׁאָהֲבָה נַפְשִׁי
רְאִיתֶם׃
4 כִּמְעַט שֶׁעָבַרְתִּי מֵהֶם עַד
שֶׁמָּצָאתִי אֵת שֶׁאָהֲבָה נַפְשִׁי
אֲחַזְתִּיו וְלֹא אַרְפֶּנּוּ עַד־
שֶׁהֲבֵיאתִיו אֶל־בֵּית אִמִּי
וְאֶל־חֶדֶר הוֹרָתִי׃

**1.** *by night on my bed.* Disappointed at the non-appearance of her lover with the coming of night, her sleep is troubled. She has feverish dreams and finally decides to go out and search for him. The pl. form of *baleloth* signifies 'the night-hours.'

*I sought him.* Repeated to emphasize her disappointment at failing to find him.

**2.** *I will rise now.* 'Come, let me arise and go about the city.' This need not be Jerusalem; it may be Shulam from which the lovers came. She is apprehensive lest harm had befallen him and she cannot rest. The exhortative form of the verb is expressive of her anxiety.

*streets . . . broad ways.* lit. 'market-places . . . open spaces.'

*I found him not.* One can detect the note of bitter disappointment in her voice.

**3.** *the watchmen.* It was natural for her to ask them to assist in the search since they patrolled the city.

*saw ye him.* The interrogative particle is absent, but it is often dropped in Hebrew. 'You must have seen him' is an alternative rendering more expressive of her agitated state of mind, implying that everybody surely knew for whom she was searching. She asks a question but does not wait for the answer, so eager is she to pursue her search.

**4.** *scarce had I passed from them.* Or, 'no sooner did I leave, when etc.' Note the abruptness of the style. Though she tells us that she put a question to the watchmen, she omits to mention the answer they gave.

*until I had brought him into my mother's house.* This is evidence that he was her acknowledged lover of whom her mother approved.

*and into . . . conceived me.* An example of the parallelism which is characteristic of Hebrew poetry.

5 'I adjure you, O daughters of Jerusalem,
By the gazelles, and by the hinds of the field,
That ye awaken not, nor stir up love,
Until it please.'

5 הִשְׁבַּעְתִּי אֶתְכֶם בְּנוֹת
יְרוּשָׁלִַם בִּצְבָאוֹת אוֹ בְּאַיְלוֹת
הַשָּׂדֶה אִם־תָּעִירוּ ׀ וְאִם־
תְּעוֹרְרוּ אֶת־הָאַהֲבָה עַד־
שֶׁתֶּחְפָּץ׃

6 Who is this that cometh up out of the wilderness
Like pillars of smoke,
Perfumed with myrrh and frankincense,
With all powders of the merchant?

6 מִי זֹאת עֹלָה מִן־הַמִּדְבָּר
כְּתִימֲרוֹת עָשָׁן מְקֻטֶּרֶת מֹר
וּלְבוֹנָה מִכֹּל אַבְקַת רוֹכֵל׃

7 Behold, it is the litter of Solomon;
Threescore mighty men are about it,
Of the mighty men of Israel.

7 הִנֵּה מִטָּתוֹ שֶׁלִּשְׁלֹמֹה שִׁשִּׁים
גִּבֹּרִים סָבִיב לָהּ מִגִּבֹּרֵי
יִשְׂרָאֵל׃

5. *I adjure you.* See on ii. 7. The verse marks the close of a section.

6-11. The rest of the chapter is devoted to a graphic description of the arrival either of the king or her lover. Some maintain that this passage is the *epithalamium* of Solomon on the occasion of his marriage to the daughter of Pharaoh. Most probably it tells of the breaking-up of the royal tent in the country and the return of the court to the royal residence in North Palestine. This section recounts the conversation that took place between the Shulammite and the attendants at the approach of the retinue. Then the court ladies again sing the glory of the king who now appears in all his regal splendour, crowned as he was by his mother *in the day of his espousals.*

6. *who is this that cometh.* Because the Hebrew for *cometh* is fem., some commentators are of the opinion that it alludes to the princess whom Solomon had married. Others maintain that it refers to the Shulammite who now approaches Jerusalem in the procession with Solomon as her consort. But the Hebrew may also express the neuter: 'What is that which cometh up?' For how could a spectator at a distance discern whether the occupant of the royal litter was a woman and whether she was perfumed with myrrh? It is more probable that *perfumed* is to be explained of the incense which was burnt before the approaching procession in accordance with Oriental custom.

*like pillars of smoke.* The word for *pillars* is found again in Joel iii. 3. The LXX renders 'palm-trees,' an analogous Hebrew word, the root-meaning being 'to be erect.'

*frankincense.* So called in Hebrew (*lebonah*) because of its white colour (*laban*). It seems to have been used extensively (cf. Isa. lxvi. 3). Frankincense was imported into Palestine from Arabia.

*with all powders.* Spices were finely crushed to make them more fragrant.

*of the merchant.* Traders who travelled from foreign lands (cf. Gen. xxxvii. 25).

7. *behold, it is the litter of Solomon.* This is the answer to the question of verse 6, and may have been spoken by the same person who asked the question or by a bystander. For *mittah,* in the sense of *litter,* cf. Amos iii. 12; Esther i. 6. Here it is best translated 'palanquin.'

*threescore mighty men are about it.* Solomon's bodyguard to protect him against nocturnal marauders; its size is an indication of his majesty.

8 They all handle the sword,
And are expert in war;
Every man hath his sword upon his thigh,
Because of dread in the night.

כֻּלָּם אֲחֻזֵי חֶרֶב מְלֻמְּדֵי 8
מִלְחָמָה אִישׁ חַרְבּוֹ עַל־יְרֵכוֹ
מִפַּחַד בַּלֵּילוֹת׃

9 King Solomon made himself a palanquin
Of the wood of Lebanon.

אַפִּרְיוֹן עָשָׂה לוֹ הַמֶּלֶךְ שְׁלֹמֹה 9
מֵעֲצֵי הַלְּבָנוֹן׃

10 He made the pillars thereof of silver,
The top thereof of gold,
The seat of it of purple,
The inside thereof being inlaid with love,
From the daughters of Jerusalem.

עַמּוּדָיו עָשָׂה כֶסֶף רְפִידָתוֹ 10
זָהָב מֶרְכָּבוֹ אַרְגָּמָן תּוֹכוֹ
רָצוּף אַהֲבָה מִבְּנוֹת יְרוּשָׁלִָם׃

11 Go forth, O ye daughters of Zion,
And gaze upon king Solomon,
Even upon the crown wherewith his mother hath crowned him in the day of his espousals,
And in the day of the gladness of his heart.

צְאֶינָה וּרְאֶינָה בְּנוֹת צִיּוֹן 11
בַּמֶּלֶךְ שְׁלֹמֹה בָּעֲטָרָה
שֶׁעִטְּרָה־לּוֹ אִמּוֹ בְּיוֹם חֲתֻנָּתוֹ
וּבְיוֹם שִׂמְחַת לִבּוֹ׃

---

8. *they all handle the sword.* Better, 'sixty valiant men, all of them with swords in their hands, trained to war, each with his sword upon his thigh, because of the fear at night with its attendant dangers' (Harper).

*in the night.* An echo of *by night on my bed* (verse 1), which is further suggested by the mention of *mittah* (a word for 'bed') for *litter*. Grätz detects a contrast to the bravery of the shepherd who ventured into the night without an armed escort. The maiden also sought her lover at night unaccompanied.

9. *a palanquin.* Hebrew *appirion* is a difficult word meaning a covered litter. 'It is like a couch long enough for the rider to recline, covered with a canopy and resting on pillars at four corners. It is hung round with curtains to exclude the sun and has a door, sometimes of lattice-work, on each side' (Ginsburg). Kimchi derives the word from *parah* 'to be fruitful,' hence *puriah* 'a bed.' Before the destruction of the Second Temple, wedding processions bore resemblance to regal cavalcades.

*wood of Lebanon.* The cedar and cypress.

10. *the top thereof.* lit. 'its spread' (see on ii. 5). The support at the back or roof of the canopy was made of gold.

*the seat of it of purple.* The royal colour.

*the inside thereof being inlaid with love.* Better, 'its centre tessellated most lovingly by the daughters of Jerusalem,' *ahabah* being construed as an adverb and the letter *mem* (*from*) in *mibenoth* (*from the daughters of*) denoting the author or instrument. Others render: 'the middle thereof is wrought, as expressive of their love, by the daughters of Jerusalem.' The interior of these litters was generally painted with borders of flowers intermingled with short sentences telling of the power of love.

11. *go forth.* The Shulammite is asked to note all this splendour, so that her love might be won over. The *daughters of Zion* is probably identical with the *daughters of Jerusalem.*

*even upon the crown.* The crown here is not a symbol of royalty, but of happiness. In ancient times garlands were worn on festive occasions, especially marriages.

*his espousals.* lit. 'his wedding.' He may have been married either that day or recently, but was still attired in the crown given to him by his mother.

## 4 CHAPTER IV ד

1 Behold, thou art fair, my love;
behold, thou art fair;
Thine eyes are as doves behind
thy veil;
Thy hair is as a flock of goats,
That trail down from mount
Gilead.

2 Thy teeth are like a flock of ewes
all shaped alike,
Which are come up from the
washing;
Whereof all are paired,
And none faileth among them.

1 הִנָּךְ יָפָה רַעְיָתִי הִנָּךְ יָפָה
עֵינַיִךְ יוֹנִים מִבַּעַד לְצַמָּתֵךְ
שַׂעְרֵךְ כְּעֵדֶר הָעִזִּים שֶׁגָּלְשׁוּ
מֵהַר גִּלְעָד׃
2 שִׁנַּיִךְ כְּעֵדֶר הַקְּצוּבוֹת שֶׁעָלוּ
מִן־הָרַחְצָה שֶׁכֻּלָּם מַתְאִימוֹת
וְשַׁכֻּלָה אֵין בָּהֶם׃

1. *behold, thou art fair.* The speaker may be Solomon who, eager to urge his suit anew, continues to extol her beauty. Some, however, maintain that the speaker is the shepherd who is now addressing his beloved after the arrival of the retinue, and this is more probable.

*thine eyes are as doves.* See on i. 15. The comparison is suggested by the innocence of the dove. It was an old custom to sing praises of the bride at her marriage.

*behind thy veil.* The veil concealed the entire face save the eyes. Perhaps the Hebrew denotes 'a hair-net' to keep her locks tidy; the root-meaning is 'to confine.'

*as a flock of goats.* Each braid of her hair is as glossy as the goat whose natural colour was black. When the sun shone upon the goat, its hair glistened with a beautiful sheen.

*that trail down.* The Hebrew word presents difficulties, occurring only here and vi. 5. Both the ancient and modern commentators vary widely in their interpretation. The best derivation is that proposed by Professor Yahuda who connected it with an Arabic root, 'to do a thing before dawn.' The picture here is of a flock of goats coming down the mountain-side in rows just before daybreak, forming white lines against the dark background in the dim light. This interpretation seems to be alluded to in the Midrashic comment on the phrase, viz. 'When a woman has a luxuriant growth of hair, she arranges it in white lines,' i.e. in plaits which show white partings in between. Render: 'thy hair is like a flock of goats that trail down in the morning twilight.'

*mount Gilead.* A chain of mountains, beyond the Jordan, intersected by numerous valleys. The tribes of Reuben, Gad and half of Manasseh found a home there (Josh. xvii. 1ff.). Gilead was renowned for its rich pasture and countless flocks. It lies within view of Jerusalem.

2. *thy teeth.* Compared here to the whiteness of newly washed wool, the colour of snow (Isa. i. 18).

*all shaped alike.* Rashi explains as 'well numbered,' Kimchi and Ibn Ezra as 'all of the same size.'

*whereof all are paired.* Like sheep, each of which keeps to its mate, so her teeth are well-paired, each upper tooth possessing a corresponding lower one. Rashi connects the word for *paired* with *methom* 'perfection,' i.e. none are decayed.

*and none faileth among them.* A play of words occurs: 'All of them (*shekullam*) are paired and none is missing (*shakkulah*) among them.'

3 Thy lips are like a thread of scarlet,
And thy mouth is comely;
Thy temples are like a pomegranate split open
Behind thy veil.

3 כְּחוּט הַשָּׁנִי שִׂפְתוֹתַיִךְ
וּמִדְבָּרֵךְ נָאוֶה כְּפֶלַח הָרִמּוֹן
רַקָּתֵךְ מִבַּעַד לְצַמָּתֵךְ׃

4 Thy neck is like the tower of David
Builded with turrets,
Whereon there hang a thousand shields,
All the armour of the mighty men.

4 כְּמִגְדַּל דָּוִיד צַוָּארֵךְ בָּנוּי
לְתַלְפִּיּוֹת אֶלֶף הַמָּגֵן תָּלוּי
עָלָיו כֹּל שִׁלְטֵי הַגִּבֹּרִים׃

5 Thy two breasts are like two fawns,
That are twins of a gazelle,
Which feed among the lilies.

5 שְׁנֵי שָׁדַיִךְ כִּשְׁנֵי עֳפָרִים תְּאוֹמֵי
צְבִיָּה הָרֹעִים בַּשּׁוֹשַׁנִּים׃

6 Until the day breathe,
And the shadows flee away,
I will get me to the mountain of myrrh,
And to the hill of frankincense.

6 עַד שֶׁיָּפוּחַ הַיּוֹם וְנָסוּ הַצְּלָלִים
אֵלֶךְ לִי אֶל־הַר הַמּוֹר וְאֶל־
גִּבְעַת הַלְּבוֹנָה׃

3. *and thy mouth is comely.* The Hebrew *midbarech* signifies 'thy speech,' or 'the instrument of thy speech,' i.e. 'mouth.' Her lips, being red and thin, are comparable to *a thread of scarlet.*

*thy temples . . . open.* Her rosy cheeks resemble the pomegranate when cut open—a favourite expression in Oriental poetry. The Hebrew for *temples* means the thin part of the skull, and Ibn Ezra translates *pelach* as 'the red flower of the pomegranate.' 'Either that the temples gleam through the slit in the veil, as the mingled white and red of the pomegranate gleam through the cracks of the rind, or if *pelach* means "a piece," then the comparison is of the cheeks to the rounded form and ruddy colour of the section of the fruit' (Harper).

4. *thy neck.* Her erect carriage and above all her neck, covered with ornaments, resemble a commanding tower adorned with trophies.

*builded with turrets.* Ibn Ezra renders: 'for the suspension of arms'; a mound (*tel*) in which swords were stored. But why compare a graceful neck to a sword? Rashi and Rashbam translate *talpioth* as if derived from the root 'to teach' (*aleph*), the first letter being elided. The rendering of the Targum, 'the instruction of the law,' may have suggested this explanation. The neck of the Shulammite is like a splendid tower built as a model for others to follow. The word is understood by the LXX as a proper noun, 'The tower of David built towards Talpioth' (cf. vii. 5).

*whereon there hang a thousand shields.* For shields used as ornaments, cf. Ezek. xxvii. 11. A *thousand* signifies a large number.

*all the armour.* 'All kinds of armour used by heroes.' To a poetical mind, a beautiful neck graced by jewels suggested a tower bedecked with shields.

5. *like two fawns,* etc. Her bosom is finely developed. Colour is added by the description *which feed among the lilies.*

6. *until the day breathe.* Or, 'cools'; see on ii. 17. Elated with joy at meeting her shepherd, she interrupts his praise for her. 'When evening comes I shall repair to the open country, where everything is sweet and fragrant like myrrh and frankincense.'

7 Thou art all fair, my love;
And there is no spot in thee.

7 כֻּלָּךְ יָפָה רַעְיָתִי וּמוּם אֵין
בָּךְ׃

8 Come with me from Lebanon, my bride,
With me from Lebanon;
Look from the top of Amana,
From the top of Senir and Hermon,
From the lions' dens,
From the mountains of the leopards.

8 אִתִּי מִלְּבָנוֹן כַּלָּה אִתִּי מִלְּבָנוֹן
תָּבוֹאִי תָּשׁוּרִי ׀ מֵרֹאשׁ אֲמָנָה
מֵרֹאשׁ שְׂנִיר וְחֶרְמוֹן מִמְּעֹנוֹת
אֲרָיוֹת מֵהַרְרֵי נְמֵרִים׃

9 Thou hast ravished my heart, my sister, my bride;
Thou hast ravished my heart with one of thine eyes,
With one bead of thy necklace.

9 לִבַּבְתִּנִי אֲחֹתִי כַלָּה לִבַּבְתִּנִי
בְּאַחַד מֵעֵינַיִךְ בְּאַחַד עֲנָק
מִצַּוְּרֹנָיִךְ׃

10 How fair is thy love, my sister, my bride!
How much better is thy love than wine
And the smell of thine ointments than all manner of spices

10 מַה־יָּפוּ דֹדַיִךְ אֲחֹתִי כַּלָּה
מַה־טֹּבוּ דֹדַיִךְ מִיַּיִן וְרֵיחַ
שְׁמָנַיִךְ מִכָּל־בְּשָׂמִים׃

11 Thy lips, O my bride, drop honey—

11 נֹפֶת תִּטֹּפְנָה שִׂפְתוֹתַיִךְ כַּלָּה

v. 8. ב"א שׂניר v. 9. באחת ק'

7. *thou art all fair.* Delighted with her promise, he continues, 'Thy beauty is indeed ravishing; I will help thee to escape from this lair of *lions* and *leopards.*'

8. The rest of the chapter describes the lover pleading with her to flee from the royal palace. Note the fervour of his pleading: Come with *me;* do not remain with him (Solomon).

*look from the top of Amana.* Better, 'depart from the top of Amana'; for the meaning of the verb, cf. Isa. lvii. 9. He urges her to leave the royal residence in Lebanon. Amana is the name of the South of the Anti-Libanus, the eastern chain of hills facing the plain of Damascus (cf. 2 Kings v. 12).

*from the top of Senir and Hermon.* The Lebanon range in the extreme North of Palestine consists of several summits, the highest of which are Hermon and Senir. Solomon had probably built royal residences there. In Deut. iv. 48 Senir is called *Sion,* and in Deut. iii. 9 we are told that the Sidonians called it *Sirion.*

9. *thou hast ravished my heart.* The reunion has endowed him with courage to carry her away from enforced confinement. It has put new heart (*lebab*) into him.

*my sister, my bride.* Repeated to express tenderness, as in v. 1.

*with one of thine eyes.* It is customary for an Eastern woman to unveil one of her eyes when addressing someone. This action would also render visible some of the ornaments worn around the neck. The *kerë* has the fem. for *one* to agree with 'eye' which in Hebrew is fem. The meaning of the *kethib* is perhaps 'with one (glance) of thine eyes.'

*with one bead of thy necklace.* Cf. Prov. i. 9. Ibn Ezra explains as 'a kind of ornamental band tied round the neck.'

10. *how fair is thy love.* Or, 'how sweet are thy caresses.' The sight of her is more refreshing than wine (cf. i. 2).

11. *thy lips . . . drop honey.* Her words

Honey and milk are under thy tongue;
And the smell of thy garments is like the smell of Lebanon.

דְּבַשׁ וְחָלָב תַּחַת לְשׁוֹנֵךְ וְרֵיחַ
שַׂלְמֹתַיִךְ כְּרֵיחַ לְבָנוֹן׃

12 A garden shut up is my sister, my bride;
A spring shut up, a fountain sealed.

12 גַּן ׀ נָעוּל אֲחֹתִי כַלָּה גַּל ׀ נָעוּל
מַעְיָן חָתוּם׃

13 Thy shoots are a park of pomegranates,
With precious fruits;
Henna with spikenard plants,

13 שְׁלָחַיִךְ פַּרְדֵּס רִמּוֹנִים עִם
פְּרִי מְגָדִים כְּפָרִים עִם־
נְרָדִים׃

14 Spikenard and saffron, calamus and cinnamon,
With all trees of frankincense;
Myrrh and aloes, with all the chief spices.

14 נֵרְדְּ ׀ וְכַרְכֹּם קָנֶה וְקִנָּמוֹן עִם
כָּל־עֲצֵי לְבוֹנָה מֹר וַאֲהָלוֹת
עִם כָּל־רָאשֵׁי בְשָׂמִים׃

are as sweet to him as the honey that drops from the honeycomb.

*and the smell of thy garments.* An allusion to the Oriental custom of perfuming clothes. Lebanon was renowned for its fragrance (cf. Hosea xiv. 7). The girl must have exchanged her humble dress for some splendid raiment worn by the ladies of the court.

**12.** *a garden shut up.* The beauty of his beloved conjures up in his ardour a garden, splendid in colour and fertility; but it is a garden secluded unto all save its lawful possessor. She is chaste and modest, just as gardens are walled in to prevent the intrusion of strangers (cf. Isa. v. 5).

*a spring shut up.* For *gal*, 'a spring,' cf. Josh. xv. 19; Judges i. 15. Water being scarce in the East, owners of fountains sealed them with clay which quickly hardened in the sun. Thus sealed they became private property.

**13.** *thy shoots are a park of pomegranates.* lit. 'thy sendings forth are,' etc. She is not like an ordinary garden, but an orchard full of the most delicious fruit, so many are her charms. *Pardes*, 'park,' is probably a word of Persian origin (cf. Eccles. ii. 5).

**14.** *spikenard.* The Hebrew *nerd* is nard-oil.

*saffron.* Obtained from the crocus in Palestine and used as a condiment. In Arabic the word means 'yellow.'

*calamus.* Hebrew *kaneh*, a plant of reed-like stem and tawny colour, well known to the ancients, which was imported into Palestine from India.

*cinnamon.* Grown in the E. Indies, and when at its full height, it reached thirty feet. 'Rabbi Huna said: Cinnamon used to grow in the Land of Israel, and goats and deer fed on it' (Midrash).

*myrrh.* This is the oil obtained from the plant.

*aloes.* Grows in India; its wood is very aromatic and held in veneration by the natives. Rabbi Joshua said: 'This is foliation—an ointment or oil prepared from the leaves of the spikenard. Why is it called *ahaloth?* Because it comes by way of a tent (*ohel*), i.e. it is imported by the Bedouin tent-dwellers.' Another Rabbi explained: 'Because its fragrance spread in the tent, i.e. its smoke when used as an incense spreads in the sacred Tent of Meeting; its fragrance is very pervasive and fills a tent' (Midrash).

*with all the chief spices.* Her charms are as rare and as much to be valued as the most precious of aromatic herbs.

15 Thou art a fountain of gardens,
A well of living waters,
And flowing streams from Lebanon.

15 מַעְיַן גַּנִּים בְּאֵר מַיִם חַיִּים
וְנֹזְלִים מִן־לְבָנוֹן׃

16 Awake, O north wind;
And come, thou south;
Blow upon my garden,
That the spices thereof may flow out.
Let my beloved come into his garden,
And eat his precious fruits.

16 עוּרִי צָפוֹן וּבוֹאִי תֵימָן הָפִיחִי
גַנִּי יִזְּלוּ בְשָׂמָיו יָבֹא דוֹדִי לְגַנּוֹ
וְיֹאכַל פְּרִי מְגָדָיו׃

## 5 CHAPTER V ה

1 I am come into my garden, my sister, my bride;
I have gathered my myrrh with my spice;

1 בָּאתִי לְגַנִּי אֲחֹתִי כַלָּה אָרִיתִי
מוֹרִי עִם־בְּשָׂמִי אָכַלְתִּי יַעְרִי

15. *a fountain of gardens.* The lover seals the charming description of his maiden's beauty by adding to the fragrant garden a fountain and a stream and cool breezes which waft the aroma of the rare spices all around. To him she is not *a sealed garden,* but one which he can enjoy as of right. The fountain of his garden is *a well of living waters,* the source of all his joy, the inspiration of his existence: she is to him what a cool fountain means to the tired and parched wayfarer.

16. *awake, O north wind.* This verse is usually explained as her answer to his glowing pæan. Touched by his longing for her, she invites him to enjoy the pleasures that are only his. *His garden* is a modest reference to herself. The north wind scatters the perfumes, so does she wish her charms to be enjoyed by him. Such words could only be spoken by a woman pining for her beloved to release her from captivity, and longing for the time when she could be wholly his. Rabbi Jochanan said: 'The Torah gives here a lesson in good breeding, viz. that the bridegroom should not enter the bridal chamber till the bride gives him permission to do so.'

## CHAPTER V

1. *I am come into my garden.* In Hebrew the perfect of the verb also expresses a definite future act. Her shepherd lover is so thrilled at the thought of coming to meet her in the garden that he imagines himself already there. Sforno, homilizing the whole of the chapter, applies this verse to the religious education of children.

*I have gathered.* The root *arah* means 'to gather fruit' (cf. Ps. lxxx. 13), and the literal translation is, 'I have plucked my myrrh with my balsam.'

I have eaten my honeycomb with my honey;
I have drunk my wine with my milk.
Eat, O friends;
Drink, yea, drink abundantly, O beloved.

עִם־דִּבְשִׁי שָׁתִיתִי יֵינִי עִם־
חֲלָבִי אִכְלוּ רֵעִים שְׁתוּ וְשִׁכְרוּ
דּוֹדִים׃

2 I sleep, but my heart waketh;
Hark! my beloved knocketh:
'Open to me, my sister, my love,
my dove, my undefiled;
For my head is filled with dew,
My locks with the drops of the night.'

2 אֲנִי יְשֵׁנָה וְלִבִּי עֵר קוֹל ׀ דּוֹדִי
דוֹפֵק פִּתְחִי־לִי אֲחֹתִי רַעְיָתִי
יוֹנָתִי תַמָּתִי שֶׁרֹּאשִׁי נִמְלָא־
טָל קְוֻצּוֹתַי רְסִיסֵי לָיְלָה׃

3 I have put off my coat;
How shall I put it on?
I have washed my feet;
How shall I defile them?

3 פָּשַׁטְתִּי אֶת־כֻּתָּנְתִּי אֵיכָכָה
אֶלְבָּשֶׁנָּה רָחַצְתִּי אֶת־רַגְלַי
אֵיכָכָה אֲטַנְּפֵם׃

v. 2. הר׳ בדגש

*my honey.* Cf. 1 Sam. xiv. 27.

*eat, O friends.* Who utters these words? Some suggest that a few friendly ladies of the court, seeing the happiness of the lovers at being together, urge them to make the most of their opportunity. According to Rashbam, it is the invitation to the friends of the lovers to participate in the marriage feast. Most commentators make *friends* agree with *beloved* (which is plural) in accordance with the context and poetic parallelism.

**2.** *I sleep.* A day of excitement is followed by troubled dreams. In verses 2-7 she relates her dream; in verse 8 she asks the ladies of the court, who have offered to assist her in the search, to tell her lover, on finding him, that she is sick with love for him. They ask (verse 9) what she can see so extraordinary in him to warrant all her excitement, which provides her with the opportunity of painting a glorious picture of his graces.

*my heart.* The heart was the seat of the passions, but also the source of intellect.

*hark! my beloved knocketh.* Seeing that the ladies are sympathetic, she tells them her dream. This translation follows the LXX which takes *dophek* as a separate clause agreeing with *dodi*, 'my beloved is knocking.' For *kol*, with the meaning *hark*, see on ii. 8.

*open to me.* With her heart awake, love conjures up many visions. Coloured by her waking thoughts, she imagines her lover calling to her.

*for my head is filled with dew.* To lend support to his plea, he mentions that he is bedrenched with dew and the moisture that drops from the night clouds. During certain months, dew falls so copiously in the East, that it saturates clothes like rain (cf. Judges vi. 38). He may have come from her mother's house in the night.

**3.** *I have put off my coat.* This was a tunic, or inner garment of linen, descending down to the ankles and taken off at night. It has been suggested that this verse should be prefaced with the words, 'I said to myself.' It is obvious that this verse records what she said in her dream, for to one awake it is not impossible to put on a coat again after having taken it off! Her reasons for not opening the door to her lover's knocking are so trivial and her difficulties such as to be insurmountable only in a dream.

*I have washed my feet.* In the East it was essential for travellers to wash their dusty feet on entering a house.

*how shall I defile them.* The word for *how* is found again only in Esther. viii. 6.

4 My beloved put in his hand by the hole of the door.
And my heart was moved for him.

4 דּוֹדִי שָׁלַח יָדוֹ מִן־הַחוֹר וּמֵעַי
הָמוּ עָלָיו׃

5 I rose up to open to my beloved;
And my hands dropped with myrrh,
And my fingers with flowing myrrh,
Upon the handles of the bar.

5 קַמְתִּי אֲנִי לִפְתֹּחַ לְדוֹדִי וְיָדַי
נָטְפוּ־מוֹר וְאֶצְבְּעֹתַי מוֹר
עֹבֵר עַל כַּפּוֹת הַמַּנְעוּל׃

6 I opened to my beloved;
But my beloved had turned away, and was gone.
My soul failed me when he spoke.
I sought him, but I could not find him;
I called him, but he gave me no answer.

6 פָּתַחְתִּי אֲנִי לְדוֹדִי וְדוֹדִי
חָמַק עָבָר נַפְשִׁי יָצְאָה בְדַבְּרוֹ
בִּקַּשְׁתִּיהוּ וְלֹא מְצָאתִיהוּ
קְרָאתִיו וְלֹא עָנָנִי׃

4. *my beloved put in his hand.* Better, 'withdrew his hand.' Hearing her lame excuses for not answering his knock, he departs, and his action causes her anxiety.

*by the hole of the door.* It would appear that an unbolted door could be opened by inserting the hand in the hole. In many cottages to-day the lifting of a latch admits to the house. As women in the East were confined to the home and secluded from the gaze of men, this verse may refer to the holes in doors from which the women could look out and speak to the men who called, without being exposed to their gaze. Her lover may have beckoned to her by putting his hand through the door, as an indication of his yearning for her, and the sight of his hand, after the long separation, stirs in her feelings of a tender nature.

*my heart.* lit. 'my bowels,' which, to the ancients, were the seat of the emotions (cf. Jer. xxxi. 19; Ps. xl. 9).

*was moved for him.* The verb *hamah*, lit. 'to make a noise,' is frequently used to describe the sound of roaring waves in troubled seas. Her agitated heart is moved like storm-tossed waves.

5. *my hands dropped with myrrh.* When the knocking ceased, she became anxious. Rushing to open the door, her hands touched the liquid scent with which her beloved had sprinkled the door, perhaps as a gesture of love, or in pursuance of a custom to anoint the door of a beloved with fragrant spices. Some commentators are of the view that she had anointed herself with myrrh before retiring for the night.

*flowing myrrh.* Others render 'liquid myrrh,' in contrast to the solidified kind. Myrrh is obtained from the shrub of that name (cf. Exod. xxx. 23 where it is termed *flowing myrrh—dror*). In her eagerness to receive him, she had sprayed herself with the perfume.

6. *but my beloved had turned away.* Imagine her grief at not finding him there! The verbs *chamak abar* (*had turned away, was gone*) are most expressive, and the omission of the particle 'and' reflects her disturbed mind.

*my soul failed me.* Her disappointment brought about a momentary loss of consciousness. She felt faint.

*when he spoke.* Rashi comments: 'Because he said, "I will not now enter, since thou didst at first refuse to open to me".' As is usual in dreams, disappointment sets in at the moment of frustration. When she first heard his voice, emotion overcame her; now that he had gone, she again felt about to swoon.

7 The watchmen that go about the city found me,
They smote me, they wounded me;
The keepers of the walls took away my mantle from me.

7 מְצָאֻנִי הַשֹּׁמְרִים הַסֹּבְבִים
בָּעִיר הִכּוּנִי פְצָעוּנִי נָשְׂאוּ
אֶת־רְדִידִי מֵעָלַי שֹׁמְרֵי
הַחֹמוֹת׃

8 'I adjure you, O daughters of Jerusalem,
If ye find my beloved,
What will ye tell him?
That I am love-sick.'

8 הִשְׁבַּעְתִּי אֶתְכֶם בְּנוֹת
יְרוּשָׁלִָם אִם־תִּמְצְאוּ אֶת־
דּוֹדִי מַה־תַּגִּידוּ לוֹ שֶׁחוֹלַת
אַהֲבָה אָנִי׃

9 'What is thy beloved more than another beloved,
O thou fairest among women?
What is thy beloved more than another beloved,
That thou dost so adjure us?'

9 מַה־דּוֹדֵךְ מִדּוֹד הַיָּפָה
בַּנָּשִׁים מַה־דּוֹדֵךְ מִדּוֹד
שֶׁכָּכָה הִשְׁבַּעְתָּנוּ׃

10 'My beloved is white and ruddy,
Pre-eminent above ten thousand.

10 דּוֹדִי צַח וְאָדוֹם דָּגוּל
מֵרְבָבָה׃

11 His head is as the most fine gold,
His locks are curled,
And black as a raven.

11 רֹאשׁוֹ כֶּתֶם פָּז קְוּצּוֹתָיו
תַּלְתַּלִּים שְׁחֹרוֹת כָּעוֹרֵב׃

**7.** *the watchmen*, etc. Those who patrol the city at night, mistaking the distraught maiden for a wanton, attempt to stop her, and when she refuses, they have recourse to violence.

*my mantle.* This word (*redid*) occurs again only in Isa. iii. 23. It was worn by Oriental ladies out of doors, and may have been a fine lawn garment thrown over the whole dress. Kimchi thinks it was a silk veil.

**8.** *I adjure you.* Only in her dream did she hesitate to welcome him; in her wakeful state she yearns for him. She asks the ladies to assist her in the search. Jewish commentators apply this verse to the intense love of Israel for God despite prolonged suffering.

*that I am love-sick.* She urges them to tell her lover, on finding him, that her delay in opening the door was caused by the effects of her ardent love for him.

**9.** *what is thy beloved more*, etc. Surprised at her great passion they taunt her. What does she see in him to excite her emotions? The question provides her with an opportunity to give a vivid account of his physical grace. Similarly, Jewish commentators point out that the nations of the world often taunt Israel by asking why they display so much loyalty to a God Who seems to have forsaken them: 'What is thy God more than other deities?'

**10.** *white and ruddy.* She depicts the clear-white complexion of his skin (cf. Lam. iv. 7).

*pre-eminent above ten thousand.* 'Just as a standard (*degel*) is raised above the head of a marching army, so does he tower above all others on account of his beauty.' *Ten thousand* expresses a very large number.

**11.** *most fine gold.* Hebrew *kethem paz*, a figure of speech for excellency. Beginning with his head, she describes in matchless imagery all the limbs of his shapely body. Ibn Ezra translates *kethem* by 'a diadem' and *paz* by 'precious stones.' Rashi renders: 'Choice things

12 His eyes are like doves
Beside the water-brooks;
Washed with milk,
And fitly set.

13 His cheeks are as a bed of spices,
As banks of sweet herbs;
His lips are as lilies,
Dropping with flowing myrrh.

14 His hands are as rods of gold
Set with beryl;
His body is as polished ivory
Overlaid with sapphires.

15 His legs are as pillars of marble,
Set upon sockets of fine gold;
His aspect is like Lebanon,
Excellent as the cedars.

12 עֵינָיו כְּיוֹנִים עַל־אֲפִיקֵי מָיִם
רֹחֲצוֹת בֶּחָלָב יֹשְׁבוֹת עַל־
מִלֵּאת׃

13 לְחָיָו כַּעֲרוּגַת הַבֹּשֶׂם מִגְדְּלוֹת
מֶרְקָחִים שִׂפְתוֹתָיו שׁוֹשַׁנִּים
נֹטְפוֹת מוֹר עֹבֵר׃

14 יָדָיו גְּלִילֵי זָהָב מְמֻלָּאִים
בַּתַּרְשִׁישׁ מֵעָיו עֶשֶׁת שֵׁן
מְעֻלֶּפֶת סַפִּירִים׃

15 שׁוֹקָיו עַמּוּדֵי שֵׁשׁ מְיֻסָּדִים
עַל־אַדְנֵי־פָז מַרְאֵהוּ כַּלְּבָנוֹן
בָּחוּר כָּאֲרָזִים׃

which kings treasure up'; and Rashbam: 'Heap of gold, pearl-like in colour.'

*his locks are curled.* His hair hangs in wavy curls from his head; lit. 'heaps upon heaps' (*taltallim*), undulating like hills (*tel*).

12. *his eyes are like doves*, etc. Like doves bathing in streams of milk. The dark iris, surrounded by the gleaming white of his eye, suggests this beautiful simile. Doves are fond of bathing and usually choose the vicinity of streams for their abode.

*and fitly set.* Neither projecting nor too deeply set, but just right; lit. 'sitting in fulness,' set like precious stones in the foil of a ring.

13. *as a bed of spices.* Or, 'balsam shrubs.' *Arugah* is a raised flower-bed (cf. Ezek. xvii. 7).

*as banks of sweet herbs.* The Hebrew for *banks* is *migdaloth*, 'towers.' Spices used to be placed in vessels in the shape of towers. The rounded form and variegated colour of his cheeks suggest this bold comparison. His beard sits perfumed on his cheeks and his breath is as sweet as the purest myrrh.

*dropping with flowing myrrh.* This refers to his lips and expresses the sweetness of his conversation.

14. *rods of gold.* lit. 'rounded cylinders,' alluding to his delicately rounded fingers, tipped with well-shaped nails, as if inlaid with precious stones.

*beryl. Tarshish* is chrysolite, first found in Tartessus in ancient Spain. In colour it is yellow and pellucid, thus suggesting the nails of the fingers which are transparently pink.

*as polished ivory.* Suggested by his white, smooth body. Her purpose is to indicate that every inch of his body is far more precious to her than all the wealth of Solomon. *Esheth* (*polished*) denotes something wrought. Rashi explains: 'to shine with brightness' (cf. Jer. v. 28).

*sapphires.* Perhaps our lapis lazuli, descriptive of the purple tunic covering his glistening skin. His body is as beautiful as a piece of ivory studded with sapphires.

15. *as pillars of marble.* His white legs, set on finely shaped feet, are like marble columns on golden pedestals.

*like Lebanon.* Descriptive of his majestic appearance. Lebanon was famed for its fertility and beauty (cf. Deut. iii. 25).

*excellent as the cedars.* These tower above all other trees (cf. Amos ii. 9). So is her beloved outstanding among all men.

16 His mouth is most sweet;
Yea, he is altogether lovely.
This is my beloved, and this is my friend,
O daughters of Jerusalem.'

16 חִכּוֹ מַמְתַקִּים וְכֻלּוֹ מַחֲמַדִּים
זֶה דוֹדִי וְזֶה רֵעִי בְּנוֹת
יְרוּשָׁלָ͏ִם׃

## 6 CHAPTER VI ו

1 'Whither is thy beloved gone,
O thou fairest among women?
Whither hath thy beloved turned him,
That we may seek him with thee?'

1 אָנָה הָלַךְ דּוֹדֵךְ הַיָּפָה בַּנָּשִׁים
אָנָה פָּנָה דוֹדֵךְ וּנְבַקְשֶׁנּוּ
עִמָּךְ׃

2 'My beloved is gone down to his garden,
To the beds of spices,
To feed in the gardens,
And to gather lilies.

2 דּוֹדִי יָרַד לְגַנּוֹ לַעֲרוּגוֹת
הַבֹּשֶׂם לִרְעוֹת בַּגַּנִּים וְלִלְקֹט
שׁוֹשַׁנִּים׃

3 I am my beloved's, and my beloved is mine,
That feedeth among the lilies.'

3 אֲנִי לְדוֹדִי וְדוֹדִי לִי הָרֹעֶה
בַּשּׁוֹשַׁנִּים׃

**16.** *his mouth is most sweet.* lit. 'his palate,' from which comes his words (cf. iv. 3). His mouth utters nothing but pleasant things. After describing the perfection of his figure, she turns to his voice which is also described in glowing terms. This touch gives animation to the beautiful statue which has been described. She concludes on a triumphant note: '*This is my beloved and this is my friend;* and now judge for yourselves wherein my beloved is more to me than any other.' She feels that she has more than answered the scornful question contained in verse 9.

## CHAPTER VI

**1.** *whither is thy beloved gone.* Touched by her ardent description, the ladies of the court are anxious to assist in the search. 'If he is so wonderful, then let us help thee to look for him.' 'Similarly have the nations taunted Israel: Where is your God to help you?' (Midrash).

**2.** *my beloved is gone down to his garden.* Perhaps jealous of the interest that has been aroused in her beloved, she offers an evasive reply, simply suggesting that he may have gone forth to his usual haunts, gathering garlands as before.

**3.** *I am my beloved's.* Bearing in mind how they formerly tried to turn away her affections from him, she gives evasive answers to their queries. So strong is her love, that his temporary disappearance only serves to make it still more overpowering. The dramatic elements which are pronounced in this chapter are intended to give unity and movement to the poem.

*that feedeth among the lilies. They* are not to search; that is *her* duty alone. Jealousy within her now speaks: 'Of what right are you so interested in him?' Perhaps the thought troubles her. Has she overstepped the mark in singing his praises and arousing the curiosity of the ladies? In fear of losing him, she retracts some of her enthusiastic statements about him.

4 Thou art beautiful, O my love, as Tirzah,
Comely as Jerusalem,
Terrible as an army with banners.

4 יָפָה אַתְּ רַעְיָתִי כְּתִרְצָה נָאוָה
כִּירוּשָׁלִָם אֲיֻמָּה כַּנִּדְגָּלוֹת׃

5 Turn away thine eyes from me,
For they have overcome me.
Thy hair is as a flock of goats,
That trail down from Gilead.

5 הָסֵבִּי עֵינַיִךְ מִנֶּגְדִּי שֶׁהֵם
הִרְהִיבֻנִי שַׂעְרֵךְ כְּעֵדֶר
הָעִזִּים שֶׁגָּלְשׁוּ מִן־הַגִּלְעָד׃

6 Thy teeth are like a flock of ewes,
Which are come up from the washing;
Whereof all are paired,
And none faileth among them.

6 שִׁנַּיִךְ כְּעֵדֶר הָרְחֵלִים שֶׁעָלוּ
מִן־הָרַחְצָה שֶׁכֻּלָּם מַתְאִימוֹת
וְשַׁכֻּלָה אֵין בָּהֶם׃

7 Thy temples are like a pomegranate split open
Behind thy veil.

7 כְּפֶלַח הָרִמּוֹן רַקָּתֵךְ מִבַּעַד
לְצַמָּתֵךְ׃

8 There are threescore queens,
And fourscore concubines,
And maidens without number.

8 שִׁשִּׁים הֵמָּה מְלָכוֹת וּשְׁמֹנִים
פִּילַגְשִׁים וַעֲלָמוֹת אֵין מִסְפָּר׃

The rest of the chapter, according to some expositors, recounts another futile attempt on the part of the infatuated Solomon to win her love for himself. Unfortunately for him the wrong moment is chosen, because she has just made another passionate declaration of her love for the shepherd, a love that is stronger than death. The king extols her physical beauty (verses 4-9) and endorses the words of the court ladies who had sung her charms. In verses 11f. the Shulammite recalls what she was doing on the fateful day when she was so praised and made her attempt to run away.

4. *as Tirzah.* The king addresses her in flattering language: 'Thou art as graceful as the beautiful town of Tirzah, as charming as Jerusalem, as captivating as a conquering army in full battle array.' Tirzah, an old Canaanite city (Josh. xii. 24), was famed for its beauty and was renowned as the royal residence of the kings of Israel after the revolt of Jeroboam. It may have been linked here with Jerusalem, instead of Samaria which was the capital of the N. Kingdom, because of the evil repute in which the latter was held after Nehemiah's day. Tirzah retained the distinction of being a royal residence until the time of Omri, who built Samaria (1 Kings xvi. 15ff.). The city was of striking beauty, as is indicated by its Hebrew name, which means 'to be pleasant.' Hence the remark of the Midrash, followed by Jewish commentators: 'Thou (Israel) art beautiful when thou performest deeds that please Me.'

*comely as Jerusalem.* A city which was called *the perfection of beauty* (cf. Lam. ii. 15).

*terrible as an army with banners.* In Prov. vii. 26 the power of a seductive woman is compared to an armed host. Here the intention of the speaker is to assert that the constancy of this country maiden was as formidable as the might of an army.

5. *for they have overcome me.* Ibn Ezra comments: 'So overwhelming is my love for thee, that I cannot look into thine eyes without being overcome.'

*thy hair . . . Gilead.* Repeated from iv. 1.

6f. Almost identical with iv. 2f.

8. Though the possessor of a harem of beautiful women, none has won the king's heart more than she. The variation of the number of his wives given

9 My dove, my undefiled, is but one;
She is the only one of her mother;
She is the choice one of her that bore her.
The daughters saw her, and called her happy;
Yea, the queens and the concubines, and they praised her.

9 אַחַת הִיא יוֹנָתִי תַמָּתִי אַחַת
הִיא לְאִמָּהּ בָּרָה הִיא
לְיוֹלַדְתָּהּ רָאוּהָ בָנוֹת
וַיְאַשְּׁרוּהָ מְלָכוֹת וּפִילַגְשִׁים
וַיְהַלְלוּהָ׃

10 Who is she that looketh forth as the dawn,
Fair as the moon,
Clear as the sun,
Terrible as an army with banners?

10 מִי־זֹאת הַנִּשְׁקָפָה כְּמוֹ־שָׁחַר
יָפָה כַלְּבָנָה בָּרָה כַּחַמָּה
אֲיֻמָּה כַּנִּדְגָּלוֹת׃

11 I went down into the garden of nuts,
To look at the green plants of the valley,
To see whether the vine budded,
And the pomegranates were in flower.

11 אֶל־גִּנַּת אֱגוֹז יָרַדְתִּי לִרְאוֹת
בְּאִבֵּי הַנָּחַל לִרְאוֹת הֲפָרְחָה
הַגֶּפֶן הֵנֵצוּ הָרִמֹּנִים׃

12 Before I was aware, my soul set me
Upon the chariots of my princely people.

12 לֹא יָדַעְתִּי נַפְשִׁי שָׂמַתְנִי
מַרְכְּבוֹת עַמִּי נָדִיב׃

here as compared with 1 Kings xi. 3 can be explained by the concluding words *and maidens without number*. The word *alamoth* denotes young women of marriageable age.

9. *is but one.* The only one of her kind (cf. 2 Sam. vii. 23); there is none like her in all his harem.

10. *that looketh forth as the dawn.* The king is citing the praise of the ladies when they first beheld her.

11. *garden of nuts.* She interrupts her royal suitor: 'Have I then gone out to meet the king and lure him to myself? When I was tending the vines and seeing what fruit and nuts were ripe in my garden, I was taken and brought to the court. Let him release me that I may return to my home.' Nuts grow plentifully in N. Palestine. The Midrash has many a fine simile in which Israel is likened to nuts, e.g. 'Just as the shell of a nut, when falling into mud, protects the kernel from becoming unclean, so has Israel preserved its purity when dispersed among the nations.'

12. This is a difficult verse. Unexpectedly and unwillingly she is brought among the aristocracy of the land, poetically called *the chariots of my princely people.* She protests: '*Before I was aware,* engaged as I was in the task allotted to me by my brothers in the garden, the servants of the king carried me away, and before I could realize it I found myself at court.'

*before I was aware.* lit. 'I did not know,' hence 'suddenly, unwittingly' (cf. Jer. l. 24).

*my princely people.* The LXX treats the words as a proper noun, *ammi nadib*, which cannot be identified. Rashi asserts that the *yad* is not the suffix 'my' but a poetical termination. He interprets: 'My soul has made me as the chariots for foreign princes to ride upon,' i.e. I have unwillingly brought a foreign yoke upon myself. That is how she feels at court in their midst, quite out of place.

1 Return, return, O Shulammite;
Return, return, that we may look upon thee.
What will ye see in the Shulammite?
As it were a dance of two companies.

1 שׁוּבִי שׁוּבִי הַשּׁוּלַמִּית שׁוּבִי
שׁוּבִי וְנֶחֱזֶה־בָּךְ מַה־תֶּחֱזוּ
בַּשּׁוּלַמִּית כִּמְחֹלַת הַמַּחֲנָיִם׃

2 How beautiful are thy steps in sandals,
O prince's daughter!
The roundings of thy thighs are like the links of a chain,
The work of the hands of a skilled workman.

2 מַה־יָּפוּ פְעָמַיִךְ בַּנְּעָלִים
בַּת־נָדִיב חַמּוּקֵי יְרֵכַיִךְ כְּמוֹ
חֲלָאִים מַעֲשֵׂה יְדֵי אָמָּן׃

3 Thy navel is like a round goblet,
Wherein no mingled wine is wanting;

3 שָׁרְרֵךְ אַגַּן הַסַּהַר אַל־יֶחְסַר

**1. *return, that we may look upon thee.*** Realizing that all his attempts have failed, the king implores her not to flee from his presence, but to allow his eyes to feast upon her beauty.

***what will ye see in the Shulammite.*** i.e. 'What canst thou see in a peasant maiden that thou art so persistent in thine attentions?' she asks the king. Shulem is a village in the plain of Esdraelon, three and a half miles north of Jezreel, lying to the west of what is called 'Little Hermon.' It may be identified with the ancient Shunem belonging to the tribe of Issachar, where the Philistines encamped before the last battle of Saul (1 Sam. xxviii. 4). It was from Shunem that Abishag hailed, and it was there Elisha found a lodging place (2 Kings iv. 8).

***as it were a dance of two companies.*** Answering her question what he can see in her, he replies, 'To see thee is like gazing at a charming view of a festive choir, expressing their joy in a sacred dance.' A.V. and R.V. render *two companies* as a place name, Mahanaim, the town whither David fled when a fugitive from Absalom (2 Sam. xvii. 24). It is situated north of the Jabbok, not far from the Jordan valley.

**2. *thy steps in sandals.*** In obedience to the king's request to retrace her steps, she comes back. Infatuated by her stately bearing and the grace of her walk, he makes still another attempt to gain her love by lauding her charms.

***O prince's daughter.*** Better, 'O born lady.' *Bath nadib* means a scion of a noble family, but may also signify the possessor of a noble character.

***the roundings of thy thighs.*** A reference to her swaying hips. The movement of her feet resembles the links of a chain. So intimate are these praises of her body, that it has been suggested that they are spoken by the ladies of the court, probably in the privacy of the women's apartments, as they dress her to appear before the king.

**3. *a round goblet.*** Hebrew *agan hasahar*, lit. 'a bowl of roundness.' 'There are places where the moon is called *sahara*. *Sahar* is an allusion to the Sanhedrin sitting in semi-circular rows, like a half moon, which is likewise the shape of the threshing-floor' (Midrash).

***mingled wine.*** It was the practice of the ancients to mix wine with spices to make it more potent.

Thy belly is like a heap of wheat
Set about with lilies.

4 Thy two breasts are like two fawns
That are twins of a gazelle.

5 Thy neck is as a tower of ivory;
Thine eyes as the pools in Heshbon,
By the gate of Bath-rabbim;
Thy nose is like the tower of Lebanon
Which looketh toward Damascus.

6 Thy head upon thee is like Carmel,
And the hair of thy head like purple;
The king is held captive in the tresses thereof.

הַמָּזֶג בִּטְנֵךְ עֲרֵמַת חִטִּים סוּגָה
בַּשּׁוֹשַׁנִּים׃
4 שְׁנֵי שָׁדַיִךְ כִּשְׁנֵי עֳפָרִים תָּאֳמֵי
צְבִיָּה׃
5 צַוָּארֵךְ כְּמִגְדַּל הַשֵּׁן עֵינַיִךְ
בְּרֵכוֹת בְּחֶשְׁבּוֹן עַל־שַׁעַר
בַּת־רַבִּים אַפֵּךְ כְּמִגְדַּל
הַלְּבָנוֹן צוֹפֶה פְּנֵי דַמָּשֶׂק׃
6 רֹאשֵׁךְ עָלַיִךְ כַּכַּרְמֶל וְדַלַּת
רֹאשֵׁךְ כָּאַרְגָּמָן מֶלֶךְ אָסוּר
בָּרְהָטִים׃

*like a heap of wheat.* In Syria, the perfect skin was considered to be that which could be compared in colour to the yellowish-white of wheat after it had been threshed and winnowed.

*set about with lilies.* 'The threshing floors in ancient times were in the open air and when wheat had been threshed out, fanned and heaped up, each heap was hedged round with thorns in order to keep off the cattle. On festal occasions the wheat was decorated with flowers. To render the compliment more flattering, the enamoured king changes the hedges of thorns to lilies' (Ginsburg). Lilies may allude to the garment about her body.

4. *like two fawns.* Cf. iv. 5 where the shepherd uses identical language.

5. *as a tower of ivory.* Cf. iv. 4. A tower-like neck has always been considered beautiful.

*thine eyes as the pools in Heshbon.* The ancient capital of Sihon, king of the Amorites, situated twenty miles east of the point where the Jordan enters the Dead Sea. Originally a Moabite city (Num. xxi. 25), it later came into the possession of the Amorites (Josh. ix. 10). Shortly before his death, Moses assigned it first to Reuben and then to the tribe of Gad. It passed hands between the Israelites and Moabites several times. For many years it was the pride of Moab, famous for its fertility, verdure and reservoirs. The soft glance of her eyes reflects the peace and beauty of the Heshbon pools.

*by the gate of Bath-rabbim.* Either a proper noun or 'the gate of the populous city,' because through it a multitude of the inhabitants pass in and out. The gates of a city were the chief place of assembly.

*thy nose is like the tower of Lebanon.* 'Since when is a prominent nose a sign of beauty?' (Rashi). The word *appech* is therefore taken to mean 'thy face.' It would seem that the comparison is between the well-proportioned nose and the beautiful projecting tower.

6. *thy head upon thee is like Carmel.* Her shapely head is poised like the summit of Carmel, overlooking the sea in N.W. Palestine in solitary majesty.

*the king . . . tresses thereof.* Common to the poetry of all times and climes is the idea of the lover held captive in a woman's tresses. Like the lashes of the eyelids, the ringlets are described as 'the net of love' (cf. Prov. vi. 25).

7 How fair and how pleasant art thou,
O love, for delights!

7 מַה־יָּפִית וּמַה־נָּעַמְתְּ אַהֲבָה
בַּתַּעֲנוּגִים׃

8 This thy stature is like to a palm-tree,
And thy breasts to clusters of grapes.

8 זֹאת קוֹמָתֵךְ דָּמְתָה לְתָמָר
וְשָׁדַיִךְ לְאַשְׁכֹּלוֹת׃

9 I said: 'I will climb up into the palm-tree,
I will take hold of the branches thereof;
And let thy breasts be as clusters of the vine,
And the smell of thy countenance like apples;

9 אָמַרְתִּי אֶעֱלֶה בְתָמָר אֹחֲזָה
בְּסַנְסִנָּיו וְיִהְיוּ־נָא שָׁדַיִךְ
כְּאֶשְׁכְּלוֹת הַגֶּפֶן וְרֵיחַ אַפֵּךְ
כַּתַּפּוּחִים׃

10 And the roof of thy mouth like the best wine,
That glideth down smoothly for my beloved,
Moving gently the lips of those that are asleep.'

10 וְחִכֵּךְ כְּיֵין הַטּוֹב הוֹלֵךְ לְדוֹדִי
לְמֵישָׁרִים דּוֹבֵב שִׂפְתֵי יְשֵׁנִים׃

11 I am my beloved's,
And his desire is toward me.

11 אֲנִי לְדוֹדִי וְעָלַי תְּשׁוּקָתוֹ׃

7. *how fair.* The rapturous description of her loveliness continues. Compared with the inanimate objects to which she had been likened, she is so full of life.

*O love, for delights.* Better, 'how surpassingly delightful is love above all other pleasures!' The king now makes a last bid for her love. Attired in costly apparel, as befits her appearance before a king, she causes the royal suitor to be more than ever enthralled with her. To his enchantment he gives utterance in terms more passionate than ever before. Again she thrusts his attentions aside and concentrates upon her lover. The king has no alternative but to withdraw and abandon her to reunion with her lover.

8. *like to a palm-tree.* The stately palm, like the tall cedar and graceful cypress, supplied favourite images to the poetic mind.

9. *I will climb up.* Proceeding with his flattery, the king tells her to what heights he would go to obtain her love.

10. *and the roof . . . wine.* Her speech was sweeter to him than the choicest wine.

*that glideth down smoothly.* Like mellow wine of prized quality (cf. Prov. xxiii. 31).

*moving gently . . . asleep.* Wine produces such animation that it often unlocks silence and causes silent lips to speak. Just as much wine causes deep sleep, coloured by pleasant dreams, so did her speech stir his pleasant emotions.

11. *I am my beloved's.* Cf. vi. 3. She openly rejects the king's wooing. None can separate her from her only beloved.

12 Come, my beloved, let us go forth into the field;
Let us lodge in the villages.

12 לְכָה דוֹדִי נֵצֵא הַשָּׂדֶה נָלִינָה
בַּכְּפָרִים׃

13 Let us get up early to the vineyards;
Let us see whether the vine hath budded,
Whether the vine-blossom be opened,
And the pomegranates be in flower;
There will I give thee my love.

13 נַשְׁכִּימָה לַכְּרָמִים נִרְאֶה אִם־
פָּרְחָה הַגֶּפֶן פִּתַּח הַסְּמָדַר
הֵנֵצוּ הָרִמּוֹנִים שָׁם אֶתֵּן אֶת־
דֹּדַי לָךְ׃

14 The mandrakes give forth fragrance,
And at our doors are all manner of precious fruits,
New and old,
Which I have laid up for thee, O my beloved.

14 הַדּוּדָאִים נָתְנוּ־רֵיחַ וְעַל־
פְּתָחֵינוּ כָּל־מְגָדִים חֲדָשִׁים
גַּם־יְשָׁנִים דּוֹדִי צָפַנְתִּי לָךְ׃

12. *come, my beloved.* She again addresses her shepherd who now reappears, and urges their departure from the palace to their former meeting-place in the fields.

*in the villages.* Some render *kefarim* by 'henna flowers,' as in iv. 13. This interpretation is unnecessary. The maiden would rather go to the villages with her lover than to Tirzah and Jerusalem.

13. *let us get up early to the vineyards.* Thrilled at the thought of her impending home-coming, she envisages the familiar scenes. But so eager is she to be home again, that she implores him to postpone his manifestation of love towards her until then.

*whether the vine-blossom be opened.* See on ii. 13 for the word *semadar.*

14. *the mandrakes.* They were believed to be helpful towards the stirring of the emotion of love (cf. Gen. xxx. 14f.). The Hebrew name for the plant, *dudaim*, is connected with *dodim* 'love.' 'Mandrakes grow low like lettuce to which they have a striking resemblance, except that they are dark green. Their flower is purple and the root is, for the most part, forked. The fruit ripens in May and in size is like a small apple. So is its colour, which is very red and its flavour very agreeable' (Ginsburg).

*which I have laid up for thee.* Fruits used to be stored on shelves or cupboards above doorways where they were left to dry and be out of reach. She assures her lover that she had put away all the good things for him only to enjoy.

1 Oh that thou wert as my brother,
That sucked the breasts of my mother!
When I should find thee without,
I would kiss thee;
Yea, and none would despise me.

1 מִי יִתֶּנְךָ כְּאָח לִי יוֹנֵק שְׁדֵי אִמִּי
אֶמְצָאֲךָ בַחוּץ אֶשָּׁקְךָ גַּם לֹא־
יָבֻזוּ לִי׃

2 I would lead thee, and bring thee into my mother's house,
That thou mightest instruct me;
I would cause thee to drink of spiced wine,
Of the juice of my pomegranate.

2 אֶנְהָגְךָ אֲבִיאֲךָ אֶל־בֵּית אִמִּי
תְּלַמְּדֵנִי אַשְׁקְךָ מִיַּיִן הָרֶקַח
מֵעֲסִיס רִמֹּנִי׃

3 His left hand should be under my head,
And his right hand should embrace me.

3 שְׂמֹאלוֹ תַּחַת רֹאשִׁי וִימִינוֹ
תְּחַבְּקֵנִי׃

4 'I adjure you, O daughters of Jerusalem:
Why should ye awaken, or stir up love,
Until it please?'

4 הִשְׁבַּעְתִּי אֶתְכֶם בְּנוֹת
יְרוּשָׁלִָם מַה־תָּעִירוּ ׀ וּמַה־
תְּעֹרְרוּ אֶת־הָאַהֲבָה עַד
שֶׁתֶּחְפָּץ׃

5 Who is this that cometh up from the wilderness,
Leaning upon her beloved?

5 מִי זֹאת עֹלָה מִן־הַמִּדְבָּר
מִתְרַפֶּקֶת עַל־דּוֹדָהּ תַּחַת

1. *Oh that thou wert as my brother.* It would appear that the course of their true love did not run smoothly even at her own home. Too many were the prying eyes and the restrictions. If he had been her brother, their companionship would have been freer and less likely to be misinterpreted.

2. *I would lead thee.* As her brother, none would question her bringing him to her home.

*that thou mightest instruct me.* Better, 'that she might instruct me.' The Hebrew can be construed as second person masc. or third fem. Her mother would teach her either to prepare for him spiced wine, or instruct her in the secrets of love.

*spiced wine.* See on vii. 3.

*juice of my pomegranate. Asis* is fermented juice obtained from crushing the fruit in a wine-press. With sherbet added to it, this was a favourite cooling drink in the Orient. She stresses *my* pomegranate, i.e. which she herself had prepared for him.

3. She loses herself in the rapturous thought of close contact with him when he supports her head in his arm. The verse is a repetition of ii. 6.

4. *I adjure you.* Cf. ii. 7, iii. 5. Now that she has rejoined her lover, she implores for the last time to be left alone with him. With this verse ends the four main sections of the Book. The rest of the chapter consists of fragments of songs then current.

5. *who is this*, etc. The lovers are seen approaching by the villagers and their curiosity is whetted. Every familiar

Under the apple-tree I awakened thee;
There thy mother was in travail with thee,
There was she in travail and brought thee forth.

6 Set me as a seal upon thy heart,
As a seal upon thine arm;
For love is strong as death,
Jealousy is cruel as the grave;
The flashes thereof are flashes of fire,
A very flame of the Lord.

7 Many waters cannot quench love,
Neither can the floods drown it;
If a man would give all the substance of his house for love,
He would utterly be contemned.

הַתַּפּוּחַ עוֹרַרְתִּיךָ שָׁמָּה
חִבְּלַתְךָ אִמֶּךָ שָׁמָּה חִבְּלָה
יְלָדַתְךָ׃

6 שִׂימֵנִי כַחוֹתָם עַל־לִבֶּךָ
כַּחוֹתָם עַל־זְרוֹעֶךָ כִּי־עַזָּה
כַמָּוֶת אַהֲבָה קָשָׁה כִשְׁאוֹל
קִנְאָה רְשָׁפֶיהָ רִשְׁפֵּי אֵשׁ
שַׁלְהֶבֶתְיָה׃

7 מַיִם רַבִּים לֹא יוּכְלוּ לְכַבּוֹת
אֶת־הָאַהֲבָה וּנְהָרוֹת לֹא
יִשְׁטְפוּהָ אִם־יִתֵּן אִישׁ אֶת־
כָּל־הוֹן בֵּיתוֹ בָּאַהֲבָה בּוֹז
יָבוּזוּ לוֹ׃

scene they pass brings back sweet memories of former meeting-places. Here they first plighted their troth, and here they must renew their love once again. On reaching her home, she reminds her brothers of their promise to reward her virtue which she guarded so zealously in the face of many temptations. The chapter ends with a visit by their friends who have come to welcome her back and before whom she declares her unswerving love for her shepherd. She tells them how Solomon, feeling frustrated that all his wealth could not make her change her affections, at last consented to her return home.

*the wilderness.* Probably refers to the plain of Esdraelon, which was uncultivated and open pasture land outside her village, between Jezreel and Shulem, which the lovers had to cross on their homeward journey.

*leaning upon her beloved.* lit. 'joined, associated, with her beloved.'

*under the apple-tree.* Where their love was first aroused.

*in travail with thee.* In the East, childbirth in the open air was not uncommon.

6. *set me as a seal.* She longs to be constantly near to him, never to be parted.

*upon thy heart.* Seals were suspended from the neck with a cord worn by a woman over her heart, and by a man on his hand. The signet-ring was a precious object and worn on the right hand (cf. Jer. xxii. 24).

*love is strong as death.* It is as irresistible as death which none can overcome.

*jealousy is cruel as the grave.* Love excites a jealousy which completely enslaves one in its sway. She is fearful lest he might not return her love but transfer his affections to another.

*a very flame.* lit. 'a flame of God (*Jah*)', i.e. of supernatural power.

7. *many waters.* This verse reaches the climax of the Book, which has dramatically been mounting to this culmination. Nothing can destroy true love, which flows spontaneously from the heart and cannot be bought even with a king's treasures, as she had convincingly shown by her recent experience.

*neither can the floods drown it.* Since love was described in the preceding verse as

Suitors have come, but the girl is too young, they think. She replies, I'm not too young — I'm only ready for the right lover.



8 We have a little sister,
And she hath no breasts;
What shall we do for our sister
In the day when she shall be spoken for?

8 אָחוֹת לָנוּ קְטַנָּה וְשָׁדַיִם אֵין
לָהּ מַה־נַּעֲשֶׂה לַאֲחֹתֵנוּ בַּיּוֹם
שֶׁיְּדֻבַּר־בָּהּ׃

9 If she be a wall,
We will build upon her a turret of silver;
And if she be a door,
We will enclose her with boards of cedar.

9 אִם־חוֹמָה הִיא נִבְנֶה עָלֶיהָ
טִירַת כָּסֶף וְאִם־דֶּלֶת הִיא
נָצוּר עָלֶיהָ לוּחַ אָרֶז׃

10 I am a wall,
And my breasts like the towers thereof;
Then was I in his eyes
As one that found peace.

10 אֲנִי חוֹמָה וְשָׁדַי כַּמִּגְדָּלוֹת אָז
הָיִיתִי בְעֵינָיו כְּמוֹצְאֵת שָׁלוֹם׃

a flame, this simile follows naturally. Homiletically interpreted, it applies to the nations of the world who did not succeed in wresting the love of God from the heart of Israel either by force or by blandishments. The Midrash adds: 'Even if the nations should open their treasuries and offer their money for one word of Torah, they would never succeed. All the temptations dangled before the eyes of Hananiah, Mishael and Azariah were of no avail.'

8. The last seven verses record her reminiscences and triumphs. She reminds her brothers how unnecessary had been their fear for her chastity when beset by temptation.

*she hath no breasts.* She is still young and undeveloped.

*what shall we do for our sister.* On her wedding day. They stipulate that their generosity will depend upon her virtue. When they first discussed this matter, she was yet of unmarriageable age.

*when she shall be spoken for.* When she will be asked in marriage (cf. I Sam. xxv. 39).

9. *if she be a wall.* The brothers are still speaking. If she will continue being virtuous, resisting all attacks on her innocence, like a battlement withstanding the invader, their wedding gift to her would be great in value.

*a turret of silver.* Women used to wear a silver horn on the head, an ornament much prized by them. The Talmud records that Rabbi Akiba made for his bride a golden ornament depicting Jerusalem.

*and if she be a door.* A door revolves on its hinges; one knocks and it is opened. If their sister yielded to temptation, they will punish her with solitary confinement for her self-protection.

*with boards of cedar.* To prevent a door from being broken into, it was barricaded with cedar planks, that wood being exceptionally hard.

10. *I am a wall.* Her proud reply is, 'I have proved as impregnable as a wall and a faithful guardian of my honour. Where is the reward you promised me?'

*my breasts like the towers thereof.* She has passed the stage of life mentioned in verse 8 and is ripe for marriage.

*as one that found peace.* After the assurance, her brothers were content and gave her the promised award.

11 Solomon had a vineyard at Baal-hamon;
He gave over the vineyard unto keepers;
Every one for the fruit thereof
Brought in a thousand pieces of silver.

11 כֶּרֶם הָיָה לִשְׁלֹמֹה בְּבַעַל
הָמוֹן נָתַן אֶת־הַכֶּרֶם לַנֹּטְרִים
אִישׁ יָבִא בְּפִרְיוֹ אֶלֶף כָּסֶף׃

12 My vineyard, which is mine, is before me;
Thou, O Solomon, shalt have the thousand,
And those that keep the fruit thereof two hundred.

12 כַּרְמִי שֶׁלִּי לְפָנָי הָאֶלֶף לְךָ
שְׁלֹמֹה וּמָאתַיִם לְנֹטְרִים אֶת־
פִּרְיוֹ׃

13 Thou that dwellest in the gardens,
The companions hearken for thy voice:
'Cause me to hear it.'

13 הַיּוֹשֶׁבֶת בַּגַּנִּים חֲבֵרִים
מַקְשִׁיבִים לְקוֹלֵךְ הַשְׁמִיעִנִי׃

14 Make haste, my beloved,
And be thou like to a gazelle or to a young hart
Upon the mountains of spices.

14 בְּרַח ׀ דּוֹדִי וּדְמֵה־לְךָ לִצְבִי
אוֹ לְעֹפֶר הָאַיָּלִים עַל הָרֵי
בְשָׂמִים׃

**11.** *Solomon had a vineyard.* She indulges in a reminiscence of her adventures. She recalls her brother's suspicions of her, and the wealth of Solomon which was used as a temptation to make her yield. The king possessed a magnificent vineyard which she had spurned with the retort, 'I am quite happy with my own humble vineyard' (verse 12).

*Baal-hamon.* The site is unidentified and is not mentioned elsewhere. Rashi believes that it was near Jerusalem and its name (lit. 'owner of a multitude') derived from the fact that it attracted crowds of visitors. It has been conjectured that it may have been Hammath in the kingdom of Aleppo.

*unto keepers.* It was the custom of *metayers* or partner-labourers (*aris*) to receive a portion of the produce, usually a third or a half, in exchange for their work.

*a thousand pieces of silver.* So plentiful was the crop that the sale of the fruit would realize this large sum. The extent of the vineyard can be gauged from the fact that it was let to many tenants, each of whom paid this sum annually.

**12.** *my vineyard.* A striking contrast to the preceding verse. Her modest vineyard belongs entirely to her and has not been loaned out to others; she is the sole owner. What she conveys is that, despite the glittering temptations, she remained loyal to her lover.

**13.** Her shepherd requests her to recount before his friends, who had gathered to greet her, some of her experiences in the palace.

*cause me to hear it.* He and his companions alike wish to hear her voice and the story she has to tell.

**14.** Embarrassed and coy, she begs him to leave her alone for a while, and when they are by themselves, she will sing to him.

*mountains of spices.* Now that they are finally united, the rugged heights are no longer barriers between them but delightful like mountains of spices. The Midrash reads a prayer into the verse: 'Mayest Thou hasten the advent of the redemption and cause Thy *Shechinah* to dwell on the mountain of spices (i.e. Moriah, as though derived from *mor*, "myrrh") and rebuild the Temple speedily in our days.'

# רות

# RUTH

INTRODUCTION AND COMMENTARY

*by*

JUDAH J. SLOTKI, M.A.

# PREFACE

JUDGING from the English translation alone, or even from the text of the Hebrew, the reader may be tempted to wonder what room there is for comment or elucidation. The simplicity of style of the Book of Ruth and the directness of its plot seem to leave little to the imagination.

That is so if we read and do not ponder. The Bible should not be so treated. Its words must be weighed and measured. Sages and scholars have vied with one another in their efforts to reveal the treasures hidden in this Book. Their meticulous and loving care, lavished upon every letter, word, turn of phrase, and every minute peculiarity of diction in this immortal Book, has disclosed a wealth of intriguing problems and a host of fascinating solutions which often lead into intricate labyrinths of exegesis. From their explorations they brought back gems of parables, homilies and allegories, with many lessons of infinite worth on good conduct and saintly living.

In the present work it was not possible to follow them in all their investigations. Much has had to be omitted in a popular Commentary. May that which has been included provide for the thirsty soul the waters of spiritual and moral uplift, and for the inquiring mind clearer understanding of the priceless words of Holy Writ!

J. J. SLOTKI

# INTRODUCTION

## NAME

Like the Book of Esther, the little volume before us derives its title from the name of the heroine whose charming personality pervades its pages.

The narrative of the drama that unfolds before our eyes was at one time preserved upon parchment in the form of a scroll, even as was, and still is, the rule in the case of its companion above mentioned. For this reason it is known in Hebrew as *Megillath Ruth*, 'the Scroll of Ruth,' and is one of the five *Megilloth* that have won for themselves a place in the sacred Scriptures.

## POSITION IN THE CANON

In the Hebrew Bible this Book finds an honoured place in the *Kethubim*, the Hagiographa, the third main division of the Holy Writings. It appears fifth, though according to the Talmud it must at one time have been first, in that division.

In the Greek translation of the Bible, the LXX, and the Authorized Version in English which follows it, *Ruth* is treated as an integral part of *Judges* and is placed immediately after it. This, however, need not be taken as evidence of an ancient tradition as to the homogeneity of the two Books. More probably it is due to a simple transfer from its proper position governed by the fact that the story of *Ruth* was laid in the time of the Judges.

## POSITION IN THE LITURGY

The Book of Ruth is prescribed for reading as part of the liturgy on Pentecost, the festival commemorating the Revelation on Mount Sinai. The connection between the Book and the festival is twofold: (*a*) the festival is, as its name *chag habbikkurim* indicates, primarily a harvest festival and the harvest figures prominently in the narrative; (*b*) the Revelation marked, as it were, the formal acceptance by Israel of that religion and law of life which were later to prove so irresistibly attractive to the heathen damsel from Moab. The privation and suffering which she faced on the thorny path of righteousness has led the Midrash to elaborate on the theme. The bearing of the story on the festival, it declares, is the moral one which teaches that the Torah can only be acquired by those who tread the road of hardship and want. The Torah, personified, is made to plead with God in these terms, 'Put my lot among the poor, for if the rich apply themselves to a mastery of me they will become arrogant.'

## LITERARY APPEAL

The Book has been fitly described by one of the greatest Gentile poets as the loveliest little epic and idyllic whole which has come down to us. It has been likened by students of comparative literature to a beautiful valley full of flowers, fertile fields and gentle brooks; and it rightly deserves to be called a wonderful story of love and holy character. It is the most enchanting short narrative in the sacred literature, a sweet pastoral idyll. No literature in the world can show a lovelier picture of womanhood.

In style it is matchless: fresh, simple and graceful. The spell of the Book is altogether irresistible, for it lies in the heroine whose name it bears; and the chief charm of Ruth herself is her unselfish and devoted love of all that is finest in the physical and spiritual world.

## SOCIAL BACKGROUND

It is not a history of public events that is presented in the pages of this immortal work, but a picture of humble village life, painted on a quiet background away from the turmoil and strife that fill the pages of the contemporary Book of Judges.

The existence of such blissful conditions in that era would be unknown to us but for the evidence of this Biblical narrative. Were it not for the testimony of the Book of Ruth, who would dream that so beautiful a society as that depicted in its chapters could flourish in those lawless times? Life in the towns was insecure, justice administered by corrupt rulers. It was, in the words of the Rabbis, a generation that judged its judges. Describing the rampant lawless-ness, the Midrash tells of men who, having been tried and convicted of crime, would turn and assault their judges. But it was a generation that had the judges it deserved. 'See who their judges were!' ironically observes a commentator, 'Gideon the son of Joash, who made an ephod for an idol, and yet he judged Israel! Samson, who was a slave of his passions, and yet he judged Israel!'

What a relief to turn to the placid scene of goodness in the small town of Bethlehem! And how happy we are to feel that the simplest country life can, and did, exist side by side with the general state of social restlessness and continuous warfare! We thank a kindly Providence for so ordaining that no times shall be so wild but that in them one might find quiet corners and green oases, all the greener for their sombre surroundings, where life might glide on in peaceful isolation from tumult and strife.

At some such quiet period in the history of the Judges, it may be assumed, the incidents recounted in the Book of Ruth took place. Israel was perhaps enjoying a momentary respite from insecurity and unrest. Their lives could apparently be lived in comparative safety, without let or hindrance, and men and women would love and work and weep and laugh and enjoy their tranquil days about the townlet of Bethlehem.

We see these folk with their time-honoured customs and family events, the toiling flockmaster, the busy reaper, the women with their cares and uncertainties, the love and labour of simple life, the sympathetic crowds that gathered to share the sorrow of the bereaved or the joy of the newly-wed, the pomp and ceremony attending the various religious and social occasions. A religious influence was evidently emanating from some central place of worship and spreading far and wide.

This was where real world history was being made. Not in the arena of battle, but in the peaceful homes of simple country folk—there nature built Israel's character and fashioned his heroes. The unimportant people who lived and died unnamed and unseeing—in their homes was shaped the course of history and there an outstanding event took place.

### HISTORICITY

Unbiased scholars are almost unanimously agreed upon the historical accuracy of the facts presented in the Book. Who can doubt them, or why should they have been invented? There would surely be little point in inventing a foreign ancestry for the greatest and most dearly loved king of Israel, even as little as in inventing, for the origin of the nation itself, the bondage in Egypt. When, then, did the events of the Book happen?

### DATE OF BOAZ

The chronological detail given in the first sentence of the Book tells us vaguely that the incident to be related occurred *in the days when the judges judged*. Four generations span the period, which may be assumed to cover at least between two and three hundred years. This period is somewhat more closely defined in the genealogical table at the end of the Book, which takes us back to the third generation before David.

We may infer, therefore, that Boaz, Ruth and their contemporaries lived between eighty and one hundred years before the birth of David. Older scholars consider it probable that the events are contemporaneous with the times of Gideon or Jephthah. Rabbinic tradition variously assigns them to the times of Barak, Ehud and Ibzan, the latter being identified with Boaz. No one, however, maintains that the Book was *written* in any of those days.

### DATE OF COMPOSITION

There is no unanimity among scholars, either ancient or modern, as to the date when the Book was written. Jewish tradition credits the authorship to Samuel whose literary works also include the Books bearing his own name as well as the Book of Judges. Modern scholarship tends to assign the authorship variously to the time of David, the period of the monarchy and a post-exilic date, before or contemporaneous with the reformation of Ezra and Nehemiah. Those who advance the last-mentioned theory argue that the Book was a favourite with such as did not share the zeal of Ezra and Nehemiah against mixed marriages.

Amid these conflicting theories we

may well stand bewildered before the question: when was the Book written? The pious Jewish reader will accept without question the tradition recorded in the Talmud. The inquiring minds will examine and weigh the evidence and form their own conclusions. This need not concern us here. The problem of authorship is secondary to an appreciation of the Book's content and message. Let us, then, consider what the author has to tell us.

### SUMMARY OF THE BOOK

*Ruth* is a perfect short historical epic in four chapters. It gives us a glimpse into the everyday life of Bethlehem, in the home and in the field, in its general gossip and its lawsuits, more than three thousand years ago. It tells us that in the time of the Judges there lived in Bethlehem of Judah a man of wealth and standing, named Elimelech, who was driven from his home by famine to take up his abode in Moab, with his wife Naomi and his two sons, Mahlon and Chilion. In exile, Elimelech dies and his sons, after marrying Moabite wives, Orpah and Ruth, also die, leaving no children. After a sojourn of ten years Naomi, widowed and childless, homeless and destitute, prepares to return to Judæa where, she learns from travelling merchants, the famine had ceased. Her daughters-in-law set out with her, but on the way Orpah is induced, after gentle persuasion from Naomi, to return to her heathen home, while Ruth clings passionately to her mother-in-law. The two women, weary and worn, opportunely arrive in Bethlehem in the early spring, at the time of the barley-harvest.

Ruth, gentle, kind, considerate and hardworking, goes out into the fields of Bethlehem to glean among the ears. She must do this in order to maintain herself and her beloved mother-in-law. Whether by chance or by Divine guidance her steps lead her into the field of Boaz, a relative of the deceased Elimelech, whose interest she arouses by her modest bearing, and who henceforth shows her more than a paternal friendliness.

At the end of about three months she proceeds, under the direction of Naomi, to the field where Boaz was winnowing the corn in the cool refreshing breeze of a Palestine summer evening and, seizing a suitable moment when Boaz had retired to rest in the threshing-floor, she reminds him that he is her nearest kinsman and that there were certain duties he owed to Naomi and herself. In the stillness of the night Boaz readily acknowledges his obligations, but reminds Ruth that there is a nearer kinsman than he, whose rights had priority over his own. He expresses his determination, in the event of the other's failure, to carry out his responsibilities to the last detail.

Next morning Boaz loses no time in going to the city-gate, where the elders used to meet for the purpose of dispensing justice and dealing with claims and litigations, and there he hails the kinsman of whom he had spoken the previous night. In the presence of a picked assembly of ten men and of the elders and other bystanders, Boaz offers this man the option of buying from Naomi the land which had belonged to Elimelech, and at the same time of marrying Ruth with the object of raising an heir to her deceased husband and assuring the continuity of the family line. The kinsman quails before the heavy responsibilities and gladly transfers his rights to Boaz who thereupon formally buys the property and marries Ruth.

The union proves happy and is crowned with the birth of a boy who grows up to become the ancestor of the royal house of David.

### AIM AND PURPOSE

What was the writer's aim and purpose in giving the Book to the world? Jewish opinion declined to believe that his motive was that of mere entertainment. 'The Books of the Torah,' said a nineteenth century commentator, 'are not in the habit of telling stories devoid of inner value.' Yet the Book contains no legal enactments, no decisions on the question of ritual cleanliness or prohibition. What purpose, then, does it serve? To teach us, is the reply, how great is the reward of those who perform deeds of kindness. The hallowing of the family is another distinct purpose in the Bible, and the beautiful example which this narrative provides of the elevating influence of domestic affection entitled it, if nothing else did, to a place in the canon. Who can lay down the Book after reading and not feel that still another of its objects is to set us upon the straight road from which we must not turn either to the right or to the left lest we meet the fate that befell Elimelech?

There is yet another purpose, a genealogical one—and on this point there is a general consensus of opinion—namely, to trace the pedigree of David. This must indeed be so, because the Book takes us into the circle of a family unknown to us and induces our participation in its sorrows and joys; but not until the end is reached do we learn that to this family belong the ancestors of David. It requires little perspicacity to see that as the genealogical details in chapter iv furnish the close of the Book, the object of the family history contained therein is unmistakably attained by these details. The author thus provides us with an answer to the question how it came about that Ruth, a daughter of Moab, left her home, found a welcome and protection in the city of David's family and by her marriage with Boaz became the ancestress of David. There is no escape from the fact that everything in the last instance leads up to David. We need not accept the rather lame theories that the Book is either a piece of political propaganda or an effort to commend the custom of levirate marriage (Deut. xxv. 5ff.).

It would, however, be unwise to suppose that the author had one aim only in view. The Book is full of ethical and religious lessons. Probably we shall be right in assuming that he aimed at inculcating not one but a number of spiritual and moral truths. His aims may be summarized as follows: (*a*) To protest against intermarriage, unless it occurs in exceptional circumstances. (*b*) To check indiscriminate proselytization. (*c*) To encourage hard work and industry. (*d*) To indicate that success attends upon the truly and objectively pious. (*e*) To emphasize the need for vigilance in the supervision of one's estates. (*f*) To instruct in moral chastity. (*g*) To impart a lesson in human kindness. In the words of a Jewish moralist of the last century, the author purposed to show that 'unto this alone does the God of the spirits of all flesh look, unto him that directs his heart to heaven (i.e. who is sincere), and this is the sole fruit of all the great sweetness of the message of this scroll, to glorify and to extol and to praise the splendour and majesty of this excellent attribute.'

### THE VALUE OF THE BOOK

Has the Book any value for the modern world? Surely, it has. Its message is as fresh and insistent to-day as when first written down in antiquity. It bears remarkable testimony to the meaning of the phrase 'religion in life.' It is, in the words of a Gentile admirer, a monument to that ethical code which could bring to perfection in the true Israelite such heartfelt piety and self-sacrificing disposition.

Not least among the features that give it value is the contribution it makes to the understanding of the social conditions of that early age, conditions which were to have a lasting influence upon civilization to the end of time. Had we only drawn our impressions of life in those days from the records of violence and crime contained in the Book of Judges, we should undoubtedly have been ready to conclude that all the gentler virtues had fled from the land, while the children of Israel were alternately struggling for their lives and liberties with the tribes of Canaan or yielding themselves to the seductions of Canaanite idolatry. The Book of Ruth raises the curtain which veiled the privacy of domestic life and discloses views of piety, integrity, affection and chastity amidst scenes of war, discord and strife. In such conditions was formed that passionate attachment of the people to the sacred soil which survived the greatest catastrophes of their history.

### LOVE OF THE HOLY LAND

Indirectly we are taught the intense love of the Israelite for Canaan; because if we but read with understanding, we cannot fail to see how devoted were the bulk of the ordinary people to their beloved land. Are we not clearly to infer that, in spite of the famine, only one family left the country, and that so grievous was this sin in the eyes of God that punishment overtook the head of the family almost instantaneously? 'It is not permitted,' declared the Rabbis, 'to emigrate from the land of Israel even to escape the pangs of famine,' unless the price of food rises inordinately. Even this is forbidden, according to one Talmudic authority, because he who does not dwell in the land of Israel is as if he worships idols.

Yet Elimelech went. From worldly considerations he forsook the land of his fathers; and what did he choose in its place? The land of Moab.

### ISRAEL AND MOAB

The relationship between the Hebrews and Moabites was often friendly, sometimes the reverse. At the time described in *Ruth* it may be assumed to have been friendly. Yet it is no wonder that tradition looked askance at Elimelech's going. The people of Moab were, of course, nearly related to the people of Israel. They were the descendants of Lot, the nephew of Abraham. They had, however, a very different history. The pure faith that had grown up in the tents of the Hebrew patriarchs and blossomed into splendour in the days of Moses had, among the Moabites, withered and died. The Moabites had been a thorn in the flesh of Israel when they came out of Egypt and had even led them away into the practice of wickedness, so that Moabites were forbidden to come into the assembly of the Lord (Deut. xxiii. 4).

Israel and Moab were separated not merely by the strip of water called the Dead Sea, but by something vaster than the ocean, a difference of religion. The journey taken by this family of Bethlehem was, therefore, not from one country to another, but from one universe of religious thought to another.

### SIGNIFICANCE OF NAMES

All the persons in the story bear names which in a measure describe their characters. Naomi personifies everything that is sweet, Elimelech the pride that goes before a fall, Mahlon the sickly, Chilion the one who disappeared or died an early death.

Almost all ancient peoples held a belief in the potency of names and often identified the name with the person, believing that the name exercised a power for good or evil over the person who bore it. To know a man's name was to secure a hold over him and the power to sway him to one's own will.

'What is in a name?' This question is discussed in the Talmud, where the advice is given that one should treat a name with respect. As proof they quote Mahlon, one of the meanings of which is 'pardon,' a name that had the effect of making him the husband of Ruth, the sin-fearing maiden. Chilion, denoting 'destruction,' married Orpah, from whom sprang the destroyer, Goliath the Philistine.

The Rabbis were not unanimous in their views on this matter. The Midrash admits that there are cases where the name seems to signify little. There are men, we are told, whose deeds are fair but whose names are ugly—e.g. the people who returned from Babylon. Others, whose names and deeds are both ugly—e.g. the spies. Others again, whose names and deeds are both fair—e.g. the tribal patriarchs; and still others whose names are fair and their deeds ugly—e.g. Esau and Ishmael. But in the name Ruth, and in her character as delineated in this Book, we have the embodiment of a great and inspiring ideal.

# RUTH

## 1 CHAPTER I א

1 AND it came to pass in the days
when the judges judged, that there
was a famine in the land. And a
certain man of Beth-lehem in Judah
went to sojourn in the field of Moab,
he, and his wife, and his two sons.
2 And the name of the man was

וַיְהִי בִּימֵי שְׁפֹט הַשֹּׁפְטִים וַיְהִי 1
רָעָב בָּאָרֶץ וַיֵּלֶךְ אִישׁ מִבֵּית
לֶחֶם יְהוּדָה לָגוּר בִּשְׂדֵי מוֹאָב
הוּא וְאִשְׁתּוֹ וּשְׁנֵי בָנָיו׃ וְשֵׁם 2

**1-5 CIRCUMSTANCES LEADING TO RUTH'S MARRIAGE**

**1.** *and it came to pass.* The common phrase employed in the Scriptures at the commencement of a Book, serving to connect the story with the events that preceded. The Midrash cites a tradition that every passage in the Bible beginning with this word, *wayehi*, tells of misfortune, the word consisting of two parts each denoting sorrow: *way* 'woe' and *hi* 'lamentation.' The misfortune here was, *there was a famine in the land.* The word, however, occurs twice in this verse, suggesting two misfortunes. The other will be indicated below.

*in the days when.* lit. 'in the days of.' This phrase is usually followed by a name, such as Amraphel (Gen. xiv. 1), Ahasuerus (Esther i. 1). Why was the name of the judge omitted here? Out of respect to his memory; for it was Ibzan, declare the Rabbis, who then held office (B.B. 91a) and he was a relative of the sinful Elimelech (Ibn Yachya).

*the judges judged.* lit. 'the judging of the judges.' It was, according to the Rabbis, a lawless generation in which the judges committed more abominations than the rest of the people, and a generation that judged its judges.

*the judges.* The period indicated was a lengthy one, extending over three hundred years, from about 1400 B.C.E. to about 1100 B.C.E. In whose days, then, did the story of Ruth occur? Rab and R. Huna placed it in the days of Barak and Deborah; R. Joshua ben Levi in those of Shamgar and Ehud; while other Rabbis regarded the story as contemporary with the judgeship of Ibzan (Judg. xii. 8) who is identified with Boaz (Ruth ii. 1) the hero of the story. A late authority (Malbim) holds the view that the events occurred, not during the rulership of any of the major judges, but in the interval between the death of one great judge and the rise to power of another. During the unrest of the interregnum lesser men, unable to exercise control, seized power and so led to utter confusion. It was the resultant chaos that brought famine to the land and exile to Elimelech.

*a famine.* One of the periodic scourges of the land in ancient times. The present famine was perhaps caused by the inroads of the marauding Midianites described in Judges vi.

*in the land. Erets Israel,* 'the land' *par excellence.*

*a certain man.* The Hebrew *ish* in Rabbinic exegesis denotes not merely a person, but rather a personage, a man of importance, either in learning or in social status; hence the inference that he was an exceedingly wealthy man, one of the city's notabilities.

*Beth-lehem.* Almost two hours' journey south of Jerusalem, in a district normally fruitful. Though one of the finest localities in Canaan he left it to stay in a foreign land. The reasons for his emigration, according to Jewish commentators, were his meanness and the insecurity of life and property which, during a famine, would be exposed to the violence of the hungry mob in the absence of a restraining authority. Nevertheless there is one redeeming feature, because he set out merely to sojourn temporarily until the famine was over, and not with the intention of settling.

Elimelech, and the name of his wife
Naomi, and the name of his two sons
Mahlon and Chilion, Ephrathites of
Beth-lehem in Judah. And they
came into the field of Moab, and
continued there. 3And Elimelech
Naomi's husband died; and she was
left, and her two sons. 4And they
took them wives of the women of
Moab; the name of the one was

הָאִישׁ אֱלִימֶלֶךְ וְשֵׁם אִשְׁתּוֹ
נָעֳמִי וְשֵׁם שְׁנֵי־בָנָיו ׀ מַחְלוֹן
וְכִלְיוֹן אֶפְרָתִים מִבֵּית לֶחֶם
יְהוּדָה וַיָּבֹאוּ שְׂדֵי־מוֹאָב
3 וַיִּהְיוּ־שָׁם׃ וַיָּמָת אֱלִימֶלֶךְ
אִישׁ נָעֳמִי וַתִּשָּׁאֵר הִיא וּשְׁנֵי
4 בָנֶיהָ׃ וַיִּשְׂאוּ לָהֶם נָשִׁים
מֹאֲבִיּוֹת שֵׁם הָאַחַת עָרְפָּה

*the field of.* lit. 'the fields of,' indicating that Elimelech did not settle in one city permanently, but moved from place to place.

*Moab.* The high plateau, 4,300 feet above the Dead Sea, to the east of it, and south of Arnon.

2. *Elimelech.* lit. 'my God is King.' The name is expounded as revealing the man's character; it signifies 'unto me (*eli*) shall the kingdom come' (Midrash), giving evidence of his arrogance. He was a descendant of Nahshon, prince of the tribe of Judah (Num. i. 7) and ancestor of the royal house of David.

*Naomi.* The name signifies 'the sweet one,' so called because her deeds were pleasant and sweet (Midrash); or 'my sweetness, or delight.'

*Mahlon and Chilion.* lit. 'sickness' and 'vanishing.' They may have been given these names because of the sad plight of the country, or as foretelling their early death and childlessness.

*Ephrathites.* i.e. hailing from Ephrath, another name for Bethlehem and later the district in which Bethlehem was situated, or Ephraimites. Another explanation is that there was a family of great distinction, belonging to the tribe of Judah, called Ephrathites who traced descent from Ephrath wife of Caleb (cf. 1 Chron. ii. 19) (Malbim).

*Beth-lehem in Judah.* To be distinguished from Bethlehem in Zebulun (Josh. xix. 15).

*and continued there.* Hebrew 'were there.' Having arrived in Moab, they decided to remain in permanent residence.

3. *Naomi's husband died.* Not from old age or infirmity, but as the result of Divine punishment for remaining away from the Holy Land.

*and she was left.* lit. 'and she remained,' in Moab. She took no heed of the Divine warning and refused to return.

4. *and they took them wives.* The sons sinned still more grievously in that they took Moabite wives. Only after their father's death, it should be noted, did the sons marry women who were not of their people.

*women of Moab.* A silent protest against intermarriage (Midrash). Jewish commentators are unanimous in this view, though they differ whether or not the wives' conversion to the faith of the Hebrews accompanied the marriage. Both opinions are supported by high authority. Legally the union was not forbidden, since the injunction against intermarriage with the Moabites applied

Orpah, and the name of the other
Ruth; and they dwelt there about ten
years. 5And Mahlon and Chilion
died both of them; and the woman
was left of her two children and of
her husband. 6Then she arose with
her daughters-in-law, that she might
return from the field of Moab; for
she had heard in the field of Moab
how that the LORD had remembered

וְשֵׁם הַשֵּׁנִית רוּת וַיֵּשְׁבוּ שָׁם
5 כְּעֶשֶׂר שָׁנִים׃ וַיָּמֻתוּ גַם־
שְׁנֵיהֶם מַחְלוֹן וְכִלְיוֹן וַתִּשָּׁאֵר
הָאִשָּׁה מִשְּׁנֵי יְלָדֶיהָ וּמֵאִישָׁהּ׃
6 וַתָּקָם הִיא וְכַלֹּתֶיהָ וַתָּשָׁב
מִשְּׂדֵי מוֹאָב כִּי שָׁמְעָה בִּשְׂדֵה
מוֹאָב כִּי־פָקַד יְהוָה אֶת־

exclusively to the males (cf. Deut. xxiii. 4).

*Orpah.* The name has been derived from *ophrah*, 'a hind,' the letters being transposed, or from a root analogous with the Arabic signifying 'ornamented with rich hair.'

*Ruth.* The name is probably a contraction of ***re'uth***, 'friendship,' which admirably summarizes her nature. Ruth was the kind of character that draws the world after her, not by a baleful gift of beauty—there is no hint that she was fair to look upon—but by the lasting qualities of unselfish devotion, of lowly serviceableness, of maidenly modesty. She is one of the characters humanity loves to remember (Hastings). Mahlon, the elder, was married to Ruth, the younger; and Chilion, the younger, to Orpah, the elder.

*about ten years.* That confirms the view that they had given up all thought of returning to the land of Israel (Malbim).

5. *Mahlon and Chilion died.* As a punishment for this sin. Mahlon died first because, being the elder, he should have exercised a restraining influence over his younger brother (Malbim).

*and the woman was left.* She was alone. There is nothing the human heart so much dreads as the thought of being utterly alone (Hastings). Yet her survival surely pointed to the saving grace of some peculiar merit which she apparently possessed. The Malbim explains that she had resolutely refused to be a willing partner in her family's misdeeds, and had never abandoned the hope of returning to Canaan.

### 6-18 RUTH ACCOMPANIES NAOMI TO BETHLEHEM

6. *then she arose with her daughters-in-law.* The resolve to leave their ill-fated domicile was equally strong in the hearts of them all, because in their minds their evil fortune was bound up with their present luckless abode.

*daughters-in-law.* The Hebrew ***kallah*** may mean 'bride' as well as 'daughter-in-law,' one being the natural outcome of the other. The name was so given because of the 'crown' (*kalil*) that adorned the bride on the day of her marriage.

*that she might return.* At first the decision to return was only Naomi's (Malbim).

*for she had heard.* Doubtless from the Jewish travellers who had brought merchandise to Moab. It does not necessarily follow from the fact that she only received the information after ten years that the famine had lasted all that time; though it would not be surprising if it had, since a famine of seven years' duration was not uncommon.

*the LORD had remembered **His people**.* It was, then, not the sufferings associated

His people in giving them bread.
7 And she went forth out of the place
where she was, and her two daughters-in-law with her; and they went
on the way to return unto the land
of Judah. 8 And Naomi said unto
her two daughters-in-law: 'Go,
return each of you to her mother's
house; the LORD deal kindly with
you, as ye have dealt with the dead,
and with me. 9 The LORD grant
you that ye may find rest, each of you
in the house of her husband.' Then
she kissed them; and they lifted up

7 עַמּוֹ לָתֵת לָהֶם לָחֶם׃ וַתֵּצֵא
מִן־הַמָּקוֹם אֲשֶׁר הָיְתָה־
שָׁמָּה וּשְׁתֵּי כַלֹּתֶיהָ עִמָּהּ
וַתֵּלַכְנָה בַדֶּרֶךְ לָשׁוּב אֶל־
8 אֶרֶץ יְהוּדָה׃ וַתֹּאמֶר נָעֳמִי
לִשְׁתֵּי כַלֹּתֶיהָ לֵכְנָה שֹּׁבְנָה
אִשָּׁה לְבֵית אִמָּהּ יַעֲשֶׂה יְהוָה
עִמָּכֶם חֶסֶד כַּאֲשֶׁר עֲשִׂיתֶם
9 עִם־הַמֵּתִים וְעִמָּדִי׃ יִתֵּן
יְהוָה לָכֶם וּמְצֶאןָ מְנוּחָה אִשָּׁה
בֵּית אִישָׁהּ וַתִּשַּׁק לָהֶן וַתִּשֶּׂאנָה

v. 8. יעשׂ ק׳

with her adopted domicile that drove her back to her former home. All she needed was just such tidings to induce her to return.

*bread.* Neither wealth nor worldly prosperity drew her on. The mere assurance of the bare necessities of life was sufficient to kindle her resolve.

7. *she went forth.* Even this simple action deserves to be recorded of so pious a woman, because the departure of the righteous has an important effect upon the city they leave behind. With them depart the city's brilliance, its glory and splendour (Midrash).

8. *go, return.* In the Orient, a parting rarely takes place in the house. The departing relative or guest is accompanied for some distance on the road by friends (Thatcher). Naomi made wise use of this custom. She knew that if she attempted to persuade her daughters-in-law to remain behind while they were still at home, they would doubtless urge her to stay with them. Now that she had left home and city far behind, she felt safe in persuading them to return (Alshich).

*her mother's house.* Ruth's father was still alive (cf. ii. 11). Why, then, to her *mother's* house? Several reasons are suggested: A proselyte has legally no father (Midrash); the mother's house or tent was the dwelling-place of the female members of the family (cf. Gen. xxiv. 28, 67); it is the mother whose love knows best how to comfort a daughter in her misfortune (Keil).

*the LORD deal kindly.* lit. 'will deal.' Naomi's statement takes the form of an asseveration. She has no doubt in her mind that Divine recompense will be given her daughters-in-law for all their kindness. They had been good wives and dutiful daughters.

9. *the LORD grant.* This is a prayer for further Divine care, over and above that which their piety had earned them.

*kissed.* A parting embrace.

their voice, and wept. 10And they
said unto her: 'Nay, but we will
return with thee unto thy people.'
11And Naomi said: 'Turn back, my
daughters; why will ye go with me?
have I yet sons in my womb, that
they may be your husbands? 12Turn
back, my daughters, go your way;
for I am too old to have a husband.
If I should say: I have hope, should
I even have a husband to-night, and
also bear sons; 13would ye tarry for
them till they were grown? would
ye shut yourselves off for them and
have no husbands? nay, my daughters; for it grieveth me much for
your sakes, for the hand of the LORD
is gone forth against me.' 14And
they lifted up their voice, and wept

10 קוֹלָן וַתִּבְכֶּינָה׃ וַתֹּאמַרְנָה
לָּהּ כִּי־אִתָּךְ נָשׁוּב לְעַמֵּךְ׃
11 וַתֹּאמֶר נָעֳמִי שֹׁבְנָה בְנֹתַי לָמָּה
תֵלַכְנָה עִמִּי הַעוֹד־לִי בָנִים
בְּמֵעַי וְהָיוּ לָכֶם לַאֲנָשִׁים׃
12 שֹׁבְנָה בְנֹתַי לֵכְןָ כִּי זָקַנְתִּי
מִהְיוֹת לְאִישׁ כִּי אָמַרְתִּי יֶשׁ־
לִי תִקְוָה גַּם הָיִיתִי הַלַּיְלָה
לְאִישׁ וְגַם יָלַדְתִּי בָנִים׃
13 הֲלָהֵן ׀ תְּשַׂבֵּרְנָה עַד אֲשֶׁר
יִגְדָּלוּ הֲלָהֵן תֵּעָגֵנָה לְבִלְתִּי
הֱיוֹת לְאִישׁ אַל בְּנֹתַי כִּי־
מַר־לִי מְאֹד מִכֶּם כִּי־יָצְאָה
14 בִי יַד־יְהוָה׃ וַתִּשֶּׂ*נָה קוֹלָן

v. 14. חסר א'

10. *and they said unto her.* Only then did they reveal their true intention.

*unto thy people.* From this Naomi understood them to convey a desire to do no more than settle among the Hebrews, not to accept their religion.

11. *turn back.* Why seek a home among a strange people who may misunderstand you and refuse to associate with you? If you hope to marry again into my family surely that is a vain hope!

*have I yet sons in my womb.* The suggestion that the young widows should wait until the hypothetical children in her womb were old enough to marry is so fantastic that the only logical interpretation of her question can be: Have I any grown-up sons whom I have hidden away in my womb, out of your sight, and whom I could produce forthwith to be your husbands?

12. *go your way.* Now she assumes a more serious tone: 'Even if you should desire to wait until I again married, had children and brought them up to a marriageable age, there is a twofold reason why you should not do so: my age, *for I am too old to have a husband*, and the prolonged waiting, *would ye tarry for them?*'

*have a husband . . . sons.* There was a belief in ancient times that a widow who resigned herself to unmarried life for a period of ten years could, after that time, no longer have children. Naomi was that day completing ten years of widowhood, so that if she married that night there was still the possibility of her having children. *Would ye tarry for them?* she asks.

14. *kissed her mother-in-law.* The LXX adds 'and returned to her people.' She is

again; and Orpah kissed her mother-
in-law; but Ruth cleaved unto her.
15 And she said: 'Behold, thy sister-
in-law is gone back unto her people,
and unto her god; return thou after
thy sister-in-law.' 16 And Ruth said:
'Entreat me not to leave thee, and
to return from following after thee;
for whither thou goest, I will go;
and where thou lodgest, I will lodge;
thy people shall be my people, and
thy God my God; 17 where thou
diest, will I die, and there will I be
buried; the LORD do so to me, and

וַתִּבְכֶּינָה עוֹד וַתִּשַּׁק עָרְפָּה
לַחֲמוֹתָהּ וְרוּת דָּבְקָה־בָּהּ׃
15 וַתֹּאמֶר הִנֵּה שָׁבָה יְבִמְתֵּךְ
אֶל־עַמָּהּ וְאֶל־אֱלֹהֶיהָ שׁוּבִי
16 אַחֲרֵי יְבִמְתֵּךְ׃ וַתֹּאמֶר רוּת
אַל־תִּפְגְּעִי־בִי לְעָזְבֵךְ
לָשׁוּב מֵאַחֲרָיִךְ כִּי אֶל־אֲשֶׁר
תֵּלְכִי אֵלֵךְ וּבַאֲשֶׁר תָּלִינִי
אָלִין עַמֵּךְ עַמִּי וֵאלֹהַיִךְ
17 אֱלֹהָי׃ בַּאֲשֶׁר תָּמוּתִי אָמוּת
וְשָׁם אֶקָּבֵר כֹּה יַעֲשֶׂה יְהוָה

the first, remarks a scholar, in a sad series of those not far from the kingdom of God who needed but a little more resolution at the critical moment and, for want of it, shut themselves out from the covenant and sank back to a world which they had half renounced (Maclaren).

**15.** *unto her god.* Known by the name 'Chemosh' (Num. xxi. 29). This suggests that she had previously abandoned idolatry (Ralbag).

*return.* The moment is tense and acutely critical. So far she had moved step by step with Orpah. Now Orpah, her sister-in-law, had gone. Behind her, in the sweet light of reminiscence is Moab, the home of her childhood, of her mother and father; the scene of her friendships, the centre of her interests. Before her lies Israel with its dark forbidding hills, its alien faces, its unknown trials (Hastings). Will Ruth follow her sister-in-law back to Moab?

**16.** The words in which Ruth's resolve is uttered constitute one of the most beautiful confessions of love in all literature, unique for its touching simplicity as well as its poignant sincerity. 'Ruth's passionate burst of tenderness is immortal' (Hastings).

*entreat me not to leave thee.* Do not put so many obstacles in the way of my embracing thy religion.

*whither thou goest, I will go.* Do not ascribe to me a motive different from thine own. I too wish to live in the land of Israel so that I may observe the commandments associated with that land.

*where thou lodgest, I will lodge.* I am prepared to be like a mere lodger, because there is but one object in my going. It is expressed in the words that follow.

*thy people . . . my God.* I have already adopted the ethical code given to thee by thy God, as well as the rites practised by thy people, and I regard myself as one of the Hebrews (Malbim).

**17.** *where thou diest, will I die.* A death that is good enough for thee is good enough for me.

*there will I be buried.* In Canaan, so as to share even in death a common lot

more also, if aught but death part
thee and me.'
18 And when she saw
that she was stedfastly minded to go
with her, she left off speaking unto
her.
19 So they two went until they
came to Beth-lehem. And it came
to pass, when they were come to
Beth-lehem, that all the city was astir
concerning them, and the women
said: 'Is this Naomi?'
20 And she
said unto them: 'Call me not
[a]Naomi, call me [b]Marah; for the
Almighty hath dealt very bitterly
with me.
21 I went out full, and the
LORD hath brought me back home
empty; why call ye me Naomi,

[a]That is, *Pleasant*. [b]That is ,*Bitter*.

לִי וְכֹה יֹסִיף כִּי הַמָּוֶת יַפְרִיד
18 בֵּינִי וּבֵינֵךְ׃ וַתֵּרֶא כִּי־
מִתְאַמֶּצֶת הִיא לָלֶכֶת אִתָּהּ
וַתֶּחְדַּל לְדַבֵּר אֵלֶיהָ׃
19 וַתֵּלַכְנָה שְׁתֵּיהֶם עַד־בֹּאָנָה
בֵּית לָחֶם וַיְהִי כְּבֹאָנָה בֵּית
לֶחֶם וַתֵּהֹם כָּל־הָעִיר עֲלֵיהֶן
וַתֹּאמַרְנָה הֲזֹאת נָעֳמִי׃
20 וַתֹּאמֶר אֲלֵיהֶן אַל־תִּקְרֶאנָה
לִי נָעֳמִי קְרֶאןָ לִי מָרָא כִּי־
21 הֵמַר שַׁדַּי לִי מְאֹד׃ אֲנִי
מְלֵאָה הָלַכְתִּי וְרֵיקָם הֱשִׁיבַנִי

v. 20 א׳ במקום ה׳

with Naomi's kith and kin. It is only proselytes of this type, whose genuineness stands out beyond doubt, who are permitted to abide beneath the wings of the *Shechinah*, the Divine Presence, and become full members of the Israelite community.

*the LORD do so to me*, etc. The idea underlying this form of oath is: May the Lord do to me such-and-such an unmentionable deed, and may He repeat it an unspecified number of times, if aught but death part us.

19-22 THEY ARRIVE IN BETHLEHEM

19. *they two.* The purpose of this expression is to indicate that both were now to be considered equals, and to demonstrate how precious the sincere proselyte is in the eyes of God (Midrash).

*all the city was astir.* As every small Eastern city or village is about the arrival of strangers, even at the present time (Thatcher). For a similar expression, cf. 1 Sam. iv. 5; 1 Kings i. 45.

*is this Naomi?* The surprise was elicited by the tragic reversal of fortune that struck the eye with such force. Here was an old woman, weary and worn, bearing the marks of sorrow and suffering. Could this be the wealthy lady of sunny disposition they had known a decade ago?

20f. Naomi's reply possesses poetic form and colour (Bertheau).

20. *the Almighty . . . with me.* What depth of suffering is compressed within the space of so few words! A Rabbi declared: all suffering is painful, but the pangs of poverty exceed them all. Other sufferings come and go and the body recovers, but the pangs of poverty make a man's eyes dim (Midrash).

21. *full.* With an abundance of wealth, blessed with a husband and family.

*empty.* Widowed and childless, lonely and poor.

seeing the LORD hath testified against me, and the Almighty hath afflicted me?' [22]So Naomi returned, and Ruth the Moabitess, her daughter-in-law, with her, who returned out of the field of Moab—and they came to Beth-lehem in the beginning of barley harvest.

יְהוָה לָמָּה תִקְרֶאנָה לִי נָעֳמִי
וַיהוָה עָנָה בִי וְשַׁדַּי הֵרַע־
22 לִי׃ וַתָּשָׁב נָעֳמִי וְרוּת
הַמּוֹאֲבִיָּה כַלָּתָהּ עִמָּהּ הַשָּׁבָה
מִשְּׂדֵי מוֹאָב וְהֵמָּה בָּאוּ בֵּית
לֶחֶם בִּתְחִלַּת קְצִיר שְׂעֹרִים׃

## 2 CHAPTER II ב

[1]And Naomi had a kinsman of her husband's, a mighty man of valour, of the family of Elimelech, and his name was Boaz. [2]And Ruth the

1 וּלְנָעֳמִי מְיֻדַּע לְאִישָׁהּ אִישׁ
גִּבּוֹר חַיִל מִמִּשְׁפַּחַת אֱלִימֶלֶךְ
2 וּשְׁמוֹ בֹּעַז׃ וַתֹּאמֶר רוּת

מודע ק׳ v. 1.

*testified.* The Hebrew verb in this context is difficult. It can denote either 'to answer, testify' (in the Qal) or 'to humble, afflict' (in the Piel). According to the former rendering the meaning would be: The Lord has testified by the affliction He has sent upon me that I have sinned against Him by emigrating to Moab. According to the latter rendering the meaning would be: The Lord has humbled me. It should be noted, however, that the Hebrew here uses the Qal.

22. *the beginning of barley harvest.* The occasion would be the commencement of the general harvesting season, because the first crop to ripen was the barley. This is about April, at the beginning of Passover, when the reaping of the *omer* (Lev. xxiii. 10) took place. The chronological detail with which the chapter ends serves as an introduction to the next chapter, which tells how Ruth availed herself of the Mosaic law providing that a share of the harvest shall be left for the poor.

## CHAPTER II

### RUTH GLEANS IN THE FIELD OF BOAZ

1. *a kinsman.* Hebrew *moda*, a noun in the abstract meaning 'familiarity,' here denotes 'an acquaintance, friend.' That Boaz, in addition, was also a relative, appears from the subsequent statement describing him as of the family of Elimelech. A Rabbinic tradition tells that Elimelech, Salmon the father of Boaz (iv. 21), the anonymous relative mentioned in chapters iii and iv, and Naomi's father were all sons of Nahshon, son of Amminadab. Boaz was accordingly Naomi's nephew.

*a mighty man of valour.* The phrase *gibbor chayil* usually signifies a brave

Moabitess said unto Naomi: 'Let me now go to the field, and glean among the ears of corn after him in whose sight I shall find favour.' And she said unto her: 'Go, my daughter.' [3]And she went, and came

הַמּוֹאֲבִיָּה אֶל־נָעֳמִי אֵלְכָה־
נָּא הַשָּׂדֶה וַאֲלַקֳטָה בַשִּׁבֳּלִים
אַחַר אֲשֶׁר אֶמְצָא־חֵן בְּעֵינָיו
3 וַתֹּאמֶר לָהּ לְכִי בִתִּי׃ וַתֵּלֶךְ

warrior, but here a man endowed with all the finest human qualities, including magnanimity and dislike of ill-gotten gains (Malbim). The possession of worldly goods is only incidental. Although Naomi could, therefore, be certain of a ready response to a request for help both for herself and Ruth, she preferred, rather than ask for charity, to maintain herself and her daughter-in-law on the share to which the Hebrew law concerning the poor entitled her.

*Boaz.* The origin of the name is doubtful. One derivation is from *bo az*, 'in him is strength.' This etymology is supported by the fact that one of the pillars in the porch of Solomon's Temple was so named. Another derivation is from an unknown root, *baaz*, corresponding to the Arabic *ba'zun*, 'to be fleet.' The Midrash, commenting on the order of the words in the phrase *his name was Boaz*, observes that it accords with the usual practice when speaking of the righteous. In the case of the wicked the order is reversed; e.g. 'Goliath was his name' (1 Sam. xvii. 4, so lit.).

2. The excitement of welcome and condolence over, Naomi and Ruth seek to settle in their homestead. But what were they to live on? Shall Naomi beg her rich nephew for support? She cannot bring herself to do this and incur the risk of being slighted as a poor relation. This brings into relief Ruth's delicate offer, of which the verse tells (Breuer).

*the Moabitess.* Here used rather as a term of commendation, to stress the nature of the woman who, with such remarkable adaptive power, could fit herself into the new conditions with ease and grace.

*let me now go.* The nobility of Ruth's character is here made still more manifest by her anxiety to spare her mother-in-law not only the possible indignity to which reference has been made, but also the humiliating gaze of those who had known her in her former affluence.

*the field.* Not to the vineyards or plantations where she would have to climb and incur danger. She would go into the safety of the fields of Bethlehem.

*glean.* The poor were by law entitled, among other privileges, to the ears of corn that fell from the hands of the reapers (Lev. xix. 9, xxiii. 22; cf. Deut. xxiv. 19).

*among the ears of corn.* The supply would be so plentiful that she would not need to struggle with the other poor for her share of the gleanings.

*find favour.* i.e. be permitted to glean unmolested. There were, we may suppose, hard-hearted owners and reapers who warned would-be gleaners off the field.

*go, my daughter.* It is more honourable to receive what is ours by right than to accept what is given us as an act of charity (Alshich). The term of maternal endearment by Naomi, say the Rabbis, is not an indication of Ruth's youth. According to the Midrash she was then forty years of age.

3. *and she went, and came.* She repeated the act of going out and coming back home again so as to familiarize herself with the bewildering network of country lanes, while at the same time making the acquaintance of decent folk to whom she could safely attach herself. What a

and gleaned in the field after the
reapers; and her hap was to light on
the portion of the field belonging
unto Boaz, who was of the family of
Elimelech. 4 And, behold, Boaz came
from Beth-lehem, and said unto the
reapers: 'The LORD be with you.'
And they answered him: 'The LORD
bless thee.' 5 Then said Boaz unto
his servant that was set over the
reapers: 'Whose damsel is this?'
6 And the servant that was set over
the reapers answered and said: 'It
is a Moabitish damsel that came

וַתָּבוֹא וַתְּלַקֵּט בַּשָּׂדֶה אַחֲרֵי
הַקֹּצְרִים וַיִּקֶר מִקְרֶהָ חֶלְקַת
הַשָּׂדֶה לְבֹעַז אֲשֶׁר מִמִּשְׁפַּחַת
4 אֱלִימֶלֶךְ׃ וְהִנֵּה־בֹעַז בָּא
מִבֵּית לֶחֶם וַיֹּאמֶר לַקּוֹצְרִים
יְהוָה עִמָּכֶם וַיֹּאמְרוּ לוֹ
5 יְבָרֶכְךָ יְהוָה׃ וַיֹּאמֶר בֹּעַז
לְנַעֲרוֹ הַנִּצָּב עַל־הַקּוֹצְרִים
6 לְמִי הַנַּעֲרָה הַזֹּאת׃ וַיַּעַן
הַנַּעַר הַנִּצָּב עַל־הַקּוֹצְרִים
וַיֹּאמַר נַעֲרָה מוֹאֲבִיָּה הִיא

tribute to a person of Moabite origin who had been brought up in a land untrammelled by the bonds of sex morality!

*her hap was to light.* As though by accident. What to the generality of mankind appears but chance is, for the righteous, the result of the guiding hand of a gracious Providence (Malbim).

4 No finer introduction could be given us to an unknown personality than that here vouchsafed to Boaz. We know, indeed, from the introductory remark to this chapter, that he is a man of importance. Now, as he appears on the scene, we learn that he combines with his wealth a rare nobility of character.

*the LORD be with you.* As an ever-sustaining help in your labours. The Rabbis assert that to Boaz is due the credit for instituting the custom of greeting in the name of God. 'It is lamentably true,' says a teacher of ethics, 'that language such as this is seldom heard in our fields while the bounty of Providence is gathering in.' Beautiful must have been the conception of Israel's religion which Ruth formed from the conversation and conduct of Boaz and his reapers (Scott).

*the LORD bless thee.* By granting a rich and abundant crop. Courtesy met courtesy. It was a charming scene and it may be reasonably assumed that there was reality in the salutation (Morison).

5. *set over the reapers.* Each overseer was in charge of forty-two workers (Midrash).

*whose damsel is this?* The question would be naturally prompted, not by her presence, but by her appearance, features and dress. A Talmudic sage explains that the interest of Boaz was aroused by her intelligent and modest behaviour. She would only pick up the ears of corn when two of them fell from the reapers' hands but not if three, as the law prescribed (Peah vi. 5). Moreover, she would never inelegantly stoop to take the gleanings, but would gather them either standing or squatting.

6. The overseer did not rightly grasp the reason for his master's interest, and his reply was almost a warning. 'She is only a Moabite girl,' he says, 'of whom nothing more is known than that she came back from Moab with Naomi.'

back with Naomi out of the field of Moab; [7]and she said: Let me glean, I pray you, and gather after the reapers among the sheaves; so she came, and hath continued even from the morning until now, save that she tarried a little in the house.' [8]Then said Boaz unto Ruth: 'Hearest thou not, my daughter? Go not to glean in another field, neither pass from hence, but abide here fast by my maidens. [9]Let thine eyes be on the field that they do reap, and go thou after them; have I not charged the young men that they shall not touch thee? and when thou art athirst, go unto the vessels, and drink of that which the young men have drawn.' [10]Then she fell on her face, and bowed down to the ground,

הַשָּׁבָה עִם־נָעֳמִי מִשְּׂדֵה
7 מוֹאָב׃ וַתֹּאמֶר אֲלַקֳטָה־נָּא
וְאָסַפְתִּי בָעֳמָרִים אַחֲרֵי
הַקּוֹצְרִים וַתָּבוֹא וַתַּעֲמוֹד
מֵאָז הַבֹּקֶר וְעַד־עַתָּה זֶה
8 שִׁבְתָּהּ הַבַּיִת מְעָט׃ וַיֹּאמֶר
בֹּעַז אֶל־רוּת הֲלוֹא שָׁמַעַתְּ
בִּתִּי אַל־תֵּלְכִי לִלְקֹט בְּשָׂדֶה
אַחֵר וְגַם לֹא־תַעֲבוּרִי מִזֶּה
וְכֹה תִדְבָּקִין עִם־נַעֲרֹתָי׃
9 עֵינַיִךְ בַּשָּׂדֶה אֲשֶׁר־יִקְצֹרוּן
וְהָלַכְתְּ אַחֲרֵיהֶן הֲלוֹא צִוִּיתִי
אֶת־הַנְּעָרִים לְבִלְתִּי נָגְעֵךְ
וְצָמִת וְהָלַכְתְּ אֶל־הַכֵּלִים
וְשָׁתִית מֵאֲשֶׁר יִשְׁאֲבוּן
10 הַנְּעָרִים׃ וַתִּפֹּל עַל־פָּנֶיהָ
וַתִּשְׁתַּחוּ אָרְצָה וַתֹּאמֶר אֵלָיו

7. *she said.* Obviously not to the overseer but in her own mind, otherwise the subsequent words *so she came and hath continued* would be unintelligible.

*in the house.* Probably one of the huts used by the reapers for rest and refreshment. The LXX translates, 'She has not rested (even) a little.' The Latin rendering is, 'She has not returned home (even) for a short time.'

8-16. The overseer's testimony to Ruth's modesty and industry could only strengthen Boaz in his decision to befriend one who was, moreover, the faithful daughter-in-law of his hard-pressed relative Naomi. The character of the man here shines out in its most resplendent light.

8. *abide here fast.* Hebrew 'cleave,' a word used by Boaz to intimate his cognizance of the incident in Moab when *Orpah kissed her mother-in-law but Ruth* cleaved *unto her* (i. 14), and his confidence in her as a woman of worth to whom one could safely cleave.

*maidens.* These would follow behind the reapers and bind the sheaves.

10. *bowed.* Deeply moved by his cordiality, she prostrated herself in humble gratitude.

and said unto him: 'Why have I
found favour in thy sight, that thou
shouldest take cognizance of me,
seeing I am a foreigner?' [11]And
Boaz answered and said unto her:
'It hath fully been told me, all that
thou hast done unto thy mother-in-
law since the death of thy husband;
and how thou hast left thy father
and thy mother, and the land of thy
nativity, and art come unto a people
that thou knowest not heretofore.
[12]The LORD recompense thy work,
and be thy reward complete from
the LORD, the God of Israel, under
whose wings thou art come to take
refuge.' [13]Then she said: 'Let me
find favour in thy sight, my lord;
for that thou hast comforted me,
and for that thou hast spoken to the
heart of thy handmaid, though I be
not as one of thy handmaidens.'
[14]And Boaz said unto her at meal-
time: 'Come hither, and eat of the

מַדּוּעַ מָצָאתִי חֵן בְּעֵינֶיךָ
11 לְהַכִּירֵנִי וְאָנֹכִי נָכְרִיָּה׃ וַיַּעַן
בֹּעַז וַיֹּאמֶר לָהּ הֻגֵּד הֻגַּד לִי
כֹּל אֲשֶׁר־עָשִׂית אֶת־חֲמוֹתֵךְ
אַחֲרֵי מוֹת אִישֵׁךְ וַתַּעַזְבִי
אָבִיךְ וְאִמֵּךְ וְאֶרֶץ מוֹלַדְתֵּךְ
וַתֵּלְכִי אֶל־עַם אֲשֶׁר לֹא־
12 יָדַעַתְּ תְּמוֹל שִׁלְשׁוֹם׃ יְשַׁלֵּם
יְהוָה פָּעֳלֵךְ וּתְהִי מַשְׂכֻּרְתֵּךְ
שְׁלֵמָה מֵעִם יְהוָה אֱלֹהֵי
יִשְׂרָאֵל אֲשֶׁר־בָּאת לַחֲסוֹת
13 תַּחַת־כְּנָפָיו׃ וַתֹּאמֶר
אֶמְצָא־חֵן בְּעֵינֶיךָ אֲדֹנִי כִּי
נִחַמְתָּנִי וְכִי דִבַּרְתָּ עַל־לֵב
שִׁפְחָתֶךָ וְאָנֹכִי לֹא אֶהְיֶה
14 כְּאַחַת שִׁפְחֹתֶיךָ׃ וַיֹּאמֶר לָהּ
בֹעַז לְעֵת הָאֹכֶל גֹּשִׁי הֲלֹם

**11.** *answered.* The Hebrew *wayya'an* signifies raising the voice. He spoke for all to hear. 'You ask me,' he said, 'what moves me to treat an unknown person with the goodwill of a friend. Did you inquire, when you left Moab, as to the conditions in which you would find yourself when you arrived in the land of the Israelites? You knew only one Hebrew woman, your mother-in-law. Yet this sole example sufficed to make you leave your paternal home and your circle of friends in order to attach yourself to a strange people' (Breuer).

**12.** *thy reward.* The promise of reward for doing good is only intended for the young or for those whose intellectual development has not reached a stage when they can appreciate the doing of good as an aim and end in itself. Ruth by her action had shown that she needed no such incentive, but that her reward was contained in the consciousness of having *come to take refuge under* (God's) *wings.*

**13.** *thou hast comforted me.* Unworthy as she felt herself to be of all the kindness she had experienced, she was deeply stirred by the comforting words which 'fell on her heart like showers on the mown grass,' and would themselves be sufficient to win her gratitude even if her benefactor did no more (Alshich).

**14.** *come hither.* She had modestly taken a seat at the foot of the table, and he invited her to sit beside him. A Rabbinic

bread, and dip thy morsel in the
vinegar.' And she sat beside the
reapers; and they reached her
parched corn, and she did eat and
was satisfied, and left thereof. 15And
when she was risen up to glean, Boaz
commanded his young men, saying:
'Let her glean even among the
sheaves, and put her not to shame.
16And also pull out some for her of
purpose from the bundles, and leave

וְאָכַלְתְּ מִן־הַלֶּחֶם וְטָבַלְתְּ
פִּתֵּךְ בַּחֹמֶץ וַתֵּשֶׁב מִצַּד
הַקֹּצְרִים וַיִּצְבָּט־לָהּ קָלִי
וַתֹּאכַל וַתִּשְׂבַּע וַתֹּתַר׃
15 וַתָּקָם לְלַקֵּט וַיְצַו בֹּעַז אֶת־
נְעָרָיו לֵאמֹר גַּם בֵּין הָעֳמָרִים
16 תְּלַקֵּט וְלֹא תַכְלִימוּהָ׃ וְגַם
שֹׁל־תָּשֹׁלּוּ לָהּ מִן־הַצְּבָתִים

פתח בס"פ v. 14.

exposition remarks: By using the word *hither* he intimated to her that the royal house of David was destined to emanate from her, the house whereof *hither* is written; as it says, *Then David the king went in and sat before the LORD; and he said: Who am I, O LORD God, and what is my house, that Thou hast brought me* hither? (2 Sam. vii. 18).

*vinegar.* The Hebrew *chomets* denotes an acid beverage (vinegar, or sour wine) mixed with a little oil, an Oriental drink still popular and very refreshing. In hot weather it is particularly beneficial, allaying thirst, cooling the body and toning up the digestive system.

*she sat beside the reapers.* She humbly declined the honour of sitting at the head of the table. Her modesty forbade her sitting *among* the reapers. A Midrashic comment is that her placing the reapers as a partition between him and her was a symbol of the partition that was to befall the kingdom of the house of David.

*they reached.* The Hebrew *wayyitsbat* occurs nowhere else in the Bible. The form is 3rd pers. sing. masc. and is explained by the Rabbis as referring to Boaz himself, thus drawing attention to his generous disposition. Good deeds were recorded in the Scriptures as an encouragement to posterity (Midrash).

*parched corn.* A famous traveller, describing his experience of a harvest in nineteenth-century Palestine, tells how at meal-time grains of corn, as yet not thoroughly dried and hardened, are roasted in a pan or on an iron plate, providing an exceedingly tasty and nourishing dish, which is eaten with, or in place of, bread (Robinson).

*she did eat . . . thereof.* Showing that Boaz must have given her a substantial quantity. This is a glowing tribute to the generosity which is characteristic of the true sons of Israel.

15. *put her not to shame.* He that puts his fellow to shame has no share in the world to come (Talmud).

16. *also pull out some for her.* This was far beyond the dictates of ordinary kindliness. When our cup runs over, observes a moralist, we let others drink the drops that fall, but not a drop from within the rim, and call it charity; when the crumbs are swept from the table, we think it generous to let the dogs eat them: as if that were charity which permits others to have what we cannot keep; which says to Ruth, 'Glean after the young men,' but forgets to say to the young men, 'Pull out some for her of purpose' (Beecher).

17-23. Ruth's humility, loyalty and piety win the heart of Boaz.

it, and let her glean, and rebuke her
not.' 17So she gleaned in the field
until even; and she beat out that
which she had gleaned, and it was
about an ephah of barley. 18And
she took it up, and went into the
city; and her mother-in-law saw
what she had gleaned; and she
brought forth and gave to her that
which she had left after she was
satisfied. 19And her mother-in-law
said unto her: 'Where hast thou
gleaned to-day? and where wrought-
est thou? blessed be he that did
take knowledge of thee.' And she
told her mother-in-law with whom
she had wrought, and said: 'The
man's name with whom I wrought
to-day is Boaz.' 20And Naomi said
unto her daughter-in-law: 'Blessed
be he of the LORD, who hath not left
off His kindness to the living and to
the dead.' And Naomi said unto
her: 'The man is nigh of kin unto us,

וַעֲזַבְתֶּם וְלִקְּטָה וְלֹא תִגְעֲרוּ־
17 בָהּ׃ וַתְּלַקֵּט בַּשָּׂדֶה עַד־
הָעָרֶב וַתַּחְבֹּט אֵת אֲשֶׁר־
לִקֵּטָה וַיְהִי כְּאֵיפָה שְׂעֹרִים׃
18 וַתִּשָּׂא וַתָּבוֹא הָעִיר וַתֵּרֶא
חֲמוֹתָהּ אֵת אֲשֶׁר־לִקֵּטָה
וַתּוֹצֵא וַתִּתֶּן־לָהּ אֵת אֲשֶׁר־
19 הוֹתִרָה מִשָּׂבְעָהּ׃ וַתֹּאמֶר לָהּ
חֲמוֹתָהּ אֵיפֹה לִקַּטְתְּ הַיּוֹם
וְאָנָה עָשִׂית יְהִי מַכִּירֵךְ בָּרוּךְ
וַתַּגֵּד לַחֲמוֹתָהּ אֵת אֲשֶׁר־
עָשְׂתָה עִמּוֹ וַתֹּאמֶר שֵׁם הָאִישׁ
אֲשֶׁר עָשִׂיתִי עִמּוֹ הַיּוֹם בֹּעַז׃
20 וַתֹּאמֶר נָעֳמִי לְכַלָּתָהּ בָּרוּךְ
הוּא לַיהוָה אֲשֶׁר לֹא־עָזַב
חַסְדּוֹ אֶת־הַחַיִּים וְאֶת־
הַמֵּתִים וַתֹּאמֶר לָהּ נָעֳמִי
קָרוֹב לָנוּ הָאִישׁ מִגֹּאֲלֵנוּ

**17.** *ephah.* Six or seven gallons liquid measure, three pecks dry measure. This would probably be enough to support both Ruth and Naomi for five days (Cook).

**18.** *brought forth.* As a pleasant surprise specially reserved for her mother-in-law (Breuer).

**19.** *where hast thou gleaned?* She guessed, from the abundance of the corn brought home and from the joy on Ruth's face, that the gleaning had been done in the field of a particularly friendly owner.

**20.** *and to the dead.* By caring for the needs of their widows.

*one of our near kinsmen.* The *goël*, 'kinsman,' had both rights and duties. He had the right of buying the property of his dead relative before it was offered for public sale; he was the avenger of the blood in the event of murder; it was his duty to redeem his relative who sold himself as a slave. Naomi recognized in Boaz the *goël* who would close the painful wound which death had torn open in the lives of two women.

one of our near kinsmen.' [21]And
Ruth the Moabitess said: 'Yea, he
said unto me: Thou shalt keep fast
by my young men, until they have
ended all my harvest.' [22]And Naomi
said unto Ruth her daughter-in-law:
'It is good, my daughter, that thou
go out with his maidens, and that
thou be not met in any other field.'
[23]So she kept fast by the maidens of
Boaz to glean unto the end of barley
harvest and of wheat harvest; and
she dwelt with her mother-in-law.

21 הוּא׃ וַתֹּאמֶר רוּת הַמּוֹאֲבִיָּה
גַּם ׀ כִּי־אָמַר אֵלַי עִם־
הַנְּעָרִים אֲשֶׁר־לִי תִּדְבָּקִין
עַד אִם־כִּלּוּ אֵת כָּל־הַקָּצִיר
22 אֲשֶׁר־לִי׃ וַתֹּאמֶר נָעֳמִי אֶל־
רוּת כַּלָּתָהּ טוֹב בִּתִּי כִּי תֵצְאִי
עִם־נַעֲרוֹתָיו וְלֹא יִפְגְּעוּ־בָךְ
23 בְּשָׂדֶה אַחֵר׃ וַתִּדְבַּק
בְּנַעֲרוֹת בֹּעַז לְלַקֵּט עַד־
כְּלוֹת קְצִיר הַשְּׂעֹרִים וּקְצִיר
הַחִטִּים וַתֵּשֶׁב אֶת־חֲמוֹתָהּ׃

## 3 CHAPTER III

[1]And Naomi her mother-in-law
said unto her: 'My daughter, shall
I not seek rest for thee, that it may

1 וַתֹּאמֶר לָהּ נָעֳמִי חֲמוֹתָהּ בִּתִּי
הֲלֹא אֲבַקֶּשׁ־לָךְ מָנוֹחַ אֲשֶׁר

22. *in any other field.* 'It is discourtesy,' remarks a religious thinker, 'where we are beholden, to alter our dependency. The very taking of their favours is a contentment to those who have already well deserved, and it is quarrel enough that their courtesy is not received. How shall God take it that, while He gives and proffers large, we run to the world that can afford us nothing but vanity and vexation?' (Hall).

23. *unto the end of . . . harvest.* A period of three months, corresponding to the time that must elapse before a female proselyte is permitted to marry. The phrasing of the last verse conveys a hint that a change of fortune awaited Ruth when the harvest was ended.

## CHAPTER III

### RUTH SEEKS BETROTHAL WITH BOAZ

True to the principle that a woman can find happiness only in the house of her husband, Naomi, when the harvest was over, is moved by no other desire than that Ruth shall find a home befitting her worth and character (Breuer).

1. *shall I not seek.* As Ruth had no mother to provide for her, Naomi felt the duty to be hers.

be well with thee? ²And now is
there not Boaz our kinsman, with
whose maidens thou wast? Behold,
he winnoweth barley to-night in the
threshing-floor. ³Wash thyself therefore, and anoint thee, and put thy
raiment upon thee, and get thee
down to the threshing-floor; but
make not thyself known unto the
man, until he shall have done eating
and drinking. ⁴And it shall be,
when he lieth down, that thou shalt
mark the place where he shall lie,
and thou shalt go in, and uncover his
feet, and lay thee down; and he will

יִֽיטַב־לָֽךְ׃ וְעַתָּה הֲלֹא בֹעַז 2
מֹֽדַעְתָּנוּ אֲשֶׁר הָיִית אֶת־
נַעֲרוֹתָיו הִנֵּה־הוּא זֹרֶה
אֶת־גֹּרֶן הַשְּׂעֹרִים הַלָּֽיְלָה׃
וְרָחַצְתְּ ׀ וָסַכְתְּ וְשַׂמְתְּ 3
שִׂמְלֹתַיִךְ עָלַיִךְ וְיָרַדְתִּי הַגֹּרֶן
אַל־תִּוָּדְעִי לָאִישׁ עַד כַּלֹּתוֹ
לֶאֱכֹל וְלִשְׁתּֽוֹת׃ וִיהִי בְשָׁכְבוֹ 4
וְיָדַעַתְּ אֶת־הַמָּקוֹם אֲשֶׁר
יִשְׁכַּב־שָׁם וּבָאת וְגִלִּית
מַרְגְּלֹתָיו וְשָׁכָבְתִּי וְהוּא יַגִּיד

v. 3. וירדת ק׳ v. 4. ושכבת ק׳

*rest.* i.e. a husband. Ruth's place was certainly not in the field. The married state, when properly entered into, writes a religious thinker, is a rest, as much as anything on earth can be so called; seeing it ought to fix the affections and form a connection for life; those are giddy indeed that marriage does not compose (Scott).

*that it may be well.* Not so much in the material, as in the spiritual, sense. Only a God-fearing husband, with a genuine understanding of human nature and the real values of life, can provide such well-being for his wife. The Jewish home has been noted for its endeavour to provide this bliss.

2. *winnoweth.* The simple manners of Boaz are here revealed. This man of wealth assists personally in the winnowing of his barley.

*to-night.* He slept in the threshing-floor either to avail himself of the cool evening breeze (beginning about 4 o'clock and lasting through the night, until about half an hour before dawn) that would carry away the chaff from the corn; or to guard his grain from thieves. The general insecurity of the times would make this a necessary precaution.

3. *anoint thee.* As was the custom of the Jewish nobility in olden days (Ibn Ezra). It was an exceptionally dangerous road along which Naomi was urging Ruth. She knew no other.

*thy raiment.* i.e. festive robes.

*get thee down.* The Rabbis inferred from this that threshing-floors were situated below the city. As a rule they were on elevated ground, but Bethlehem being built on two hills, Ruth would naturally have to go down in order to get to the threshing-floor.

4. *feet.* The Hebrew signifies 'the place where the feet are.'

*lay thee down.* Perhaps, observes one writer, the assurance which long trial had given her of the good behaviour and firm chastity of her daughter-in-law, together with her persuasion of the

tell thee what thou shalt do.' 5 And
she said unto her: 'All that thou
sayest unto me I will do.' 6 And she
went down unto the threshing-floor,
and did according to all that her
mother-in-law bade her. 7 And
when Boaz had eaten and drunk, and
his heart was merry, he went to lie
down at the end of the heap of corn;
and she came softly, and uncovered
his feet, and laid her down. 8 And
it came to pass at midnight, that
the man was startled, and turned
himself; and, behold, a woman lay
at his feet. 9 And he said: 'Who art
thou?' And she answered: 'I am
Ruth thy handmaid; spread therefore thy skirt over thy handmaid; for
thou art a near kinsman.' 10 And he

5 לָךְ אֵת אֲשֶׁר תַּעֲשִׂין׃ וַתֹּאמֶר
אֵלֶיהָ כֹּל אֲשֶׁר־תֹּאמְרִי *
6 אֶעֱשֶׂה׃ וַתֵּרֶד הַגֹּרֶן וַתַּעַשׂ
כְּכֹל אֲשֶׁר־צִוַּתָּה חֲמוֹתָהּ׃
7 וַיֹּאכַל בֹּעַז וַיֵּשְׁתְּ וַיִּיטַב לִבּוֹ
וַיָּבֹא לִשְׁכַּב בִּקְצֵה הָעֲרֵמָה
וַתָּבֹא בַלָּט וַתְּגַל מַרְגְּלֹתָיו
8 וַתִּשְׁכָּב׃ וַיְהִי בַּחֲצִי הַלַּיְלָה
וַיֶּחֱרַד הָאִישׁ וַיִּלָּפֵת וְהִנֵּה
9 אִשָּׁה שֹׁכֶבֶת מַרְגְּלֹתָיו׃ וַיֹּאמֶר
מִי־אָתְּ וַתֹּאמֶר אָנֹכִי רוּת
אֲמָתֶךָ וּפָרַשְׂתָּ כְנָפֶךָ עַל־
10 אֲמָתְךָ כִּי גֹאֵל אָתָּה׃ וַיֹּאמֶר

v. 5. אלי קרי ולא כתיב

religious gravity of Boaz, made her think that design safe, which to others would have been perilous (Hall).

5. *unto me.* A masoretic addition, absent from the Hebrew text.

*I will do.* Ruth's conduct must not be judged by modern standards, but by those of the times in which she lived. She is fulfilling a duty of love and piety towards the dead by approaching Boaz and reminding him of his obligation as a kinsman (Nowack).

6. Only after reaching the threshing-floor did she do as Naomi had bidden. This saved her from the curious glances which a festively dressed woman would certainly attract. Though she was not carrying out the letter of Naomi's instructions she was certainly complying with the spirit, for only in this way could she avoid becoming known to the man.

7. *merry.* This expression does not necessarily imply excess. It can even denote gladness without reference to eating and drinking. This is the sense in which the Talmud understands the word.

8. *was startled.* At the thought that possibly a night-demon was at his feet.

*behold, a woman.* Her voice would betray her; or her face and clothes in the light of the moon (Ibn Ezra).

9. *skirt.* lit. 'wing,' a metaphor borrowed from the winged kingdom and used as a symbol of marriage. According to some authorities the Hebrew *kanaph* is here, as often elsewhere, intended to be understood in the sense of corner of the garment. The custom of placing the corner of the garment over a maiden as a token of marriage is known among the Arabs.

said: 'Blessed be thou of the LORD,
my daughter; thou hast shown more
kindness in the end than at the beginning, inasmuch as thou didst not
follow the young men, whether poor
or rich. [11]And now, my daughter,
fear not; I will do to thee all that
thou sayest; for all the men in the
gate of my people do know that thou
art a virtuous woman. [12]And now it
is true that I am a near kinsman;
howbeit there is a kinsman nearer
than I. [13]Tarry this night, and it
shall be in the morning, that if he
will perform unto thee the part of a
kinsman, well; let him do the kinsman's part; but if he be not willing
to do the part of a kinsman to thee,
then will I do the part of a kinsman
to thee, as the LORD liveth; lie down

בְּרוּכָה אַתְּ לַיהוָה בִּתִּי
הֵיטַבְתְּ חַסְדֵּךְ הָאַחֲרוֹן מִן־
הָרִאשׁוֹן לְבִלְתִּי־לֶכֶת אַחֲרֵי
הַבַּחוּרִים אִם־דַּל וְאִם־
11 עָשִׁיר׃ וְעַתָּה בִּתִּי אַל־
תִּירְאִי כֹּל אֲשֶׁר־תֹּאמְרִי
אֶעֱשֶׂה־לָּךְ כִּי יוֹדֵעַ כָּל־
שַׁעַר עַמִּי כִּי אֵשֶׁת חַיִל אָתְּ׃
12 וְעַתָּה כִּי אָמְנָם כִּי אם גֹּאֵל
אָנֹכִי וְגַם יֵשׁ גֹּאֵל קָרוֹב מִמֶּנִּי׃
13 לִינִי ׀ הַלַּיְלָה וְהָיָה בַבֹּקֶר
אִם־יִגְאָלֵךְ טוֹב יִגְאָל
וְאִם־לֹא יַחְפֹּץ לְגָאֳלֵךְ
וּגְאַלְתִּיךְ אָנֹכִי חַי־יְהוָה

v. 12. כתיב ולא קרי   v. 13. ב׳ רבתי

*a near kinsman.* It was, therefore, his legal right and duty to purchase her husband's estate (Lev. xxv. 25). She asks him to acquire her, too, so that the name of the departed might be perpetuated through the union.

**10.** *at the beginning.* When she decided to abandon home and fortune in order to attach herself to her mother-in-law.

**11.** *fear not.* He reassured her that he was not merely putting her off with fair words.

**12.** *nearer than I.* A brother of Elimelech; whereas Boaz was only a nephew. Tradition makes Boaz at this time an octogenarian! (Midrash).

**13.** *if he will perform . . . kinsman, well.* The Hebrew *tob yig'al* may mean, 'Let Tob perform.' From this it is inferred by some that Tob was the name of the anonymous kinsman.

*then will I.* In every undertaking, remarks a religious teacher, we should be diligent in using proper means and then leave the issue to God's decision.

*as the LORD liveth.* 'Where the thought of a living God governs the relationship between the sexes, a man and a woman may meet in the hour of midnight in a lonely threshing-floor and part from each other as pure as when they came' (Breuer).

until the morning.' [14]And she lay
at his feet until the morning; and
she rose up before one could discern
another. For he said: 'Let it not be
known that the woman came to the
threshing-floor.' [15]And he said:
'Bring the mantle that is upon thee,
and hold it'; and she held it; and he
measured six measures of barley, and
laid it on her; and he went into the
city. [16]And when she came to her
mother-in-law, she said: 'Who art
thou, my daughter?' And she told
her all that the man had done to her.

14 שִׁכְבִי עַד־הַבֹּקֶר׃ וַתִּשְׁכַּב
מַרְגְּלוֹתָו עַד־הַבֹּקֶר וַתָּקָם
בְּטֶרֶום יַכִּיר אִישׁ אֶת־רֵעֵהוּ
וַיֹּאמֶר אַל־יִוָּדַע כִּי־בָאָה
15 הָאִשָּׁה הַגֹּרֶן׃ וַיֹּאמֶר הָבִי
הַמִּטְפַּחַת אֲשֶׁר־עָלַיִךְ
וְאֶחֳזִי־בָהּ וַתֹּאחֶז בָּהּ וַיָּמָד
שֵׁשׁ־שְׂעֹרִים וַיָּשֶׁת עָלֶיהָ וַיָּבֹא
16 הָעִיר׃ וַתָּבוֹא אֶל־חֲמוֹתָהּ
וַתֹּאמֶר מִי־אַתְּ בִּתִּי וַתַּגֶּד־
לָהּ אֵת כָּל־אֲשֶׁר עָשָׂה־לָהּ׃

v. 14. מרגלותיו ק׳ v. 14. יתיר ו׳ v. 15. ב״א וְאֶחֳזִי

14. *before.* The Hebrew *beterem* has an apparently superfluous *vav*, which commentators explain as an allusion to the six (the numerical value of *vav*) hours which Ruth spent in the threshing-floor.

*said.* In his mind, i.e. thought. According to Rabbinic comment he was addressing himself to God. 'All that night Boaz was prostrate in prayer, saying: Sovereign of the Universe! Thou knowest that I have had no physical contact with her. I pray Thee, let it not be known that the woman came into the threshing-floor, so that the name of Heaven be not profaned through me.'

15. *six measures of barley.* The measure is not stated. The Targum renders, 'six seahs of barley,' i.e. two ephahs, too heavy a load for a woman to carry. It therefore adds that Ruth received miraculous strength for the occasion. The Hebrew has 'six barley (grains)', a phrase which the Rabbis interpreted metaphorically as alluding to the six righteous men destined to issue from this marriage, viz. David, Hananiah, Mishael, Azariah, Daniel and the Messiah.

*laid it on her.* Probably on her head. Oriental women can carry great weights in this manner.

*he went into the city.* He accompanied her to the city gate, lest she be molested (Midrash).

16. *who art thou?* It was still dark and difficult to recognize even familiar faces. The expression might also mean: Are you one dishonoured or one protected as a wife? We see here Naomi's anxiety to discover how her hazardous plan had worked.

17. *to me.* This is absent from the masoretic text. Its insertion by the masoretes is explained as indicating that though the words were addressed to her, they were intended as a message for Naomi.

17 הָאִישׁ׃ וַתֹּאמֶר שֵׁשׁ־הַשְּׂעֹרִים
הָאֵלֶּה נָתַן לִי כִּי אָמַר *
אַל־תָּבוֹאִי רֵיקָם אֶל־
18 חֲמוֹתֵךְ׃ וַתֹּאמֶר שְׁבִי בִתִּי
עַד אֲשֶׁר תֵּדְעִין אֵיךְ יִפֹּל
דָּבָר כִּי לֹא יִשְׁקֹט הָאִישׁ כִּי
אִם־כִּלָּה הַדָּבָר הַיּוֹם׃

* v. 17. אלי קרי ולא כתיב

[17]And she said: 'These six measures of barley gave he me; for he said to me: Go not empty unto thy mother-in-law.' [18]Then said she: 'Sit still, my daughter, until thou know how the matter will fall; for the man will not rest, until he have finished the thing this day.'

## 4 CHAPTER IV ד

1 וּבֹעַז עָלָה הַשַּׁעַר וַיֵּשֶׁב שָׁם
וְהִנֵּה הַגֹּאֵל עֹבֵר אֲשֶׁר דִּבֶּר־
בֹּעַז וַיֹּאמֶר סוּרָה שְׁבָה־פֹּה

[1]Now Boaz went up to the gate, and sat him down there; and, behold, the near kinsman of whom Boaz spoke came by; unto whom he said: 'Ho, such a one! turn aside, sit

18. *the man will not rest.* He will do all in his power to fulfil his promise. The Rabbis assert: The yea of the righteous is yea, and their nay, nay (Midrash).

## CHAPTER IV

### BOAZ MARRIES RUTH

1. *went up.* The next morning. The fulfilment of a task, especially if undertaken on solemn oath, declare the Rabbis, should not be delayed, lest it be altogether prevented by force of circumstances.

*to the gate.* This was a fairly large edifice, where men might sit in the comfort of the shade during the heat of the day. In front of it was a broad open space. This was the market-place where the court normally held its sessions and people met for the interchange of news and the settlement of disputes.

*such a one.* If we assume that his name was Tob (see on iii. 13), the explanation of this phrase may be that the name is withheld out of deference to his position, he being a person of note who should not have selfishly refused to discharge his duty as a kinsman. If, on the other hand, it was not Tob, then we must suppose that the name was unknown or unnecessary for the understanding of the story.

*turn aside.* The authoritative tone of voice reveals the influential position held by Boaz, who was a judge. He was evidently dispensing with the customary forms of polite address, as appears from the omission of *na*, 'please.'

*sit down.* The matter on which your aid is sought is one of great moment and requires calm thought and sedate judgment (Yavets).

down here.' And he turned aside,
and sat down. 2And he took ten men
of the elders of the city, and said:
'Sit ye down here.' And they sat
down. 3And he said unto the near
kinsman: 'Naomi, that is come
back out of the field of Moab, selleth
the parcel of land, which was our
brother Elimelech's; 4and I thought
to disclose it unto thee, saying:
Buy it before them that sit here,
and before the elders of my people.
If thou wilt redeem it, redeem it; but
if it will not be redeemed, then tell
me, that I may know; for there is
none to redeem it beside thee; and
I am after thee.' And he said: 'I
will redeem it.' 5Then said Boaz:
'What day thou buyest the field of
the hand of Naomi—hast thou also
bought of Ruth the Moabitess, the
wife of the dead, to raise up the
name of the dead upon his inherit-

2 פְּלֹנִי אַלְמֹנִי וַיָּסַר וַיֵּשֵׁב׃ וַיִּקַּח
עֲשָׂרָה אֲנָשִׁים מִזִּקְנֵי הָעִיר
וַיֹּאמֶר שְׁבוּ־פֹה וַיֵּשֵׁבוּ׃
3 וַיֹּאמֶר לַגֹּאֵל חֶלְקַת הַשָּׂדֶה
אֲשֶׁר לְאָחִינוּ לֶאֱלִימֶלֶךְ
מָכְרָה נָעֳמִי הַשָּׁבָה מִשְּׂדֵה
4 מוֹאָב׃ וַאֲנִי אָמַרְתִּי אֶגְלֶה
אָזְנְךָ לֵאמֹר קְנֵה נֶגֶד הַיֹּשְׁבִים
וְנֶגֶד זִקְנֵי עַמִּי אִם־תִּגְאַל גְּאָל
וְאִם־לֹא יִגְאַל הַגִּידָה לִּי
וְאֵדְעָ כִּי אֵין זוּלָתְךָ לִגְאוֹל
וְאָנֹכִי אַחֲרֶיךָ וַיֹּאמֶר אָנֹכִי
5 אֶגְאָל׃ וַיֹּאמֶר בֹּעַז בְּיוֹם־
קְנוֹתְךָ הַשָּׂדֶה מִיַּד נָעֳמִי וּמֵאֵת
רוּת הַמּוֹאֲבִיָּה אֵשֶׁת־הַמֵּת
קָנִיתִי לְהָקִים שֵׁם־הַמֵּת עַל־

v. 4. ואדעה ק׳ v. 5. קנית ק׳

2. *ten men.* The quorum required for the recital of the marriage benedictions. Boaz held them in readiness for the pending ceremony. It is the concern of the community that a family threatened with extinction shall be duly rebuilt by those whose duty it is to do so. Hence the wide publicity Boaz gave to the proceedings.

*elders.* Heads of leading families in the city.

*sit.* The Rabbis inferred from this that it is impolite to sit in the presence of a superior until invited to do so.

3. *selleth.* lit. 'hath sold.' The context requires the translation to be either 'intends to sell' or 'has offered for sale,' because in fact Naomi had not yet sold the field, as appears from verse 5.

*brother.* Not necessarily in the literal sense, but rather a relative in general.

4. *I will redeem.* His readiness to fulfil his obligation in the first instance was doubtless due to his belief that the property belonged solely to Naomi, and that his duty would end with the purchase of the field from her. On learning that the transaction would include marriage with Ruth and its attendant responsibilities, he withdrew.

5. *to raise up the name of the dead.* The property would not be in their kinsman's name, but in that of the widow whom he will marry.

ance?' 6And the near kinsman said:
'I cannot redeem it for myself, lest I
mar mine own inheritance; take
thou my right of redemption on thee;
for I cannot redeem it.'—7Now this
was the custom in former time in
Israel concerning redeeming and
concerning exchanging, to confirm
all things: a man drew off his shoe,
and gave it to his neighbour; and
this was the attestation in Israel.—
8So the near kinsman said unto Boaz:
'Buy it for thyself.' And he drew
off his shoe. 9And Boaz said unto
the elders, and unto all the people:
'Ye are witnesses this day, that I
have bought all that was Elimelech's,

נַחֲלָתוֹ׃ וַיֹּאמֶר הַגֹּאֵל לֹא 6
אוּכַל לִגְאָול־לִי פֶּן־אַשְׁחִית
אֶת־נַחֲלָתִי גְּאַל־לְךָ אַתָּה
אֶת־גְּאֻלָּתִי כִּי לֹא־אוּכַל
לִגְאֹל׃ וְזֹאת לְפָנִים בְּיִשְׂרָאֵל 7
עַל־הַגְּאוּלָּה וְעַל־הַתְּמוּרָה
לְקַיֵּם כָּל־דָּבָר שָׁלַף אִישׁ
נַעֲלוֹ וְנָתַן לְרֵעֵהוּ וְזֹאת
הַתְּעוּדָה בְּיִשְׂרָאֵל׃ וַיֹּאמֶר 8
הַגֹּאֵל לְבֹעַז קְנֵה־לָךְ וַיִּשְׁלֹף
נַעֲלוֹ׃ וַיֹּאמֶר בֹּעַז לַזְּקֵנִים 9
וְכָל־הָעָם עֵדִים אַתֶּם הַיּוֹם
כִּי קָנִיתִי אֶת־כָּל־אֲשֶׁר

v. 6. יתירו׳

6. *mar mine own inheritance.* The process, besides causing a taint in the family pedigree, will render me also penniless. According to the Targum his refusal was due to his being already married.

*take thou my right of redemption.* The greater the selfishness of the egoist the more generous the dose of altruism he allots to others (Breuer.)

7. *redeeming.* This refers to a sale. The words 'redemption' and 'exchange' are used here in a general signification for all cases of buying or selling land (Wright). *exchanging.* Perhaps some such transfer of right as that made by the anonymous kinsman to Boaz.

*drew off his shoe.* A symbolic act of legal transfer. The custom is also known among the Indians, the ancient Germans and the Arabs. The Hebrew *na'al,* 'shoe,' is explained by some commentators as 'glove' (Targum and Yavets). This form of acquisition later gave way to others, such as by means of money-payment, by deed or by virtue of *Chazakah,* i.e. for instance, a fixed period of undisputed possession (B.B. III, 1). A distinction must be made between drawing off the shoe in this ceremony and in that of *chalitsah* (Deut. xxv. 9).

8. *his shoe.* It is not clear whose shoe is intended, whether that of Boaz or the kinsman. The Targum favours the former who was the purchaser. The LXX adds 'and gave it to him.'

9. *all the people.* The ceremony had attracted the townspeople of Bethlehem who had formerly shown a sympathetic interest in the two stricken women on their return from Moab, and who now witnessed the hour of restoration to their rightful place in the community.

and all that was Chilion's and
Mahlon's, of the hand of Naomi.
10 Moreover Ruth the Moabitess, the
wife of Mahlon, have I acquired to
be my wife, to raise up the name of
the dead upon his inheritance, that
the name of the dead be not cut off
from among his brethren, and from
the gate of his place; ye are witnesses this day.' 11 And all the people
that were in the gate, and the elders,
said: 'We are witnesses. The LORD
make the woman that is come into
thy house like Rachel and like Leah,
which two did build the house of
Israel; and do thou worthily in
Ephrath, and be famous in Beth-
lehem; 12 and let thy house be like the
house of Perez, whom Tamar bore
unto Judah, of the seed which the
LORD shall give thee of this young

לֶאֱלִימֶלֶךְ וְאֵת כָּל־אֲשֶׁר
לְכִלְיוֹן וּמַחְלוֹן מִיַּד נָעֳמִי׃
10 וְגַם אֶת־רוּת הַמֹּאֲבִיָּה אֵשֶׁת
מַחְלוֹן קָנִיתִי לִי לְאִשָּׁה
לְהָקִים שֵׁם־הַמֵּת עַל־
נַחֲלָתוֹ וְלֹא־יִכָּרֵת שֵׁם־הַמֵּת
מֵעִם אֶחָיו וּמִשַּׁעַר מְקוֹמוֹ
11 עֵדִים אַתֶּם הַיּוֹם׃ וַיֹּאמְרוּ
כָּל־הָעָם אֲשֶׁר־בַּשַּׁעַר
וְהַזְּקֵנִים עֵדִים יִתֵּן יְהוָה אֶת־
הָאִשָּׁה הַבָּאָה אֶל־בֵּיתֶךָ
כְּרָחֵל ׀ וּכְלֵאָה אֲשֶׁר בָּנוּ
שְׁתֵּיהֶם אֶת־בֵּית יִשְׂרָאֵל
וַעֲשֵׂה־חַיִל בְּאֶפְרָתָה וּקְרָא
12 שֵׁם בְּבֵית לָחֶם׃ וִיהִי בֵיתְךָ
כְּבֵית פֶּרֶץ אֲשֶׁר־יָלְדָה תָמָר
לִיהוּדָה מִן־הַזֶּרַע אֲשֶׁר יִתֵּן
יְהוָה לְךָ מִן־הַנַּעֲרָה הַזֹּאת׃

**10.** *moreover Ruth.* There is a delicacy in the manner in which Boaz mentions the acquisition of Ruth. He does not refer to it in the same breath as he speaks of his purchase of the property, but gives to the act a due weight and importance all its own; as if to stress the distinction between acquiring a wife and mere chattels. Although the same legal terminology is employed, the analogy ends there and never in Jewish law is the wife regarded as anything but a partner in the sacred duty of building a home.

*to raise . . . inheritance.* The constant association of the remarried widow with the property of her departed husband kept alive in people's minds the dead man's memory.

**11.** *all the people.* Though Boaz had addressed the elders first, the crowd were too excited to wait until their turn came to respond.

*Rachel . . . Leah.* The founders of the family of Jacob and the matriarchs in Israel.

**12.** *Perez.* He, too, was the offspring of a marriage contracted in circumstances similar to those of Boaz (Gen. xxxviii).

woman.' [13]So Boaz took Ruth, and
she became his wife; and he went
in unto her, and the LORD gave her
conception, and she bore a son.
[14]And the women said unto Naomi:
'Blessed be the LORD, who hath not
left thee this day without a near
kinsman, and let his name be famous
in Israel. [15]And he shall be unto
thee a restorer of life, and a nourisher
of thine old age; for thy daughter-in-
law, who loveth thee, who is better
to thee than seven sons, hath borne
him.' [16]And Naomi took the child,
and laid it in her bosom, and
became nurse unto it. [17]And the
women her neighbours gave it a

וַיִּקַּח בֹּעַז אֶת־רוּת וַתְּהִי־לוֹ 13
לְאִשָּׁה וַיָּבֹא אֵלֶיהָ וַיִּתֵּן יְהֹוָה
לָהּ הֵרָיוֹן וַתֵּלֶד בֵּן׃
וַתֹּאמַרְנָה הַנָּשִׁים אֶל־נָעֳמִי 14
בָּרוּךְ יְהֹוָה אֲשֶׁר לֹא הִשְׁבִּית
לָךְ גֹּאֵל הַיּוֹם וְיִקָּרֵא שְׁמוֹ
בְּיִשְׂרָאֵל׃ וְהָיָה לָךְ לְמֵשִׁיב 15
נֶפֶשׁ וּלְכַלְכֵּל אֶת־שֵׂיבָתֵךְ כִּי
כַלָּתֵךְ אֲשֶׁר־אֲהֵבַתֶךְ יְלָדַתּוּ
אֲשֶׁר־הִיא טוֹבָה לָךְ מִשִּׁבְעָה
בָּנִים׃ וַתִּקַּח נָעֳמִי אֶת־הַיֶּלֶד 16
וַתְּשִׁתֵהוּ בְחֵיקָהּ וַתְּהִי־לוֹ
לְאֹמֶנֶת׃ וַתִּקְרֶאנָה לוֹ 17
הַשְּׁכֵנוֹת שֵׁם לֵאמֹר יֻלַּד־בֵּן

13. *Boaz took Ruth.* A worthy match; a woman of valour wed to a man of valour.

*gave her conception.* The peculiar construction of the text leads a Midrash to explain that a miracle occurred, whereby a new womb was given her. It was surely Divine intervention which enabled her to have children by the elderly Boaz and not by the young Mahlon.

14. *this day.* The phrase is superfluous and induced the Rabbis to make the following observation: As the day (i.e. the sun) holds dominion in the skies, so shall your seed produce one (viz. the Messiah) who will hold sway over Israel for ever.

*a near kinsman.* lit. 'redeemer'; not Boaz, but the new-born son who removed the stigma of childlessness from Naomi.

*let his name be famous.* The Hebrew is literally 'his name shall be called,' i.e. it will be on the lips of all.

15. *seven sons.* The number is not to be taken literally but as an indication of multitude. A mother of many sons is a happy mother; but happier still is Naomi who has a daughter-in-law in whose child she finds consolation in her old age for the loss of her own sons, and a new hope of becoming the ancestress of a family in Israel.

16. *bosom.* As a sign that the son of Ruth was also her son.

17. *the women.* These are consistently

name, saying: 'There is a son born to Naomi'; and they called his name Obed; he is the father of Jesse, the father of David.

[18]Now these are the generations of Perez: Perez begot Hezron; [19]and Hezron begot Ram, and Ram begot Amminadab; [20]and Amminadab begot Nahshon, and Nahshon begot [a]Salmon; [21]and Salmon begot Boaz, and Boaz begot Obed; [22]and Obed begot Jesse, and Jesse begot David.

[a] Heb. *Salmah.*

לְנָעֳמִי וַתִּקְרֶאנָה שְׁמוֹ עוֹבֵד
הוּא אֲבִי־יִשַׁי אֲבִי דָוִד׃
18 וְאֵלֶּה תּוֹלְדוֹת פָּרֶץ פֶּרֶץ
19 הוֹלִיד אֶת־חֶצְרוֹן׃ וְחֶצְרוֹן
הוֹלִיד אֶת־רָם וְרָם הוֹלִיד
20 אֶת־עַמִּינָדָב׃ וְעַמִּינָדָב
הוֹלִיד אֶת־נַחְשׁוֹן וְנַחְשׁוֹן
21 הוֹלִיד אֶת־שַׂלְמָה׃ וְשַׂלְמוֹן
הוֹלִיד אֶת־בֹּעַז וּבֹעַז הוֹלִיד
22 אֶת־עוֹבֵד׃ וְעֹבֵד הוֹלִיד
אֶת־יִשָׁי וְיִשַׁי הוֹלִיד אֶת־
דָּוִד׃

described as interested in all Naomi's affairs.

*a son born to Naomi.* A Talmudic comment asks, Was it Naomi who bore him? Surely it was Ruth! The reply is, Ruth indeed gave him birth, but Naomi brought him up; hence he was called her son.

*Obed.* An apt name for one who was expected by all to *serve* both God and men, even as his father and mother had done, and in keeping with the traditions of their exalted family.

18. *generations of Perez.* There may have been a family book for the house of Perez in which their genealogies were preserved.

19. *Ram.* In the LXX the name appears as Aram.

20. *Salmon.* In 1 Chron. ii. 11 he is called Salma.

21. *begot Boaz.* There is a non-Jewish tradition that the mother of Boaz was Rahab, famous for her part in Joshua's conquest of Jericho.

22. *Jesse begot David.* Thus the descent of the great king and poet in Israel is traced to Moabite ancestry. The Rabbis, recalling David's conquest and suppression of the children of Moab (2 Sam. viii. 2), were led to quote the proverb, 'From the very forest itself comes the handle of the axe that fells it.' Tradition ascribes to Ruth unusual longevity. She did not die, says a Midrashic comment, until after beholding her royal descendant Solomon sitting and judging the case of the harlots (1 Kings iii. 16ff.).

Everything leads up, in the last instance, to David, and so the whole purpose of the Book is achieved in the final verse of this chapter.

This is the only place in תנ״ך except for Gen. 2.4 that the word Toldot appears with the "full" spelling. In @ 50 other instances, either of these is used. — תולדות v. 18; תלדות / תולדת

Midrash: After Eden, the world is imperfect until the messiah, who will come from the line of David.

# איכה

# LAMENTATIONS

INTRODUCTION AND COMMENTARY

*by*

REV. DR. S. GOLDMAN, M.A., D.PHIL.

איכה is traditionally ascribed to Jeremiah (or his scribe).

But Jeremiah didn't live to see 586 BCE, which Lamentations describes

1010 BCE - David united the tribes → the Kingdom of Israel

960 - Solomon took over

937 - Rehoboam taxed the people even more than Solomon, so the kingdom split

Jeroboam → Northern Kingdom - Israel (or Ephraim)
Rehoboam → Southern Kingdom - Judah (the Royal House of David)

721 - Israel destroyed by the Assyrians, people dispersed (10 tribes are lost) replaced by Assyrians, Samaritans (from capital, Samaria)

626 - Babylonian Empire crushes the Assyrians, Judah pays tribute to Babylonia

→ Jeremiah prophesies Babylonian exile

Buttressed religious reformation

597 - First Babylonian exile (the king is taken), Zedekiah is put on throne as a puppet - last king

~~Jeremiah is also exiled, but the Babylonians~~
The Babylonians leave Jeremiah ~~[illegible]~~ alone, but he is kidnapped to Egypt, where he dies before

586 BCE - T. I destroyed, the major Babylonian exile occurs

70 CE - T. II destroyed

## INTRODUCTION

### THE TITLE

LAMENTATIONS, in the Hebrew Bible, is the third of the Five Scrolls. Its Hebrew title, *Echah*, is derived from the initial word of the book, but its contents are best indicated by the name by which it is known in Rabbinic literature, *kinoth*, 'Lamentations, or Elegies.'

### AUTHORSHIP

The authorship of this small book is—by a very old tradition, traces of which may perhaps be found in 2 Chronicles xxxv. 25—ascribed to Jeremiah, and this ascription is generally accepted in the Synagogue. It is a bitter and tragic conclusion to the prophet's life-work. Against his whole nature, which was tender and sensitive, but because of the evils of his age, he had perforce to be a prophet of woe and calamity; and he lived to see and bewail the destruction of Judea and Jerusalem which he had so clearly foreseen. But there is no note of self-vindication or self-righteousness in *Lamentations*. The dire fulfilment of his prophecies fills Jeremiah only with grief.

### THE THEME

The theme of the Book is simple. It is a lament for Judea and Jerusalem, which had been destroyed by the Babylonians in 586 B.C.E., and for the sufferings of their inhabitants during and after the siege, together with a confession of the sins of the people and their leaders, which, in the prophet's mind, had been the cause of the calamity—a noble insistence on resignation to God's will—and the prayer that God might again look with favour on Israel and restore them to grace. The theme is repeated in each of the five distinct elegies which make up the Book; for each of the chapters is to be considered a poem complete in itself, and it is fruitless to attempt to find logical coherence or development between one chapter and the next. Even within each of the separate poems there is an absence of plan or structure; instead the thought moves this way and that, as indeed might be expected in poems which are the spontaneous outpourings of a grief-stricken heart.

### THE STRUCTURE

Four of the five poems are alphabetic in structure, chapters i, ii and iv, each having twenty-two verses beginning with successive letters of the alphabet, and chapter iii, with its sixty-six verses, following a triple alphabet. Chapter v, though not alphabetic, has as many verses (22) as there are letters in the alphabet. Such alphabetic forms were a useful *aide-memoire* when manuscripts were rare and expensive, and the work had to be used for liturgical purposes. But the alphabetic structure of *Lamentations* has been considered by some to be an artificiality which belies the sincerity and spontaneity of the grief which the poet expresses. Yet the naturalness and reality of the emotion are unmistakable, and seem completely unhampered by the limitations which the special form might be supposed to set. A possible explanation may be that, in his first grief-stricken composition of the elegies in which he gave unhampered utterance to his emotion, Jeremiah did not use the alphabetic form, but that he adopted this form in revising the elegies for liturgical use.

The rhythm of *Lamentations* i to iv is not that usually found in Hebrew verse. It has been fittingly called the 'limping' or 'elegiac' metre, and it 'gives the impression of sorrow in short clauses which seem to sob as they are uttered.' The Book is read in synagogues on the Fast of the Ninth of Ab, when the destruction of both Temples is commemorated, and is chanted to a haunting melody of poignant beauty.

# LAMENTATIONS

## 1 CHAPTER I א

1 How doth the city sit solitary,
That was full of people!
How is she become as a widow!
She that was great among the nations,
And princess among the provinces,
How is she become tributary!
2 She weepeth sore in the night,
And her tears are on her cheeks;
She hath none to comfort her
Among all her lovers;
All her friends have dealt treacherously with her,
They are become her enemies.

1 אֵיכָה ׀ יָשְׁבָה בָדָד הָעִיר
רַבָּתִי עָם הָיְתָה כְּאַלְמָנָה
רַבָּתִי בַגּוֹיִם שָׂרָתִי בַּמְּדִינוֹת
הָיְתָה לָמַס׃
2 בָּכוֹ תִבְכֶּה בַּלַּיְלָה וְדִמְעָתָהּ
עַל לֶחֱיָהּ אֵין־לָהּ מְנַחֵם
מִכָּל־אֹהֲבֶיהָ כָּל־רֵעֶיהָ
בָּגְדוּ בָהּ הָיוּ לָהּ לְאֹיְבִים׃

v. 1. פתח בס״ף

THIS chapter can be divided into two main sections, the principle of division being not so much the nature of the contents, as the fact that in verses 1-11 Jeremiah is the speaker, whereas in verses 12-22 Jerusalem itself takes up the lament. The theme throughout is the distress of Jerusalem and its inhabitants, with a strong sense of the grievousness of the sin which had incurred such suffering. The theme is expressed in a series of unconnected utterances, as if the poet's mind is agitated by a multitude of distressing thoughts, each struggling for simultaneous expression.

### 1-11 THE POET LAMENTS

**1.** *how.* The Hebrew word *Echah* is a characteristic opening for an elegy (cf. Deut. i. 12; Isa. i. 21).

*sit solitary.* Jerusalem, both as the capital city and as the centre for worship, was normally a very crowded place, and its emptiness was therefore the most striking and pathetic feature of its desolation. There are few more saddening spectacles on earth than a deserted city.

*as a widow.* A frequent Biblical image for loneliness and misery. The Midrash stresses the word *as*, i.e. her desolation was not permanent but temporary.

*princess among the provinces . . . tributary.* Judea, which had once received the tribute of other nations, is now herself a subject state. By *provinces* such nations as Moab and Edom, which were subject to Israel in the days of David and Solomon, are most likely meant.

In A.V. and R.V. there is a departure from the Massoretic division of this verse which results in a threefold division more in accord with the rhythm of the rest of the chapter. If adopted, the translation would read: 'How doth the city sit solitary, that was full of people! How is she become as a widow, that was great among the nations! How is the princess among the provinces become a tributary!'

**2.** *in the night.* The time of natural silence, when it might be expected that the sound of weeping as well would be

3 Judah is gone into exile because of affliction,
And because of great servitude;
She dwelleth among the nations,
She findeth no rest;
All her pursuers overtook her
Within the straits.

4 The ways of Zion do mourn,
Because none come to the solemn assembly;
All her gates are desolate,
Her priests sigh;
Her virgins are afflicted,
And she herself is in bitterness.

5 Her adversaries are become the head,
Her enemies are at ease;

3 גָּלְתָה יְהוּדָה מֵעֹנִי וּמֵרֹב
עֲבֹדָה הִיא יָשְׁבָה בַגּוֹיִם לֹא
מָצְאָה מָנוֹחַ כָּל־רֹדְפֶיהָ
הִשִּׂיגוּהָ בֵּין הַמְּצָרִים׃
4 דַּרְכֵי צִיּוֹן אֲבֵלוֹת מִבְּלִי בָּאֵי
מוֹעֵד כָּל־שְׁעָרֶיהָ שׁוֹמֵמִין
כֹּהֲנֶיהָ נֶאֱנָחִים בְּתוּלֹתֶיהָ
נּוּגוֹת וְהִיא מַר־לָהּ׃
5 הָיוּ צָרֶיהָ לְרֹאשׁ אֹיְבֶיהָ שָׁלוּ

stilled, and when the sound is all the more harrowing. Rashi notes that the Temple was destroyed at night.

*her lovers.* This is a favourite phrase of Jeremiah for the neighbouring peoples with whom Judea attempted to form alliances against Babylonia—Egypt, Edom, Moab, Ammon, Tyre and Sidon (cf. verse 19; Jer. xxvii. 3).

*dealt treacherously . . . enemies.* Far from saving Judah, the attempts at forming a confederacy against Babylonia had brought on Jerusalem the vengeance of Nebuchadnezzar. At the hour of need, Judah found herself deserted of her allies, and some, jackal-like, greedily helped the Babylonians in spoiling her.

3. *gone into exile because of affliction.* This must refer, not to the Babylonian captivity, but to those of the inhabitants who voluntarily exiled themselves to Egypt to escape from the affliction and servitude imposed by the Babylonians after the destruction of Jerusalem. Jeremiah himself was compelled to join them (Jer. xliif.).

*dwelleth among the nations . . . findeth no rest.* Words true of all the long history of Israel's exile. R. Simeon b. Lakish said, 'If she had found rest, she would not have longed to return to Jerusalem.'

*overtook her within the straits.* This might be understood literally, as referring to the actual overtaking of the fugitives in narrow defiles; but probably the figurative sense of dangers and difficulties overtaking and hemming in the people is to be preferred.

4. *the ways . . . assembly.* The roads leading to Jerusalem, usually so thronged with pilgrims, are desolate and *mourn.*

*her gates are desolate.* The spaces within and without the gates of Eastern cities were the recognized places of concourse. There the elders and judges sat; there the markets were held; and there citizens gathered together for friendly meeting and exchange of news.

*her priests sigh.* For the loss of the Temple.

*afflicted.* In the sense of 'grieved,' at the loss of prospective husbands.

5. *the head.* i.e. on top. Perhaps a reference to Deut. xxviii. 44, *He shall be the head and thou shalt be the tail,* is intended.

*at ease.* A bitter contrast with the condition of Judah.

For the LORD hath afflicted her
For the multitude of her transgressions;
Her young children are gone into captivity
Before the adversary.

כִּי־יְהוָה הוֹגָהּ עַל־רֹב
פְּשָׁעֶיהָ עוֹלָלֶיהָ הָלְכוּ שְׁבִי
לִפְנֵי־צָר׃

6 And gone is from the daughter of Zion
All her splendour;
Her princes are become like harts
That find no pasture,
And they are gone without strength
Before the pursuer.

6 וַיֵּצֵא *מִן־בַּת־צִיּוֹן כָּל־
הֲדָרָהּ הָיוּ שָׂרֶיהָ כְּאַיָּלִים
לֹא־מָצְאוּ מִרְעֶה וַיֵּלְכוּ
בְלֹא־כֹחַ לִפְנֵי רוֹדֵף׃

7 Jerusalem remembereth
In the days of her affliction and of her anguish
All her treasures that she had
From the days of old;
Now that her people fall by the hand of the adversary,
And none doth help her,
The adversaries have seen her,
They have mocked at her desolations.

7 זָכְרָה יְרוּשָׁלִַם יְמֵי עָנְיָהּ
וּמְרוּדֶיהָ כֹּל מַחֲמֻדֶיהָ אֲשֶׁר
הָיוּ מִימֵי קֶדֶם בִּנְפֹל עַמָּהּ
בְּיַד־צָר וְאֵין עוֹזֵר לָהּ רָאוּהָ
צָרִים שָׂחֲקוּ עַל־מִשְׁבַּתֶּהָ׃

8 Jerusalem hath grievously sinned,
Therefore she is become as one unclean;
All that honoured her despise her,

8 חֵטְא חָטְאָה יְרוּשָׁלִַם עַל־כֵּן
לְנִידָה הָיָתָה כָּל־מְכַבְּדֶיהָ

v. 6. מבת ק'

*the LORD hath afflicted her.* This is the first mention of the doctrine which is elaborated in greater detail in later chapters, a doctrine consistently taught by the prophets, viz. that the evils which had befallen the country were God's punishment for its iniquities.

*young children.* The suffering of children in the siege and captivity are always uppermost in Jeremiah's mind, and wring from him some of his most heart-broken cries.

6. *splendour.* The following words suggest that the author has in mind the splendour of the royal court, and the whole sentence may be a reference to the flight and capture of king Zedekiah (Jer. xxxix. 4f.).

*that find no pasture.* And therefore have no strength to flee.

7. *Jerusalem remembereth.* A true picture of grief. The mourner lacerates herself by contrasting her former happy state with her present unhappy condition.

*treasures.* i.e. prosperous and happy times.

*the adversaries have seen her.* Better, 'now that the adversaries have seen her and have mocked at her desolations.'

Because they have seen her nakedness;
She herself also sigheth,
And turneth backward.

הִזִּיל֙וּהָ כִּי־רָא֣וּ עֶרְוָתָ֔הּ גַּם־
הִ֥יא נֶאֶנְחָ֖ה וַתָּ֥שָׁב אָחֽוֹר׃

9 Her filthiness was in her skirts,
She was not mindful of her end;
Therefore is she come down wonderfully,
She hath no comforter.
'Behold, O LORD, my affliction,
For the enemy hath magnified himself.'

9 טֻמְאָתָ֣הּ בְּשׁוּלֶ֗יהָ לֹ֤א זָֽכְרָה֙
אַחֲרִיתָ֔הּ וַתֵּ֣רֶד פְּלָאִ֔ים אֵ֥ין
מְנַחֵ֖ם לָ֑הּ רְאֵ֤ה יְהוָה֙ אֶת־
עָנְיִ֔י כִּ֥י הִגְדִּ֖יל אוֹיֵֽב׃

10 The adversary hath spread out his hand
Upon all her treasures;
For she hath seen that the heathen
Are entered into her sanctuary,
Concerning whom Thou didst command
That they should not enter into Thy congregation.

10 יָדוֹ֙ פָּ֣רַשׂ צָ֔ר עַ֖ל כָּל־
מַחֲמַדֶּ֑יהָ כִּי־רָאֲתָ֤ה גוֹיִם֙ בָּ֣אוּ
מִקְדָּשָׁ֔הּ אֲשֶׁ֣ר צִוִּ֔יתָה לֹא־
יָבֹ֥אוּ בַקָּהָ֖ל לָֽךְ׃

11 All her people sigh,
They seek bread;
They have given their pleasant things for food

11 כָּל־עַמָּ֤הּ נֶאֱנָחִים֙ מְבַקְּשִׁ֣ים
לֶ֔חֶם נָתְנ֧וּ מַחֲמוֹדֵּיהֶ֛ם בְּאֹ֖כֶל

יתיר ו׳ v. 11.

8. *nakedness.* They have seen through her brave outward appearance to the wickedness lying beneath. The image of this verse is that of a woman, once honoured and accepted by all, who has been discovered in sin and is now shunned as one unclean.

*sigheth . . . turneth backward.* The image of a shunned woman is continued. It is as if she has come forward to greet an old acquaintance, but she is spurned and turns away with a sigh.

9. *her filthiness was in her skirts.* Her sins were now public for all to see.

*not mindful of her end.* Heedless of the inevitable consequences of her sins.

*wonderfully.* i.e. astonishingly.

*behold, O LORD, my affliction.* The city itself breaks in with a panting cry of distress and prayer, as in verse 11.

10. *treasures.* In this context, the word refers to the treasures of the Sanctuary, the holy and precious vessels.

*heathen are entered.* No worse humiliation could befall the Hebrews than this. It was forbidden even for an Israelite who was not a priest to enter the Sanctuary.

*that they should not enter into Thy congregation.* Cf. Deut. xxiii. 4. The reason was not so much a patriotic desire to preserve the integrity of the nation, as a religious dread of idolatry and anxiety to preserve the purity of the religion.

11. *pleasant things.* The Hebrew word is the same as that translated *treasures* in verse 10. The meaning is therefore that the people, in the scarcity of siege conditions, had given up their most valuable possessions for bread.

To refresh the soul.
'See, O LORD, and behold,
How abject I am become.'

12 'Let it not come unto you, all ye that pass by!
Behold, and see
If there be any pain like unto my pain,
Which is done unto me,
Wherewith the LORD hath afflicted me
In the day of His fierce anger.

13 From on high hath He sent fire
Into my bones, and it prevaileth against them;
He hath spread a net for my feet,
He hath turned me back;
He hath made me desolate
And faint all the day.

14 The yoke of my transgressions is impressed by His hand;
They are knit together,
They are come up upon my neck;
He hath made my strength to fail;
The Lord hath delivered me into their hands,
Against whom I am not able to stand.

לְהָשִׁיב נָפֶשׁ רְאֵה יְהוָה
וְהַבִּיטָה כִּי הָיִיתִי זוֹלֵלָה׃
12 *לוֹא אֲלֵיכֶם כָּל־עֹבְרֵי דֶרֶךְ
הַבִּיטוּ וּרְאוּ אִם־יֵשׁ מַכְאוֹב
כְּמַכְאֹבִי אֲשֶׁר עוֹלַל לִי אֲשֶׁר
הוֹגָה יְהוָה בְּיוֹם חֲרוֹן אַפּוֹ׃
13 מִמָּרוֹם שָׁלַח־אֵשׁ בְּעַצְמֹתַי
וַיִּרְדֶּנָּה פָּרַשׂ רֶשֶׁת לְרַגְלַי
הֱשִׁיבַנִי אָחוֹר נְתָנַנִי שֹׁמֵמָה
כָּל־הַיּוֹם דָּוָה׃
14 נִשְׂקַד עֹל פְּשָׁעַי בְּיָדוֹ יִשְׂתָּרְגוּ
עָלוּ עַל־צַוָּארִי הִכְשִׁיל כֹּחִי
נְתָנַנִי אֲדֹנָי בִּידֵי לֹא־אוּכַל
קוּם׃

v. 12. ל׳ זעירא

*see, O LORD, and behold.* Another ejaculated cry from the city (cf. verse 9), this time serving as a transition to the change of speaker in the second part of the poem.

12-22 JERUSALEM TAKES UP THE LAMENT

12. *let it not come unto you.* lit. 'not to you.' There is much difference of opinion among commentators as to the correct rendering of this phrase. The Talmud and older Jewish commentators take it to be a statement, and deduce from it the rule that a man in trouble should wish that like trouble never come upon others. The English versions read a question into the words: 'Is it nothing to you?' a rendering which, while more poignant and effective, is nevertheless less close to the original.

13. In three successive figures of fire, net and sickness, Jeremiah graphically expresses the calamities which have befallen the city.

*He sent fire.* The Midrash takes this literally to mean that God had himself set fire to the Temple, so that the heathen might not boast that he had destroyed it.

14. *yoke.* A complicated figure, the meaning of which is that God had, as it were, knitted together the transgressions of Jerusalem into a yoke which He had placed on her neck to weigh her down therewith.

15 The Lord hath set at nought
All my mighty men in the midst of me;
He hath called a solemn assembly against me
To crush my young men;
The Lord hath trodden as in a winepress
The virgin daughter of Judah.'

15 סִלָּה כָל־אַבִּירַי ׀ אֲדֹנָי
בְּקִרְבִּי קָרָא עָלַי מוֹעֵד
לִשְׁבֹּר בַּחוּרָי גַּת דָּרַךְ אֲדֹנָי
לִבְתוּלַת בַּת־יְהוּדָה׃

16 'For these things I weep;
Mine eye, mine eye runneth down with water;
Because the comforter is far from me,
Even he that should refresh my soul;
My children are desolate,
Because the enemy hath prevailed.'

16 עַל־אֵלֶּה ׀ אֲנִי בוֹכִיָּה עֵינִי ׀
עֵינִי יֹרְדָה מַּיִם כִּי־רָחַק
מִמֶּנִּי מְנַחֵם מֵשִׁיב נַפְשִׁי הָיוּ
בָנַי שׁוֹמֵמִים כִּי גָבַר אוֹיֵב׃

17 Zion spreadeth forth her hands;
There is none to comfort her;
The LORD hath commanded concerning Jacob,
That they that are round about him should be his adversaries;
Jerusalem is among them
As one unclean.

17 פֵּרְשָׂה צִיּוֹן בְּיָדֶיהָ אֵין מְנַחֵם
לָהּ צִוָּה יְהוָה לְיַעֲקֹב סְבִיבָיו
צָרָיו הָיְתָה יְרוּשָׁלִַם לְנִדָּה
בֵּינֵיהֶם׃

18 'The LORD is righteous;
For I have rebelled against His word;
Hear, I pray you, all ye peoples,
And behold my pain:
My virgins and my young men
Are gone into captivity.

18 צַדִּיק הוּא יְהוָה כִּי־פִיהוּ
מָרִיתִי שִׁמְעוּ־נָא כָל־*עַמִּים
וּרְאוּ מַכְאֹבִי בְּתוּלֹתַי וּבַחוּרַי
הָלְכוּ בַשֶּׁבִי׃

v. 18. העמים ק׳

15. *solemn assembly.* This is a tragic inversion of the usual joyful and happy purpose of a solemn assembly.

*as in a winepress.* The shedding of blood is compared with the squeezing out of the juice of grapes in a winepress.

*the virgin daughter of Judah.* i.e. Jerusalem, which was considered inviolate (cf. iv. 12).

16. *the comforter . . . my soul.* From these words some derived the opinion that the name of the Messiah would be *Menahem*, i.e. 'comforter' (Talmud).

17. In a parenthetic verse, Jeremiah himself takes up the lament.

*spreadeth forth her hands.* A gesture at once of grief and entreaty.

*they that are round about him.* The neighbouring peoples, who ought to be sympathetic, gloat over the spectacle of Israel's misfortunes.

18. *the LORD is righteous.* The age-old Jewish cry in adversity, an expression of resignation and unquestioning acceptance of God's righteous judgment.

19 I called for my lovers,
But they deceived me;
My priests and mine elders
Perished in the city,
While they sought them food
To refresh their souls.

19 קָרָאתִי לַמְאַהֲבַי הֵמָּה רִמּוּנִי
כֹּהֲנַי וּזְקֵנַי בָּעִיר גָּוָעוּ כִּי־
בִקְשׁוּ אֹכֶל לָמוֹ וְיָשִׁיבוּ אֶת־
נַפְשָׁם׃

20 Behold, O LORD, for I am in distress,
Mine inwards burn;
My heart is turned within me,
For I have grievously rebelled.
Abroad the sword bereaveth,
At home there is the like of death.

20 רְאֵה יְהוָה כִּי־צַר־לִי מֵעַי
חֳמַרְמָרוּ נֶהְפַּךְ לִבִּי בְּקִרְבִּי
כִּי מָרוֹ מָרִיתִי מִחוּץ שִׁכְּלָה־
חֶרֶב בַּבַּיִת כַּמָּוֶת׃

21 They have heard that I sigh,
There is none to comfort me;
All mine enemies have heard of my trouble, and are glad,
For Thou hast done it;
Thou wilt bring the day that Thou hast proclaimed,
And they shall be like unto me.

21 שָׁמְעוּ כִּי נֶאֱנָחָה אָנִי אֵין
מְנַחֵם לִי כָּל־אֹיְבַי שָׁמְעוּ
רָעָתִי שָׂשׂוּ כִּי אַתָּה עָשִׂיתָ
הֵבֵאתָ יוֹם־קָרָאתָ וְיִהְיוּ
כָמוֹנִי׃

22 Let all their wickedness come before Thee;
And do unto them,
As Thou hast done unto me
For all my transgressions;
For my sighs are many,
And my heart is faint.'

22 תָּבֹא כָל־רָעָתָם לְפָנֶיךָ
וְעוֹלֵל לָמוֹ כַּאֲשֶׁר עוֹלַלְתָּ לִי
עַל כָּל־פְּשָׁעָי כִּי־רַבּוֹת
אַנְחֹתַי וְלִבִּי דַוָּי׃

**19.** *lovers.* See on verse 2. Judah had appealed for help to its allies, especially to Egypt, but in vain.

**20.** *inwards.* lit. 'bowels,' which, in Biblical thought, is one of the seats of emotion.

*the like of death.* i.e. terror, starvation and pestilence. For the whole phrase, cf. Deut. xxxii. 25, *Without shall the sword bereave, and in the chambers terror.*

**21.** *for Thou hast done it.* Their enemies derive special satisfaction from the knowledge that the God of the Hebrews, who had so often helped them to defeat their foes, had now brought this calamity upon them.

*Thou wilt bring the day.* Rashi and Ibn Ezra both translate this phrase as a wish, 'Mayest Thou bring the day.'

*that Thou hast proclaimed.* A reference to the prophetic promises of Israel's restoration and punishment on his enemies.

**22.** *come before Thee.* i.e. come in judgment before Thee.

1 How hath the Lord covered with a cloud
The daughter of Zion in His anger!
He hath cast down from heaven unto the earth
The beauty of Israel,
And hath not remembered His footstool
In the day of His anger.

1 אֵיכָה יָעִיב בְּאַפּוֹ | אֲדֹנָי אֶת־
בַּת־צִיּוֹן הִשְׁלִיךְ מִשָּׁמַיִם
אֶרֶץ תִּפְאֶרֶת יִשְׂרָאֵל וְלֹא־
זָכַר הֲדֹם־רַגְלָיו בְּיוֹם אַפּוֹ׃

2 The Lord hath swallowed up unsparingly
All the habitations of Jacob;
He hath thrown down in His wrath
The strongholds of the daughter of Judah;
He hath brought them down to the ground;
He hath profaned the kingdom and the princes thereof.

2 בִּלַּע אֲדֹנָי *לֹא חָמַל אֵת כָּל־
נְאוֹת יַעֲקֹב הָרַס בְּעֶבְרָתוֹ
מִבְצְרֵי בַת־יְהוּדָה הִגִּיעַ
לָאָרֶץ חִלֵּל מַמְלָכָה וְשָׂרֶיהָ׃

3 He hath cut off in fierce anger
All the horn of Israel;
He hath drawn back His right hand
From before the enemy;
And He hath burned in Jacob like a flaming fire,
Which devoureth round about.

3 גָּדַע בָּחֳרִי־אַף כֹּל קֶרֶן
יִשְׂרָאֵל הֵשִׁיב אָחוֹר יְמִינוֹ
מִפְּנֵי אוֹיֵב וַיִּבְעַר בְּיַעֲקֹב
כְּאֵשׁ לֶהָבָה אָכְלָה סָבִיב׃

v. 2. ולא ק׳

A DESCRIPTION in greater detail of the calamity which had befallen Judea.

### 1-13 THE DESOLATION OF JUDEA AND JERUSALEM

1. *with a cloud.* The figure would appear more striking to a Palestinian, to whom a cloud was a comparatively rare phenomenon, than to us.

*the daughter of Zion . . . the beauty of Israel.* i.e. Jerusalem.

*from heaven unto the earth.* Expressing both the suddenness and the extent of the degradation.

*footstool.* The Sanctuary (cf. Ps. cxxxii. 7).

2. *habitations.* The Hebrew word is one which is used particularly of the abodes of shepherds, and thus refers to the open villages of Judea, as opposed to the *strongholds* in the following phrase.

*profaned.* The nation which was to be a *kingdom of priests and a holy nation* (Exod. xix. 6) had become profane.

3. *horn.* The horn, which is the animal's weapon, is a favourite figure for strength

4 He hath bent His bow like an enemy,
Standing with His right hand as an adversary,
And hath slain all that were pleasant to the eye;
In the tent of the daughter of Zion
He hath poured out His fury like fire.

4 דָּרַךְ קַשְׁתּוֹ כְּאוֹיֵב נִצָּב יְמִינוֹ
כְּצָר וַיַּהֲרֹג כֹּל מַחֲמַדֵּי־עָיִן
בְּאֹהֶל בַּת־צִיּוֹן שָׁפַךְ כָּאֵשׁ
חֲמָתוֹ׃

5 The Lord is become as an enemy,
He hath swallowed up Israel;
He hath swallowed up all her palaces,
He hath destroyed his strongholds;
And He hath multiplied in the daughter of Judah
Mourning and moaning.

5 הָיָה אֲדֹנָי ׀ כְּאוֹיֵב בִּלַּע
יִשְׂרָאֵל בִּלַּע כָּל־אַרְמְנוֹתֶיהָ
שִׁחֵת מִבְצָרָיו וַיֶּרֶב בְּבַת־
יְהוּדָה תַּאֲנִיָּה וַאֲנִיָּה׃

6 And He hath stripped His tabernacle, as if it were a garden,
He hath destroyed His place of assembly;
The LORD hath caused to be forgotten in Zion
Appointed season and sabbath,
And hath rejected in the indignation of His anger
The king and the priest.

6 וַיַּחְמֹס כַּגַּן שֻׂכּוֹ שִׁחֵת מֹעֲדוֹ
שִׁכַּח יְהוָה ׀ בְּצִיּוֹן מוֹעֵד
וְשַׁבָּת וַיִּנְאַץ בְּזַעַם־אַפּוֹ מֶלֶךְ
וְכֹהֵן׃

in the Bible. Here it should be interpreted as every means of defence, especially the fortresses.

*drawn back.* Instead of using it in defence of His people. In this and the following two verses, Jeremiah, using boldly anthropomorphic language, adopts the metaphor of an attack by a cruel enemy to describe God's punishment.

4. *His right hand as an adversary.* That *right hand,* which had been the symbol of the Almighty's help in Israel's history, was now turned against them.

5. *Israel.* A generic term for the Hebrews, not to be understood here as referring specifically to the Northern Kingdom.

*mourning and moaning.* The translation is an effort to represent two Hebrew words which are not only synonymous, but have also the same sound. Poetically, it is a most effective and poignant phrase.

6. This verse describes the climax of the destruction. Villages and strongholds, king and priests, princes and commoners, had been destroyed; but the deadliest blow was the destruction of the Temple.

*tabernacle.* The Temple, which is compared with a rough booth in a garden, so quickly was the magnificent structure destroyed.

*appointed season and sabbath.* Neither could now be observed with the Temple ritual that accompanied them. It may be, as well, that in the period immediately following the destruction of the Temple, the minds of the people were so distraught with grief and bewilderment that for a time the actual observance of holy days was abandoned.

7 The Lord hath cast off His altar,
He hath abhorred His sanctuary,
He hath given up into the hand of the enemy
The walls of her palaces;
They have made a noise in the house of the LORD,
As in the day of a solemn assembly.

7 זָנַח אֲדֹנָי ׀ מִזְבְּחוֹ נִאֵר מִקְדָּשׁוֹ
הִסְגִּיר בְּיַד־אוֹיֵב חוֹמֹת
אַרְמְנוֹתֶיהָ קוֹל נָתְנוּ בְּבֵית־
יְהוָה כְּיוֹם מוֹעֵד׃

8 The LORD hath purposed to destroy
The wall of the daughter of Zion;
He hath stretched out the line,
He hath not withdrawn
His hand from destroying;
But He hath made the rampart and wall to mourn,
They languish together.

8 חָשַׁב יְהוָה ׀ לְהַשְׁחִית חוֹמַת
בַּת־צִיּוֹן נָטָה קָו לֹא־הֵשִׁיב
יָדוֹ מִבַּלֵּעַ וַיַּאֲבֶל־חֵל וְחוֹמָה
יַחְדָּו אֻמְלָלוּ׃

9 Her gates are sunk into the ground;
He hath destroyed and broken her bars;
Her king and her princes are among the nations,

9 טָבְעוּ בָאָרֶץ שְׁעָרֶיהָ אִבַּד
וְשִׁבַּר בְּרִיחֶיהָ מַלְכָּהּ וְשָׂרֶיהָ

ט׳ זעירא v. 9.

7. *palaces.* lit. 'high buildings.' In the present context, the Temple buildings are probably meant.

*noise . . . solemn assembly.* See on i. 15. The shouts of triumph of the enemy are likened to the joyous, festal sounds of the Temple worshippers (Rashi).

8. *wall.* i.e. the city, of which it was, from the military point of view, the most important part.

*stretched out the line.* As a builder does when constructing. With his usual strong sense of tragic contrast, Jeremiah depicts the Almighty as showing as much precision in destruction as a builder does in construction.

*rampart and wall to mourn.* The personification of inanimate objects is a characteristic feature of this Book.

9. *sunk into the ground.* They have disappeared as completely as if they had been swallowed up by the earth.

*among the nations.* In exile and captivity.

*instruction is no more.* The Hebrew word is *torah,* the basic meaning of which is instruction. The duty of teaching religious law and giving decisions thereon rested with the priests; in the case of civil law, the administration was in the hands of the king and his officers. Thus the whole system of legal administration had ceased with the exile of the king, his officers and the priests cf. Ezek. vii. 26, *Instruction shall perish from the priest, and counsel from the elders*).

*her prophets find no vision from the LORD.* Some have found it difficult to reconcile this lament with Jeremiah's repeated denunciation of the prophets of his time (cf. especially Jer. xxiii). Would the cessation of their visions, it is asked, have appeared to him a calamity? The answer is twofold: (1) We have no reason for assuming that *all* the prophets who were Jeremiah's contemporaries

Instruction is no more;
Yea, her prophets find
No vision from the LORD.

בַגּוֹיִם אֵין תּוֹרָה גַּם־נְבִיאֶיהָ
לֹא־מָצְאוּ חָזוֹן מֵיְהוָה׃

10 They sit upon the ground, and keep silence,
The elders of the daughter of Zion;
They have cast up dust upon their heads,
They have girded themselves with sackcloth;
The virgins of Jerusalem hang down
Their heads to the ground.

10 יֵשְׁבוּ לָאָרֶץ יִדְּמוּ זִקְנֵי בַת־
צִיּוֹן הֶעֱלוּ עָפָר עַל־רֹאשָׁם
חָגְרוּ שַׂקִּים הוֹרִידוּ לָאָרֶץ
רֹאשָׁן בְּתוּלֹת יְרוּשָׁלִָם׃

11 Mine eyes do fail with tears,
Mine inwards burn,
My liver is poured upon the earth,
For the breach of the daughter of my people;
Because the young children and the sucklings swoon
In the broad places of the city.

11 כָּלוּ בַדְּמָעוֹת עֵינַי חֳמַרְמְרוּ
מֵעַי נִשְׁפַּךְ לָאָרֶץ כְּבֵדִי עַל־
שֶׁבֶר בַּת־עַמִּי בֵּעָטֵף עוֹלֵל
וְיוֹנֵק בִּרְחֹבוֹת קִרְיָה׃

12 They say to their mothers:
'Where is corn and wine?'
When they swoon as the wounded
In the broad places of the city,
When their soul is poured out
Into their mothers' bosom.

12 לְאִמֹּתָם יֹאמְרוּ אַיֵּה דָּגָן וָיָיִן
בְּהִתְעַטְּפָם כֶּחָלָל בִּרְחֹבוֹת
עִיר בְּהִשְׁתַּפֵּךְ נַפְשָׁם אֶל־
חֵיק אִמֹּתָם׃

were unrighteous; there were most likely true prophets of the Lord, whose names and messages have not survived. (2) Even the rebukes which Jeremiah administers to the prophets for their unfaithfulness suggest that he accredits them with important duties, and the gifts with which to execute them; it is the abuse of their proper function and their failure to seek the true message of God, which he condemns. In iv. 13 (and frequently in Jeremiah), prophets and priests are equally chastised for their sinful lives. Just as it is not the office of the priests which is condemned, but their failure properly to fulfil their duties, so, it could well be argued, it is not the office of the prophets which is condemned but their faulty fulfilment of the duties of that office.

10. *the elders.* Each city and district had a ruling body of elders, who are now silent, with no function to perform.

*cast up dust upon their heads.* A sign of mourning (cf. Ezek. xxvii. 30; Job ii. 12).

11f. Jeremiah breaks down at the most pitiful picture of all, that of children swooning in the streets and dying of hunger, in the famine during and after the siege.

11. *liver.* In Biblical thought, the liver is one of the seats of emotion.

12. *corn and wine.* A general term for solid and liquid food, and indicating the people's sustenance (cf. Deut. xi. 14).

*soul is poured out.* i.e. they die.

13 What shall I take to witness for thee? what shall I liken to thee,
O daughter of Jerusalem?
What shall I equal to thee, that I may comfort thee,
O virgin daughter of Zion?
For thy breach is great like the sea;
Who can heal thee?

14 Thy prophets have seen visions for thee
Of vanity and delusion;
And they have not uncovered thine iniquity,
To bring back thy captivity;
But have prophesied for thee burdens
Of vanity and seduction.

15 All that pass by clap
Their hands at thee;
They hiss and wag their head

13 מָה־אֲעוֹדֵךְ מָה אֲדַמֶּה־לָּךְ
הַבַּת יְרוּשָׁלִַם מָה אַשְׁוֶה־לָּךְ
וַאֲנַחֲמֵךְ בְּתוּלַת בַּת־צִיּוֹן
כִּי־גָדוֹל כַּיָּם שִׁבְרֵךְ מִי
יִרְפָּא־לָךְ׃

14 נְבִיאַיִךְ חָזוּ לָךְ שָׁוְא וְתָפֵל
וְלֹא־גִלּוּ עַל־עֲוֺנֵךְ לְהָשִׁיב
שְׁבִיתֵךְ וַיֶּחֱזוּ לָךְ מַשְׂאוֹת שָׁוְא
וּמַדּוּחִים׃

15 סָפְקוּ עָלַיִךְ כַּפַּיִם כָּל־עֹבְרֵי
דֶרֶךְ שָׁרְקוּ וַיָּנִעוּ רֹאשָׁם עַל־

v. 13. אעידך ק׳ v. 14. שבותך ק׳

**13.** The meaning of the verse is: Can I point to any other nation which has suffered a calamity equal to yours, and comfort you with the thought that you are not alone in your grief?

**14 THE FAULT OF THE PROPHETS**

The prophets have to bear the largest share of the blame for the calamity. Their message had been the false one of *Ye shall not see the sword, neither shall ye have famine; but I will give you assured peace in this place* (Jer. xiv. 13). Had they exposed the sins of the people fearlessly, and foretold the evil consequences that would befall them, instead of indulging in vain and soothing prophecies which lulled the people into a false sense of security and righteousness, the calamity might have been avoided.

*visions for thee.* i.e. devised with the express purpose to please thee (cf. Micah iii. 5).

*uncovered thine iniquity.* Exposed and rebuked the people's sins.

*to bring back thy captivity.* If this translation is accepted, the meaning must be 'to save thee from going into captivity.' Probably a preferable rendering is that suggested by Rashi, 'to bring thee back in repentance.'

*burdens.* i.e. prophecies.

**15-17 MALICIOUS GLEE OF THE ENEMY**

**15.** *clap their hands . . . hiss and wag their head.* Gestures of malicious joy and contempt.

At the daughter of Jerusalem:
'Is this the city that men called
The perfection of beauty,
The joy of the whole earth?'

בַּת יְרוּשָׁלָ͏ִם הֲזֹאת הָעִיר
שֶׁיֹּאמְרוּ כְּלִילַת יֹפִי מָשׂוֹשׂ
לְכָל־הָאָרֶץ׃

16 All thine enemies have opened
Their mouth wide against thee;
They hiss and gnash the teeth;
They say: 'We have swallowed
her up;
Certainly this is the day that we
looked for;
We have found, we have seen it.'

16 פָּצוּ עָלַיִךְ פִּיהֶם כָּל־אֹיְבַיִךְ
שָׁרְקוּ וַיַּחַרְקוּ־שֵׁן אָמְרוּ
בִּלָּעְנוּ אַךְ זֶה הַיּוֹם שֶׁקִּוִּינֻהוּ
מָצָאנוּ רָאִינוּ׃

17 The LORD hath done that which
He devised;
He hath performed His word
That He commanded in the days
of old;
He hath thrown down unsparingly
And He hath caused the enemy to
rejoice over thee,
He hath exalted the horn of thine
adversaries.

17 עָשָׂה יְהוָה אֲשֶׁר זָמָם בִּצַּע
אֶמְרָתוֹ אֲשֶׁר צִוָּה מִימֵי־קֶדֶם
הָרַס וְלֹא חָמָל וַיְשַׂמַּח עָלַיִךְ
אוֹיֵב הֵרִים קֶרֶן צָרָיִךְ׃

18 Their heart cried unto the Lord:
'O wall of the daughter of Zion,
Let tears run down like a river
Day and night;
Give thyself no respite;
Let not the apple of thine eye
cease.

18 צָעַק לִבָּם אֶל־אֲדֹנָי חוֹמַת
בַּת־צִיּוֹן הוֹרִידִי כַנַּחַל
דִּמְעָה יוֹמָם וָלַיְלָה אַל־תִּתְּנִי
פוּגַת לָךְ אַל־תִּדֹּם בַּת־
עֵינֵךְ׃

*that men called the perfection of beauty.* The enemies of the Jews derive cruel pleasure from reminding them of the very high esteem in which they had held Jerusalem (cf. Ps. l. 2).

**16f.** The order of the letters Pe and Ayin is reversed in these two verses, as also in the two following chapters. This unusual order has never been satisfactorily explained.

**16.** *have opened their mouth wide.* To swallow up Israel, as a ravening lion (cf. Ps. xxii. 14).

*gnash the teeth.* In triumphant rage.

**17.** *that He commanded in the days of old.* In the Torah, in the threats of punishment for disobedience (Lev. xxvi. and Deut. xxviii).

### 18-19 CALL ON ZION TO SUPPLICATE THE LORD

**18.** There is an abrupt transition from verse 17 to verse 18, as frequently in this Book (*see* Introduction).

*their heart.* i.e. the heart of the people of Judah.

*unto the LORD.* The cry, though directly to Zion, is ultimately addressed to the Lord.

*wall.* See on verse 8.

*apple of thine eye.* The pupil of the eye, a poetical expression for the whole eye, employed to denote an object requiring the utmost care.

| | |
|---|---|
| 19 Arise, cry out in the night,<br>At the beginning of the watches;<br>Pour out thy heart like water<br>Before the face of the Lord;<br>Lift up thy hands toward Him<br>For the life of thy young children,<br>That faint for hunger<br>At the head of every street.' | 19 קוּמִי ׀ רֹנִּי בַלַּיִל* לְרֹאשׁ<br>אַשְׁמֻרוֹת שִׁפְכִי כַמַּיִם לִבֵּךְ<br>נֹכַח פְּנֵי אֲדֹנָי שְׂאִי אֵלָיו כַּפַּיִךְ<br>עַל־נֶפֶשׁ עוֹלָלַיִךְ הָעֲטוּפִים<br>בְּרָעָב בְּרֹאשׁ כָּל־חוּצוֹת׃ |
| 20 'See, O Lord, and consider,<br>To whom Thou hast done thus!<br>Shall the women eat their fruit,<br>The children that are dandled in the hands?<br>Shall the priest and the prophet be slain<br>In the sanctuary of the Lord? | 20 רְאֵה יְהוָה וְהַבִּיטָה לְמִי<br>עוֹלַלְתָּ כֹּה אִם־תֹּאכַלְנָה<br>נָשִׁים פִּרְיָם עֹלְלֵי טִפֻּחִים<br>אִם־יֵהָרֵג בְּמִקְדַּשׁ אֲדֹנָי כֹּהֵן<br>וְנָבִיא׃ |
| 21 The youth and the old man lie<br>On the ground in the streets;<br>My virgins and my young men<br>Are fallen by the sword;<br>Thou hast slain them in the day of Thine anger;<br>Thou hast slaughtered unsparingly. | 21 שָׁכְבוּ לָאָרֶץ חוּצוֹת נַעַר וְזָקֵן<br>בְּתוּלֹתַי וּבַחוּרַי נָפְלוּ בֶחָרֶב<br>הָרַגְתָּ בְּיוֹם אַפֶּךָ טָבַחְתָּ לֹא<br>חָמָלְתָּ׃ |

* בלילה ק׳ v. 19.

**19.** *at the beginning of the watches.* The night was divided into three equal periods, each known as a *watch.* This phrase has been interpreted to mean at the beginning of each watch, i.e. intermittently through the night, or, in the first watch, when people enjoy their first sleep.

*pour out thy heart like water.* A wonderfully expressive description of sincere and heartfelt prayer.

*young children that faint for hunger.* Jeremiah returns again and again to this terrible subject, so had the horror of it imprinted itself on his mind.

### 20-22 ZION'S SUPPLICATION

**20.** *consider to whom.* God is asked to remember that the people whom He is afflicting are His chosen people.

*shall the women eat their fruit.* The extremity of horror in the inhuman conditions which starvation creates. The deed is so unthinkable that the Rabbis in the Midrash shrank from accepting this sentence literally, and attempted to interpret it figuratively. But that such abominable things could happen is vouched for by the incident recorded in 2 Kings vi. 26-9.

**21.** *Thou hast slain them.* To Jeremiah, the Babylonians are no more than the instruments of God's anger, and it is as if the Almighty Himself had slain them.

22 Thou hast called, as in the day of
a solemn assembly,
My terrors on every side,
And there was none in the day of
the LORD's anger
That escaped or remained;
Those that I have dandled and
brought up
Hath mine enemy consumed.'

22 תִּקְרָא כְיוֹם מוֹעֵד מְגוּרַי
מִסָּבִיב וְלֹא הָיָה בְּיוֹם אַף־
יְהוָה פָּלִיט וְשָׂרִיד אֲשֶׁר־
טִפַּחְתִּי וְרִבִּיתִי אֹיְבִי כִלָּם׃

Again, an alphabetic acrostic, but in tercets

## 3 CHAPTER III ג

1 I am the man that hath seen
affliction
By the rod of His wrath.

1 אֲנִי הַגֶּבֶר רָאָה עֳנִי בְּשֵׁבֶט
עֶבְרָתוֹ׃

2 He hath led me and caused me to
walk
In darkness and not in light.

2 אוֹתִי נָהַג וַיֹּלַךְ חֹשֶׁךְ וְלֹא־
אוֹר׃

22. *solemn assembly.* See on i. 15.

*terrors on every side.* A phrase constantly on Jeremiah's lips (cf. Jer. vi. 25, xx. 3).

*those that I have dandled.* Zion speaks of her inhabitants, who were born and reared in her, as a mother would speak of her children.

## CHAPTER III

Two interpretations of this chapter are possible: that it is a description of the personal experiences of Jeremiah, or a personification, in one individual, of the experiences of the whole people. The second interpretation is here adopted, for the following reasons: (1) A continuation of the themes of chapters i and ii is more appropriate than a sudden transition to the lamenting of personal woe; (2) the appearance of the first person plural in verses 42ff. supports the view that the people, not the prophet, is the subject of the chapter; and (3), although much in this chapter would be a true description of Jeremiah's own hard life, there are nevertheless passages which, as a description of Jeremiah's personal sufferings, would be an overstatement.

This chapter is a triple acrostic, each letter of the alphabet in turn supplying the first letter of three verses. In the translation, the verses are grouped alphabetically; but the sense division is not determined by the alphabetic form, and runs across the alphabetic groupings.

1-20. The sufferings of the people are described as if they were the experiences of one man, in a succession of vivid figures — darkness, disease, imprisonment, ambush.

1. *seen.* i.e. experienced.

*affliction.* The calamities which reached their climax in the capture and destruction of Jerusalem.

3 Surely against me He turneth His hand
Again and again all the day.

3 אַךְ בִּי יָשֻׁב יַהֲפֹךְ יָדוֹ כָּל־
הַיּוֹם׃

4 My flesh and my skin hath He worn out;
He hath broken my bones.

4 בִּלָּה בְשָׂרִי וְעוֹרִי שִׁבַּר
עַצְמוֹתָי׃

5 He hath builded against me, and compassed me
With gall and travail.

5 בָּנָה עָלַי וַיַּקַּף רֹאשׁ וּתְלָאָה׃

6 He hath made me to dwell in dark places,
As those that have been long dead.

6 בְּמַחֲשַׁכִּים הוֹשִׁיבַנִי כְּמֵתֵי
עוֹלָם׃

7 He hath hedged me about, that I cannot go forth;
He hath made my chain heavy.

7 גָּדַר בַּעֲדִי וְלֹא אֵצֵא הִכְבִּיד
נְחָשְׁתִּי׃

8 Yea, when I cry and call for help,
He shutteth out my prayer.

8 גַּם כִּי אֶזְעַק וַאֲשַׁוֵּעַ שָׂתַם
תְּפִלָּתִי׃

9 He hath enclosed my ways with hewn stone,
He hath made my paths crooked.

9 גָּדַר דְּרָכַי בְּגָזִית נְתִיבֹתַי
עִוָּה׃

10 He is unto me as a bear lying in wait,
As a lion in secret places.

10 דֹּב אֹרֵב הוּא לִי אֲרִיה
בְּמִסְתָּרִים׃

ארי ק' v. 10.

4. *my flesh and my skin hath He worn out.* The language of these verses is highly figurative, and it is perhaps fruitless to attempt to find the reality behind each of the figures of speech. What matters is the cumulative effect, the total picture, of a people broken by suffering, perplexed and dismayed, and turning helplessly this way and that, with no escape.

5. *gall.* i.e. bitterness. The people is, as it were, imprisoned in suffering and misery.

6. *long dead.* The word *long* hardly adds anything to the meaning of *dead*, and a preferable translation may be 'for ever dead.'

7. *hedged me about.* As if a traveller were suddenly hemmed in by a high hedge.

*chain.* Fetters.

8. *shutteth out my prayer.* Even heaven seemed closed to them.

9. *made my paths crooked.* Figuratively, for the path of life, which, instead of being smooth and straightforward, is tortuous and perplexing.

10. In a bold figure, the Almighty, in His affliction of Israel, is likened to a beast of prey.

11 He hath turned aside my ways, and pulled me in pieces;
He hath made me desolate.

11 דְּרָכַי סוֹרֵר וַיְפַשְּׁחֵנִי שָׂמַנִי שֹׁמֵם׃

12 He hath bent His bow, and set me
As a mark for the arrow.

12 דָּרַךְ קַשְׁתּוֹ וַיַּצִּיבֵנִי כַּמַּטָּרָא לַחֵץ׃

13 He hath caused the arrows of His quiver
To enter into my reins.

13 הֵבִיא בְּכִלְיוֹתָי בְּנֵי אַשְׁפָּתוֹ׃

14 I am become a derision to all my people,
And their song all the day.

14 הָיִיתִי שְּׂחֹק לְכָל־עַמִּי נְגִינָתָם כָּל־הַיּוֹם׃

15 He hath filled me with bitterness,
He hath sated me with wormwood.

15 הִשְׂבִּיעַנִי בַמְּרוֹרִים הִרְוַנִי לַעֲנָה׃

16 He hath also broken my teeth with gravel stones,
He hath made me to wallow in ashes.

16 וַיַּגְרֵס בֶּחָצָץ שִׁנָּי הִכְפִּישַׁנִי בָּאֵפֶר׃

17 And my soul is removed far off from peace,
I forgot prosperity.

17 וַתִּזְנַח מִשָּׁלוֹם נַפְשִׁי נָשִׁיתִי טוֹבָה׃

18 And I said: 'My strength is perished,
And mine expectation from the LORD.'

18 וָאֹמַר אָבַד נִצְחִי וְתוֹחַלְתִּי מֵיְהוָה׃

11. *turned aside my ways.* As the presence of a wild animal in a man's path would make him turn aside.

12f. The figure changes to that of a hunter.

14. *a derision to all my people.* The word *my* need not be accepted as proof that this chapter is to be interpreted as the personal experience of Jeremiah. The phrase *my people* is still consistent with the view that we have in this chapter the individualization of the nation's experiences. As an individual is to the people of his own country, so a nation is to the peoples of the world; and the meaning behind the figure would be that 'Israel is become a derision to the peoples of the earth.'

16. *broken my teeth.* The Midrash thinks that a historical fact is preserved in these words, that the Jews, on their way into exile, were compelled to bake their bread in pits dug in the ground, so that their bread was mixed with grit. This verse is the origin of the custom, which some observe, of eating a piece of bread dipped in ashes after the meal preparatory to the Fast of the Ninth of Ab.

17. *prosperity.* Better, 'happiness.'

18. *expectation.* In the depth of suffering, even hope was lost.

19 Remember mine affliction and mine anguish,
The wormwood and the gall.

20 My soul hath them still in remembrance,
And is bowed down within me.

21 This I recall to my mind,
Therefore have I hope.

22 Surely the LORD's mercies are not consumed,
Surely His compassions fail not.

23 They are new every morning;
Great is Thy faithfulness.

24 'The LORD is my portion,' saith my soul;
'Therefore will I hope in Him.'

25 The LORD is good unto them that wait for Him,
To the soul that seeketh Him.

26 It is good that a man should quietly wait
For the salvation of the LORD.

27 It is good for a man that he bear
The yoke in his youth.

19 זְכָר־עָנְיִי וּמְרוּדִי לַעֲנָה וָרֹאשׁ׃

20 זָכוֹר תִּזְכּוֹר וְתָשִׁיחַ עָלַי נַפְשִׁי׃

21 זֹאת אָשִׁיב אֶל־לִבִּי עַל־כֵּן אוֹחִיל׃

22 חַסְדֵי יְהוָה כִּי לֹא־תָמְנוּ כִּי לֹא־כָלוּ רַחֲמָיו׃

23 חֲדָשִׁים לַבְּקָרִים רַבָּה אֱמוּנָתֶךָ׃

24 חֶלְקִי יְהוָה אָמְרָה נַפְשִׁי עַל־כֵּן אוֹחִיל לוֹ׃

25 טוֹב יְהוָה לְקֹוָו לְנֶפֶשׁ תִּדְרְשֶׁנּוּ׃

26 טוֹב וְיָחִיל וְדוּמָם לִתְשׁוּעַת יְהוָה׃

27 טוֹב לַגֶּבֶר כִּי־יִשָּׂא עֹל בִּנְעוּרָיו׃

v. 20. ותשוח ק׳

**21-42 GOD'S MERCY NEVER FAILS**

In a wonderful series of verses, the doctrine of hope even in suffering is elaborated. As God's chastisement, affliction is not unending; if He punishes, He also forgives. Man therefore should never consider himself abandoned of God, but seek God's pardon through repentance.

21. *this.* Rashi comments: All the verses 22-38.

22. *the LORD'S mercies are not consumed.* One can set no limit to God's mercies; they are inexhaustible.

23. *new every morning.* Renewed daily.

*faithfulness.* Unchanging constancy.

25. *that wait for Him.* That have faith and confidence in Him.

26. *quietly.* Submissively and uncomplainingly.

27. *the yoke.* Of God's discipline (Ibn Ezra).

*in his youth.* When his passions are strongest and therefore most in need of discipline.

28 Let him sit alone and keep silence,
Because He hath laid it upon him.

28 יֵשֵׁב בָּדָד וְיִדֹּם כִּי נָטַל עָלָיו׃

29 Let him put his mouth in the dust,
If so be there may be hope.

29 יִתֵּן בֶּעָפָר פִּיהוּ אוּלַי יֵשׁ
תִּקְוָה׃

30 Let him give his cheek to him that smiteth him,
Let him be filled full with reproach.

30 יִתֵּן לְמַכֵּהוּ לֶחִי יִשְׂבַּע
בְּחֶרְפָּה׃

31 For the LORD will not cast off
For ever.

31 כִּי לֹא יִזְנַח לְעוֹלָם אֲדֹנָי׃

32 For though He cause grief, yet will He have compassion
According to the multitude of His mercies.

32 כִּי אִם־הוֹגָה וְרִחַם כְּרֹב
חֲסָדָו׃

33 For He doth not afflict willingly,
Nor grieve the children of men.

33 כִּי לֹא עִנָּה מִלִּבּוֹ וַיַּגֶּה בְּנֵי־
אִישׁ׃

חסדיו ק' v. 32.

**28.** *let him sit alone.* He who has experienced misfortune.

*keep silence.* A regular expression of the Psalmists for resignation to God's will.

*laid it.* viz. His chastisement.

**29.** *put his mouth in the dust.* The eastern way of expressing absolute submission.

**30.** *give his cheek to him that smiteth him.* Cf. Isa. l. 6. Let him submit to his chastisement.

**31-33.** These verses state the two thoughts which are the grounds for a spirit of resignation in suffering: (1) God's punishment is limited in time, and will be followed by a renewal of mercy, and (2) God does not afflict capriciously.

**33.** *willingly.* The word thus translated means literally 'out of His own heart, or mind,' and the sense of the verse is: 'God does not devise afflictions and griefs without relation to a man's conduct. God causes the affliction, but man has brought it upon himself.'

*grieve.* i.e. willingly grieve.

**34-36.** These verses are intelligible in themselves, but it is not easy to interpret them in relation to their context. One interpretation is that three types of wrong-doing are enumerated, and of all it is said, *the LORD approveth not*; and the argument is that, if God cannot condone injustice in man, He cannot Himself be guilty of it; therefore God's chastisement is just, and the sufferer can afford to be patient. But if this is what the author intended to say, one would expect him to state it more clearly and explicitly. It would probably be better, following Rashi, to treat these verses as a continuation of the argument in verse 33, and to translate the last phrase as 'the Lord doth not see fit,' instead of *the LORD approveth not.* The meaning of the paragraph would then be: 'The Lord doth not see fit to crush men capriciously under foot, or to wrest their rights and treat them unjustly.'

34 To crush under foot
All the prisoners of the earth,

35 To turn aside the right of a man
Before the face of the Most High,

36 To subvert a man in his cause,
The Lord approveth not.

37 Who is he that saith, and it cometh to pass,
When the Lord commandeth it not?

38 Out of the mouth of the Most High proceedeth not
Evil and good?

34 לְדַכֵּא תַּחַת רַגְלָיו כֹּל אֲסִירֵי אָרֶץ׃

35 לְהַטּוֹת מִשְׁפַּט־גָּבֶר נֶגֶד פְּנֵי עֶלְיוֹן׃

36 לְעַוֵּת אָדָם בְּרִיבוֹ אֲדֹנָי לֹא רָאָה׃

37 מִי זֶה אָמַר וַתֶּהִי אֲדֹנָי לֹא צִוָּה׃

38 מִפִּי עֶלְיוֹן לֹא תֵצֵא הָרָעוֹת וְהַטּוֹב׃

36. ע׳ זעירא

34. *prisoners of the earth.* Why should prisoners be specially mentioned? Would it not be equally wrong to crush any innocent man underfoot? These questions would be answered, and an excellent sense given to the verse, if the phrase is interpreted as a vivid poetical image for *mankind*, i.e. those who are tied to the earth, *earth-bound.*

35. If these verses are interpreted as describing actions which God would not see fit to do, the phrase *before the face of the Most High* presents a difficulty, because the sentence suggests that the one who 'turns aside the right of a man' is other than the Most High. But the difficulty is present only as long as we read the verse as if it were 'to turn aside before the face of the Most High the right of a man.' The Hebrew words, however, can equally be read with the meaning 'to turn aside the right which a man has before the face of the Most High,' i.e. a man's God-given or *natural* rights. With this interpretation, which makes excellent sense, the difficulty vanishes.

*to turn aside the right of a man.* i.e. to defraud a man of his legal rights.

36. *to subvert a man in his cause.* To deny a man justice by obtaining an unrighteous decision in law against him. In this context, 'to condemn a man unjustly.'

*the Lord approveth not.* Better, 'the Lord doth not see fit.'

37f. Like Isaiah xlv. 7, these verses are a distinct argument against those who would ascribe the source of evil to a power other than God. If they were right, if evil were produced by some malignant power in the universe, one would have good cause for despair. But since evil, as well as good, is determined of the Lord, and since God is just and beneficent, one must be patient.

37. Nothing can happen against God's will.

39 Wherefore doth a living man complain,
A strong man because of his sins?

39 מַה־יִּתְאוֹנֵן אָדָם חָי גֶּבֶר עַל־
חֲטָאָו׃

40 Let us search and try our ways,
And return to the LORD.

40 נַחְפְּשָׂה דְרָכֵינוּ וְנַחְקֹרָה
וְנָשׁוּבָה עַד־יְהוָה׃

41 Let us lift up our heart with our hands
Unto God in the heavens.

41 נִשָּׂא לְבָבֵנוּ אֶל־כַּפָּיִם אֶל־
אֵל בַּשָּׁמָיִם׃

42 We have transgressed and have rebelled;
Thou hast not pardoned.

42 נַחְנוּ פָשַׁעְנוּ וּמָרִינוּ אַתָּה לֹא
סָלָחְתָּ׃

43 Thou hast covered with anger and pursued us;
Thou hast slain unsparingly.

43 סַכּוֹתָה בָאַף וַתִּרְדְּפֵנוּ הָרַגְתָּ
לֹא חָמָלְתָּ׃

44 Thou hast covered Thyself with a cloud,
So that no prayer can pass through.

44 סַכֹּתָה בֶעָנָן לָךְ מֵעֲבוֹר
תְּפִלָּה׃

45 Thou hast made us as the off-scouring and refuse
In the midst of the peoples.

45 סְחִי וּמָאוֹס תְּשִׂימֵנוּ בְּקֶרֶב
הָעַמִּים׃

חטאיו ק' v. 39.

**39.** Since suffering is God's just punishment for his sins, man has no cause to complain.

*living man.* The Midrash remarks: 'He should be thankful that he is alive.' Life itself is a great gift from God for which a man should be eternally grateful.

**40-42** REPENTANCE WILL BRING PARDON

**40.** The remedy lies in our own hands.

**41.** *lift up our heart with our hands.* Pray sincerely, with our hearts as well as with our hands. 'A man's prayer is not heard unless he puts his soul into his hands' (Talmud).

**42.** There is a note of finality in this verse, as if the author is saying, 'That is the end of the matter.' It is a complete and succinct summary of the doctrine of the preceding section. The people has sinned, and God has been unable to withhold punishment, for there was no ground for pardon. In the Hebrew, the pronouns *we* and *thou* are emphatic.

**43-54** RENEWED EXPRESSIONS OF SUFFERING

**43.** *covered with anger.* Cf. the image in ii. 1.

**44.** *no prayer can pass through.* Until the sins of the people have been expiated, God is inexorable (cf. Isa. lix. 2, *Your sins have hid His face from you, that He will not hear*).

46 All our enemies have opened their mouth
Wide against us.

46 פָּצוּ עָלֵינוּ פִּיהֶם כָּל־אֹיְבֵינוּ׃

47 Terror and the pit are come upon us,
Desolation and destruction.

47 פַּחַד וָפַחַת הָיָה לָנוּ הַשֵּׁאת
וְהַשָּׁבֶר׃

48 Mine eye runneth down with rivers of water,
For the breach of the daughter of my people.

48 פַּלְגֵי־מַיִם תֵּרַד עֵינִי עַל־
שֶׁבֶר בַּת־עַמִּי׃

49 Mine eye is poured out, and ceaseth not,
Without any intermission,

49 עֵינִי נִגְּרָה וְלֹא תִדְמֶה מֵאֵין
הֲפֻגוֹת׃

50 Till the LORD look forth,
And behold from heaven.

50 עַד־יַשְׁקִיף וְיֵרֶא יְהוָה
מִשָּׁמָיִם׃

51 Mine eye affected my soul,
Because of all the daughters of my city.

51 עֵינִי עוֹלְלָה לְנַפְשִׁי מִכֹּל בְּנוֹת
עִירִי׃

52 They have chased me sore like a bird,
That are mine enemies without cause.

52 צוֹד צָדוּנִי כַּצִּפּוֹר אֹיְבַי חִנָּם׃

53 They have cut off my life in the dungeon,
And have cast stones upon me.

53 צָמְתוּ בַבּוֹר חַיָּי וַיַּדּוּ־אֶבֶן
בִּי׃

46. Cf. ii. 16.

47. *terror and the pit . . . desolation and destruction.* The Hebrew words are *pachad wa-phachath, ha-sheth we-ha-shaver.* It is impossible to reproduce this effective assonance in translation, and this verse is a good illustration of the truth that no translation can do full justice to the Hebrew of the Bible.

48. *breach.* In the Hebrew, the word thus translated is the same as that for *destruction* in the preceding verse.

49. *mine eye is poured out.* As if the eye itself were dissolved in tears.

51. *affected my soul.* i.e. affected me, made me ill.

52-57. This group of verses in particular has been taken by some to refer to the personal experiences of Jeremiah and his persecution at the hand of his own countrymen. Jeremiah was cast into a pit (Jer. xxxviii. 6—the Hebrew word there, as here, is *bor*); but there is no record that stones were cast on him, and the pit had no water in it, only mire. There is, of course, no compulsion to take the phrases *cast stones upon me* and *waters flowed over my head* literally; but if a figurative interpretation is adopted, one can just as well interpret the passage as a figurative personification of the sufferings of the whole people. (See Introduction to this chapter.)

54 Waters flowed over my head;
I said: 'I am cut off.'

54 צָֽפוּ־מַ֥יִם עַל־רֹאשִׁ֖י אָמַ֥רְתִּי
נִגְזָֽרְתִּי׃

55 I called upon Thy name, O LORD,
Out of the lowest dungeon.

55 קָרָ֤אתִי שִׁמְךָ֙ יְהוָ֔ה מִבּ֖וֹר
תַּחְתִּיּֽוֹת׃

56 Thou heardest my voice; hide not
Thine ear at my sighing, at my cry.

56 קוֹלִ֖י שָׁמָ֑עְתָּ אַל־תַּעְלֵ֧ם
אָזְנְךָ֛ לְרַוְחָתִ֖י לְשַׁוְעָתִֽי׃

57 Thou drewest near in the day that I called upon Thee;
Thou saidst: 'Fear not.'

57 קָרַ֙בְתָּ֙ בְּי֣וֹם אֶקְרָאֶ֔ךָּ אָמַ֖רְתָּ
אַל־תִּירָֽא׃

58 O Lord, Thou hast pleaded the causes of my soul;
Thou hast redeemed my life.

58 רַ֧בְתָּ אֲדֹנָ֛י רִיבֵ֥י נַפְשִׁ֖י גָּאַ֥לְתָּ
חַיָּֽי׃

59 O LORD, Thou hast seen my wrong;
Judge Thou my cause.

59 רָאִ֤יתָה יְהוָה֙ עַוָּ֣תָתִ֔י שָׁפְטָ֖ה
מִשְׁפָּטִֽי׃

53. *cut off my life.* Taken away the possibility of the enjoyment of life.

*cast stones upon me.* The Hebrew might equally well be translated 'cast a stone upon me,' i.e. covered the mouth of the dungeon with a stone. But it is preferable to take the words as a figure of speech for persecution.

54. *waters flowed over my head.* A figurative phrase, meaning intense distress (cf. Ps. lxix. 2, *The waters are come in even unto the soul*).

### 55-66 PRAYER FOR RETRIBUTION

55. *lowest dungeon.* The lowest depths of misery.

56. The prayer, *hide not Thine ear*, seems unnecessary and even conflicting after the statement *Thou heardest my voice*; and further, the interpretation of verses 56-59a which is given by this translation, viz. that they describe a response on the part of God to a prayer for relief from present troubles, is contradictory to the sense of the whole of the rest of the Book, which is that relief had not yet come and Israel's prayers had not yet been answered. It is better, therefore, to accept Rashi's interpretation, that the verbs in these verses are imperfects; and the sense of the passage is: 'Thou wert used (in the past) to hear my voice, to draw near, to say "Fear not"; Thou wert used to plead the causes of my soul, to redeem my life, to see my wrong. Judge now my cause.' Whether the experiences described in these verses be individual or collective, the meaning would be the same, that in the past God answered their prayers; may He do so in their present grievous troubles.

*at my sighing, at my cry.* An alternative rendering is 'at my cry for relief.'

58. *pleaded the causes of my soul.* i.e. taken my part.

59. *my wrong.* In the sense of 'the wrong done to me.'

60 Thou hast seen all their vengeance
And all their devices against me.

60 רָאִיתָה כָּל־נִקְמָתָם כָּל־
מַחְשְׁבֹתָם לִי׃

61 Thou hast heard their taunt, O LORD,
And all their devices against me;

61 שָׁמַעְתָּ חֶרְפָּתָם יְהוָה כָּל־
מַחְשְׁבֹתָם עָלָי׃

62 The lips of those that rose up against me,
And their muttering against me all the day.

62 שִׂפְתֵי קָמַי וְהֶגְיוֹנָם עָלַי כָּל־
הַיּוֹם׃

63 Behold Thou their sitting down, and their rising up;
I am their song.

63 שִׁבְתָּם וְקִימָתָם הַבִּיטָה אֲנִי
מַנְגִּינָתָם׃

64 Thou wilt render unto them a recompense, O LORD,
According to the work of their hands.

64 תָּשִׁיב לָהֶם גְּמוּל יְהוָה
כְּמַעֲשֵׂה יְדֵיהֶם׃

65 Thou wilt give them hardness of heart,
Thy curse unto them.

65 תִּתֵּן לָהֶם מְגִנַּת־לֵב תַּאֲלָתְךָ
לָהֶם׃

66 Thou wilt pursue them in anger, and destroy them
From under the heavens of the LORD.

66 תִּרְדֹּף בְּאַף וְתַשְׁמִידֵם מִתַּחַת
שְׁמֵי יְהוָה׃

**60-63.** A description of the crimes of the enemy for which retribution is sought.

**63.** *their sitting down and their rising up.* A comprehensive expression for all their activities.

*I am their song.* The subject of their taunting songs of contempt and triumph.

**65.** *hardness of heart.* lit. 'a covering of the heart,' interpreted by some as 'obstinacy,' and by others as 'blindness of heart.' But in the present context, Rashi's interpretation is to be preferred—the dulness of a heart which has been so affected by sorrows that it can feel no more.

1 How is the gold become dim!
How is the most fine gold changed!
The hallowed stones are poured out
At the head of every street.

1 אֵיכָה יוּעַם זָהָב יִשְׁנֶא הַכֶּתֶם
הַטּוֹב תִּשְׁתַּפֵּכְנָה אַבְנֵי־קֹדֶשׁ
בְּרֹאשׁ כָּל־חוּצוֹת׃

2 The precious sons of Zion,
Comparable to fine gold,
How are they esteemed as earthen pitchers,
The work of the hands of the potter!

2 בְּנֵי צִיּוֹן הַיְקָרִים הַמְסֻלָּאִים
בַּפָּז אֵיכָה נֶחְשְׁבוּ לְנִבְלֵי־
חֶרֶשׂ מַעֲשֵׂה יְדֵי יוֹצֵר׃

3 Even the jackals draw out the breast,
They give suck to their young ones;
The daughter of my people is become cruel,
Like the ostriches in the wilderness.

3 גַּם־תַּנִּין* חָלְצוּ שַׁד הֵינִיקוּ
גּוּרֵיהֶן בַּת־עַמִּי לְאַכְזָר
כִּי *עֵנִים בַּמִּדְבָּר׃

4 The tongue of the sucking child cleaveth
To the roof of his mouth for thirst;
The young children ask bread,
And none breaketh it unto them.

4 דָּבַק לְשׁוֹן יוֹנֵק אֶל־חִכּוֹ
בַּצָּמָא עוֹלָלִים שָׁאֲלוּ לֶחֶם
פֹּרֵשׂ אֵין לָהֶם׃

v. 3. תנים ק׳ v. 3. כיענים ק׳

A REPETITION, in more harrowing detail, of the themes of chapters i. and ii.

**1-10 MISERIES OF THE SIEGE**

1. *gold . . . fine gold . . . hallowed stones.* These expressions should not be taken literally, but as verse 2 confirms, figuratively for the people themselves. The people of Zion were to the other peoples of the earth as gold to base metal, but they have been treated as dross.

*the hallowed stones are poured out.* Better, 'how are the hallowed stones poured out.'

3. *cruel.* In the stress of famine, mothers consumed such little food as there was and allowed their children to go hungry (Rashi).

*ostriches.* The ostrich was proverbially cruel to its young (cf. Job xxxix. 13-16.)

4. *for thirst.* Famine and troubles had staunched the mother's milk.

5 They that did feed on dainties
Are desolate in the streets;
They that were brought up in scarlet
Embrace dunghills.

5 הָאֹכְלִים לְמַעֲדַנִּים נָשַׁמּוּ
בַּחוּצוֹת הָאֱמֻנִים עֲלֵי תוֹלָע
חִבְּקוּ אַשְׁפַּתּוֹת׃

6 For the iniquity of the daughter of my people is greater
Than the sin of Sodom,
That was overthrown as in a moment,
And no hands fell upon her.

6 וַיִּגְדַּל עֲוֺן בַּת־עַמִּי מֵחַטַּאת
סְדֹם הַהֲפוּכָה כְמוֹ־רָגַע
וְלֹא־חָלוּ בָהּ יָדָיִם׃

7 Her princes were purer than snow,
They were whiter than milk,
They were more ruddy in body than rubies,
Their polishing was as of sapphire;

7 זַכּוּ נְזִירֶיהָ מִשֶּׁלֶג צַחוּ מֵחָלָב
אָדְמוּ עֶצֶם מִפְּנִינִים סַפִּיר
גִּזְרָתָם׃

8 Their visage is blacker than coal;
They are not known in the streets;
Their skin is shrivelled upon their bones;
It is withered, it is become like a stick.

8 חָשַׁךְ מִשְּׁחוֹר תָּאֳרָם לֹא נִכְּרוּ
בַּחוּצוֹת צָפַד עוֹרָם עַל־
עַצְמָם יָבֵשׁ הָיָה כָעֵץ׃

9 They that are slain with the sword are better
Than they that are slain with hunger;
For these pine away, stricken through,
For want of the fruits of the field.

9 טוֹבִים הָיוּ חַלְלֵי־חֶרֶב
מֵחַלְלֵי רָעָב שֶׁהֵם יָזוּבוּ
מְדֻקָּרִים מִתְּנוּבֹת שָׂדָי׃

5. *in scarlet.* In rich and costly clothing.

*embrace.* Lie prostrate on.

6. Since the sufferings of Jerusalem are greater than those of Sodom, which perished in a moment, without prolonged agonies, it is inferred that the iniquity of Jerusalem must have been proportionately greater.

7f. The terrible contrast between the former and present appearance of the nobility is a stark witness of the ravages of the famine.

8. *blacker than coal.* lit. 'blacker than blackness.'

9. The swift death of the sword was preferable to the lingering death of famine.

10 The hands of women full of compassion
Have sodden their own children;
They were their food
In the destruction of the daughter of my people.

יְדֵ֗י נָשִׁים֙ רַחֲמָ֣נִיּ֔וֹת בִּשְּׁל֖וּ 10
יַלְדֵיהֶ֑ן הָי֤וּ לְבָרוֹת֙ לָ֔מוֹ
בְּשֶׁ֖בֶר בַּת־עַמִּֽי׃

11 The LORD hath accomplished His fury,
He hath poured out His fierce anger;
And He hath kindled a fire in Zion,
Which hath devoured the foundations thereof.

כִּלָּ֤ה יְהוָה֙ אֶת־חֲמָת֔וֹ שָׁפַ֖ךְ 11
חֲר֣וֹן אַפּ֑וֹ וַיַּצֶּת־אֵ֣שׁ בְּצִיּ֔וֹן
וַתֹּ֖אכַל יְסֹדֹתֶֽיהָ׃

12 The kings of the earth believed not,
Neither all the inhabitants of the world,
That the adversary and the enemy would enter
Into the gates of Jerusalem.

לֹ֤א הֶאֱמִ֙ינוּ֙ מַלְכֵי־אֶ֔רֶץ *וּכֹ֖ל 12
יֹשְׁבֵ֣י תֵבֵ֑ל כִּ֤י יָבֹא֙ צַ֣ר וְאוֹיֵ֔ב
בְּשַׁעֲרֵ֖י יְרוּשָׁלִָֽם׃

13 It is because of the sins of her prophets,
And the iniquities of her priests,
That have shed the blood of the just
In the midst of her.

מֵחַטֹּ֣את נְבִיאֶ֔יהָ עֲוֺנֹ֖ת כֹּהֲנֶ֑יהָ 13
הַשֹּׁפְכִ֥ים בְּקִרְבָּ֖הּ דַּ֥ם
צַדִּיקִֽים׃

14 They wander as blind men in the streets,
They are polluted with blood,
So that men cannot
Touch their garments.

נָע֤וּ עִוְרִים֙ בַּֽחוּצ֔וֹת נְגֹֽאֲל֖וּ 14
בַּדָּ֑ם בְּלֹ֣א יֽוּכְל֔וּ יִגְּע֖וּ
בִּלְבֻשֵׁיהֶֽם׃

כל ק' v. 12.

**10.** Cf. ii. 20 and Jer. xix. 9.

*full of compassion.* i.e. hitherto compassionate or naturally compassionate.

**11-16** THE SUFFERING IS GOD'S PUNISHMENT

**11.** *accomplished.* Not 'finished,' but 'poured out in full measure.'

**12.** Since Jerusalem had been captured twice before, foreign kings would hardly have believed that it was completely impregnable. This verse, therefore, is probably to be understood as an ironic reference to the false confidence of its inhabitants in the city's impregnability.

**14.** After the fall of the city, the guilty men, fearing the wrath of the inhabitants, wander blindly through the streets, not knowing where to seek refuge (cf. Deut. xxviii. 29).

15 'Depart ye! unclean!' men cried unto them,
'Depart, depart, touch not';
Yea, they fled away and wandered;
Men said among the nations:
'They shall no more sojourn here.'

16 The anger of the LORD hath divided them;
He will no more regard them;
They respected not the persons of the priests,
They were not gracious unto the elders.

17 As for us, our eyes do yet fail
For our vain help;
In our watching we have watched
For a nation that could not save.

18 They hunt our steps,
That we cannot go in our broad places;
Our end is near, our days are fulfilled;
For our end is come.

19 Our pursuers were swifter
Than the eagles of the heaven;
They chased us upon the mountains,
They lay in wait for us in the wilderness.

15 סוּרוּ טָמֵא קָרְאוּ לָמוֹ סוּרוּ
סוּרוּ אַל־תִּגָּעוּ כִּי נָצוּ גַּם־
נָעוּ אָמְרוּ בַּגּוֹיִם לֹא יוֹסִפוּ
לָגוּר׃

16 פְּנֵי יְהוָה חִלְּקָם לֹא יוֹסִיף
לְהַבִּיטָם פְּנֵי כֹהֲנִים לֹא נָשָׂאוּ
*זְקֵנִים לֹא חָנָנוּ׃

17 עוֹדֵ*ינָה תִּכְלֶינָה עֵינֵינוּ אֶל־
עֶזְרָתֵנוּ הָבֶל בְּצִפִּיָּתֵנוּ צִפִּינוּ
אֶל־גּוֹי לֹא יוֹשִׁעַ׃

18 צָדוּ צְעָדֵינוּ מִלֶּכֶת
בִּרְחֹבֹתֵינוּ קָרַב קִצֵּנוּ מָלְאוּ
יָמֵינוּ כִּי־בָא קִצֵּנוּ׃

19 קַלִּים הָיוּ רֹדְפֵינוּ מִנִּשְׁרֵי
שָׁמָיִם עַל־הֶהָרִים דְּלָקֻנוּ
בַּמִּדְבָּר אָרְבוּ לָנוּ׃

v. 16. וזקנים ק׳   v. 17. עודינו ק׳

15. *depart ye! unclean!* The citizens shrink from the guilty men as from lepers, as if physical contact with them would be contamination (cf. Lev. xiii. 45).

*fled away and wandered.* They attempted to take refuge in other lands, but even abroad men would have none of them and would not allow them to settle.

16. *divided.* i.e. scattered them among the nations.

*priests.* This, in contrast with verse 13, must refer to *good* priests. The second half of this verse states the reason for God's anger.

17-20 HOPELESSNESS OF HUMAN AID

17. *a nation that could not save.* Egypt, with whom Zedekiah attempted to form an alliance against Babylonia (see Jer. xxxvii. 7).

18f. A description of the hunted state of the Jews who remained in Judea under Babylonian occupation.

19. *pursuers.* Pursuing those who went into hiding, or attempted to flee the country.

20 The breath of our nostrils, the anointed of the LORD,
Was taken in their pits;
Of whom we said: 'Under his shadow
We shall live among the nations.'

21 Rejoice and be glad, O daughter of Edom,
That dwellest in the land of Uz:
The cup shall pass over unto thee also;
Thou shalt be drunken, and shalt make thyself naked.

22 The punishment of thine iniquity is accomplished, O daughter of Zion,
He will no more carry thee away into captivity;
He will punish thine iniquity, O daughter of Edom,
He will uncover thy sins.

20 רוּחַ אַפֵּינוּ מְשִׁיחַ יְהוָה נִלְכַּד
בִּשְׁחִיתוֹתָם אֲשֶׁר אָמַרְנוּ
בְּצִלּוֹ נִחְיֶה בַגּוֹיִם׃

21 שִׂישִׂי וְשִׂמְחִי בַּת־אֱדוֹם
יוֹשֶׁבְתִּי* בְּאֶרֶץ עוּץ גַּם־עָלַיִךְ
תַּעֲבָר־כּוֹס תִּשְׁכְּרִי
וְתִתְעָרִי׃

22 תַּם־עֲוֺנֵךְ בַּת־צִיּוֹן לֹא יוֹסִיף
לְהַגְלוֹתֵךְ פָּקַד עֲוֺנֵךְ בַּת־
אֱדוֹם גִּלָּה עַל־חַטֹּאתָיִךְ׃

v. 21. יתיר י'

**20.** *breath of our nostrils, the anointed of the LORD.* King Zedekiah, who was captured in the plain of Jericho when attempting to escape across the Jordan, and blinded and imprisoned by Nebuchadnezzar (Jer. lii. 7-11). This apparently favourable judgment, contrasted with the unfavourable judgments on Zedekiah in Jeremiah (e.g. xxxvii. 2), and Kings (2 Kings xxiv. 19), has given much trouble to commentators. Some have attempted to escape the difficulty by attributing the reference to king Josiah. But, in fact, the verse is a tribute, not to Zedekiah, but to his kingship. Whatever his failings, he was still the Lord's anointed and of the House of David, and, so it was thought, the one on whom centred the people's hopes for a continued national identity when the State had been destroyed. We might compare the honour which Elijah paid to Ahab in virtue of his office (1 Kings xviii. 46).

### 21-22 PUNISHMENT OF EDOM

**21.** Edom had refused to join the Egyptian alliance against Babylonia, and, as a reward, when Judea was conquered, Nebuchadnezzar gave the rural districts over to the Edomites as a prey (cf. Ezek. xxv. 12-14, xxxv. 5; Obad. 11-14). Israel could not forgive this infamous conduct, and prophets and Psalmists alike invoked God's vengeance on Edom (cf. with this passage Jer. xlix. 7-13).

*rejoice and be glad.* The words are ironical: 'Rejoice while you can, for your rejoicing will be short-lived.'

*the cup.* Of punishment and destruction.

**22.** The connection between this and the preceding verse is that, in the punishment of his enemies, Israel will see a sign of the restoration of Divine favour.

1 Remember, O LORD, what is come upon us;
Behold, and see our reproach.

2 Our inheritance is turned unto strangers,
Our houses unto aliens.

3 We are become orphans and fatherless,
Our mothers are as widows.

4 We have drunk our water for money;
Our wood cometh to us for price.

5 To our very necks we are pursued;
We labour, and have no rest.

1 זְכֹר יְהוָה מֶה־הָיָה לָנוּ
הַבִּיטָ* וּרְאֵה אֶת־חֶרְפָּתֵנוּ׃
2 נַחֲלָתֵנוּ נֶהֶפְכָה לְזָרִים בָּתֵּינוּ
לְנָכְרִים׃
3 יְתוֹמִים הָיִינוּ *אֵין אָב אִמֹּתֵינוּ
כְּאַלְמָנוֹת׃
4 מֵימֵינוּ בְּכֶסֶף שָׁתִינוּ עֵצֵינוּ
בִּמְחִיר יָבֹאוּ׃
5 עַל צַוָּארֵנוּ נִרְדָּפְנוּ יָגַעְנוּ *לֹא
הוּנַח־לָנוּ׃

v. 1. הביטה ק׳ v. 3. ואין ק׳ v.5. ולא ק׳

THIS chapter is rightly regarded more as a prayer than as a lament. It is a sorrowful account of the condition of Judah, laid before God in order to secure His compassion.

**1-18 PERSECUTION OF THE REMNANT IN JUDEA**

2. *inheritance.* i.e. land. It was the established practice in those days to colonize a conquered land with foreigners (cf. Deut. xxviii. 33).

3. *orphans and fatherless.* i.e. fatherless orphans.

4. A dear price had to be paid to the conquerors for even the commonest necessities of life.

5. *to our very necks we are pursued.* This may be a reference to the barbarous practice of riding across the bodies of conquered foes, as depicted in some of the Assyrian inscriptions (cf. Isa. li. 23).

6 We have given the hand to Egypt,
And to Assyria, to have bread enough.

6 מִצְרַיִם נָתַנּוּ יָד אַשּׁוּר לִשְׂבֹּעַ
לָחֶם׃

7 Our fathers have sinned, and are not;
And we have borne their iniquities.

7 אֲבֹתֵינוּ חָטְאוּ *אֵינָם *אֲנַחְנוּ
עֲוֹנֹתֵיהֶם סָבָלְנוּ׃

8 Servants rule over us;
There is none to deliver us out of their hand.

8 עֲבָדִים מָשְׁלוּ בָנוּ פֹּרֵק אֵין
מִיָּדָם׃

9 We get our bread with the peril of our lives
Because of the sword of the wilderness.

9 בְּנַפְשֵׁנוּ נָבִיא לַחְמֵנוּ מִפְּנֵי
חֶרֶב הַמִּדְבָּר׃

10 Our skin is hot like an oven
Because of the burning heat of famine.

10 עוֹרֵנוּ כְּתַנּוּר נִכְמָרוּ מִפְּנֵי
זַלְעֲפוֹת רָעָב׃

11 They have ravished the women in Zion,
The maidens in the cities of Judah.

11 נָשִׁים בְּצִיּוֹן עִנּוּ בְּתֻלֹת בְּעָרֵי
יְהוּדָה׃

12 Princes are hanged up by their hand;
The faces of elders are not honoured.

12 שָׂרִים בְּיָדָם נִתְלוּ פְּנֵי זְקֵנִים
לֹא נֶהְדָּרוּ׃

v. 7. ואינם ק׳ v. 7. ואנחנו ק׳

6. *given the hand to.* Submitted to.

*Egypt.* A reference to those who escaped to Egypt (Jer. xliii. 5-7).

*Assyria.* Babylonia is meant, but there are parallels in the Bible for this usage (e.g. Jer. ii. 18).

7. The doctrine in this verse is not that children are *punished* for the fathers' sins: Jeremiah explicitly denied that doctrine (xxxi. 29f.); but that the evil consequences of sin are inevitably felt by many generations.

8. *servants.* Better, 'slaves,' who had risen, through ability or favour, to high office among the Babylonians.

9. *get our bread with the peril of our lives.* Every excursion into the fields to bring in food meant exposure to the depredations of ravaging bands of Babylonians or their followers.

10. *our skin is hot.* The fever brought on by hunger is meant.

12. *their hand.* i.e. the hand of the slaves mentioned in verse 8.

13 The young men have borne the mill,
And the children have stumbled under the wood.

14 The elders have ceased from the gate,
The young men from their music.

15 The joy of our heart is ceased;
Our dance is turned into mourning.

16 The crown is fallen from our head;
Woe unto us! for we have sinned.

17 For this our heart is faint,
For these things our eyes are dim;

18 For the mountain of Zion, which is desolate,
The foxes walk upon it.

19 Thou, O Lord, art enthroned for ever,
Thy throne is from generation to generation.

20 Wherefore dost Thou forget us for ever,
And forsake us so long time?

13 בַּחוּרִים טְחוֹן נָשָׂאוּ וּנְעָרִים
בָּעֵץ כָּשָׁלוּ׃
14 זְקֵנִים מִשַּׁעַר שָׁבָתוּ בַּחוּרִים
מִנְּגִינָתָם׃
15 שָׁבַת מְשׂוֹשׂ לִבֵּנוּ נֶהְפַּךְ לְאֵבֶל
מְחוֹלֵנוּ׃
16 נָפְלָה עֲטֶרֶת רֹאשֵׁנוּ אוֹי־
נָא לָנוּ כִּי חָטָאנוּ׃
17 עַל־זֶה הָיָה דָוֶה לִבֵּנוּ עַל־
אֵלֶּה חָשְׁכוּ עֵינֵינוּ׃
18 עַל הַר־צִיּוֹן שֶׁשָּׁמֵם שׁוּעָלִים
הִלְּכוּ־בוֹ׃
19 אַתָּה יְהוָה לְעוֹלָם תֵּשֵׁב
כִּסְאֲךָ לְדוֹר וָדוֹר׃
20 לָמָּה לָנֶצַח תִּשְׁכָּחֵנוּ תַּעַזְבֵנוּ
לְאֹרֶךְ יָמִים׃

13. *borne the mill.* Carried the heavy mill-stones in forced labour for the conquerors.

*under the wood.* When carrying fuel.

14. *from the gate.* See on i. 4.

16. *the crown.* i.e. our national prestige and prosperity.

17-22 PRAYER FOR RESTORATION OF DIVINE FAVOUR

18. *the foxes walk upon it.* Without fear of human encounter.

19f. God endures for ever; will His anger against Israel likewise endure for ever? (Ibn Ezra). Or it may be that the appeal is to God's constancy: 'Thou hast promised that, as Thou art enduring, so Thy promise (to restore Israel) is enduring' (Rashi).

21 Turn Thou us unto Thee, O LORD, and we shall be turned;
Renew our days as of old.

22 Thou canst not have utterly rejected us,
And be exceeding wroth against us!

Turn Thou us unto Thee, O LORD, and we shall be turned;
Renew our days as of old.

21 הֲשִׁיבֵ֨נוּ יְהוָ֤ה ׀ אֵלֶ֙יךָ֙ וְֽנָשׁ֔וּבָ*
חַדֵּ֥שׁ יָמֵ֖ינוּ כְּקֶֽדֶם׃
22 כִּ֚י אִם־מָאֹ֣ס מְאַסְתָּ֔נוּ קָצַ֥פְתָּ
עָלֵ֖ינוּ עַד־מְאֹֽד׃

השיבנו יהוה אליך ונשובה חדש ימינו כקדם׃

v. 21. ונשובה ק׳

21. *turn Thou us.* Help us to return.

*as of old.* When we enjoyed Thy favour.

22. *Thou canst not.* This translation, while making good sense, is etymologically without parallel, and can only be defended if the sentence be understood as an asseveration. Translations more in accordance with Hebrew usage are: (1) 'Unless Thou hast utterly rejected us and art exceedingly wroth against us'; (2) 'But if Thou hast utterly rejected us, Thou hast (already) been exceedingly wroth against us' (Ibn Ezra).

In accordance with the Jewish custom of not concluding on an unpleasant note, verse 21 is repeated at the conclusion of the Book. A similar repetition occurs at the end of Isaiah, Malachi and Ecclesiastes.

# קהלת

# ECCLESIASTES

INTRODUCTION AND COMMENTARY

*by*

RABBI DR. VICTOR E. REICHERT, D.D.

*and*

THE REV. DR. A. COHEN, M.A., Ph.D., D.H.L.

# PREFACE

A WORD of explanation is necessary to account for the dual authorship of this Commentary. Rabbi Dr. Victor Reichert, of Cincinnati, undertook the task and produced a most painstaking piece of work.

It did not, however, fit into the plan and scope of the present series in two respects. He collected an abundance of Rabbinic material which, though valuable, was too long for insertion and was not always helpful to the modern reader who seeks an understanding of the text. He also, as a rule, commented upon the verse as a whole rather than upon its words and phrases.

In these circumstances I had the invidious duty of subtracting from what he had prepared and making additions. I trust that the resultant composite work which, owing to the factor of distance, he was not able to see before publication, is as acceptable to him as collaboration has been pleasing to me.

In some respects *Ecclesiastes* is the most difficult Book of the Bible for the commentator. Its complexities and obscurities are so many and often baffling that the assumption of dogmatic certainty is unwise and unwarranted. My co-author and I can only plead that no effort has been spared to make this elusive Book understandable to and appreciated by the reader.

A. COHEN

# INTRODUCTION

In the Introduction to his volume of literary essays *The New Spirit*, Havelock Ellis writes: 'The old cycles are for ever renewed, and it is no paradox that he who would advance can never cling too close to the past. The thing that has been is the thing that will be again; if we realize that, we may avoid many of the disillusions, miseries, insanities, that for ever accompany the throes of new birth. Set your shoulder joyously to the world's wheel: you may spare yourself some unhappiness if, beforehand, you slip the Book of Ecclesiastes beneath your arm.'

We have here suggested the charm and the fascination of this remarkable Book. Throughout the centuries, it has preserved its freshness, the vivid, alive quality of a thinker who faced the inexorable vanities of life and yet, somehow, never lost the joy of living. The juxtaposition of piety and scepticism, irreconcilable as they may appear, seems to belong to the whole paradox of the Jewish mind. Faith and Reason write one upon the other in the palimpsest of our past. Perhaps it was to strike the balance of sanity that the Fathers of the Synagogue chose the recital of *Ecclesiastes*, with its melancholy refrain *Vanity of vanities, all is vanity*, on the Festival of Tabernacles when the Jew is commanded to rejoice. At all events, it is hard to escape the judgment that the major emphasis of Jewish thinking has indeed been that of setting our shoulders joyously to the world's wheel. That we have spared ourselves some unhappiness by, beforehand, slipping the Book of Ecclesiastes beneath our arm, seems likewise true.

A large part of the perennial fascination of this Book derives from the baffling problems that encompass it. Who was its author? When and where was it written? What is its message?

Endless have been the efforts to unravel these mysteries. The final and absolute word yet remains to be said in answer to these questions. The ancients accepted uncritically the thin disguise that this composition came from the pen of King Solomon. This view is now abandoned. We may be grateful that it once found acceptance because the prestige of this presumption helped to win it a place in the sacred Canon.

If not Solomon, who then? Ecclesiastes has been defined to mean a 'member of an assembly.' Set against the internal evidence of the Book, the title, harsh and forbidding, does not carry us far to the light. Nor does the conjectural translation, 'The Preacher,' help us any better. If Koheleth was a preacher, he certainly defied all the conventions of his calling and broke the mould when his day was done. We come nearer the truth when we think of Koheleth as a daring teacher, restless and courageous in his search for the abiding meaning of life. He looks out on life with wide open eyes, hating hypocrisy and sham, despising injustice and wrong. He knows the sadness of things, but the mood of dejection never freezes over him. Thus he can speak of the joy and beauty of life and set it against the haunting echo of the world's vanity.

When and where did Koheleth write? Again we are confronted with endless contradiction and conjecture. Alexandria has been suggested as best suited to the cultural mood of the Book, but the evidence is not conclusive. It may have been Jerusalem. Grätz placed its time as late as Herod. Renan thought it belonged before 100 B.C.E. If one can speak of a consensus amid a wide, bewildering range of guesses, the period between 300 and 250 B.C.E. seems most probable. It is hard to escape the feeling that we have before us a post-exilic literary product.

Finally, what is the message of Koheleth? What is this Book really about? One looks in vain for the sustaining integrity of mood and thought that we expect in a contemporary literary product. We are constantly confronted with contradiction. Faith and futility struggle together in this spiritual tug of war. It may be that Koheleth, like a wise teacher seeking to awake thought and reflection rather than to stifle discussion and strait-jacket investigation, deliberately set mood against mood. We probably shall never really know.

Long ago the sages of the Talmud worried over the juxtaposition of piety and heterodoxy. In the Tractate Sabbath 30*b* we read: 'Rab Judah the son of R. Samuel b. Shilath said in Rab's name: The sages wished to hide the Book of Ecclesiastes (exclude it from the Canon and make it apocryphal) because its words are self-contradictory; yet why did they not hide it? Because its beginning is religious teaching and its end is religious teaching.' Like Dr. Israel Levine, they saw in Koheleth a rebel returning to Faith.

There is an indefinable charm about this *Journal Intime.* The pronoun 'I' is never obtrusive and offensive. The note of personal confession brings a warm, human touch to this adventure after life's meaning. And although Stoic fatalism and Epicurean hedonism have their say, yet in the end we rise to the higher synthesis of reverence for God and obedience to His commandments, for that is the whole duty of man.

Koheleth was not only a searching seeker for truth. He was a great poet. There is a sad music to his poem on old age and death in the twelfth chapter of the Book which is one of the immortal beauty places in the Hebrew Bible.

*Of making many books there is no end.* But, then, Koheleth himself wrote, and a grateful posterity will for ever be glad that he did.

V. R.

For practically all modern authorities on the Bible, the authorship of *Ecclesiastes* is a closed question so far as the traditional view, that King Solomon wrote it, is concerned. Even the late Professor Schechter said, 'That tradition cannot be maintained in all its statements need not be denied . . . Solomon cannot be held responsible for the scepticism of the Book of Ecclesiastes' (*Studies in Judaism,* II, p. 39). In the standpoint adopted above, Dr. Reichert has undoubtedly the vast majority of scholars on his side.

The vast majority of scholars—but not all. It is only fair to state the case for Solomonic authorship as it has been presented, for example, by J. D. Eisenstein in the Hebrew Encyclopædia, *Otsar Yisrael.* The additions of the present writer are inserted between square brackets.

A main argument advanced against the identification of Koheleth with Solomon is the strong influence of Greek philosophic teaching evident in some of the points of view expressed in the Book, and such ideas were unknown among the Hebrews in the time of the Israelite king. But is it certain that the first philosophers originated among the Greeks? If it be not agreed that earlier philosophers existed among the Israelites, certain it is that the Greek thinkers were preceded by the *magicians* and *wise men* of Egypt (Gen. xli. 8) and no doubt also by the sages of Assyria and Babylonia. May not these have had an effect upon Hebrew thinkers?

[The alleged influence of Stoic and Epicurean doctrine upon the author is an assumption and far from being proved. A modern commentator like the Rev. A. Lukyn Williams, who does not accept the Solomonic authorship, yet writes: 'The fact of the matter is that we cannot look upon Koheleth as a philosopher in the technical sense of the word. If he had any training in Greek philosophy, his Book shows hardly any sign of its effect upon him. The passages which have been adduced in favour of his possessing deep philosophical thought, and of his regarding the universe in a strictly philosophical way, have been for the most part wrested from their context, and in other cases do not bear the weight that has been laid upon them' (p. xxxv). He goes on to assert that the cast of Koheleth's mind was essentially Hebraic.]

The experiences of Solomon, as recorded in 1 Kings, are the same as those ascribed to himself by Koheleth. The luxury of his household, his numerous wives, the buildings he erected, his reputation for outstanding wisdom—all these foundations upon which the king's fame rested find reflection in the person of Koheleth as delineated in the Book. Likewise the follies to which he became addicted later in his reign find a parallel there. Koheleth depicts the conditions of life in the country as unsettled and the people as existing under hardships; here too confirmation may be found in the history of Solomon. The statement, *And he* [*Rezon*] *was an adversary to Israel all the days of Solomon, beside the mischief that Hadad did; and he abhorred Israel* (1 Kings xi. 25), is an indication that all was not well with the Israelites while he was on the throne, and for many life must have been intolerable. Their dissatisfaction is also evident from the complaint they made to his successor, Rehoboam, *Thy father made our yoke grievous* (1 Kings xii. 4). Note must further be taken of the verdict passed upon him, *When Solomon was old, his wives turned away his heart after other gods; and his heart was not whole with the LORD his God* (1 Kings xi. 4). All these circumstances are faithfully mirrored in the Book, and there is no other man known in the annals of Israel who corresponds to the person of Koheleth.

It is assumed by the critics that several writers are responsible for the Book in its present form. [The German commentator, Siegfried, claims to have discovered traces of five different hands in it.] According to Grätz, the original author was a member of the sect of Essenes who drew a sombre picture of life. A Greek author annotated his treatise with marginal comments combating his views with Epicurean ideas. Finally a Pharisee, shocked by the heresies it contained, corrected them with orthodox Jewish sentiments.

As for this theory, what can one think of the editor who mixed up these discordant elements in so extraordinary a manner? Why did he not compile each writer's statements into a separate document? And why did he not reveal the secret of the mixture for which he was responsible? It is far more probable that one man wrote a kind of drama in which three separate characters speak, but all their opinions emanate from a single mind. Thus King Solomon collected divergent views and weighed them one against the other, until he arrived at the conclusion, *Fear God, and keep His commandments; for this is the whole of man.*

The critics further argue for a late date from the style of the language in which Aramaic [and supposedly Greek] words occur, as well as terms and grammatical constructions which are common in Mishnaic Hebrew. It is possible that King Hezekiah and his literary collaborators made linguistic changes in the text when they edited it. But it is more proper to contend that our knowledge of Hebrew is insufficient to make possible a decision about the lateness of any particular word or phrase, because many terms which are found in the Mishnah but not in the Bible are in fact old.

[Every reader of the Book with a knowledge of Hebrew must admit that the literary style, except in the proverbial citations, differs widely from that of the rest of the Bible. This may well be accounted for by the fact that the contents of the Book are unique in the Hebrew Scriptures. The argumentation, which is its principal feature, is far removed from the declamation of the prophets, the song and prayer of the Psalmists, or the annals of the historians. No other records of the Hebrew thinkers, who reflected upon the meaning and purpose of life, have been preserved and for that reason comparison is impossible. It may well be that in the Book we have the common speech of the people as against the more polished style of the literary writers.]

---

Interesting and important as the critical questions raised by the Book may be, they should not be allowed to divert the reader's attention from the spiritual journey which is traced in its chapters through the labyrinth of doubt and disillusionment to the goal of restful Faith. The true character of the document is well described in these words: 'This is a soul's diary, not the morbid confessions of egotism like Rousseau's *Confessions* . . . but the frank story of struggle with and triumph over temperament. The writer gives us the benefit of his experience' (Devine, p. 4).

That spiritual journey is not along a straight road, but winds backwards and forwards. Hence the apparent contradictions and repetitions which are frequently met with. They are natural and inevitable as mood succeeds mood, and doubts, temporarily stifled, reassert themselves. Boldness of reasoning and humility of disposition are the two characteristics of Koheleth which contend for mastery within the arena of his mind and heart. To read the Book from this point of view is like sitting at the ring-side and watching a thrilling bout. For long the issue remains in doubt. Often Faith appears defeated under the blows of hard facts; in the end it triumphs.

A. C.

# ECCLESIASTES

## 1 CHAPTER I א

1 The words of Koheleth, the son of David, king in Jerusalem.

2 Vanity of vanities, saith Koheleth;
Vanity of vanities, all is vanity.

1 דִּבְרֵי קֹהֶלֶת בֶּן־דָּוִד מֶלֶךְ
2 בִּירוּשָׁלִָם׃ הֲבֵל הֲבָלִים
אָמַר קֹהֶלֶת הֲבֵל הֲבָלִים

1. *the words of*. Rashi asserts: 'Wherever Scripture uses the phrase *the words of*, the purpose is to speak words of reproof or admonition.' There is a Midrashic teaching that in the case of three prophets, because their messages consist of chiding and rebuke, their prophecies depend on themselves. That is to say, the Books of other prophets begin with a phrase which is indicative of Divine origin; e.g. *The word of the LORD* or *The Vision* (cf. Isa. i. 1; Hosea i. 1). But not so in the following three instances: *The words of Koheleth*, *The words of Amos* and *The words of Jeremiah*. From a critical point of view, this is only a literary and stylistic peculiarity; but there is a beautiful thought implied, viz. the words inspired by God are gentle and compassionate, and not characterized by bitterness.

*Koheleth*. The Rabbis asked why Solomon was called Koheleth and answered because his words were spoken in 'the assembly' (*kahal*). The feminine form of the word is explained on the supposition that it personifies 'wisdom' (which is feminine in Hebrew) who is the speaker in the Book; or more probably it is to be regarded, according to Hebrew usage, as a neuter adjective with the meaning 'the type of speaker in an assembly.' On his identity, see the Introduction.

*the son of David*. The Midrash emphasizes the fact that Koheleth was a king, the son of a king, a sage, the son of a sage, a righteous man, the son of a righteous man. It is possible that this Rabbinic characterization is to be connected with a report in the Talmud (Shabbath 30*b*) that some Rabbis wished to exclude this Book from the Scriptures because they found in it passages that contradicted one another and also statements that might undermine faith. For this reason, in their praise of the Book other Rabbis implied that all its words were conducive to righteousness, especially since Koheleth was the son of David, a wise and righteous king, and the fruit does not fall far from the tree. Just as the words of David (the Psalms) were upright and without blemish, so were the words of Koheleth.

*king in Jerusalem*. The phrase is to be attached to Koheleth, not David. There is a Talmudic tradition that at first Solomon ruled over the whole earth, afterwards over all Israel, and finally over Jerusalem alone. Rashi comments that Koheleth is described as *king in Jerusalem* as a tribute to his wisdom, since it was a city famed for the wisdom of its inhabitants.

### 2-11 THE AUTHOR'S INTRODUCTION

Everything is vanity, and endless repetition is the story both of nature and man.

2. *vanity of vanities*. The word *hebel* is to be reckoned as occurring seven times in the verse, each plural denoting two. The number seven corresponds to the days of the world's creation. Koheleth, accordingly, pronounces the judgment that the seven days of the creation were

3 What profit hath man of all his labour
Wherein he laboureth under the sun?

4 One generation passeth away, and another generation cometh;
And the earth abideth for ever.

5 The sun also ariseth, and the sun goeth down,
And hasteth to his place where he ariseth.

3 הַכֹּל הָבֶל׃ מַה־יִּתְרוֹן לָאָדָם
בְּכָל־עֲמָלוֹ שֶׁיַּעֲמֹל תַּחַת
4 הַשָּׁמֶשׁ׃ דּוֹר הֹלֵךְ וְדוֹר בָּא
5 וְהָאָרֶץ לְעוֹלָם עֹמָדֶת׃ וְזָרַח
הַשֶּׁמֶשׁ וּבָא הַשָּׁמֶשׁ וְאֶל־
מְקוֹמוֹ שׁוֹאֵף זוֹרֵחַ הוּא שָׁם׃

the height of vanity. Literally the word signifies 'a breath,' that which lacks substance; and the phrase indicates the superlative degree like 'song of songs,' 'holy of holies.'

*all is vanity.* A Rabbi taught that Koheleth spoke of seven vanities to correspond to the seven stages of man which he experiences in his lifetime. At one year old he is like a king, everyone embraces and pays deference to him. At two and three years he is like a pig, groping in the gutters. At ten, he skips like a young goat. At twenty he neighs like a horse and seeks a wife. After marriage he bears burdens like an ass and hardens his face like a dog in search of sustenance. In old age he is like an ape!

3. *profit.* An important word for the understanding of Koheleth's philosophy, occurring ten times in the Book and nowhere else in the Bible. It is the criterion by which he tests the value of objects and experiences. Being a false standard, it leads him to false conclusions. The literal meaning of the word is 'surplus,' in a balance sheet. 'It was probably one of the words which the commerce of the Jews, after the captivity, had brought into common use. The question is in substance, almost in form, identical with that of our times, " Is life worth living? " ' (Plumptre). In Hebrew a question is sometimes used to express an emphatic denial. *What profit?* really means 'there is certainly no profit.'

*labour.* Better, 'toil,' since the Hebrew term implies hard and wearying work.

*under the sun.* This phrase is found twenty-nine times in this Book to express the earthly scene of man's activities and vicissitudes. An analogous phrase was current among the Greeks, but it would be hazardous to deduce, as many modern commentators do, that it was borrowed and rendered into Hebrew. It has been found on Phoenician inscriptions, and is a variant of *under* (*the*) *heaven* (verse 13, ii. 3, iii. 1) which is common in the Bible.

4. *one generation . . . cometh.* The Hebrew is more terse and forceful, 'a generation goeth and a generation cometh.' His first reflection is upon the transitory character of human life. The earth is the stage upon which man plays his rôle; but when his part is ended, he leaves the stage.

*the earth abideth.* 'In contrast to the changing life of men, the author thinks of the earth as stable and an abiding background for the ever-varying pageantry of human life, which changes with such kaleidoscopic rapidity' (Martin).

*for ever.* Here the meaning is: for an indefinite time as compared with the limited term of man's existence.

5. *the sun also ariseth.* lit. 'and the sun ariseth.' In the same manner that one

6 The wind goeth toward the south,
And turneth about unto the north;
It turneth about continually in its circuit,
And the wind returneth again to its circuits.

7 All the rivers run into the sea,
Yet the sea is not full;
Unto the place whither the rivers go,
Thither they go again.

6 הוֹלֵךְ֙ אֶל־דָּר֔וֹם וְסוֹבֵ֖ב אֶל־
צָפ֑וֹן סוֹבֵ֤ב ׀ סֹבֵב֙ הוֹלֵ֣ךְ
הָר֔וּחַ וְעַל־סְבִיבֹתָ֖יו שָׁ֥ב
7 הָרֽוּחַ׃ כָּל־הַנְּחָלִים֙ הֹלְכִ֣ים
אֶל־הַיָּ֔ם וְהַיָּ֖ם אֵינֶ֣נּוּ מָלֵ֑א
אֶל־מְק֗וֹם שֶׁ֤הַנְּחָלִים֙ הֹֽלְכִ֔ים
שָׁ֛ם הֵ֥ם שָׁבִ֖ים לָלָֽכֶת׃

generation moves on to make place for another, the sun appears in the heavens only to set before the rising moon. The Psalmist was moved to exclaim *The heavens declare the glory of God* (Ps. xix. 2), but Koheleth detected there only evidence of purposeless motion. The ethical bent of Judaism is discernible in the interpretation of a Rabbi who read into the verse something profounder than the wearisome cycle of the sun in its orbit: 'It intends to teach us that no sooner does the sun of one righteous person set, then the sun of another righteous person arises.' In this sense the statement loses its pessimism; the quality of goodness endures in the human race.

*hasteth.* lit. 'panteth,' as though it hurried to set. In Ps. xix. 6 the sun is said to rejoice *as a strong man to run his course.* Similarly the sun has apparently no desire to remain, but is eager to reach its appointed goal.

6. *the wind.* Like the sun, the wind too is an illustration of the monotonous mutability and yet static law of nature. There is only the spectacle of endless, wearisome repetition. The language of the original breathes 'the languor of one who was weary with watching the endless and yet monotonous changes' (Plumptre).

*south . . . north.* In Cant. iv. 16 the north and south winds are evoked. The explanation that these are the directions from which the wind usually blows in Palestine is incorrect, and more probably south and north are mentioned to supplement the east and west referred to in the previous verse (Ginsburg).

*it turneth about continually.* The constant change of wind suggests to the mind of Koheleth a comparison with the round of man's duties and activities. The Hebrew is most vivid and a literal translation is, 'going to the south and turning about to the north, turning about, turning about, goeth the wind.'

7. *all the rivers.* The thought is not that the streams return from the abyss by subterranean channels, nor is the reference to the evaporation of the sea which forms into clouds and falls as rain (cf. Job xxxvi. 27f.). He confines himself to the phenomenon that the sea is the source of rivers which return to the sea. It is probable that Koheleth, like some Greek naturalists, thought of the waters of the ocean seeping through the cracks in the earth and providing a supply to wells and streams.

*is not full.* Commentators quote the exact parallel which is found in the *Clouds* of Aristophanes, 'The sea, though all the rivers flow to it, increaseth not in volume.' It is not extraordinary that the same impression should have been made upon a Hebrew observer.

8 All things toil to weariness;
Man cannot utter it,
The eye is not satisfied with seeing,
Nor the ear filled with hearing.

9 That which hath been is that which shall be,
And that which hath been done is that which shall be done;
And there is nothing new under the sun.

10. Is there a thing whereof it is said:
'See, this is new'?—it hath been already, in the ages which were before
us. 11. There is no remembrance

8 כָּל־הַדְּבָרִים יְגֵעִים לֹא־
יוּכַל אִישׁ לְדַבֵּר לֹא־תִשְׂבַּע
עַיִן לִרְאוֹת וְלֹא־תִמָּלֵא אֹזֶן
9 מִשְּׁמֹעַ׃ מַה־שֶּׁהָיָה הוּא
שֶׁיִּהְיֶה וּמַה־שֶּׁנַּעֲשָׂה הוּא
שֶׁיֵּעָשֶׂה וְאֵין כָּל־חָדָשׁ תַּחַת
10 הַשָּׁמֶשׁ׃ יֵשׁ דָּבָר שֶׁיֹּאמַר
רְאֵה־זֶה חָדָשׁ הוּא כְּבָר הָיָה
לְעֹלָמִים אֲשֶׁר הָיָה מִלְּפָנֵנוּ׃
11 אֵין זִכְרוֹן לָרִאשֹׁנִים וְגַם

8. *all things.* i.e. there are many other illustrations to be drawn from nature which have the same peculiarity. The Hebrew may also signify 'all words'; the sense would then be: the power of speech possessed by man is unequal to the task of describing the uselessness of everything in the universe.

*the eye . . . hearing.* Two different explanations have been offered for the last two lines of the verse. The meaning may be that neither the eye nor the ear of man is able to take in all this weariness. A more natural interpretation is that 'the meaningless rounds of nature communicate themselves to the spirit of man, so that eye and ear enter upon endless courses of seeing and hearing that never satisfy' (Barton). The Jewish commentators understand the verse in a spiritual sense. Rashi comments that if a man exchanges preoccupation with the Torah for profane, empty talk, then he toils to weariness, and can never attain anything. If his eye is busied with the externalities of sight, the eye will not be satisfied; and if the ear with mere listening, his ear will never be filled.

9. *that which hath been.* The monotonous sameness which Koheleth found in natural phenomena he likewise detects in human life. All movement is in a circle without any progress being achieved. Everywhere and always there is sameness and no novelty.

10. *see, this is new.* He meets the challenge that his statement is too sweeping and new things are made or discovered, by dogmatically asserting that, in reality, they are old. This point of view was held by the Stoics. Marcus Aurelius, for example, wrote, 'They that come after us will see nothing new, and they who went before us saw nothing more than we have seen.' A modern commentator remarked, 'We who are proud of our modern civilization are continually discovering that many of our most vaunted novelties were known to the ancient world' (Martin).

11. *there is no remembrance of them.* With these words Koheleth sums up the prologue with its theme of the vanity of life and the endless, monotonous cycle of nature. Things seem new only because

of them of former times; neither
shall there be any remembrance of
them of latter times that are to come,
among those that shall come after.

12. I Koheleth have been king over
Israel in Jerusalem. 13. And I
applied my heart to seek and to
search out by wisdom concerning all
things that are done under heaven;
it is a sore task that God hath given
to the sons of men to be exercised
therewith. 14. I have seen all the

לאחרנים שיהיו לא־יהיה
להם זכרון עם שיהיו
12 לאחרנה׃ אני קהלת הייתי
מלך על־ישראל בירושלם׃
13 ונתתי את־לבי לדרוש
ולתור בחכמה על כל־אשר
נעשה תחת השמים הוא ׀
ענין רע נתן אלהים לבני
14 האדם לענות בו׃ ראיתי

men have forgotten what went before. This fact creates another of the ideas which haunt his mind and induce a pessimistic mood. Not only is man a transient creature (verse 4), but he lives to no purpose in that he passes into oblivion. That is true of those who preceded him, and it will be true of those who succeed him. Consequently any distinction which he gains is only of temporary worth and, for that reason, in reality valueless.

### 12-18 VANITY OF THE QUEST FOR WISDOM

The author, speaking in the person of king Solomon, relates his search for wisdom to discover whether it held a permanent satisfaction in life. What he found was, in the words of an Arabic proverb, that 'a wise man is never happy.' The Midrash points out that the Book should properly have begun here, because Koheleth passed judgment in the prologue before describing his several quests; and the answer is given that the Torah does not always follow a chronological order.

12. *have been king.* According to a Rabbinic tradition, Koheleth went through three turns of fortune: king, commoner and again king; wise, foolish and again wise; rich, poor and again rich. Ibn Ezra finds in the past tense of the verb evidence that Solomon wrote the Book in old age at the end of his reign. The statement is not decisive either way on the question of the author's identity. 'It would, perhaps, be too much to say that this mode of introducing himself is so artificial as to exclude, as some have thought, the authorship of the historical Solomon. Louis XIV's way of speaking of himself "Quand j'etois roi" may well have had its parallel in the old age of another king weary of the trappings and the garb of majesty. As little, however, can they be held to prove that authorship' (Plumptre).

*king.* Holding that powerful office, he had the fullest opportunities to conduct his experiments with the best chance of success.

13. *I applied my heart.* lit. 'I gave my heart'; applied myself diligently and to the utmost of my powers. It is a favourite phrase of the author and occurs again in verse 17, viii. 9, 16.

*by wisdom.* 'The censure here is not upon *absolute* wisdom, for this the sacred writer praises in the sequel; but upon wisdom acquired for the purpose of guiding in the gratification of his desires, and for finding in it solid happiness' (Ginsburg).

*under heaven.* A variant of *under the sun*

works that are done under the sun; and, behold, all is vanity and a striving after wind.

15 That which is crooked cannot be made straight;
And that which is wanting cannot be numbered.

16. I spoke with my own heart, saying: 'Lo, I have gotten great wisdom, more also than all that were before me over Jerusalem'; yea, my heart hath had great experience of wisdom and knowledge. 17. And I applied

אֶת־כָּל־הַמַּעֲשִׂים שֶׁנַּעֲשׂוּ
תַּחַת הַשָּׁמֶשׁ וְהִנֵּה הַכֹּל הֶבֶל
15 וּרְעוּת רוּחַ׃ מְעֻוָּת לֹא־יוּכַל
לִתְקֹן וְחֶסְרוֹן לֹא־יוּכַל
16 לְהִמָּנוֹת׃ דִּבַּרְתִּי אֲנִי עִם־
לִבִּי לֵאמֹר אֲנִי הִנֵּה הִגְדַּלְתִּי
וְהוֹסַפְתִּי חָכְמָה עַל כָּל־
אֲשֶׁר־הָיָה לְפָנַי עַל־יְרוּשָׁלִָם
וְלִבִּי רָאָה הַרְבֵּה חָכְמָה
17 וָדָעַת׃ וָאֶתְּנָה לִבִּי לָדַעַת

(verse 3). His search embraced all the usual pursuits of man.

*a sore task.* That is his final summing up which he states before recounting the inquiry that led to it.

*God hath given.* In spite of his bitter dissatisfaction it does not enter his mind to deny the existence of God. However unsatisfactory life may appear to be and however heavy the burdens it places upon men, everything has been ordained by Him. It is to be noted that Koheleth always designates the Deity as *Elohim* and never uses the Tetragrammaton, an indication that he thinks of Him throughout the Book as the Ruler of the universe, not as the God of Israel.

14. *all the works that are done.* His condemnation is all-embracing. He finds nothing in man's labours and activities which he can exclude from his pessimistic verdict. The noun and verb perhaps have the meaning common in Rabbinic Hebrew, 'all the occurrences that occur.' If taken in their usual sense, the remark of Martin is apposite: 'Surely nothing can be sadder than to say that all the works of human enterprise are perfectly fruitless—that life, therefore, both theoretically and practically, is a mockery.'

*a striving after wind.* The vivid expression is one of Koheleth's favourite ways of describing the futility and emptiness of his quest. To reach a satisfying goal is as hopeless as to catch the wind which, if one caught, would be of no use to him. It occurs seven times in the Book. Another possible translation is 'a feeding on wind,' which does not relieve the pangs of hunger (cf. *feedeth on folly*, Prov. xv. 14).

15. This verse is in poetical form and may be a proverb quoted by the author. It expresses the mood in which he conducts his examination. He sees many things in human society which are *crooked*, but how they are to be *made straight* baffles him; similarly he detects so many deficiencies that they cannot be numbered.

16. *I spoke with my own heart.* i.e. I communed within myself, I reflected.

*I have gotten.* The subject is emphatic in the Hebrew.

*all that were . . . Jerusalem.* The capital

my heart to know wisdom, and to know madness and folly—I perceived that this also was a striving after wind.

18 For in much wisdom is much vexation;
And he that increaseth knowledge increaseth sorrow.

חָכְמָה וְדַעַת הֹלֵלוֹת וְשִׂכְלוּת
יָדַעְתִּי שֶׁגַּם־זֶה הוּא רַעְיוֹן
18 רוּחַ׃ כִּי בְּרֹב חָכְמָה רָב־
כָּעַס וְיוֹסִיף דַּעַת יוֹסִיף
מַכְאוֹב׃

## 2 CHAPTER II ב

1. I said in my heart: 'Come now, I will try thee with mirth, and enjoy pleasure'; and, behold, this also was vanity. 2. I said of laughter: 'It

1 אָמַרְתִּי אֲנִי בְּלִבִּי לְכָה־נָּא
אֲנַסְּכָה בְשִׂמְחָה וּרְאֵה בְטוֹב
2 וְהִנֵּה גַם־הוּא הָבֶל׃ לִשְׂחוֹק

was famed as a city of wisdom (see on i. 1) and in former times was the home of renowned sages (1 Kings v. 11).

*hath had great experience of.* lit. 'hath seen much of.' Maimonides remarked that the verb alludes to 'intellectual perception.'

17. *and to know madness and folly.* For the purpose of a complete investigation, he did not restrict himself to the study of wisdom, but also included the manifestations of its opposite as displayed by his fellow-men.

*striving.* Not the same word as in verse 14, but it occurs again in iv. 16.

18. Like verse 15, this verse is also in poetical form and is possibly a proverbial saying. It tells of the disappointment which the search for knowledge brings in its train; it seems to lead nowhere. The possession of wisdom merely serves to reveal more realistically the imperfections of the world order, thereby increasing one's weariness and unhappiness.

## CHAPTER II

### 1-11 VANITY OF WORLDLY PLEASURES

DISCOVERING the vanity of the pursuit of wisdom, Koheleth turns to wine and the pleasures that earth affords to the wealthy. These, too, give only temporary satisfaction; in the end they prove to be vain and profitless. The details fit in exactly with what is known of Solomon. Koheleth either describes his personal experience, or attributes to himself what had been related of the Israelite king.

1. *I said in my heart.* Since I have found disillusionment in the acquisition of wisdom.

*come, now.* Cf. Isa. i. 18, a call to action.

*mirth.* lit. 'gladness,' meaning that which gives pleasure to the physical senses. The Midrash and later Jewish expositors hold that the allusion is more particularly to indulgence in wine.

*enjoy pleasure.* lit. 'look upon what is good,' i.e. participate in the dissipations of men who are not guided by wisdom. Jastrow explains that the phrase is 'a is mad'; and of mirth: 'What doth it accomplish?' 3. I searched in my heart how to pamper my flesh with wine, and, my heart conducting itself with wisdom, how yet to lay hold on folly, till I might see which it was best for the sons of men that they should do under the heaven the few days of their life. 4. I made me great works; I builded me houses; I planted me vineyards; 5. I made me gardens and parks, and I planted trees in them of all kinds of fruit;

אָמַרְתִּי מְהוֹלָל וּלְשִׂמְחָה
3 מַה־זֹּה עֹשָׂה׃ תַּרְתִּי בְלִבִּי
לִמְשׁוֹךְ בַּיַּיִן אֶת־בְּשָׂרִי וְלִבִּי
נֹהֵג בַּחָכְמָה וְלֶאֱחֹז בְּסִכְלוּת
עַד | אֲשֶׁר אֶרְאֶה אֵי־זֶה טוֹב
לִבְנֵי הָאָדָם אֲשֶׁר יַעֲשׂוּ תַּחַת
הַשָּׁמַיִם מִסְפַּר יְמֵי חַיֵּיהֶם׃
4 הִגְדַּלְתִּי מַעֲשָׂי בָּנִיתִי לִי בָּתִּים
5 נָטַעְתִּי לִי כְּרָמִים׃ עָשִׂיתִי לִי
גַּנּוֹת וּפַרְדֵּסִים וְנָטַעְתִּי בָהֶם

perfect equivalent to our colloquial "having a good time,"' and adds, 'Koheleth is not afraid of using the expressive slang of his day.'

2. *laughter.* Merriment and frivolity, in contrast to the serious mood of a sage.

*it is mad.* There is no sense in it.

*what doth it accomplish?* What is the use of it? The answer is nothing. 'Koheleth does not denounce innocent cheerfulness and pleasure, for this he himself recommends in the sequel. What he repudiates is, that rational man, seeing the inability of wisdom to calm the mind saddened by the admonition of everything around that it has no abiding place here, and aching after solid happiness, should betake himself to pleasure and mirth, in the vain hope thereby to quiet the voice of reason' (Ginsburg).

3. *to pamper.* lit. 'to draw, drag along.' Its force here is' to attract' as in Rabbinic Hebrew.

*my heart . . . wisdom.* Rather, 'my heart guiding (me) with wisdom,' i.e. he did not plunge blindly into dissipation, but consciously experimented with it to understand its effects.

*folly.* The opposite of the life controlled by wisdom.

*the few days.* lit. 'the (limited) number of the days.'

4. *I made me great works.* The Hebrew is 'I magnified my works,' which means that he constructed on a large scale. To increase his pleasure, he surrounded himself with objects which added to his physical comfort.

*houses.* Cf. 1 Kings vii. 1ff., 8, ix. 17ff., for an account of Solomon's vast building operations.

*vineyards.* Cf. Cant. viii. 11. During Solomon's reign *every man* (dwelt) *under his vine and under his fig-tree* (1 Kings v. 5).

5. *parks.* Hebrew *pardes,* a Persian word from which 'paradise' is derived (again Cant. iv. 13; Nehem. ii. 8).

6. I made me pools of water, to water therefrom the wood springing up with trees; 7. I acquired men-servants and maid-servants, and had servants born in my house; also I had great possessions of herds and flocks, above all that were before me in Jerusalem; 8. I gathered me also silver and gold, and treasure such as kings and the provinces have as their own; I got me men-singers and

6 עֵ֥ץ כָּל־פֶּֽרִי׃ עָשִׂ֥יתִי לִ֖י
בְּרֵכ֣וֹת מָ֑יִם לְהַשְׁק֣וֹת מֵהֶ֔ם
7 יַ֖עַר צוֹמֵ֥חַ עֵצִֽים׃ קָנִ֙יתִי֙
עֲבָדִ֣ים וּשְׁפָח֔וֹת וּבְנֵי־בַ֖יִת
הָ֣יָה לִ֑י גַּם֩ מִקְנֶ֨ה בָקָ֧ר וָצֹ֛אן
הַרְבֵּ֥ה הָ֣יָה לִ֔י מִכֹּ֥ל שֶׁהָי֖וּ
8 לְפָנַ֥י בִּירוּשָׁלִָֽם׃ כָּנַ֤סְתִּי לִי֙
גַּם־כֶּ֣סֶף וְזָהָ֔ב וּסְגֻלַּ֥ת מְלָכִ֖ים
וְהַמְּדִינ֑וֹת עָשִׂ֨יתִי לִ֜י שָׁרִ֣ים

6. *pools of water.* Not to depend upon the rain-fall which may be deficient, he had excavations made in which water was collected and stored to supply the young trees with life-giving moisture. The *king's pool* (Nehem. ii. 14) is called by Josephus 'Solomon's Pool' (War, V. iv. 2).

7. *men-servants and maid-servants.* A large retinue of servants was required for the upkeep of the many, huge palaces, parks, etc. The Queen of Sheba was amazed at *the sitting of his* (Solomon's) *servants and the attendance of his ministers* (1 Kings x. 5).

*and had servants . . . house.* A paraphrase of the Hebrew which is literally 'and children of the house were to me.' Besides the slaves he bought, he also possessed the children born to them. The latter were held to be of a higher status and were assigned more responsible tasks in connection with the household (cf. Gen. xiv. 14, xv. 3).

*great possessions of herds and flocks.* To feed his army of dependants, Solomon required daily *ten fat oxen, and twenty oxen out of the pastures, and a hundred sheep*, etc. (1 Kings v. 3).

8. *silver and gold.* This may mean the precious metal in the form of ingots, but also vessels of silver and gold such as befitted a monarch. When the king of Assyria imposed upon Hezekiah a tribute of *three hundred talents of silver and thirty talents of gold,* he paid it partly from *the treasures of the king's house* (2 Kings xviii. 14f.). This Israelite king also displayed to the messengers of the Babylonian king *all his treasure-house, the silver and the gold* (2 Kings xx. 13).

*and treasure . . . own.* More lit. 'and the possession of kings and the provinces,' i.e. levies exacted from tributary rulers and countries. It was said of Solomon that he received gold *of all the kings of the mingled people and of the governors of the country* (1 Kings x. 15). The Hebrew word *segullah,* translated 'peculiar treasure' by A.V. and R.V., signifies 'property.' It occurs in the phrase *peculiar people* applied to Israel as God's possession.

*I got me.* lit. 'I made for myself.' The verb is employed here with the meaning 'acquired' (cf. *and the souls that they had gotten* (lit. made) *in Haran,* Gen. xii. 5).

*men-singers and women-singers.* To entertain the guests with music at the banquets held by the king (cf. Isa. v. 12; Amos vi. 5) as well as for his own pleasure.

women-singers, and the delights of the sons of men, women very many. 9. So I was great, and increased more than all that were before me in Jerusalem; also my wisdom stood me in stead. 10. And whatsoever mine eyes desired I kept not from them; I withheld not my heart from any joy, for my heart had joy of all my labour; and this was my portion from all my labour. 11. Then I looked on all the

וְשָׁרוֹת וְתַעֲנֻגוֹת בְּנֵי הָאָדָם
9 שִׁדָּה וְשִׁדּוֹת׃ וְגָדַלְתִּי
וְהוֹסַפְתִּי מִכֹּל שֶׁהָיָה לְפָנַי
בִּירוּשָׁלָםִ אַף חָכְמָתִי עָמְדָה
10 לִּי׃ וְכֹל אֲשֶׁר שָׁאֲלוּ עֵינַי לֹא
אָצַלְתִּי מֵהֶם לֹא־מָנַעְתִּי
אֶת־לִבִּי מִכָּל־שִׂמְחָה כִּי־
לִבִּי שָׂמֵחַ מִכָּל־עֲמָלִי וְזֶה־
הָיָה חֶלְקִי מִכָּל־עֲמָלִי׃
11 וּפָנִיתִי אֲנִי בְּכָל־מַעֲשַׂי שֶׁעָשׂוּ

*delights*. The word connotes sensual indulgences.

*women very many*. An obscure phrase. A.V. 'musical instruments' follows Kimchi, and R.V. 'concubines' is derived from Ibn Ezra who connects *shiddah* with the root *shadad* '(women) taken by violence.' The context seems to indicate the occupants of the royal harem. The phraseology, which is literally 'a concubine and concubines,' may be compared with *a damsel, two damsels* (Judges v. 30), i.e. several damsels.

**9.** *I was great, and increased*. The Hebrew verbs are like those in i. 16, *I have gotten great wisdom*, and are deliberately repeated to point out that as he exceeded all predecessors in wisdom, he also surpassed them in material splendour. Jastrow sees in the verse a 'sarcastic touch, that the greatness of kings consists in having large possessions and in surrounding themselves with luxuries, slaves and courtesans'; but this may be reading into the words what is not implicit in them.

*stood me in stead*. lit. 'stood to (or, for) me.' The translation of A.J. means that his wisdom helped him to acquire his unequalled status. Others take it to signify that he did not lose his hold on wisdom while surrounded by inducements to indulge in dissipation (A.V. and R.V. 'remained with me'; see on verse 3).

**10.** *desired*. lit. 'asked.' He went to the extreme and threw off all restraint to his desires by gratifying every whim. His object was to discover whether this course made living worth while.

*joy*. The same Hebrew word as *mirth* in verse 1.

*had joy of all my labour*. His efforts to sink himself in debauchery were successful and he experienced all the sensations to be gained from this way of life.

*portion*. The reward which accrued from his endeavours.

**11.** *I looked*. lit. 'I turned,' which means 'I turned to look,' to take stock of the situation. 'It implies that Koheleth turned from the absorption of his active material labours and his sensual pleasures to consider the meaning of them all, and finds that, like the delights of wisdom, the delights of possession are but vanity' (Barton).

works that my hands had wrought, and on the labour that I had laboured to do; and, behold, all was vanity and a striving after wind, and there was no profit under the sun.

12. And I turned myself to behold wisdom, and madness and folly; for what can the man do that cometh after the king? even that which hath been already done. 13. Then I saw that wisdom excelleth folly, as far as light excelleth darkness.

יָדַי וּבֶעָמָל שֶׁעָמַלְתִּי לַעֲשׂוֹת
וְהִנֵּה הַכֹּל הֶבֶל וּרְעוּת רוּחַ
וְאֵין יִתְרוֹן תַּחַת הַשָּׁמֶשׁ׃
12 וּפָנִיתִי אֲנִי לִרְאוֹת חָכְמָה
וְהוֹלֵלוֹת וְסִכְלוּת כִּי ׀ מֶה
הָאָדָם שֶׁיָּבוֹא אַחֲרֵי הַמֶּלֶךְ
אֵת אֲשֶׁר־כְּבָר עָשׂוּהוּ׃
13 וְרָאִיתִי אָנִי שֶׁיֵּשׁ יִתְרוֹן
לַחָכְמָה מִן־הַסִּכְלוּת
כִּיתְרוֹן הָאוֹר מִן־הַחֹשֶׁךְ׃

*the works.* As detailed in verses 4ff.

*the labour.* The care and thought expended in the preparation and execution of the designs.

**12-17 WISDOM AND FOLLY EQUALLY VAIN**

In this section Koheleth dwells more fully than in i. 17f., on the lesson he drew from his search for wisdom and folly. There he stated the conclusion that no happiness resulted from wisdom and knowledge, but he had not summed them up against folly to estimate whether the former possessed any superiority over the latter. This he proceeds to do in the following verses.

12. *I turned myself.* The same verb as *I looked* in verse 11 with the same meaning.

*wisdom . . . folly.* As in i. 17.

*for what . . . done.* lit. 'for what the man who will come after the king? that which they have already done.' The general sense is evident although the exact translation is uncertain. The subject of *I turned* is emphasized in the Hebrew, and so presents a contrast to what follows: I, the king, with every advantage at my command, have made this investigation. Of what use is it for a commoner to repeat the experiment after me? He can only go over the same ground with smaller resources at his disposal. The impersonal subject, 'they have already made,' may be the Hebrew idiom to denote the passive, *that which hath been already done*; but some MSS. point the verb as singular, *asahu*, 'which he hath already done' (the Jewish commentator, Sforno, appears to have had this reading), giving the translation, 'for what can a (common) man (do) that cometh after the king? (Only) what he (the king) hath already done.' He cannot do any more, so the inquiry must be considered final.

13. *then I saw.* The *I* is emphatic. 'I the doubter and explorer. For I have taken nothing on credit. I have myself investigated the matter' (Williams).

*wisdom excelleth folly.* More lit. 'there is profit to wisdom over folly,' the Hebrew word, *yithron*, being the same as in i. 3. A man of Koheleth's intellect and insight could not possibly decide that wisdom and folly were on precisely the same level. The possession of wisdom was unquestionably an advantage in the battle of life, and the wise man was more often the victor than the fool.

14 The wise man, his eyes are in his head;
But the fool walketh in darkness.

And I also perceived that one event
happeneth to them all. 15. Then
said I in my heart: 'As it happeneth
to the fool, so will it happen even to
me; and why was I then more wise?'
Then I said in my heart, that this
also is vanity. 16. For of the wise

14 הֶחָכָם עֵינָיו בְּרֹאשׁוֹ וְהַכְּסִיל
בַּחֹשֶׁךְ הוֹלֵךְ וְיָדַעְתִּי גַם־אָנִי
שֶׁמִּקְרֶה אֶחָד יִקְרֶה אֶת־
15 כֻּלָּם׃ וְאָמַרְתִּי אֲנִי בְּלִבִּי
כְּמִקְרֵה הַכְּסִיל גַּם־אֲנִי
יִקְרֵנִי וְלָמָּה חָכַמְתִּי אֲנִי אָז
יֹתֵר וְדִבַּרְתִּי בְלִבִּי שֶׁגַּם־זֶה
16 הָבֶל׃ כִּי אֵין זִכְרוֹן לֶחָכָם

*as far as light excelleth darkness.* lit. 'like the profit of the light over the darkness,' making a comparison with two conditions which are diametrically opposite, one having an obvious advantage over the other.

**14.** The first half of the verse is doubtless a proverb in the form of a poetical couplet. '*Light* and *darkness*, used in the preceding verse to show the superiority of wisdom over folly in the abstract, have suggested in this verse the figurative use of "open and closed eyes," to illustrate these qualities as manifest in the concrete' (Ginsburg).

*his eyes are in his head.* He foresees the end of his action before he begins it and desists if it will prove injurious (Rashi). Ibn Ezra's explanation is preferable: he keeps his eyes open and makes for his desired goal by the most direct route.

*walketh in darkness.* Groping his way uncertainly and falling over stumbling-blocks.

*and I also perceived.* Better, 'but even I perceived'; although he admits the superiority of wisdom, he cannot overlook a factor which counteracts its advantage when one takes the long view.

*one event happeneth to them all.* Ultimately the possessor of wisdom and the fool have a like end, because death is the fate which overtakes them both. This reflection is often in the author's mind to depress him (cf. iii. 19, ix. 2f.).

**15.** *as it happeneth.* The fool will die and so will I, notwithstanding my wisdom.

*why was I then more wise?* Of what use were my labours to excel in wisdom and knowledge?

*this also is vanity.* viz. the effort and ambition to become wise.

**16.** *for of the wise . . . ever.* lit. 'for there is no remembrance to the wise man (equally) with the fool for ever.' Sooner or later they are both forgotten. Here, as in i. 11, his mind is troubled by the reflection that when life is over, nothing of it remains in the memory of man. He feels that to be true of the wise and foolish alike. Other Biblical writers did draw a distinction: *The righteous shall be had in everlasting remembrance* (Ps. cxii. 6), *The memory of the righteous shall be for a blessing; but the name of the wicked shall rot* (Prov. x. 7).

man, even as of the fool, there is no remembrance for ever; seeing that in the days to come all will long ago have been forgotten. And how must the wise man die even as the fool!

17. So I hated life; because the work that is wrought under the sun was grievous unto me; for all is vanity and a striving after wind.

18. And I hated all my labour wherein I laboured under the sun, seeing that I must leave it unto the man that shall be after me. 19. And who knoweth whether he will be a wise man or a fool? yet will he have rule over all my labour wherein I

עִם־הַכְּסִיל לְעוֹלָם בְּשֶׁכְּבָר
הַיָּמִים הַבָּאִים הַכֹּל נִשְׁכָּח
וְאֵיךְ יָמוּת הֶחָכָם עִם־
17 הַכְּסִיל׃ וְשָׂנֵאתִי אֶת־הַחַיִּים
כִּי רַע עָלַי הַמַּעֲשֶׂה שֶׁנַּעֲשָׂה
תַּחַת הַשָּׁמֶשׁ כִּי־הַכֹּל הֶבֶל
18 וּרְעוּת רוּחַ׃ וְשָׂנֵאתִי אֲנִי אֶת־
כָּל־עֲמָלִי שֶׁאֲנִי עָמֵל תַּחַת
הַשָּׁמֶשׁ שֶׁאַנִּיחֶנּוּ לָאָדָם שֶׁיִּהְיֶה
19 אַחֲרָי׃ וּמִי יוֹדֵעַ הֶחָכָם יִהְיֶה
אוֹ סָכָל וְיִשְׁלַט בְּכָל־עֲמָלִי

*all will long ago have been forgotten.* 'It is easy to discover flaws in the logic of the pessimist. The night is never so dark as it appears to him. *For of the wise man, even as of the fool, there is no remembrance for ever*, he says. And, whilst he is speaking, he is impersonating Solomon, whose wisdom has immortalized him!' (Devine). But what if it is Solomon himself speaking?

*and how.* An exclamation denoting a complaint (cf. *how then comfort ye me in vain?* Job xxi. 34).

17. *so I hated life.* Life as he interpreted it at that stage was hateful to him, because its content appeared meaningless and purposeless. Existence terminated in death which put the seal upon every human activity and deprived every good quality of its value. 'As a matter of fact, Koheleth loves life, and this inconsistency, of which there are other examples, adds to the charm of the Book. *A living dog*, runs a passage that has become famous, *is better than a dead lion* (ix. 4)' Jastrow).

*the work that is wrought.* See on i. 14.

*grievous unto me.* lit. 'evil upon me.' irksome and distasteful.

### 18-23 FUTILITY OF TOIL

Besides the thought that, in spite of a man's achievements, his destiny is to be forgotten, another consideration crosses the speaker's mind to intensify his depression, viz. he worked hard and sagaciously, but the fruits of his toil may pass into the hands of an heir who will deal with them unwisely.

18. *all my labour.* He thinks of his constructive works which are enumerated in verses 4ff.

*leave it unto the man.* His complaint now is not that death deprives him of ownership, although this idea will occur later (cf. v. 14), but the type of man who may be his heir.

19. *who knoweth.* An expression used by Koheleth to denote a doubt. They who identify him with Solomon find in the verse the father's concern about Rehoboam who was the successor to the throne. Otherwise, the words have to be interpreted as a general experience.

have laboured, and wherein I have shown myself wise under the sun. This also is vanity. 20. Therefore I turned about to cause my heart to despair concerning all the labour wherein I had laboured under the sun. 21. For there is a man whose labour is with wisdom, and with knowledge, and with skill; yet to a man that hath not laboured therein shall he leave it for his portion. This also is vanity and a great evil. 22. For what hath a man of all his labour, and of the striving of his heart, wherein he laboureth under the sun? 23. For all his days are pains, and his occu-

שֶׁעָמַלְתִּי וְשֶׁחָכַמְתִּי תַּחַת
20 הַשָּׁמֶשׁ גַּם־זֶה הָבֶל׃ וְסַבּוֹתִי
אֲנִי לְיַאֵשׁ אֶת־לִבִּי עַל כָּל־
הֶעָמָל שֶׁעָמַלְתִּי תַּחַת הַשָּׁמֶשׁ׃
21 כִּי־יֵשׁ אָדָם שֶׁעֲמָלוֹ בְּחָכְמָה
וּבְדַעַת וּבְכִשְׁרוֹן וּלְאָדָם
שֶׁלֹּא עָמַל־בּוֹ יִתְּנֶנּוּ חֶלְקוֹ
22 גַּם־זֶה הֶבֶל וְרָעָה רַבָּה׃ כִּי
מֶה־הֹוֶה לָאָדָם בְּכָל־עֲמָלוֹ
וּבְרַעְיוֹן לִבּוֹ שֶׁהוּא עָמֵל
23 תַּחַת הַשָּׁמֶשׁ׃ כִּי כָל־יָמָיו

**20.** *I turned about.* This is not the same verb as in verses 11f. which connotes a mental turning. Here it expresses a turning of the body. He is like a traveller who turns round to survey the country through which he is passing and feels appalled at what he sees, and asks himself whether his journey is worth the discomforts he has to endure.

**21.** *for there is.* Rather, 'for should there be a man whose labour has been with wisdom.'

*skill.* The noun *kishron* recurs in iv. 4, v. 10, and is restricted to this Book. The root meaning is 'to be proper,' and here the signification is 'advantage'; he toiled successfully.

*a man that hath not laboured.* Since the estate comes to him as an inheritance, he does not prize it as highly as does the person who worked to build it up, and may therefore squander it.

**22.** *what hath a man.* Viewed from this angle, the toiler exhausts his mind and strength to no enduring purpose. The corrective, which is inculcated by the Rabbis, that a man should work for posterity, even as his predecessors toiled for his benefit, is left out of the argument. The Midrash, however, explained *I turned about* (verse 20) as 'I reconsidered,' and declared that Koheleth adopted that standpoint eventually. In this connection it related that the Emperor Hadrian saw a very aged man planting some young trees. 'How old are you?' he asked, and received the reply, 'I am one hundred years.' 'And do you expect to eat the fruit of the trees you are planting?' he inquired. The old man answered, 'If I am worthy, I shall eat; if not, as my forefathers toiled for me, I toil for my children.'

**23.** *all his days.* The contrast is *even in the night*; therefore, as Ibn Ezra comments, *days* must indicate the hours when a man is awake and works. He translates: 'for during all his day-time his occupation (produces) pains and vexation.'

pation vexation; yea, even in the
night his heart taketh no rest. This
also is vanity.

24. There is nothing better for a
man than that he should eat and
drink, and make his soul enjoy
pleasure for his labour. This also I
saw, that it is from the hand of God.
25. For who will eat, or who will
enjoy, if not I? 26. For to the man

מַכְאוֹבִים וָכַעַס עִנְיָנוֹ גַּם־
בַּלַּיְלָה לֹא־שָׁכַב לִבּוֹ גַּם־זֶה
24 הֶבֶל הוּא׃ אֵין־טוֹב בָּאָדָם
שֶׁיֹּאכַל וְשָׁתָה וְהֶרְאָה אֶת־
נַפְשׁוֹ טוֹב בַּעֲמָלוֹ גַּם־זֹה
רָאִיתִי אָנִי כִּי מִיַּד הָאֱלֹהִים
25 הִיא׃ כִּי מִי יֹאכַל וּמִי יָחוּשׁ
26 חוּץ מִמֶּנִּי׃ כִּי לְאָדָם שֶׁטּוֹב

*taketh no rest.* His worries, connected with his schemes, disturb his sleep.

24-26 ENJOY LIFE AS FAR AS POSSIBLE

24. *there is nothing better for a man.* So A.V. and R.V., but this translation does not correspond to the Hebrew. Rashi understood the first clause as a question, 'Is there no good in man that he (just) eats and drinks?' i.e. he should have other aims in living, and Rashi quotes as a parallel, *Did not thy father eat and drink, and do justice and righteousness?* (Jer. xxii. 15). This interpretation, however, does not agree with the mood of Koheleth. Ibn Ezra's rendering is better, 'There is no good in man (except) that he eat and drink.' Notwithstanding the emptiness of labour when one considers what is to become of it after the toiler's death, the proper course to adopt is to enjoy its fruits as long as one may.

*and make his soul enjoy pleasure.* lit. 'and show his soul good,' *soul* being employed in the sense of 'appetite, physical desire' as often in Proverbs (x. 3, xiii. 25, xxvii. 7).

*I saw.* I perceived, understood (as in i. 16).

*it is from the hand of God.* The Creator's will is that man should find pleasure in life from the work of his hands. 'The contradiction to verses 1, 2, 11 is only apparent, not real. Material pleasures cannot, it is true, yield absolute happiness; but *in practice* it is possible to derive much happiness from them' (Williams).

25. *for who will eat.* Better, 'for who should eat and who enjoy except me?' He means, since he has worked to accumulate all these objects which give delight to the senses, it would be absurd if he did not exercise his right to participate in them.

26. This verse, with the exception of the final clause, is best understood as parenthetical and the reader should think of it as though printed within brackets. It illustrates the statement *it is from the hand of God* (verse 24). As in i. 13 Koheleth here has the awareness that the universe is controlled by its Creator and human life is directed by Him. The good man's lot is awarded by Him, as also the fate of the wicked person who

that is good in His sight He giveth wisdom, and knowledge, and joy; but to the sinner He giveth the task, to gather and to heap up, that he may leave to him that is good in the sight of God. This also is vanity and a striving after wind.

לְפָנָיו נָתַן חָכְמָה וְדַעַת
וְשִׂמְחָה וְלַחוֹטֶא נָתַן עִנְיָן
לֶאֱסֹף וְלִכְנוֹס לָתֵת לְטוֹב
לִפְנֵי הָאֱלֹהִים גַּם־זֶה הֶבֶל
וּרְעוּת רוּחַ׃

## 3 CHAPTER III ג

1. To every thing there is a season, and a time to every purpose under the heaven:

2 A time to be born, and a time to die;
A time to plant, and a time to pluck up that which is planted;

1 לַכֹּל זְמָן וְעֵת לְכָל־חֵפֶץ
תַּחַת הַשָּׁמָיִם׃
2 עֵת לָלֶדֶת וְעֵת לָמוּת
עֵת לָטַעַת וְעֵת לַעֲקוֹר
נָטוּעַ׃

accumulates wealth which he is not permitted to enjoy and ultimately passes into the possession of the virtuous. For this last thought, cf. Prov. xiii. 22, xxviii. 8; Job xxvii. 16f.

*this also is vanity.* The reference is to verse 24. Even the adoption of the rule to draw personal pleasure from one's labour fails to yield satisfaction.

## CHAPTER III

### 1-15 EVERYTHING IS ORDAINED

One interpretation of this section is that 'it is wisdom to do the right thing at the right time' (Plumptre), but it does not fit into the train of thought which Koheleth is pursuing. More acceptable is the view that he gives another argument to establish the futility of all work and effort, and this he finds in the doctrine of determinism. All the events of life are part of a fixed scheme; they happen to the human being whether he wills them or not; therefore individual effort is abortive.

1. *a season.* The Hebrew word is only found in the later Books of the Bible and denotes 'a fixed period.'

*a time.* i.e. an appointed time.

*purpose.* lit. 'desire, pleasure,' then the enterprise in which one takes pleasure, 'affairs' (cf. Isa. lviii. 3, 13, where it is translated *business*).

2. *a time to be born . . . die.* The list begins with the two most important events in a person's existence, birth and death, which are beyond his control. The possibility of determining the time of death by suicide is not taken into consideration. A Rabbi homiletically eliminated the fatalistic implication of the statement by explaining: Happy the man whose hour of death is like the hour of his birth; as he was pure at birth so should he be pure at the time of death.

*to plant . . . pluck up.* An analogy to

3 A time to kill, and a time to heal;
A time to break down, and a time to build up;

4 A time to weep, and a time to laugh;
A time to mourn, and a time to dance;

5 A time to cast away stones, and a time to gather stones together;
A time to embrace, and a time to refrain from embracing;

3 עֵת לַהֲרוֹג וְעֵת לִרְפּוֹא
עֵת לִפְרוֹץ וְעֵת לִבְנוֹת׃
4 עֵת לִבְכּוֹת וְעֵת לִשְׂחוֹק
עֵת סְפוֹד וְעֵת רְקוֹד׃
5 עֵת לְהַשְׁלִיךְ אֲבָנִים
וְעֵת כְּנוֹס אֲבָנִים
עֵת לַחֲבוֹק
וְעֵת לִרְחֹק מֵחַבֵּק׃

human life is found in the world of vegetation. There, too, the times are ordained for sowing seed and harvesting the growth of the field.

3. *to kill . . . heal.* That life can be ended by an act of violence might be adduced as a contradiction of the assertion that there is *a time to die*; but Koheleth insists that death is never premature, and if a man is killed, that is his predetermined end. Should, however, he recover from the wound or from an illness which might have been fatal, that also is not accidental but ordained.

*break down . . . build up.* As with the fate of the individual, so it is with the house in which he dwells. If it is destroyed or collapses, or if it is built, that is not the effect of caprice but of design.

4. *to weep . . . laugh.* Over calamities or strokes of good fortune respectively.

*to mourn . . . dance.* In domestic events of sorrow or joy. Ginsburg suggests that the verb *dance* (Hebrew *rekod*) is used instead of a more general word 'to rejoice' because of its assonance with *sephod, to mourn.* Dancing was a conspicuous feature at marriages, and may be mentioned here to lead on to the thought of the next verse.

5. *to cast away stones.* Many conjectures have been made to explain these words. The Targum and Ibn Ezra think of building materials as being at one time thrown aside as unwanted and at another time needed. Many moderns refer to 2 Kings iii. 19, 25 where a practice is mentioned of a victorious army throwing stones on fields to destroy their fertility; *to gather stones* would then signify clearing the fields to restore their productivity. All such interpretations fail to provide a connection with the latter half of the verse. The Midrash has a noteworthy comment. It apparently identifies *abanim* (stones) with the word *obnayim* in Exod. i. 16, usually translated *the birthstool.* This term is plausibly explained by the Rabbis as the organ by which the sex of the newly born child is discovered; and here the phrase *cast away stones* is held to be an idiomatic expression for carnal intercourse, with the remark: 'There is a time to cast the testes, when thy wife is clean (menstrually); and there is a time to conserve the testes, when thy wife is unclean.' The marital act is, accordingly, controlled by circumstances.

*to embrace.* The Targum understands the allusion to be to marital intercourse (cf. its use in Prov. v. 20). This was

6 A time to seek, and a time to lose;
A time to keep, and a time to cast away;
7 A time to rend, and a time to sew;
A time to keep silence, and a time to speak;
8 A time to love, and a time to hate;
A time for war, and a time for peace.
9. What profit hath he that worketh in that he laboureth? 10. I have seen the task which God hath given to the sons of men to be exercised therewith. 11. He hath made every thing beautiful in its time; also

6 עֵת לְבַקֵּשׁ וְעֵת לְאַבֵּד
עֵת לִשְׁמוֹר
וְעֵת לְהַשְׁלִיךְ׃
7 עֵת לִקְרוֹעַ וְעֵת לִתְפּוֹר
עֵת לַחֲשׁוֹת וְעֵת לְדַבֵּר׃
8 עֵת לֶאֱהֹב וְעֵת לִשְׂנֹא
עֵת מִלְחָמָה וְעֵת שָׁלוֹם׃
9 מַה־יִּתְרוֹן הָעוֹשֶׂה בַּאֲשֶׁר
10 הוּא עָמֵל׃ רָאִיתִי אֶת־הָעִנְיָן
אֲשֶׁר נָתַן אֱלֹהִים לִבְנֵי הָאָדָם
11 לַעֲנוֹת בּוֹ׃ אֶת־הַכֹּל עָשָׂה

interdicted in a time of war or a solemn fast (cf. 2 Sam. xi. 6ff.; Joel ii. 16).

6. *to seek . . . lose.* 'Even the ever-changing desire in man to seek after new objects, and carelessly losing them as soon as they are obtained, the whimsical grasping of a thing and then to reject it, all these are not done from choice, but are predetermined' (Ginsburg).

*to keep . . . away.* To cherish an object and guard it against theft, or to discard it as no longer of value.

7. *to rend . . . sew.* In agreement with the Targum the reference is best understood to be to the practice of rending a garment in the time of sorrow or bereavement (cf. Gen. xxxvii. 29, xliv. 13; Judges xi. 35; 2 Sam. i. 2, etc.), which was later sewn together when the feeling of grief had lessened in intensity.

*to keep silence.* When under the strain of deep emotion (cf. Lev. x. 3; Job ii. 12f.). Only when one is able, in such circumstances, to think calmly, is it proper for him to speak.

8. *to love . . . hate.* The friendly or unfriendly relationship between individuals is a matter which can be decided by conditions that may not have been created by them.

*for war . . . peace.* What is true of individuals holds good also of nations.

9. *what profit.* As usual (see on i. 3) Koheleth uses the question to state a denial. Since events occur in one's life, whether he wishes them to happen or not, it is useless to put forward any effort to avert fate.

10. The wording of the verse is repeated from i. 13 with the significant omission of the adjective in *sore task*, and Ibn Ezra is right in connecting the sentence with what follows: (Since) *I have seen the task* . . . (I appreciate that) *He hath made every thing beautiful.* He has pondered over the problem why man's labours, although imposed upon him by God, prove ineffective as a means of yielding him lasting satisfaction.

11. *every thing beautiful.* Cf. the Divine

He hath set the world in their heart,
yet so that man cannot find out the
work that God hath done from the
beginning even to the end. 12 I
know that there is nothing better for
them, than to rejoice, and to get
pleasure so long as they live. 13. But
also that every man should eat and
drink, and enjoy pleasure for all his

יָפֶה בְעִתּוֹ גַּם אֶת־הָעֹלָם נָתַן
בְּלִבָּם מִבְּלִי אֲשֶׁר לֹא־יִמְצָא
הָאָדָם אֶת־הַמַּעֲשֶׂה אֲשֶׁר־
עָשָׂה הָאֱלֹהִים מֵרֹאשׁ וְעַד־
12 סוֹף׃ יָדַעְתִּי כִּי אֵין טוֹב בָּם
כִּי אִם־לִשְׂמוֹחַ וְלַעֲשׂוֹת טוֹב
13 בְּחַיָּיו׃ וְגַם כָּל־הָאָדָם
שֶׁיֹּאכַל וְשָׁתָה וְרָאָה טוֹב

judgment upon creation in Gen. i. 31. 'In spite of man's perception of "eternity" (see the next note) and his desire to understand it, the various parts that make up God's work are, in their multitude and variety, altogether beyond his grasp. Man's delight in each detail and yet his inability to know the whole, and his consequent failure to be satisfied, are expressed by Koheleth with singular vividness in this verse' (Williams).

*also He hath set the world in their heart.* The Hebrew word *olam* is variously interpreted *world* or 'eternity,' but the latter is the only signification it has in the Bible. God has endowed man with the sense of a future. He knows he is more than the creature of a day, and this consciousness is a cause of his dissatisfaction with the transitory experiences which take place within the span of his lifetime.

*yet so that man cannot find out.* Notwithstanding this Divine endowment, it is beyond man's powers to gain an understanding of God's scheme of the universe.

*the work that God hath done.* Cf. viii. 17 for an elaboration of this part of the verse. The words do not mean the creation of the material world, but His government of it and the purposes that underlie the scheme of life which is His gift to man.

*from the beginning even to the end.* An idiom for 'in its entirety,' referring to *the work* (cf. *the beginning . . . and the end*, x. 13).

12. *nothing better for them.* This is the deduction he draws from his contemplation of the fact that *the sons of men* have not the capacity to comprehend God's *work.*

*to rejoice, and to get pleasure.* He reverts to his statement in ii. 24. *To get pleasure* is literally 'to do good,' but it does not possess an ethical connotation.

*so long as they live.* Notwithstanding the sense of eternity with which man is equipped, he should consider only the period of his life on earth as a time for self-enjoyment.

13. *but also.* Better, 'and also,' i.e. furthermore, continuing the statement of the preceding verse.

*enjoy pleasure.* lit. 'see good' (see on ii. 1). 'In Koheleth's view, God's one good gift to man is the bit of healthy animal life which comes with the years of vigour (cf. xi. 9-xii. 6)' (Barton).

*the gift of God.* An additional reason is

**labour, is the gift of God. 14. I know that, whatsoever God doeth, it shall be for ever; nothing can be added to it, nor any thing taken from it; and God hath so made it, that men should fear before Him. 15. That which is hath been long ago, and that which is to be hath already been; and God seeketh that which is pursued.**

**16. And moreover I saw under the**

בְּכָל־עֲמָלוֹ מַתַּת אֱלֹהִים
14 הִיא׃ יָדַעְתִּי כִּי כָּל־אֲשֶׁר
יַעֲשֶׂה הָאֱלֹהִים הוּא יִהְיֶה
לְעוֹלָם עָלָיו אֵין לְהוֹסִיף
וּמִמֶּנּוּ אֵין לִגְרֹעַ וְהָאֱלֹהִים
15 עָשָׂה שֶׁיִּרְאוּ מִלְּפָנָיו׃ מַה־
שֶּׁהָיָה כְּבָר הוּא וַאֲשֶׁר לִהְיוֹת
כְּבָר הָיָה וְהָאֱלֹהִים יְבַקֵּשׁ
16 אֶת־נִרְדָּף׃ וְעוֹד רָאִיתִי

given why man should make his lifetime as enjoyable as possible: the means of enjoyment are provided by God and intended by Him to be used. This thought is in line with the declaration of the Psalmist that God made *wine that maketh glad the heart of man* (civ. 15), but it is not identical with the doctrine of hedonism which regards pleasures as the aim of life. Judaism only condemns abuse, not the moderate use, of comforts.

**14.** *I know that.* As in verse 12, the verb introduces a deduction from verses 1-9.

*it shall be for ever.* The conditions imposed by God upon the scheme of human life are fixed for all time and unchangeable. It is useless, therefore, for man to attempt by his endeavours to alter them by addition or subtraction. His course is to submit to them.

*that men should fear before Him.* By *fear* is meant reverential awe. Unlike the Greeks who held that the human being was in every respect a helpless prisoner of forces which he was unable to control, Koheleth believed that he had the power of moral freedom and should learn the lesson from the circumstances in which he was bound that he had the duty to utilize them in 'the fear of the Lord.' As the Rabbis taught, 'Everything is in the hands of God except the fear of God.'

**15.** *that which is . . . already been.* An inference from his line of argument confirms his earlier statement in i. 9.

*God seeketh that which is pursued.* This is the literal rendering of the text, and is explained by Rashi: To punish the pursuer (persecutor); therefore what profit has the evil-doer in what he commits, seeing that his end is to be held to account for his deed? R.V. translates, 'God seeketh again that which is passed away,' and Ginsburg, 'God recalleth what is past.' 'This term (*pursued*),' he writes, 'is here designedly chosen because of its connection with time, whose rapid march overtakes and speedily leaves behind every event which God has predetermined for every season.' According to this interpretation, God exacts a reckoning from man for his actions, although circumstances have been ordained by Him, because the human being possesses freedom of will.

### 16-22 MAN'S INHUMANITY: HIS COMMON FATE WITH THE BEAST

The conclusion that the proper course

sun, in the place of justice, that
wickedness was there; and in the
place of righteousness, that wickedness was there. 17. I said in my
heart: 'The righteous and the wicked
God will judge; for there is a time
there for every purpose and for every
work.' 18. I said in my heart: 'It is
because of the sons of men, that God

תַּחַת הַשֶּׁמֶשׁ מְקוֹם הַמִּשְׁפָּט
שָׁמָּה הָרֶשַׁע וּמְקוֹם הַצֶּדֶק
17 שָׁמָּה הָרָשַׁע׃ אָמַרְתִּי אֲנִי
בְּלִבִּי אֶת־הַצַּדִּיק וְאֶת־
הָרָשָׁע יִשְׁפֹּט הָאֱלֹהִים כִּי־
עֵת לְכָל־חֵפֶץ וְעַל כָּל־
18 הַמַּעֲשֶׂה שָׁם׃ אָמַרְתִּי אֲנִי
בְּלִבִּי עַל־דִּבְרַת בְּנֵי הָאָדָם

to follow is to enjoy one's life is strengthened by two facts of experience: first, justice being perverted by the men in authority, contrary to the will of God, it is useless to pursue wisdom and righteousness. Secondly, nobody knows what is in store for him when he departs from earth; his end is the same as that of the animal.

16. *the place of justice.* The courts of law where truth alone should bear sway and every man receive his due.

*wickedness was there.* Bribery or partiality decided a verdict; the innocent were condemned and the guilty acquitted.

*the place of righteousness.* Either the statement is repeated for the sake of emphasis in different words, or the allusion is to the council chamber, national or municipal, where policy is discussed. It should be a *place of righteousness*, but it is not. The picture of corrupt administration which is drawn does not correspond to what is known of Solomon's reign.

17. *I said in my heart.* The words that follow are Koheleth's reaction to the sight of injustice.

*righteous . . . wicked.* The terms have their juridical meaning of 'innocent, guilty.'

*God will judge.* He is the supreme Judge of the universe, and in that capacity He will right the wrongs which are committed by venal judges.

*there.* A.J. is ambiguous, and the literal translation is, 'for a time for every purpose and for every work there.' The word is vague in the sentence and, according to Plumptre, 'may refer to the unfathomed depths of the Divine judgment which works, through long delay, at its appointed time.' Rashi understands it as 'an unspecified time.' The Targum and Ibn Ezra see in the word an allusion to the Judgment after death, and Ginsburg accepts this interpretation.

18. *it is because of the sons of men.* The phrase should be attached to what precedes: 'I said in my heart concerning the sons of men.'

*that God may sift . . . beasts.* The translation is hardly intelligible. As for the general sense, modern commentators like Grätz and Barton connect this verse with verse 16 and take it to mean: the corruption in civil and religious affairs is God's way of showing that men, despite their intelligence and assumed authority, are really only on a level with the beasts. A noteworthy explanation is may sift them, and that they may see that they themselves are but as beasts.' 19. For that which befalleth the sons of men befalleth beasts; even one thing befalleth them; as the one dieth, so dieth the other; yea, they have all one breath; so that man hath no pre-eminence above a beast; for all is vanity.

לְבָרָם הָאֱלֹהִים וְלִרְאוֹת
19 שְׁהֶם־בְּהֵמָה הֵמָּה לָהֶם׃ כִּי
מִקְרֶה בְנֵי־הָאָדָם וּמִקְרֶה
הַבְּהֵמָה וּמִקְרֶה אֶחָד לָהֶם
כְּמוֹת זֶה כֵּן מוֹת זֶה וְרוּחַ
אֶחָד לַכֹּל וּמוֹתַר הָאָדָם מִן־
הַבְּהֵמָה אָיִן כִּי הַכֹּל הָבֶל׃

offered by Eitan to overcome the difficulty of the verb translated *sift* and the last clause which, apparently, is lit. 'and to see that they a beast they are to them.' The *lamed* of *lebaram* he understands as 'surely' on the analogy of Arabic and Assyrian; *baram*, following the Syriac Version, is construed as *beraam* (with elision of the *aleph*), 'He created them'; *hem* (they) he connects with an Arabic noun signifying 'straying of the mind, stupidity.' His rendering is: 'truly God has created them to show that they have the stupidity of beasts,' i.e. that they are stupid like beasts. But this translation ignores the *and* in *and that they may see*. Adopting Eitan's original suggestions, we may translate: 'truly God hath created them, and it is (for them) to see that they indeed (*hemmah* emphasizes the suffix of *lahem*) possess the stupidity of a beast.' The intention would then be: Men pride themselves on being a special creature of God, formed in His image; but if they examined the way they conduct themselves, they would become conscious that they behave with the same lack of reason as an irrational animal. Hence their pride is ill-founded.

**19.** Another resemblance between man and the beast is added; but the dark pessimism of Koheleth in this passage contrasts sharply with the main stream of confident faith of Judaism in the higher destiny of man.

*for that which befalleth.* A closer rendering of the Hebrew is given in R.V. margin, 'For the sons of men are a chance, and the beasts are a chance, and one chance is to them.' They are alike in that they are subject to the same doom passed upon them by fate, viz. death.

*as the one dieth . . . other.* The phenomenon of death is identical with both, a statement which suggests a parallel with *but man abideth not in honour; he is like the beasts that perish* (Ps. xlix. 13). A noteworthy difference, however, is to be detected. The Psalmist refers only to men who *trust in their wealth* (verse 7) and he has the conviction *God will redeem my soul from the power of the nether-world* (verse 16). In the present verse, on the other hand, Koheleth does not go beyond the fact that the same end comes to man and beast.

*they have all one breath.* He evidently has in mind, God *breathed into his nostrils the breath of life* (Gen. ii. 7). Since death means the same to both, that which constitutes life is also the same in both.

*man hath no pre-eminence.* Identical in all these respects, there is no feature which places the human being upon a higher level.

20. All go unto one place; all are of the dust, and all return to dust.

21. Who knoweth the spirit of man whether it goeth upward, and the spirit of the beast whether it goeth downward to the earth? 22. Wherefore I perceived that there is nothing better, than that a man should rejoice in his works; for that is his portion; for who shall bring him to see what shall be after him?

20 הַכֹּל הוֹלֵךְ אֶל־מָקוֹם אֶחָד
הַכֹּל הָיָה מִן־הֶעָפָר וְהַכֹּל
21 שָׁב אֶל־הֶעָפָר׃ מִי יוֹדֵעַ
רוּחַ בְּנֵי הָאָדָם הָעֹלָה הִיא
לְמָעְלָה וְרוּחַ הַבְּהֵמָה
הַיֹּרֶדֶת הִיא לְמַטָּה לָאָרֶץ׃
22 וְרָאִיתִי כִּי אֵין טוֹב מֵאֲשֶׁר
יִשְׂמַח הָאָדָם בְּמַעֲשָׂיו כִּי־
הוּא חֶלְקוֹ כִּי מִי יְבִיאֶנּוּ
לִרְאוֹת בְּמֶה שֶׁיִּהְיֶה אַחֲרָיו׃

20. *all go unto one place.* Koheleth must have known of the Hebraic doctrine of Sheol as the abode of the dead; but his purpose is to drive home his point of the equal destiny of man and beast. Alike they come from the dust and revert to dust. The wording is reminiscent of Gen. iii. 19 (cf. also Ps. civ. 29, cxlvi. 4; Job x. 9, xxxiv. 15). In addition we have the declaration, 'All things that are of the earth turn to the earth again' (Ecclus. xl. 11, xli. 10). Therefore his words would not sound strange to a Hebrew who believed in immortality.

21. *who knoweth?* i.e. nobody knows. He does not deny, but for the present assumes an agnostic attitude.

*the spirit.* The same Hebrew word as that translated *breath* in verse 19 with the same meaning. Having demonstrated that *as the one dieth so dieth the other*, he now proceeds to deal with his assertion *they have all one breath.*

*goeth upward . . . downward.* He obviously asks his sceptical question because there was a current belief that there was this difference of destiny.

22. *wherefore I perceived.* He draws the conclusion from his argument. Man does not know what follows death; but he does know that before its advent he has the opportunity and capacity to experience pleasure. Let him act upon this knowledge.

*portion.* Cf. ii. 10. That is what life offers to man, and he should take it.

*for who shall bring . . . him?* Nobody can take him, while he is alive, to catch a glimpse of what awaits him in the hereafter.

1. But I returned and considered
all the oppressions that are done
under the sun; and behold the tears
of such as were oppressed, and they
had no comforter; and on the side of
their oppressors there was power,
but they had no comforter. 2. Wherefore I praised the dead that are
already dead more than the living
that are yet alive; 3. but better than

1 וָשַׁבְתִּי אֲנִי וָאֶרְאֶה אֶת־כָּל־
הָעֲשֻׁקִים אֲשֶׁר נַעֲשִׂים תַּחַת
הַשָּׁמֶשׁ וְהִנֵּה ׀ דִּמְעַת הָעֲשֻׁקִים
וְאֵין לָהֶם מְנַחֵם וּמִיַּד
עֹשְׁקֵיהֶם כֹּחַ וְאֵין לָהֶם
2 מְנַחֵם׃ וְשַׁבֵּחַ אֲנִי אֶת־הַמֵּתִים
שֶׁכְּבָר מֵתוּ מִן־הַחַיִּים אֲשֶׁר
3 הֵמָּה חַיִּים עֲדֶנָה׃ וְטוֹב

**1-3** SUFFERINGS OF THE OPPRESSED

In iii. 16 Koheleth had remarked upon the state of injustice which prevailed, and he reverts to the subject. 'We can see in this element of despair, that which was the beginning of a better life. The man was passing, to use modern terms, from egoism to altruism, thinking more of the misery of others than of his own enjoyment' (Plumptre).

1. *but I returned and considered.* A Hebrew idiom for 'I reconsidered.' His mind had previously given a passing thought to this evil; now it dwells upon it again to estimate its effect upon the value of living.

*oppressions.* The heavy disabilities and extortions which the masses were compelled to endure at the hands of the few who misused the power and authority wherewith they had been invested.

*tears.* The Hebrew is singular in a collective sense. For these men and women life was so embittered that they found the world indeed 'a vale of tears.'

*no comforter.* 'No avenger,' explains Jastrow, but more probably the word is to be understood literally: nobody had any sympathy with them in their plight. The lack of a sympathizer was keenly felt by the ancient Hebrew in time of trouble (cf. (*I looked*) *for comforters, but I found none*, Ps. lxix. 21; *She hath none to comfort her*, Lam. i. 2). It is still regarded by Jews as a religious duty to visit and condole with a mourner.

*and on the side . . . power.* Better, 'and from the hand of their oppressors (came) power,' i.e. the exercise of ruthless might.

*but they had no comforter.* The phrase is repeated to underline the distressing circumstance.

2f. A parallel to this pessimistic evaluation of human existence occurs in Job iii. 11ff. What a self-condemnation he pronounces if the speaker is Solomon since, as king, he was responsible for the conditions in his kingdom! But, in fact, as remarked on ii. 17, this is only a passing phase in his mental pilgrimage, and he expresses an opposite opinion later in the Book. With the statement of verse 3 may be compared this passage from the Talmud: 'For two and a half years the School of Shammai and the

they both is he that hath not yet
been, who hath not seen the evil work
that is done under the sun.

4. Again, I considered all labour
and all excelling in work, that it is a
man's rivalry with his neighbour.
This also is vanity and a striving after
wind.
5 The fool foldeth his hands together,
And eateth his own flesh.

מִשְּׁנֵיהֶם אֵת אֲשֶׁר־עֲדֶן לֹא
הָיָה אֲשֶׁר לֹא־רָאָה אֶת־
הַמַּעֲשֶׂה הָרָע אֲשֶׁר נַעֲשָׂה
תַּחַת הַשָּׁמֶשׁ׃ וְרָאִיתִי אֲנִי 4
אֶת־כָּל־עָמָל וְאֵת כָּל־
כִּשְׁרוֹן הַמַּעֲשֶׂה כִּי הִיא
קִנְאַת־אִישׁ מֵרֵעֵהוּ גַּם־זֶה
הֶבֶל וּרְעוּת רוּחַ׃ הַכְּסִיל 5
חֹבֵק אֶת־יָדָיו וְאֹכֵל אֶת־

School of Hillel were in dispute, the former asserting that it were better for man not to have been created than to have been created, and the latter maintaining that it is better for man to have been created than not to have been created. They finally took a vote and decided that it were better for man not to have been created than to have been created, but now that he has been created, let him investigate his past deeds (and, if he find them at fault, make the necessary amends) or, as others say, let him examine his future actions (before committing them)' (Erub. 13*b*). The point of this discussion is the tendency of the human being to sin and so earn for himself God's disapproval. Here, too, it is the evil in man which asserts itself that leads Koheleth to his conclusion that it were better not to have been born.

### 4-6 THE EVIL OF RIVALRY

4. *again, I considered.* lit. 'and I saw.' Once more he meditates upon the worth of human endeavour.

*excelling.* The Hebrew word is the same as *skill* in ii. 21 (see note), and in this passage signifies the sincerity and application which a man devotes to his task to make a success of it.

*a man's rivalry with his neighbour.* Or, more lit., 'from jealousy of one toward the other' (Ginsburg). The incentive to work is not the accomplishment of something worth doing but the desire to outdo one's fellow-man; thereby life becomes a competition instead of mutual co-operation. 'It is curious to find how very modern this conception is. It would make a splendid motto for a Socialist address against the evils of competition' (Martin).

5. This and the next verses are proverbs in poetical form. Two interpretations are placed on the verse, depending upon the way the second clause is understood. (1) The *fool* is the indolent person who does not appreciate the necessity to work hard for a livelihood. He *foldeth his hands* in idleness (cf. Prov. vi. 10, xxiv. 33) when he should be up and doing, and as a consequence reduces himself to poverty. He *eateth his own flesh* then means he starves himself and hastens his death. The objection to this reading of the text is that it does not connect with the point made by Koheleth in the previous verse concerning rivalry. (2) The *fool* is the opposite type to the alert and active workman who is eager to beat his competitor; he is a slothful person of

6 Better is a handful of quietness,
Than both the hands full of labour
and striving after wind.

7. Then I returned and saw vanity
under the sun. 8. There is one that
is alone, and he hath not a second;
yea, he hath neither son nor brother;
yet is there no end of all his labour,
neither is his eye satisfied with riches:
'for whom then do I labour, and
bereave my soul of pleasure?' This

6 בְּשָׂרוֹ׃ טוֹב מְלֹא כַף נָחַת
מִמְּלֹא חָפְנַיִם עָמָל וּרְעוּת
7 רוּחַ׃ וְשַׁבְתִּי אֲנִי וָאֶרְאֶה הֶבֶל
8 תַּחַת הַשָּׁמֶשׁ׃ יֵשׁ אֶחָד וְאֵין
שֵׁנִי גַּם בֵּן וָאָח אֵין־לוֹ וְאֵין
קֵץ לְכָל־עֲמָלוֹ גַּם־עֵינָיו*
לֹא־תִשְׂבַּע עֹשֶׁר וּלְמִי ׀ אֲנִי
עָמֵל וּמְחַסֵּר אֶת־נַפְשִׁי
מִטּוֹבָה גַּם־זֶה הֶבֶל וְעִנְיַן רָע

v. 8. עינו ק׳

phlegmatic temperament who prefers a minimum of exertion (*foldeth his hands*). For all that, 'he eateth his meat' (so translate), he sits down to his meals (cf. Exod. xvi. 8; Isa. xxii. 13). Of what use, then, is this keen rivalry which motivates industry?

6. Koheleth quotes this saying as expressing the standpoint with which he is in agreement. Be satisfied, he urges, with half the earnings if this is secured with *quietness*, lit. 'restfulness (of mind),' which competition makes impossible, rather than double the amount when this results from worrying toil and an empty ambition. A less probable interpretation places this verse in the mouth of the fool.

### 7-8 VANITY OF A LONELY MISER

7. *then I returned and saw.* The intention is well expressed in the rendering: 'I saw another futile thing under the sun' (Moffatt). 'From jealousy Koheleth proceeds to avarice, as the two features are intimately connected with each other; both are described as the cause of hard labour, undertaken in spite of the immutably fixed order of things, and as neglecting the enjoyment of the present, which is the only portion of man' (Ginsburg).

8. A graphic picture of the miser is drawn whose sole aim, for which he sacrifices all else, is to pile up and hoard riches.

*that is alone.* The words do not occur in the Hebrew text but add to the force of *there is one.*

*a second.* Ibn Ezra understands this of a wife, but the Hebrew word is masculine. More probably it signifies, as Rashi explains, that he toils alone, without a partner or assistant, so that he may retain all the profits.

*neither son nor brother.* Koheleth states the extreme case, where a person has nobody whom he can regard as his heir.

*his eye.* Following the *kerë*, the *kethib* being plural. The *eye* is mentioned as the organ which excites desire. The miser's eye is never contented with what he has and longs for more.

*for whom then I do labour.* Koheleth puts himself in the position of such a man and imagines him, in a moment of reflection, asking the question.

*bereave my soul.* i.e. deny myself.

also is vanity, yea, it is a grievous business. 9. Two are better than one; because they have a good reward for their labour. 10. For if they fall, the one will lift up his fellow; but woe to him that is alone when he falleth, and hath not another to lift him up. 11. Again, if two lie together, then they have warmth; but how can one be warm alone? 12. And if a man prevail against him that is alone, two shall withstand him; and a threefold cord is not quickly broken.

9 הוּא׃ טוֹבִים הַשְּׁנַיִם מִן־
הָאֶחָד אֲשֶׁר יֵשׁ־לָהֶם שָׂכָר
10 טוֹב בַּעֲמָלָם׃ כִּי אִם־יִפֹּלוּ
הָאֶחָד יָקִים אֶת־חֲבֵרוֹ וְאִילוֹ
הָאֶחָד שֶׁיִּפּוֹל וְאֵין שֵׁנִי
11 לַהֲקִימוֹ׃ גַּם אִם־יִשְׁכְּבוּ
שְׁנַיִם וְחַם לָהֶם וּלְאֶחָד אֵיךְ
12 יֵחָם׃ וְאִם־יִתְקְפוֹ הָאֶחָד
הַשְּׁנַיִם יַעַמְדוּ נֶגְדּוֹ וְהַחוּט
הַמְשֻׁלָּשׁ לֹא בִמְהֵרָה יִנָּתֵק׃

**9-12** BENEFITS OF COMPANIONSHIP

The miserable lot of the miser leads Koheleth to meditate upon the advantages which result from fellowship.

9. *two are better than one.* In undertaking a piece of work, and not labouring alone.

*they have a good reward.* Such co-operation brings greater profits, even when divided, than each earns by his solitary efforts.

10. *if they fall.* Other advantages are mentioned. The 'fall' may be metaphorical: if one fails in his work, the other comes to his assistance; or it may be understood literally: should two men travel together and one slips, his companion helps him to his feet.

*but woe to him.* The Hebrew is one word, but some MSS. read it as two. That it is to be regarded as such is indicated by the double accentuation.

11. The illustration is again taken from companion travellers who huddle together in the cold nights which follow the heat of the day in the Orient. Less acceptable is Rashi's explanation which refers to the cohabitation of husband and wife.

12. *if a man prevail.* Or, 'overpower.' Still another illustration from travel. A person journeying by himself is liable to be attacked by bandits. If he is accompanied, there is less danger of assault; and should it happen, the two together have a better chance of overcoming the attacker.

*and a threefold . . . broken.* Probably a proverbial saying quoted to round off the argument. A cord woven from three strands will hold a greater strain than if it had two. If the companionship of another has these advantages, how much more so the fellowship of two others! The value of friends is often urged in Jewish literature. The Talmud has an anecdote of a man who fell asleep for seventy years and on waking found himself solitary and unknown. In desperation he cried to God, 'Either give me companionship or death.' Ibn Gabirol, in his *Choice of Pearls,* includes these aphorisms: 'I find all worldly possessions and treasures perishable; but there is no treasure like instruction, no stronghold

13. Better is a poor and wise child
than an old and foolish king, who
knoweth not how to receive admonition any more. 14. For out of
prison he came forth to be king;
although in his kingdom he was
born poor. 15. I saw all the living

13 טוֹב יֶלֶד מִסְכֵּן וְחָכָם מִמֶּלֶךְ
זָקֵן וּכְסִיל אֲשֶׁר לֹא־יָדַע
14 לְהִזָּהֵר עוֹד׃ כִּי־מִבֵּית
הָסוּרִים יָצָא לִמְלֹךְ כִּי גַּם
15 בְּמַלְכוּתוֹ נוֹלַד רָשׁ׃ רָאִיתִי

like companions'; 'A friendless man is like a left hand bereft of the right.'

### 13-16 THE VANITY OF ROYAL POPULARITY

The commentators who see in this section an allusion to an actual event are in hopeless disagreement over the identity of the king referred to. More probably Koheleth states a hypothetical case of the instability of the throne which finds many illustrations in history.

13. *a poor and wise child.* Better, 'a poor but wise youth.' The Hebrew word *yeled* is used of Joseph when he was seventeen (Gen. xxxvii. 30) and the friends of Rehoboam when he was over forty years old (1 Kings xii. 8). Being *poor*, he lacked power and influence, and so offers a contrast to a *king* who was an autocrat.

*and foolish.* Better, 'but foolish.' Even with the experience of age he had not acquired wisdom.

*receive admonition any more.* i.e. he is now too old to learn and remains steeped in folly. The Midrash gives the verse a homiletical interpretation: The *poor and wise child* is the Good Inclination in the human being. Why is it called *child*? Because it attaches itself to a person only from the age of thirteen years onward (the age of puberty). Why is it called *poor*? Because all do not obey it. Why is it called *wise*? Because it teaches the right way. The *old and foolish king* is the Evil Inclination. Why is it called *king*? Because all obey it. Why is it called *old*? Because it attaches itself to a man from youth to old age. Why is it called *foolish*? Because it teaches the way of evil.

14. The Hebrew is capable of various translations owing to the ambiguity of the subjects of the verbs. Ibn Ezra connects the verse with the foregoing and understands it as relating to the *child*. Although (like Joseph) he may be in a prison during his youth, yet through his wisdom he can rise to the highest office in the land. It is preferable, however, to interpret the verse as illustrating by a concrete though hypothetical example the general statement which had just been made. 'The history of all nations shows that some, who have been born in meanness and poverty, have, by wisdom and magnanimity, raised themselves to honour and riches, whilst others, who have inherited kingdoms and renown, have, by their foolish and selfish conduct, been reduced to dishonour and poverty' (Ginsburg).

*for.* The conjunction gives the reason why *a poor and wise child* is superior to *an old and foolish king*.

*out of prison . . . king.* Better, 'out of prison one has come to be king'; he started with every disadvantage yet climbed to the top.

*although . . . poor.* Render, 'for even in his (own) kingdom one has become poor.' The conjunction *for* has the same force as at the beginning of the verse. 'Become'

that walk under the sun, that they
were with the child, the second, that
was to stand up in his stead.
16. There was no end of all the
people, even of all them whom he
did lead; yet they that come after
shall not rejoice in him. Surely this
also is vanity and a striving after
wind.
17. Guard thy foot when thou

אֶת־כָּל־הַחַיִּים הַמְהַלְּכִים
תַּחַת הַשָּׁמֶשׁ עִם הַיֶּלֶד הַשֵּׁנִי
16 אֲשֶׁר יַעֲמֹד תַּחְתָּיו׃ אֵין־קֵץ
לְכָל־הָעָם לְכֹל אֲשֶׁר־הָיָה
לִפְנֵיהֶם גַּם הָאַחֲרוֹנִים לֹא
יִשְׂמְחוּ־בוֹ כִּי־גַם־זֶה הֶבֶל
17 וְרַעְיוֹן רוּחַ׃ שְׁמֹר רַגְלֶיךָ

v. 17. יתיר י'

is lit. 'born,' but it is given this meaning by the Targum and Rashi. The sense is: a king may be deposed and become a beggar in his own kingdom.

15. *I saw . . . sun.* To make his argument more forceful, he pictures all the population (*all the living*) flocking to the standard of the new king.

*the child, the second.* Some take this to refer to the successor of the foolish king who is described as *second* because he followed him on the throne. Others (e.g. *Metsudath David*) interpret it as the supplanter of the young man who seized the throne from the old king. This strengthens the point Koheleth is making. The first king becomes unpopular, and the people acclaim a young successor; but he in turn loses favour with his subjects and they applaud a new hero. The history of Saul, David and Absalom exemplifies the truth of what he says.

16. *no end of all the people.* A graphic description of the acclaim with which the new king was greeted at the commencement of his reign.

*whom he did lead.* lit. 'he was before them, an abbreviation of the idiom 'go out and come in before' (cf. I Sam. xviii. 16), denoting leadership.

*they that come after.* Usually understood as 'the next generation'; but the intention is well paraphrased in 'yet later on men lost all interest in him' (Moffatt).

17 MORALITY AND DIVINE WORSHIP

In the English Version this verse begins chapter v and it appears to be connected with what follows in subject-matter. The Hebrew division is supported by the LXX and Vulgate. Ginsburg suggests this link with the foregoing and the next chapter: 'Since all things are under the control of an Omnipotent Power, so that no exertion of ours can secure for us lasting good, or avert the evils common to all men, Koheleth submits that the best thing we can do is to submit to the laws of God, and serve Him acceptably upon Whom we inevitably depend.'

*guard thy foot.* Perhaps an idiomatic expression like 'watch your step,' i.e. do not go astray morally (cf. *I have refrained my feet from every evil way*, Ps. cxix. 101). The teaching is: when you feel the urge to worship your Maker (*when thou goest to the house of God*), remember that man honours Him by ethical conduct.

goest to the house of God, and be ready to hearken: it is better than when fools give sacrifices; for they know not that they do evil.

כַּאֲשֶׁר תֵּלֵךְ אֶל־בֵּית הָאֱלֹהִים וְקָרוֹב לִשְׁמֹעַ מִתֵּת הַכְּסִילִים זָבַח כִּי־אֵינָם יוֹדְעִים לַעֲשׂוֹת רָע׃

*and be ready . . . sacrifices.* Rather, 'for to be near to hearken is better than the offering of a sacrifice by fools.' As in Proverbs the *fool* is morally, as well as intellectually, defective. The sacrifice by such a person is an inferior act of worship as compared with readiness to obey God's precepts (cf. *to obey is better than sacrifice,* 1 Sam. xv. 22).

*for they know not . . . evil.* Ginsburg's translation, 'they who obey know not to do evil,' besides being grammatically questionable, is not true in fact; the morally good know to do evil but resist the temptation. The clause must be related to *fools*: owing to their obtuseness, they commit sin; lit. 'they know not (hence it is their practice) to do evil.' Noteworthy is the Talmudic treatment of this verse: What means that which is written, *Guard thy foot when thou goest to the house of God*? Guard thyself so that thou sinnest not; but if thou sinnest, bring an offering into My presence. *And be ready to hearken*—be ready to hearken to the words of the sages; for if they sin, they bring an offering and repent. *It is better than when fools give sacrifices*—be not like the fools who sin and bring an offering without repenting. *For they know not to do evil* (*sic.*)—if so they are righteous! Nay, the meaning is, be not like the fools who sin and bring an offering and know not whether they bring it for the good they have done or for the evil they have committed. The Holy One, blessed be He, says, 'They are unable to discern between good and evil, and they bring an offering into My presence!' (Ber 23*a*). This Rabbinic interpretation stresses the integral connection between Divine worship and morality.

1. Be not rash with thy mouth, and let not thy heart be hasty to utter a word before God; for God is in heaven, and thou upon earth; therefore let thy words be few.

2 For a dream cometh through a
multitude of business;
And a fool's voice through a multitude of words.

3. When thou vowest a vow unto

1 אַל־תְּבַהֵל עַל־פִּיךָ וְלִבְּךָ
אַל־יְמַהֵר לְהוֹצִיא דָבָר
לִפְנֵי הָאֱלֹהִים כִּי הָאֱלֹהִים
בַּשָּׁמַיִם וְאַתָּה עַל־הָאָרֶץ
עַל־כֵּן יִהְיוּ דְבָרֶיךָ מְעַטִּים׃
2 כִּי בָּא הַחֲלוֹם בְּרֹב עִנְיָן וְקוֹל
3 כְּסִיל בְּרֹב דְּבָרִים׃ כַּאֲשֶׁר

**1-6 VANITY OF NUMEROUS SUPPLICATIONS**

ON the subject of worshipping God, Koheleth contends that, inasmuch as He is the Controller of man's fortunes, it is useless for him to importune God with lengthy prayers and many petitions. He knows what He has in store for each of His creatures and His will is inflexible.

1. *be not rash with thy mouth.* Rashi explains the verse as a warning against rebellious speech in criticism of God when He permits evils to happen in the world. Similarly Jehudah Halevi, in his *al-Khazari*, comments, 'A person who is convinced of the justice of the Creator and His all-embracing wisdom will pay no attention to apparent cases of injustice on earth.' The Talmud, Ibn Ezra and Sforno, with greater probability, interpret the statement as relating to man's prayers. A better translation is, 'Do not make thy mouth precipitate with the utterance of supplications.'

*let not thy heart be hasty.* This clause repeats the thought of the first. The *heart* is the organ which directs human action and prompts speech. It should put a curb upon desires and their expression by the tongue.

*before God.* i.e. in the worship of Him which takes the form of prayer.

*God is in heaven.* The point is not the remoteness of God from the scene of human activity which makes prayer to Him futile, but His infinite greatness and majesty before which man is a very humble creature. Therefore a petition should be addressed to Him in brief terms.

2. A proverb quoted by Koheleth to support the plea just made.

*a dream cometh.* When a man's mind is preoccupied with many concerns which worry him during the day, they disturb his rest at night. He dreams upon his bed instead of sleeping peacefully.

*a fool's voice.* In like manner the fool is possessed of too many words, which result in the obscuring of the message he wishes to convey. It is the evil excess that is the moral of the proverb, and is applied to prayer. The Talmud observes that Moses' petition on behalf of Miriam, *Heal her now, O God, I beseech Thee* (Num. xii. 13), consisting in the Hebrew of only five monosyllables, was favourably answered.

God, defer not to pay it; for He hath no pleasure in fools; pay that which thou vowest. 4. Better is it that thou shouldest not vow, than that thou shouldest vow and not pay. 5. Suffer not thy mouth to bring thy flesh into guilt, neither say thou before the messenger, that it was an error; wherefore should God be

תִּדֹּר נֶדֶר לֵאלֹהִים אַל־
תְּאַחֵר לְשַׁלְּמוֹ כִּי אֵין חֵפֶץ
בַּכְּסִילִים אֵת אֲשֶׁר־תִּדֹּר
4 שַׁלֵּם׃ טוֹב אֲשֶׁר לֹא־תִדֹּר
5 מִשֶּׁתִּדּוֹר וְלֹא תְשַׁלֵּם׃ אַל־
תִּתֵּן אֶת־פִּיךָ לַחֲטִיא אֶת־
בְּשָׂרֶךָ וְאַל־תֹּאמַר לִפְנֵי
הַמַּלְאָךְ כִּי שְׁגָגָה הִיא לָמָּה

3. *when thou vowest . . . pay it.* Almost quoted verbatim from Deut. xxiii. 22. Commentators regard this verse as distinct from what precedes. Rashness in prayer having been deprecated, a warning is uttered against rashness in vowing. It is possible, however, that there is an interrelationship of ideas in that when one is prolix in supplication, he is likely to include in it a promise to carry out a certain obligation if God grants him his request.

*for He hath no pleasure in fools.* This translation agrees with Rashi's explanation, 'The Holy One, blessed be He, hath no pleasure in wicked men who vow but do not fulfil.' But the Hebrew is lit. 'for there is no pleasure in fools,' and an allusion to God would have been included if that were intended. Ginsburg's rendering, 'for fools have no fixed will,' is preferable, and that interpretation is found in *Metsudath David.* Do not defer fulfilment of a vow because *fools*, and most men in this respect are within that category, are of unstable purpose. In a moment of exaltation a vow is made, but the fervour quickly evaporates and the inclination to pay the vow disappears (cf. Prov. xx. 25).

4. Vows are not obligatory as a part of His worship, and no wrong is done if they are not made (cf. *If thou shalt forbear to vow, it shall be no sin in thee,* Deut. xxiii. 23). Consequently it is better to avoid the possibility of the sin of non-fulfilment by refraining from a vow.

5. *thy mouth.* By uttering a vow.

*thy flesh.* 'An equivalent of the whole nature, which is thus led into evil ways by the rashness of a careless vow' (Martin). There may also be the implied idea that though one organ, the mouth, was involved in the sin, yet the whole body will have to bear the punishment.

*the messenger.* According to Rabbinic tradition the allusion is to the 'angel' (so A.V., R.V.) appointed by God as superintendent over the Temple; but was this belief current in the writer's days? Rashi and *Metsudath David* define the term as the Temple-official whose duty was to collect what had been vowed.

*that it was an error.* Omit *that* in translation. The words are those actually spoken by the defaulter. His plea is that he uttered his vow by mistake and it was not intentionally made.

angry at thy voice, and destroy the work of thy hands? 6. For through the multitude of dreams and vanities there are also many words; but fear thou God.

7. If thou seest the oppression of the poor, and the violent perverting of justice and righteousness in the state, marvel not at the matter; for one higher than the high watcheth, and there are higher than they. 8. But the profit of a land every way

יִקְצֹף הָאֱלֹהִים עַל־קוֹלֶךָ
6 וְחִבֵּל אֶת־מַעֲשֵׂה יָדֶיךָ׃ כִּי
בְרֹב חֲלֹמוֹת וַהֲבָלִים
וּדְבָרִים הַרְבֵּה כִּי אֶת־
7 הָאֱלֹהִים יְרָא׃ אִם־עֹשֶׁק רָשׁ
וְגֵזֶל מִשְׁפָּט וָצֶדֶק תִּרְאֶה
בַמְּדִינָה אַל־תִּתְמַהּ עַל־
הַחֵפֶץ כִּי גָבֹהַּ מֵעַל גָּבֹהַּ
8 שֹׁמֵר וּגְבֹהִים עֲלֵיהֶם׃ וְיִתְרוֹן

*thy voice.* Which dishonoured Him by making a vow in connection with His service and then saying *it was an error.*

*destroy the work of thy hands.* The man's sacrilegious conduct was motivated by reluctance to deliver to the Temple that part of his possessions which had been promised. His punishment will be still greater loss.

6. Koheleth summarizes the moral of the section in this verse. It should be translated: 'for (the penalty just described is the effect of) the multitude of dreams and vanities and many words.' The meaning of *dreams* is determined by its use in verse 2. Excessive concern with business to acquire much wealth, the vain pursuit after worldly possessions, and lengthy prayers which led to the making of a vow and its non-payment—these were the faults that aroused God's anger and incurred the penalty He inflicted.

*but fear thou God.* Make this principle the rule of living and the guiding force of action, and you will escape the effects of His wrath.

7-8 CORRUPTION OF GOVERNMENT

Ginsburg tries to find a connection between what follows and what precedes; but a new section begins with this verse and extends to vi. 9 in which the vanity of riches is dealt with again. It is introduced by two verses describing the heavy extortions imposed by governors on the people, robbing them of their means.

7. *oppression of the poor.* Through their exploitation by officials who leave them barely enough to live on.

*violent perverting of justice.* lit. 'robbery of justice,' the deprivation of right and justice as the effect of bribery.

*marvel not at the matter.* The Targum, Rashi, Ibn Ezra and others interpret this phrase as 'do not wonder that God permits it.' It should rather be understood as 'do not be surprised at what happens.'

*for one higher . . . than they.* The older commentators took this to mean that God is supreme over all earthly rulers; He watches their actions and eventually punishes them. Much more likely we have a graphic description of the system of government which is responsible for is a king that maketh himself servant to the field.

9. He that loveth silver shall not be satisfied with silver; nor he that loveth abundance, with increase; this also is vanity. 10. When goods increase, they are increased that eat them; and what advantage is there to the owner thereof, saving the beholding of them with his eyes?

11. Sweet is the sleep of a labour-

אֶרֶץ בַּכֹּל הִ*יא מֶלֶךְ לְשָׂדֶה
9 נֶעֱבָד׃ אֹהֵב כֶּסֶף לֹא־יִשְׂבַּע
כֶּסֶף וּמִי־אֹהֵב בֶּהָמוֹן לֹא
10 תְבוּאָה גַּם־זֶה הָבֶל׃ בִּרְבוֹת
הַטּוֹבָה רַבּוּ אוֹכְלֶיהָ וּמַה־
כִּשְׁרוֹן לִבְעָלֶיהָ כִּי אִם־
11 רְאִ*ית עֵינָיו׃ מְתוּקָה שְׁנַת

v. 8. הוא ק׳ v. 10. ראות ק׳

the corrupt state of affairs. 'For there is a superior (official) watching a superior (official), and above them are (still) higher officials.' Set in authority over the people is an official who enriches himself at their expense; he is watched by a more authoritative governor who also has his share of the spoils; and above them are other officers of the State who likewise have to be satisfied. 'As each officer was an oppressor, no wonder that the poor peasant—the lowest stratum of the heap—should be squeezed' (Barton).

8. An obscure and difficult verse which has been variously explained. The simplest interpretation is that proposed by Williams who translates: 'And the profit of (the) land is among the whole (of them, i.e. the grasping officials); even the wild land when cultivated has a king,' i.e. not only do all the officials take their share of extortion, but even wild land falls under the exactions of the state directly it is cultivated. *Field* means an uncultivated tract of land, as in 2 Sam. xvii. 8. The verb translated *maketh himself servant* is the same as in *there was not a man to till the ground* (Gen. ii. 5).

9-16 THE VANITY OF RICHES

9. *that loveth silver.* The man who makes the acquisition of money his life's purpose is never satisfied with what he has and longs to increase his hoard.

*with increase.* i.e. 'shall not be satisfied with increase.' A better rendering is 'he who loveth abundance (has) no increase,' i.e. none which he reckons of any real account (Williams). The truth of this characterization was later taught by a Rabbi in the aphorism, 'Who is rich? He who rejoiceth in his portion' (Aboth).

10. *when goods increase.* lit. 'when that which is good (viz. prosperity) increaseth'; as a man grows richer.

*they are increased that eat them.* His family, servants and friends multiply to have a share in his possessions.

*advantage.* Hebrew *kishron* (see on ii. 21).

*the beholding of them with his eyes.* The only satisfaction he has is the sight of his riches. He is unable to enjoy them because they are eaten up by his numerous dependants.

ing man, whether he eat little or
much; but the satiety of the rich will
not suffer him to sleep.

12. There is a grievous evil which I
have seen under the sun, namely,
riches kept by the owner thereof to
his hurt; 13. and those riches perish
by evil adventure; and if he hath
begotten a son, there is nothing in
his hand. 14. As he came forth of
his mother's womb, naked shall he
go back as he came, and shall take

הָעֹבֵד אִם־מְעַט וְאִם־
הַרְבֵּה יֹאכֵל וְהַשָּׂבָע לֶעָשִׁיר
12 אֵינֶנּוּ מַנִּיחַ לוֹ לִישׁוֹן׃ יֵשׁ רָעָה
חוֹלָה רָאִיתִי תַּחַת הַשָּׁמֶשׁ
עֹשֶׁר שָׁמוּר לִבְעָלָיו לְרָעָתוֹ׃
13 וְאָבַד הָעֹשֶׁר הַהוּא בְּעִנְיַן רָע
וְהוֹלִיד בֵּן וְאֵין בְּיָדוֹ מְאוּמָה׃
14 כַּאֲשֶׁר יָצָא מִבֶּטֶן אִמּוֹ עָרוֹם

**11.** *a labouring man.* Rashi defines the Hebrew more exactly as 'one who tills the ground.' He has no large possessions to worry over, whether they will be stolen or expropriated by corrupt officials. He is able to lie down at night without cares to prevent his sleeping.

*satiety of the rich.* i.e. the abundance of property belonging to a rich man.

**12.** *a grievous evil.* Again in verse 15, lit. 'a sick evil.' Another form of the word occurs in the phrase *my wound is grievous* (Jer. x. 19, xiv. 17).

*kept by the owner . . . hurt.* Instead of spending the money on his personal comfort, a man hoards it. This he does *to his hurt*, either because of his ceaseless anxiety lest it be stolen, or it may be lost to him through some cause or other. *Metsudath David* suggests that the report that he possesses this wealth may be the occasion of a false charge made against him by a ruler who aimed at confiscating it. Others interpret the verse as applying to a man who does not spend on himself in order to leave as much as possible to his heir. Should, then, the fortune be lost, its owner suffers *hurt* in the bitter disappointment he feels. Ginsburg varies this interpretation by understanding *owner* as the heir who may come to harm (*his hurt*) on inheriting a large sum of money for which he did not have to work. Although this is often true in fact, it is doubtful whether *owner* can refer to the heir. It usually denotes the original possessor.

**13.** *by evil adventure.* i.e. in a business venture which fails.

*in his hand.* viz. the father's hand, to bequeath to his son.

**14.** *as he came forth . . . came.* Almost identical with *naked came I out of my mother's womb, and naked shall I return thither* (Job i. 21), but, as Williams well observes, the thought is different: 'For to say specifically of the parsimonious person that he will not carry material wealth away with him when he dies is a mere truism, for it is self-evident of all, rich and poor alike. It must state something of him which is not universally applicable. This is that when he is dying he gets no gain for all his trouble. A man may have at that time the satisfaction of having done well in life, but this niggardly man will not, for his money has been lost.'

*naked shall he go back.* To the earth, strikingly described as 'the mother of all things' (Ecclus. xl. 1; cf. *I was made in*

nothing for his labour, which he may
carry away in his hand. 15. And
this also is a grievous evil, that in all
points as he came, so shall he go;
and what profit hath he that he
laboureth for the wind? 16. All his
days also he eateth in darkness, and
he hath much vexation and sickness
and wrath.

17. Behold that which I have seen:
it is good, yea, it is comely for one

יָשׁוּב לָלֶכֶת כְּשֶׁבָּא וּמְאוּמָה
לֹא־יִשָּׂא בַעֲמָלוֹ שֶׁיֹּלֵךְ בְּיָדוֹ׃
15 וְגַם־זֹה רָעָה חוֹלָה כָּל־עֻמַּת
שֶׁבָּא כֵּן יֵלֵךְ וּמַה־יִּתְרוֹן לוֹ
16 שֶׁיַּעֲמֹל לָרוּחַ׃ גַּם כָּל־יָמָיו
בַּחֹשֶׁךְ יֹאכֵל וְכָעַס הַרְבֵּה
17 וְחָלְיוֹ וָקָצֶף׃ הִנֵּה אֲשֶׁר־
רָאִיתִי אָנִי טוֹב אֲשֶׁר־יָפֶה
לֶאֱכוֹל וְלִשְׁתּוֹת וְלִרְאוֹת

*secret and curiously wrought in the lowest parts of the earth*, Ps. cxxxix. 15).

*in his hand.* In his possession. The Midrash illustrates the verse with the parable: It is like a fox who found a vineyard which was fenced in on all sides. There was one hole through which he wanted to enter, but he was unable to do so. He fasted for three days until he became lean, and so got through the hole. Then he ate of the grapes and became fat again, so that when he wished to leave the vineyard he could not pass through the gap. He fasted another three days until he grew sufficiently thin, and went out. When he was outside, he gazed at the vineyard and exclaimed, 'All that is inside is indeed beautiful, but what advantage has one from you? As he enters so he leaves.' Such is the world.

**15.** *in all points.* In exactly the same material condition, penniless.

*he came.* Barton considers the 'father,' mentioned in verse 13, to be the subject; but more likely Koheleth is uttering a reflection upon men in general.

*the wind.* Exemplifying what is elusive, unsubstantial, and cannot be grasped.

**16.** *he eateth in darkness.* This verse concludes the section dealing with the miser and sums up his condition of living. Ibn Ezra explains *darkness* in a literal sense: he is so engrossed in money-making throughout the day, that he only sits down to his meal in the darkness of night. It is better to understand the word metaphorically: not as referring to the 'self-denial and mental distresses of those who are bent upon the accumulation of wealth,' but the gloom of poverty, although his money could have brought light into his life (cf. *his lamp shall be put out in the blackest darkness*, Prov. xx. 20, signifying he will be reduced to extreme poverty). An Arab proverb, 'he sleeps in darkness,' means that the man is poor.

*and sickness.* lit. 'and his sickness.' It 'stands for *we-choli lo*, lit. "and grief is for him," i.e. "and he has grief" ' (Ginsburg). The *sickness* is primarily of the mind, but eventually the body is affected.

*wrath.* The Hebrew word *ketseph* is always used in the Bible of God except here and Esther i. 18. Perhaps its significance in these passages is 'chagrin.'

**17-19** ENJOY LIFE

After meditating upon the foolishness of the miser's mode of existence, Koheleth comes back to the conclusion forced upon him in his previous reflections, that the sensible course to follow is to draw out of life whatever enjoyment it affords (cf. ii. 24, iii. 22). We shall hear the same note struck again in viii. 15, ix. 7, xi. 7ff.

to eat and to drink, and to enjoy pleasure for all his labour, wherein he laboureth under the sun, all the days of his life which God hath given him; for this is his portion. 18. Every man also to whom God hath given riches and wealth, and hath given him power to eat thereof, and to take his portion, and to rejoice in his labour—this is the gift of God. 19. For let him remember the days of his life that they are not many; for God answereth him in the joy of his heart.

טוֹבָה בְכָל־עֲמָלוֹ ׀ שֶׁיַּעֲמֹל
תַּֽחַת־הַשֶּׁמֶשׁ מִסְפַּר יְמֵי־
חַיָּו אֲשֶׁר־נָֽתַן־לוֹ הָאֱלֹהִים
18 כִּי־הוּא חֶלְקֽוֹ׃ גַּם כָּל־
הָאָדָם אֲשֶׁר נָֽתַן־לוֹ הָאֱלֹהִים
עֹשֶׁר וּנְכָסִים וְהִשְׁלִיטוֹ לֶאֱכֹל
מִמֶּנּוּ וְלָשֵׂאת אֶת־חֶלְקוֹ
וְלִשְׂמֹחַ בַּעֲמָלוֹ זֹה מַתַּת
19 אֱלֹהִים הִֽיא׃ כִּי לֹא הַרְבֵּה
יִזְכֹּר אֶת־יְמֵי חַיָּיו כִּי
הָאֱלֹהִים מַעֲנֶה בְּשִׂמְחַת לִבּֽוֹ׃

It should be noted that 'the Hebrew writer, while frankly recognizing man's lowly place in the scheme of things, and enjoining the pursuit of natural pleasures, goes on to find the ultimate sanction of that enjoyment *in a religious setting*' (Levine).

17. *I have seen.* In the Hebrew the subject is emphasized (as in ii. 24).

*it is good, yea, it is comely.* A more exact translation is, 'behold, that which I have seen good is that it is comely.'

*enjoy pleasure.* See on ii. 1.

*all the days of his life.* See on ii. 3.

*this is his portion.* As in iii. 22.

18. *to whom God hath given riches.* As in Deut. viii. 18, prosperity is bestowed upon man by God, and His intention must have been that the fortunate person should make use of what He had granted and not just hoard it.

19. *for let him . . . many.* This is the meaning attached to the words by the Jewish commentators and many moderns. Life is short, so enjoy the few years at your disposal. A.V. and R.V. render, 'for he shall not much remember the days of his life,' i.e. a man will not worry about life's brevity.

*answereth.* An impossible translation, since the verb is causative in form. The verb *anah*, as well as its noun *inyan*, is always employed in this Book to denote 'to be occupied with a task' (cf. i. 13, iii. 10). Ginsburg is, therefore, probably correct in translating, 'that God causeth him to work for the enjoyment of his heart.'

1. There is an evil which I have seen under the sun, and it is heavy upon men: 2. a man to whom God giveth riches, wealth, and honour, so that he wanteth nothing for his soul of all that he desireth, yet God giveth him not power to eat thereof, but a stranger eateth it; this is vanity, and it is an evil disease. 3. If a man beget a hundred children, and live many years, so that the days of his years are many, but his soul have not

1 יֵשׁ רָעָה אֲשֶׁר רָאִיתִי תַּחַת
הַשָּׁמֶשׁ וְרַבָּה הִיא עַל־
2 הָאָדָם׃ אִישׁ אֲשֶׁר יִתֶּן־לוֹ
הָאֱלֹהִים עֹשֶׁר וּנְכָסִים וְכָבוֹד
וְאֵינֶנּוּ חָסֵר לְנַפְשׁוֹ ׀ מִכֹּל
אֲשֶׁר־יִתְאַוֶּה וְלֹא־יַשְׁלִיטֶנּוּ
הָאֱלֹהִים לֶאֱכֹל מִמֶּנּוּ כִּי אִישׁ
נָכְרִי יֹאכְלֶנּוּ זֶה הֶבֶל וָחֳלִי
3 רָע הוּא׃ אִם־יוֹלִיד אִישׁ
מֵאָה וְשָׁנִים רַבּוֹת יִחְיֶה וְרַב ׀
שֶׁיִּהְיוּ יְמֵי־שָׁנָיו וְנַפְשׁוֹ לֹא־

**1-9 WEALTH WITHOUT ENJOYMENT**

1. *it is heavy upon men.* lit. 'it is much upon men,' which Rashi interprets as 'it is prevalent among men'; but the preposition *upon* is against it. A similar phrase occurs in viii. 6, *the evil of man is great upon him.*

2. The wording of the verse is reminiscent of v. 18, although the situation is different. In the former passage God *hath given him power to eat thereof,* while here He denies him the opportunity.

*honour.* In such a context, the Hebrew word *kabod* stands for 'splendour, luxury' (cf. Ps. xlix. 17).

*soul.* In the sense of 'desire, appetite.'

*God giveth him not power.* The contrast of the next verse suggests that the circumstance here is that he dies early in manhood and childless.

*a stranger.* He has no son to be his heir.

3. *a hundred children.* The word *children* does not occur in the text but has to be supplied (cf. 1 Sam. ii. 5). *Hundred* merely represents a large number (cf. Gen. xxvi. 12; 2 Sam. xxiv. 3; Prov. xvii. 10) and it is unnecessary to assume that numerous grandchildren are included. Koheleth states a case which is the opposite of the one he cited in the preceding verse: a man who has an abundance of heirs.

*and live many years.* Unlike the man described in the last verse who died young.

*so that the days . . many.* This translation makes the phrase mere tautology. Render: 'however many be the days of his years,' i.e. think of him as living as long as you please.

*but his soul . . . good.* If for any reason

enough of good, and moreover he have no burial; I say, that an untimely birth is better than he; 4. for it cometh in vanity, and departeth in darkness, and the name thereof is covered with darkness; 5. moreover it hath not seen the sun nor known it; this hath gratification rather than the other; 6. yea, though he live a thousand years twice told, and enjoy no good; do not all go to one place?

תִשְׂבַּע מִן־הַטּוֹבָה וְגַם־
קְבוּרָה לֹא־הָיְתָה לּוֹ אָמַרְתִּי
4 טוֹב מִמֶּנּוּ הַנָּפֶל׃ כִּי־בַהֶבֶל
בָּא וּבַחֹשֶׁךְ יֵלֵךְ וּבַחֹשֶׁךְ שְׁמוֹ
5 יְכֻסֶּה׃ גַּם־שֶׁמֶשׁ לֹא־רָאָה
6 וְלֹא יָדָע נַחַת לָזֶה מִזֶּה׃ וְאִלּוּ
חָיָה אֶלֶף שָׁנִים פַּעֲמַיִם וְטוֹבָה
לֹא רָאָה הֲלֹא אֶל־מָקוֹם

he lacks the capacity to experience the enjoyment to be derived from wealth and he feels dissatisfaction.

*moreover he have no burial.* Better, 'and even were he to have no burial'; were he never to die. This seems the appropriate sense in the context. The usual complaint is that man does not live long enough to have the fullest pleasure from his possessions. Koheleth, therefore, suggests the other extreme, viz. an endless life without the means of full enjoyment. The explanation which takes the phrase to refer to the honourable disposal of the body at death does not agree with the argument.

*an untimely birth.* A stillborn child which has never lived at all.

4. *in vanity.* Ginsburg renders 'in nothingness' which he explains as 'a mere nothing in size and form.' The Hebrew rather means that the stillborn child comes into the world to no purpose.

*departeth in darkness.* The verb indicates burial (as in v. 14) and *darkness* describes the private interment without the presence of mourners. Such is still the practice among Jews with a stillborn child.

*the name . . . darkness.* As *Metsudath David* remarks, the child has no name given to it, and the phrase is to be understood metaphorically: it is quickly and completely forgotten. This kind of nonexistence, declares Koheleth, is preferable to an unending or long life without satisfaction.

5. *seen the sun.* An idiom for the state of living (again vii. 11, xi. 7; cf. Job iii. 16, *as infants that never saw light*).

*nor known it.* The Hebrew lacks anything corresponding to *it.* Ibn Ezra translates, 'it knew nothing,' it was never a conscious being. Thereby it escaped all the vexations and frustrations which are the normal experience.

*this hath gratification.* From this standpoint the stillborn child has a better lot than the person who lives long.

6. *a thousand years twice told.* More than double the longest age on record, that of Methuselah (Gen. v. 27).

*enjoy no good.* Longevity without physical enjoyment is profitless.

*do not all go to one place?* The end is the same for those who die young or old, viz. return to the dust (cf. iii. 20).

7 All the labour of man is for his
mouth,
And yet the appetite is not filled.

8. For what advantage hath the wise
more than the fool? or the poor man
that hath understanding, in walking
before the living? 9. Better is the
seeing of the eyes than the wandering
of the desire; this also is vanity and
a striving after wind.

10. Whatsoever cometh into being,

7 אֶחָד הַכֹּל הוֹלֵךְ׃ כָּל־עֲמַל
הָאָדָם לְפִיהוּ וְגַם־הַנֶּפֶשׁ לֹא
8 תִמָּלֵא׃ כִּי מַה־יּוֹתֵר לֶחָכָם
מִן־הַכְּסִיל מַה־לֶּעָנִי יוֹדֵעַ
9 לַהֲלֹךְ נֶגֶד הַחַיִּים׃ טוֹב
מַרְאֵה עֵינַיִם מֵהֲלָךְ־נָפֶשׁ
גַּם־זֶה הֶבֶל וּרְעוּת רוּחַ׃
10 מַה־שֶּׁהָיָה כְּבָר נִקְרָא שְׁמוֹ

**7.** A proverb quoted to substantiate the view that the stillborn child *hath gratification rather than the other* (verse 5). The former does not know unsatisfied desire.

*for his mouth.* For self-indulgence.

*appetite.* lit. 'soul,' as in verse 2.

**8.** *what advantage . . . fool?* Cf. ii. 15f. where the point common to both was death; here it is the fact that alike they cannot gratify their longings.

*or the poor . . . living?* The clause is obscure, and it has been suggested that the comparative preposition *min* should be repeated after *the poor man.* The translation would then be, 'or (what advantage hath) the poor man more than he who knoweth to walk before the living?' *Living* signifies 'people in general' as in iv. 15, and 'he who knoweth' etc. indicates an important personage in the community. But if this were the intention, the terms would have been reversed: 'or he who knoweth . . . over the poor man?' As in the first clause the contrast is between a person of superior quality and one of inferior quality, it is natural to expect the same in the second clause. It is preferable, therefore, to translate, 'Or (what advantage) hath the poor man who knoweth to walk before the living (more than the fool who hath not this knowledge)?' The former, in his poverty, has learnt to accommodate himself to his circumstances and make the best of his lot, while the fool is afflicted by an insatiable hunger for more than he has. Nevertheless, they are similar in that they both lead cheerless lives because their appetites remain unsatisfied.

**9.** *the seeing of the eyes.* That which the eyes see and can be enjoyed.

*the wandering of the desire.* The quest of longings which may prove in vain. The moral is expressed in the English proverb, 'A bird in the hand is worth two in the bush.'

*this also is vanity.* viz. to enjoy *the seeing of the eyes,* since it does not put an end to the hunger for desires unattained.

### 10-12 VANITY OF MAN'S STRUGGLE AGAINST FATE

Koheleth now repeats the point he had made in iii. 9ff. Man's dissatisfaction is due to the circumstance that he is a mortal creature, and for that reason is unable to achieve all his wishes.

**10.** *whatsoever cometh into being.* Render, with the R.V. margin: 'whatsoever he be, his name was given him long ago, and

the name thereof was given long ago,
and it is foreknown what man is;
neither can he contend with Him
that is mightier than he. 11. Seeing
there are many words that increase
vanity, what is man the better?
12. For who knoweth what is good
for man in his life, all the days of his
vain life which he spendeth as a
shadow? for who can tell a man
what shall be after him under the
sun?

וְנוֹדָע אֲשֶׁר־הוּא אָדָם וְלֹא־
יוּכַל לָדִין עִם שֶׁהַתַּקִּיף*
מִמֶּנּוּ׃ כִּי יֵשׁ־דְּבָרִים הַרְבֵּה 11
מַרְבִּים הָבֶל מַה־יֹּתֵר
לָאָדָם׃ כִּי מִי־יוֹדֵעַ מַה־ 12
טּוֹב לָאָדָם בַּחַיִּים מִסְפַּר
יְמֵי־חַיֵּי הֶבְלוֹ וְיַעֲשֵׂם כַּצֵּל
אֲשֶׁר מִי־יַגִּיד לָאָדָם מַה־
יִּהְיֶה אַחֲרָיו תַּחַת הַשָּׁמֶשׁ׃

* v. 10. יתיר ה׳

it is known that he is man,' i.e. the human being is nothing more than *adam*, the very name describing his condition as a being formed *of the dust of the ground* (*adamah*, Gen. ii. 7). When God created the first man, He willed that he was to be mortal.

*contend with Him.* By printing *Him* with a capital, A. J. takes the word to allude to God; but *takkif* is nowhere else applied to the Deity. Translate, 'contend with what is mightier than he,' viz. death. It is so understood by Rashi and other Jewish commentators.

11. *words.* The Hebrew means 'words' or 'things.' If it is taken in the former sense, Koheleth maintains that the more man complains about his fate, the more useless it is to do so because it will not help him in the least. If the latter signification is accepted, the vanity of wealth is again proclaimed, since it cannot avert his fate.

12. *who knoweth what is good.* A final reason for uncomplaining submission to the fixed order of things is the impossibility of defining the *good* in life. Many answers had been advanced, but none proved satisfactory under examination.

*as a shadow.* Cf. Ps. cxliv. 4; Job viii. 9; 1 Chron. xxix. 15.

*after him.* 'The uncertainty of the future creates a part of the difficulty of telling what is good for man' (Barton). This is the only explanation possible in view of the addition *under the sun* which makes it clear that the instability of his fortune upon earth is meant.

טוב שם משמן טוב!



1 A good name is better than precious oil;
And the day of death than the day of one's birth.

2 It is better to go to the house of mourning,
Than to go to the house of feasting;
For that is the end of all men,
And the living will lay it to his heart.

1 טוֹב* שֵׁם מִשֶּׁמֶן טוֹב וְיוֹם הַמָּוֶת
2 מִיּוֹם הִוָּלְדוֹ׃ טוֹב לָלֶכֶת
אֶל־בֵּית־אֵבֶל מִלֶּכֶת אֶל־
בֵּית מִשְׁתֶּה בַּאֲשֶׁר הוּא סוֹף
כָּל־הָאָדָם וְהַחַי יִתֵּן אֶל־

* ט׳ רבתי v. 1.

**1-12** THE THINGS THAT ARE BETTER

THE whole of this section, with the exception of verses 10 and 12, consists of a series of poetical proverbs. A connecting link is the initial word *tob* (*it is better*) which occurs in verses 1, 2, 3, 5, 8 and 11. In the comparison preference is given to what accords with the more serious attitude to life.

1. *a good name.* The Hebrew is simply 'a name' but, as in Proverbs xxii. 1, it is the equivalent of 'good repute.' After describing all else as vanity, Koheleth discovers one aim to be worth while, viz. to have the esteem of one's fellows.

*precious oil.* lit. 'good oil' (cf. *thy name is as ointment poured forth*, Cant. i. 3). There is a noteworthy assonance in the Hebrew for *name* (*shem*) and *oil* (*shemen*). Perfumed oil was profusely employed in the Orient to overcome the odour of perspiration and was considered a great luxury.

*the day of death.* To a man who has so lived that he gained for himself *a good name*, death means nothing else than the victorious end of the adventure which is life. He is then in better state than at the time of his birth when he started out on his adventure, not knowing what may be in store for him. The Midrash illustrates the clause with the parable: It is as if there were two ocean-going ships, one leaving the harbour and the other entering it. As the one sailed out of the harbour the bystanders all rejoiced, but none displayed any joy over the one which was entering the harbour. A shrewd man remarked, 'There is no cause to rejoice over the ship which is leaving because nobody knows what storms it may encounter; but when a ship returns in safety, that is an occasion for rejoicing.' Similarly, when a person dies all should rejoice that he reached his haven with a good name and in peace.

2. *the house of mourning.* The practice among Jews, to observe mourning for seven days after the burial of a near relative, dates from early times (cf. Gen. l. 10), and 'seven days are the days of mourning for the dead' (Ecclus. xxii. 12). To visit the mourner was held to be a meritorious act. It comforted the bereaved, but also induced in the visitor a consciousness of life's brevity and frailty. Such reflections served a better purpose than the frivolity which pervaded a place of feasting.

*that is the end of all men.* It is well to be mindful of the fact, and a visit to a house of mourning is a reminder (cf. Ps. xc. 12 and the Rabbinic aphorism, 'Reflect upon three things, and thou wilt not come within the power of sin: know whence thou comest, and whither thou art going, and before Whom thou wilt in future have to give account and reckoning,' Aboth).

*lay it to his heart.* He will give serious consideration to the truth that not only does life end, but the value of *a good name* is the sole possession of value at that time.

3 Vexation is better than laughter;
For by the sadness of the countenance the heart may be gladdened.
4 The heart of the wise is in the house of mourning;
But the heart of fools is in the house of mirth.
5 It is better to hear the rebuke of the wise,
Than for a man to hear the song of fools.
6 For as the crackling of thorns under a pot,
So is the laughter of the fool;
This also is vanity.
7 Surely oppression turneth a wise man into a fool;

לִבּוֹ׃ טוֹב כַּעַס מִשְּׂחוֹק כִּי 3
בְרֹעַ פָּנִים יִיטַב לֵב׃ לֵב 4
חֲכָמִים בְּבֵית אֵבֶל וְלֵב
כְּסִילִים בְּבֵית שִׂמְחָה׃ טוֹב 5
לִשְׁמֹעַ גַּעֲרַת חָכָם מֵאִישׁ שֹׁמֵעַ
שִׁיר כְּסִילִים׃ כִּי כְקוֹל 6
הַסִּירִים תַּחַת הַסִּיר כֵּן שְׂחֹק
הַכְּסִיל וְגַם־זֶה הָבֶל׃ כִּי 7

3. *vexation.* This verse is part of the theme which began with the opening of the chapter and is continued in the next verse; this fact must determine the use of the Hebrew word here. *Vexation* is clearly unsuitable. In Job vi. 2 it occurs (with a slightly different spelling) as a parallel to *calamity* with the meaning 'grief.' It defines the emotion aroused in a house of mourning.

*laughter.* A frivolous frame of mind (see on ii. 2). His point is that only when one is in a serious mood does he feel disposed to think seriously about life.

*the sadness of the countenance.* lit. 'the evil of the countenance' (cf. the question addressed by Joseph to Pharaoh's butler and baker after their dreams, *wherefore look ye so sad to-day?* Gen. xl. 7, lit. 'why is your countenance evil?'). The phrase, therefore, implies a brooding mind reflected in a troubled look on the face.

*the heart may be gladdened.* Better, 'the heart is improved' (Ginsburg). Rashi comments: the heart of man will be turned to better his ways.

4. *the heart of the wise . . . mourning.* Their thoughts are upon the day of death (Rashi). Their mind is attuned to the seriousness which is natural in a house of bereavement and it influences their way of living.

*the heart of fools . . . mirth.* The careless mood in a place of revelry appeals to the disposition of fools; they face life in that reckless spirit.

5. *better to hear the rebuke of the wise.* After dealing with the silent reproof which the man of understanding receives by contact with death, Koheleth deals with the beneficial effects which may be gained by listening to a sage's admonition. To have one's conduct criticized hurts, but it is the way to moral improvement.

*than for a man to hear.* Or, 'than (to be) a man hearing.'

*the song of fools.* Ehrlich explains *song* as 'fulsome praise' which conceals one's faults and so tends to confirm them.

6. *crackling of thorns under a pot.* The Hebrew has a play on words: *thorns* is *sirim* and *pot* is *sir.* English commentators try to reproduce the original by the translation, 'the crackling of nettles under a kettle.' To use thorns as fuel for cooking is not satisfactory; they flame up quickly, but as quickly are burnt to ashes before the process of cooking is finished (cf. Ps. lviii. 10, cxviii. 12). It is the same with *the laughter of the fool,* understood by Ehrlich as 'the applause of fools'; it serves no useful purpose.

*this also is vanity.* That likewise is to be included in the list of things to be

And a gift destroyeth the understanding.
8 Better is the end of a thing than the beginning thereof;
And the patient in spirit is better than the proud in spirit.
9 Be not hasty in thy spirit to be angry;
For anger resteth in the bosom of fools.
10. Say not thou: 'How was it that

הָעֹשֶׁק יְהוֹלֵל חָכָם וִיאַבֵּד
8 אֶת־לֵב מַתָּנָה׃ טוֹב אַחֲרִית
דָּבָר מֵרֵאשִׁיתוֹ טוֹב אֶרֶךְ־
9 רוּחַ מִגְּבַהּ רוּחַ׃ אַל־תְּבַהֵל
בְּרוּחֲךָ לִכְעוֹס כִּי כַעַס בְּחֵיק
10 כְּסִילִים יָנוּחַ׃ אַל־תֹּאמַר

stamped with the word *vanity*. Another suggestion is to connect the clause with the next verse.

7. Jastrow's translation, 'for extortion deprives a wise man of reason, and a bribe corrupts the mind,' gives the sense of the text exactly. There is, however, a difficulty in the conjunction 'for' which A. J. renders *surely*. It is the same initial word as in the preceding verse, and appears to imply a sequence of thought which Plumptre understands to be: the *song* and *laughter* of fools, i.e. evil-doers, lead to selfish luxury, and therefore to all forms of unjust gains. More probably we have here a common literary device called 'chiasmus,' according to which words or phrases are arranged 'crosswise.' In verse 5 there is mention of *the wise* and then of *fools*. In the succeeding verse the order is reversed: first there is a statement about *the fool* followed by one about *a wise man*.

*oppression*. The tyrannical use of power for self-enrichment.

*turneth a wise man into a fool*. Such an abuse of power is completely demoralizing, and if practised by a wise man will neutralize all his wisdom so that he behaves like a fool.

*a gift*. A bribe to pervert justice (Exod. xxiii. 8; Deut. xvi. 19).

8. *end of a thing*. As was observed on vi. 11 the Hebrew can signify 'thing' or 'word.' If we adopt the former, the statement means 'at the beginning of the thing we do not know what will be at its end; but when its end is good, it is concluded with good' (Rashi). This interpretation does not fit the second half of the verse. It is therefore better to translate, 'Better is the end of a word (or, words, collectively).' Only rarely is a man able to judge what will be the ultimate effect of a remark. He may make a perfectly innocuous observation which can nevertheless have serious consequences. The moral is to be exceedingly cautious in speech, and, so far as possible, foresee what effect it will produce before uttering it.

*the patient in spirit*. i.e. the man who can control his temper and not make a rash retort when provoked for which he will afterwards be sorry.

*the proud in spirit*. A person of this temperament treats his fellow-man with contempt and does not weigh his words.

9. *be not hasty . . . angry*. As it is necessary to control one's words, there is equal necessity to control one's emotions. The person who readily gives way to vexation stands in his own light.

*anger resteth in the bosom of fools*. i.e. vexation (so render) finds a resting-

מֶה הָיָה שֶׁהַיָּמִים הָרִאשֹׁנִים
הָיוּ טוֹבִים מֵאֵלֶּה כִּי לֹא
מֵחָכְמָה שָׁאַלְתָּ עַל־זֶה׃
11 טוֹבָה חָכְמָה עִם־נַחֲלָה וְיֹתֵר
12 לְרֹאֵי הַשָּׁמֶשׁ׃ כִּי בְּצֵל
הַחָכְמָה בְּצֵל הַכָּסֶף וְיִתְרוֹן
דַּעַת הַחָכְמָה תְּחַיֶּה בְעָלֶיהָ׃

the former days were better than these?' for it is not out of wisdom that thou inquirest concerning this.

11 Wisdom is good with an inheritance,
Yea, a profit to them that see the sun.

12. For wisdom is a defence, even as money is a defence; but the excellency of knowledge is, that wisdom preserveth the life of him that hath it.

place there. Wise men banish it from their hearts, fools welcome it. For the use of the verb, cf. *in the heart of him that hath discernment wisdom resteth* (Prov. xiv. 33).

**10.** *the former days were better.* The verse is usually interpreted as a warning against praising 'the good old times' to which men are so prone. If this is the intention, the sentence is disjointed and can only be suited to the context with difficulty. If, however, the previous verse deprecated a readiness to feel vexation, this verse is a natural sequel. It is unwise, urges Koheleth, when troubles come upon you, to grow peevish and imagine that your past life was free of these trials. The earlier years were probably no better than the present, so do not give way to vexation.

*not out of wisdom.* But out of folly, and it is only in a fool's bosom that vexation finds an abode, raising the querulous complaint about the hard times of the present as compared with the easy times of the past.

*concerning this.* viz. this phenomenon that the former days were better.

**11.** *wisdom is good with an inheritance.* Plumptre does not think the verse expresses the cynical idea that 'wisdom is all very well if you have property to fall back upon.' He finds a more satisfactory meaning by construing the preposition as denoting comparison, 'wisdom is good as an inheritance'; but the preposition cannot have this force. The Midrash comments: 'Wisdom is good when it is an inheritance (i.e. when it is acquired through successive generations of teachers, or transmitted from father to son for several generations; it will then be free from error).' It also gives the phrase its literal interpretation which is rather practical than cynical, 'Wisdom is good when there is an inheritance together with it,' in agreement with the teaching, 'Excellent is the study of Torah together with a worldly occupation' (Aboth). The combination of the two is what is commended.

*a profit.* It is certainly an advantage for a man to be equipped with wisdom (cf. ii. 13f.).

*that see the sun.* Living persons (cf. vi. 5). Williams has this note: 'What fresh statement do these words add to the preceding? Hence translate, "with regard to (i.e. in the opinion of) them that see the sun." Ibn Ezra comments: for men honour him for his wealth.'

**12.** *for wisdom is a defence.* More lit. 'for (to be) in the shade of wisdom (is to be) in the shade of money.' 'Shade' is a common metaphor for a place of shelter from danger (cf. Isa. xxxii. 2; Ps. xvii. 8, xci. 1). The Wisdom writers appre-

13. Consider the work of God; for
who can make that straight, which
He hath made crooked? 14. In the
day of prosperity be joyful, and in
the day of adversity consider; God
hath made even the one as well as
the other, to the end that man
should find nothing after him.

13 רְאֵה אֶת־מַעֲשֵׂה הָאֱלֹהִים כִּי
מִי יוּכַל לְתַקֵּן אֵת אֲשֶׁר עִוְּתוֹ׃
14 בְּיוֹם טוֹבָה הֱיֵה בְטוֹב וּבְיוֹם
רָעָה רְאֵה גַּם אֶת־זֶה לְעֻמַּת־
זֶה עָשָׂה הָאֱלֹהִים עַל־דִּבְרַת
שֶׁלֹּא יִמְצָא הָאָדָם אַחֲרָיו

ciated the fact that money has advantages and can bring a measure of security from rapacious governors (cf. Prov. xiii. 8); but, asserts Koheleth, the same power of affording protection is held by wisdom. Later he speaks of *a man poor and wise, and he by his wisdom delivered the city* (ix. 15).

*excellency.* Better, 'advantage,' a key-word of this Book. Wisdom, he claims, is superior to money as a *defence.*

*preserveth the life.* It is doubtful whether the phrase can mean 'wisdom has a pre-eminence over riches inasmuch as it has the power of affecting the inner man, it makes him serene and cheerful, which the former cannot do' (Ginsburg); or, 'it quickens those who have it to a new and higher life' (Plumptre). Simpler is the explanation of *Metsudath David*: wisdom can be the means of saving a man's life when it is in danger, whereas riches may be the cause of the owner's death at the hands of men who seek to rob him.

**13-14** SUBMIT TO WHAT GOD HAS WILLED

**13.** *consider.* lit. 'see,' and it is well remarked, 'This word may be regarded as summing up much of the practical philosophy of this Book. The writer advises us not to perplex ourselves too much about the mysteries of the universe, but by observing and reflecting upon God's methods, seek to discover how we may rule our lives in accordance with the Divine will' (Martin). This attitude towards speculation about the problems of life is the one adopted by the large majority of the Talmudical Rabbis.

*straight . . . crooked.* The language and thought recall i. 15. Whatever God has ordained is immutable, and it is futile for man to think of 'rectifying' His work.

**14.** *in the day of prosperity be joyful.* lit. 'in the day of good (fortune) be in good'; i.e. enjoy any period of good fortune that comes to you because it is God's doing (cf. 'Defraud not thyself of a good day; and let not the portion of a good desire pass thee by,' Ecclus. xiv. 14). Talmudical teaching on this subject reads, 'In the Hereafter a man will have to give judgment and reckoning for all that his eye saw but he did not eat.'

*consider.* The same word as in the last verse; it is repeated to indicate the point of view there expressed. If bad times come, do not be depressed and complain; that also is His will.

*the one as well as the other.* lit. 'this corresponding to this.' God's plan was not to make human life an unbroken spell of happiness or calamity, but both are constituents of life in His scheme and they interchange.

*to the end . . . after him.* In consequence of this plan, the human being cannot forecast what lies in store for him in the future, whether his prosperity will last or whether his ill-luck will end. That being so, submit to your fate; make the most of the good fortune while you can, and do not be excessively worried when times are bad.

15. All things have I seen in the
days of my vanity; there is a righteous man that perisheth in his righteousness, and there is a wicked man
that prolongeth his life in his evil-
doing. 16. Be not righteous overmuch; neither make thyself overwise; why shouldest thou destroy
thyself? 17. Be not overmuch

מְאוּמָה׃ אֶת־הַכֹּל רָאִיתִי 15
בִּימֵי הֶבְלִי יֵשׁ צַדִּיק אֹבֵד
בְּצִדְקוֹ וְיֵשׁ רָשָׁע מַאֲרִיךְ
בְּרָעָתוֹ׃ אַל־תְּהִי צַדִּיק 16
הַרְבֵּה וְאַל־תִּתְחַכַּם יוֹתֵר
לָמָּה תִּשּׁוֹמֵם׃ אַל־תִּרְשַׁע 17

**15-22 SOME RULES OF LIVING.** By advising submission to the order of things in the world, Koheleth did not imply that man must be completely passive. Within circumscribed limits he has freedom of movement and action, as well as the choice between alternative courses. He accordingly prescribes a few guiding principles.

15. *all things.* In the course of his career he took note of all the varied phenomena which the world presents, and he goes on to mention one that had impressed him deeply.

*in the days of my vanity.* If the Hebrew is so understood, the reference must be to the period when he made his series of experiments (ii. 1ff.), but this is very improbable. According to a common idiom the phrase means 'my vain days,' i.e. my swiftly passing days (*Metsudath David*).

*there is a righteous man.* Koheleth was disturbed by this anomaly as were other Hebrew thinkers; it is the theme of Ps. lxxiii. and the Book of Job.

*prolongeth his life.* The words *his life* do not occur in the text but are obviously intended.

16. *be not righteous overmuch.* Koheleth is a fearless thinker and moves on to his logical deductions wherever they may lead him. Since it is a fact that righteous men perish in their righteousness, he draws the conclusion that excessive piety is not a means for securing a long and happy life.

*neither make thyself overwise.* He has admitted that wisdom has advantages over folly, but he has also proved by experience that wisdom is ultimately a vanity. Consequently he advises against devoting too much effort to becoming wise.

*why shouldest thou destroy thyself?* This translation hardly yields sense. In agreement with *Metsudath David* Ginsburg renders 'for thou wilt only make thyself to be forsaken,' i.e. by being over-righteous and very wise, one alienates the friendship of ordinary men and is left solitary and wretched. Barton likewise remarks, 'The world often hates its greatest men and makes marks of them. In one sense it is not good to be ahead of one's times.' It is better to adopt the meaning which this form of the verb has in other passages, viz. *and was astonished* (Isa. lix. 16, lxiii. 5), *my heart within me is appalled* (Ps. cxliii. 4). Translate: 'why shouldest thou be overcome with amazement?' If, he argues, you are excessively righteous or wise and obtain no reward for your virtue in a long and happy life, your mind will be filled with amazement at your lot and your heart greatly disturbed.

wicked, neither be thou foolish;
why shouldest thou die before thy
time? 18. It is good that thou
shouldest take hold of the one; yea,
also from the other withdraw not
thy hand; for he that feareth God
shall discharge himself of them all.

19. Wisdom is a stronghold to the
wise man more than ten rulers that

הַרְבֵּה וְאַל־תְּהִי סָכָל לָמָּה
18 תָמוּת בְּלֹא עִתֶּךָ׃ טוֹב אֲשֶׁר
תֶּאֱחֹז בָּזֶה וְגַם־מִזֶּה אַל־תַּנַּח
אֶת־יָדֶךָ כִּי־יְרֵא אֱלֹהִים
19 יֵצֵא אֶת־כֻּלָּם׃ הַחָכְמָה תָּעֹז
לֶחָכָם מֵעֲשָׂרָה שַׁלִּיטִים אֲשֶׁר

**17.** *be not overmuch wicked.* Despite the truth that wicked men sometimes live long, it is nevertheless a fact that evil may be the cause of a premature death. Remember, he contends, that vice shortens life. 'There is no question of Koheleth's indirectly permitting a little sin, though he says in verse 20 that some sin is in fact inevitable. Observe also, that, probably by a subconscious shrinking from apparent encouragement to sin, he avoids the word "sin" (*techeta*) here. For the word *wicked* (*tirsha*) stands in more direct contrast to *righteous* (verse 16), and perhaps means the wilful rejection of the many regulations of the Law. Do not cast off its restraints too far' (Williams).

*neither be thou foolish.* Even if wisdom can bring one disappointment, it is true that through folly a man may take a dangerous course with fatal consequences.

*die before thy time.* Koheleth contradicts his earlier statement that the time of a man's death is fixed (iii. 2). Previously he had made generalizations, now he deals with concrete facts.

**18.** *it is good . . . thy hand. The one* and *the other* are literally 'this' and 'this,' and are most naturally referred to the two contrasting rules he had just mentioned, viz. *be not righteous overmuch* and *be not overmuch wicked.* By accepting only one of them, harmful consequences will ensure. If the former only is followed, the man's trust in Divine Providence may be undermined; if the latter, he will incur the penalty of sin. The wise procedure is, therefore, to cling to both.

*he that feareth God.* With this influence in his life, man avoids the harmful extreme in both directions: he will be deterred from heinous sin and avoid the menace to his faith if ill-fortune comes upon him.

*shall discharge himself of them all.* lit. 'will go forth with all of them,' which Rashi well explains: by means of both these rules he will fulfil his duty in the matter of righteousness and wickedness in a proper manner. This sense of the verb 'go forth' is common in Rabbinic Hebrew.

**19.** *wisdom.* If, as is probable, this verse is to be linked on to the preceding, the term here applies to the principles of action which had been laid down. There may also be a connection with *he that feareth God* in accordance with the fundamental teaching of the school to which Koheleth belonged, *The fear of the LORD is the beginning of wisdom* (Ps. cxi. 10; cf. Prov. i. 7).

*a stronghold.* The rules of wise conduct he has expounded afford protection to a man.

*ten rulers.* As Ibn Ezra remarks, *ten* stands for 'any number, many.' While it is true that 'many heads are better than one,' and consultation between many leaders increases the chance of safety are in a city. 20. For there is not a righteous man upon earth, that doeth good, and sinneth not.

21. Also take not heed unto all words that are spoken, lest thou hear thy servant curse thee; 22. for oftentimes also thine own heart knoweth that thou thyself likewise hast cursed others.

23. All this have I tried by wis-

20 הָיוּ בָּעִיר׃ כִּי אָדָם אֵין צַדִּיק
בָּאָרֶץ אֲשֶׁר יַעֲשֶׂה־טּוֹב וְלֹא
21 יֶחֱטָא׃ גַּם לְכָל־הַדְּבָרִים
אֲשֶׁר יְדַבֵּרוּ אַל־תִּתֵּן לִבֶּךָ
אֲשֶׁר לֹא־תִשְׁמַע אֶת־עַבְדְּךָ
22 מְקַלְלֶךָ׃ כִּי גַּם־פְּעָמִים
רַבּוֹת יָדַע לִבֶּךָ אֲשֶׁר גַּם־אַתָּ*
23 קִלַּלְתָּ אֲחֵרִים׃ כָּל־זֹה

v. 22 אתה ק'

when a city is threatened by attack, nevertheless *wisdom*, as here defined, stands a man in even better stead when he is assailed by the complexities of life.

20. *for*. The conjunction indicates a sequence of thought, but what it is has been variously explained. The suggestion that such is the conclusion to be drawn from the narrative of Abraham's intercession on behalf of Sodom (Gen. xviii. 32), identified with the *city* with *ten rulers*, is far-fetched. Ibn Ezra connects with verse 16, *be not righteous overmuch*, making the words a warning that such an ideal is unattainable. More probably it follows on verse 18: despite the fact that a man fears God, he is certain to fall into sin during his lifetime, and for that reason requires the protective power of *wisdom*.

*that doeth good, and sinneth not*. i.e. always does good and never sins (Ibn Ezra); a reminiscence of 1 Kings viii. 46.

21. *all words that are spoken*. Better, 'all words that (men) speak (about thee).' Inasmuch as all men have faults, it is foolish to be eager to know what people are saying about you. You are likely to hear censure rather than commendation, because a man's sins and not his good deeds are more usually the topic of conversation.

*lest thou hear thy servant curse thee*. 'No man is a hero to his valet, and if he is anxious to know his servant's estimate of him, he may discover, however wise and good he strives to be, that it may find utterance in a curse and not a blessing' (Plumptre).

22. Although A.J. follows the order of the Hebrew words, the sense is better reproduced in 'for thine own heart knoweth that even thou too hast oftentimes cursed others.' The truth of verse 21 is verified by an appeal to the practice of those to whom it is addressed.

*heart*. Corresponds here to 'conscience.'

### 23-29 VANITY OF SEARCH FOR WISDOM AND A GOOD WOMAN

23. *all this*. He alludes to the rules of conduct he had so far formulated in this chapter. He had tested them and found them satisfactory.

dom; I said: 'I will get wisdom'; but it was far from me. 24. That which is is far off, and exceeding deep; who can find it out? 25. I turned about, and applied my heart to know and to search out, and to seek wisdom and the reason of things, and to know wickedness to be folly, and foolishness to be madness;

נִסִּיתִי בַחָכְמָה אָמַרְתִּי
אֶחְכָּמָה וְהִיא רְחוֹקָה מִמֶּנִּי׃
24 רָחוֹק מַה־שֶּׁהָיָה וְעָמֹק ׀ עָמֹק
25 מִי יִמְצָאֶנּוּ׃ סַבּוֹתִי אֲנִי וְלִבִּי
לָדַעַת וְלָתוּר וּבַקֵּשׁ חָכְמָה
וְחֶשְׁבּוֹן וְלָדַעַת רֶשַׁע כֶּסֶל

*I will get wisdom.* But when he passed beyond these concrete precepts and wandered into the realm of speculation to comprehend the scheme of the universe and God's government thereof, he discovered that he was seeking to reach out to the unattainable. A similar confession is made in Job xxviii. 12ff. (cf. the statement of Moses, *The secret things belong unto the LORD our God; but the things that are revealed belong unto us and to our children for ever, that we may do all the words of this law,* Deut. xxix. 28).

**24.** The text is literally, 'far (is) that which has been, and deep, deep; who can find it?' Ginsburg is of opinion that the repetition of *deep* implies a repetition of *far,* and he translates, 'Far remaineth what was far, and deep, deep.' Preference should be given to Barton and Jastrow who render, 'Far off is that which exists and very deep.' It is the same expression of man's helplessness before the infinite greatness of the universe as we find beautifully conveyed in Job xi. 7f.

**25.** Realizing that to understand the ultimate perplexities of the universe is beyond his powers, Koheleth turns again to the problems of life which have been exercising his attention.

*I turned about, and applied my heart.* This translation evades the difficulty of the text which is lit., 'I and my heart turned about,' a phrase which is without parallel. A number of MSS. read *belibbi* for *welibbi,* i.e. 'I turned about in my heart.' But, as Plumptre observes, the expression 'harmonizes with the common mode of speech, familiar enough in the poetry of all times and countries, furnishing a title ("My Soul and I") to a poem of Whittier's, in which a man addresses his heart or soul, as something distinguishable from himself. Here the thought implied seems to be that of an intense retrospective consciousness of the experience, or experiment, of life which the seeker is about to narrate.'

*to know and to search out, and to seek.* The accumulation of verbs denotes the painstaking and thorough character of his investigation (cf. i. 13).

*wisdom and the reason of things.* lit. 'wisdom and reckoning,' which Ginsburg explains as an idiom for 'practical wisdom.' The second noun is repeated in verse 27, and the probability is that the same meaning is to be found in both passages. Its literal interpretation, 'reckoning,' 'what it adds up to,' is most suitable.

*wickedness to be folly.* Or, 'the wickedness of folly.'

*foolishness to be madness.* The same Hebrew terms as in i. 17, ii. 12.

26. and I find more bitter than death
the woman, whose heart is snares
and nets, and her hands as bands;
whoso pleaseth God shall escape
from her; but the sinner shall be
taken by her. 27. Behold, this have
I found, saith Koheleth, adding one
thing to another, to find out the
account; 28. which yet my soul

26 וְהַסְּכָלוּת הוֹלֵלוֹת׃ וּמוֹצֶא
אֲנִי מַר מִמָּוֶת אֶת־הָאִשָּׁה
אֲשֶׁר־הִיא מְצוֹדִים וַחֲרָמִים
לִבָּהּ אֲסוּרִים יָדֶיהָ טוֹב לִפְנֵי
הָאֱלֹהִים יִמָּלֵט מִמֶּנָּה וְחוֹטֵא
27 יִלָּכֶד בָּהּ׃ רְאֵה זֶה מָצָאתִי
אָמְרָה קֹהֶלֶת אַחַת לְאַחַת
28 לִמְצֹא חֶשְׁבּוֹן׃ אֲשֶׁר עוֹד־

**26.** Some commentators find in the verse a wholesale condemnation of woman, but this is contrary to the plain statement of the text and his recommendation in ix. 9. The author of Proverbs has very harsh things to say about a bad woman (ii. 18f., vii. 25ff.), but praises the good woman (xi. 16, xii. 4, xviii. 22, xix. 14, xxxi. 10ff.). The phrases which Koheleth employs indicate that he has the former class in mind.

*more bitter than death.* Cf. Prov. v. 4f. of association with an abandoned woman.

*whose heart is snares and nets.* Or, 'who is snares and her heart nets.' This is descriptive of the unscrupulous type of woman who sets out to lure a man into her toils to his undoing.

*her hands as bands.* Holding the victim prisoner within her clutches (cf. Prov. vii. 22).

*whoso pleaseth God.* lit. 'he who is good before God' (cf. ii. 26). A man whose aim is to act with His approval will have the strength to resist such a temptress. The words contradict the suggestion that Koheleth spoke from bitter personal experience; he makes a general observation.

*the sinner.* Since like is attracted to like, only an evil-doer will be attracted by a debased woman. The mention of the *sinner* seems to agree with the interpretation that Koheleth is referring only to a vicious woman.

**27.** *saith Koheleth.* Here the verb is feminine in agreement with the feminine form of the subject, but in xii. 8 the verb is masculine. As Rashi points out, this is not an uncommon feature in Hebrew literary style.

*adding one thing to another.* lit. 'one to one.'

*the account.* Rather, 'the total' (see on verse 25). 'The allegation made in the foregoing verse respecting the great wickedness of woman, Koheleth here assures us, is not owing to his ignoring the faults of his own sex, but is the result of unbiased and minute observations of both sexes. Having examined both men and women, and taken everything (*adding one thing to another*) belonging to their respective conditions into consideration, he now tells us both what he has found and what he has not found among them to substantiate the foregoing assertion' (Ginsburg).

sought, but I found not; one man
among a thousand have I found;
but a woman among all those have I
not found. 29. Behold, this only
have I found, that God made man
upright; but they have sought out
many inventions.

בִּקְשָׁה נַפְשִׁי וְלֹא מָצָאתִי
אָדָם אֶחָד מֵאֶלֶף מָצָאתִי
וְאִשָּׁה בְכָל־אֵלֶּה לֹא
29 מָצָאתִי׃ לְבַד רְאֵה־זֶה
מָצָאתִי אֲשֶׁר עָשָׂה הָאֱלֹהִים
אֶת־הָאָדָם יָשָׁר וְהֵמָּה בִקְשׁוּ
חִשְּׁבֹנוֹת רַבִּים׃

**28.** *one man among a thousand.* i.e. one upright man in a large number of men.

*but a woman among all those.* He does not say that no upright woman exists, but that she is a greater rarity than a good man. It would appear from the Book of Proverbs that the times were licentious and the general standard of morality was low among women.

**29.** *man.* i.e. the human species. God created both man and woman upright; the degeneracy displayed by both, and by woman to a greater degree, is not to be attributed to their Maker.

*many inventions.* God had endowed them with faculties and instincts which He designed for the perpetuation of the human race and its true progress; but these have been corrupted and employed for base ends. In the same spirit the Rabbis declared that even 'the evil inclination' was created for a good purpose, for 'were it not for that impulse, a man would not build a house, marry a wife, beget children or conduct business affairs,' i.e. social life could not exist. John Ruskin discovered in this verse an incentive to better living: 'You have had false prophets among you, who have told you that all men are nothing but fiends and wolves—half beast, half devil. Believe that, and indeed you may sink to that. But refuse that and have faith that God made you upright though you have sought out many inventions; so you will strive daily to become what your Maker meant and means you to be.'

1. Who is the wise man? and who
knoweth the interpretation of a
thing?

A man's wisdom maketh his face
to shine,
And the boldness of his face is
changed.

2. I [counsel thee]: keep the king's
command, and that in regard of the
oath of God. 3. Be not hasty to go

1 מִ֚י כְּהֶ֣חָכָ֔ם וּמִ֥י יוֹדֵ֖עַ פֵּ֣שֶׁר
דָּבָ֑ר חָכְמַ֤ת אָדָם֙ תָּאִ֣יר פָּנָ֔יו
2 וְעֹ֥ז פָּנָ֖יו יְשֻׁנֶּֽא׃ אֲנִי֙ פִּי־מֶ֣לֶךְ
שְׁמֹ֔ר וְעַ֕ל דִּבְרַ֖ת שְׁבוּעַ֥ת
3 אֱלֹהִֽים׃ אַל־תִּבָּהֵ֤ל מִפָּנָיו֙

**1-9 WISE RELATIONSHIP WITH A KING**

AFTER a brief tribute to the pre-eminence of a wise man, Koheleth gives sound advice on the attitude one should adopt towards the king. At a time when a person's life and fortune might depend upon royal caprice, the Wisdom writers felt it necessary to dwell upon this subject (cf. Prov. xvi. 14, xix. 12, xxiv. 21, xxv. 6f.).

1. *who is the wise man?* As frequently, the author states an emphatic negative in the form of a question: there is nobody the equal of a wise man.

*and who knoweth.* Ibn Ezra, *Metsudath David* and moderns interpret the Hebrew 'and who is as the man that knoweth.'

*the interpretation.* The Hebrew word *pesher* occurs only here, but is found several times in the Aramaic portions of Daniel, usually for interpretation of a dream, corresponding to the Hebrew *pathar*. Here the application is wider: who can compare with a man possessing sagacity and insight so that he successfully grapples with the difficult problems that come before him?

*a man's wisdom.* The rest of the verse is a proverbial saying.

*maketh his face to shine.* Or, 'illuminateth his face.' When a man possesses wisdom it is reflected in the happy and serene look on his face.

*the boldness of his face.* Usually the phrase indicates 'impudence,' but here it has the same meaning as in Deut. xxviii. 50, *a nation of fierce countenance.* A cultured mind lends a benign and attractive expression to the face, and removes the forbidding look which repels.

2. *I [counsel thee].* The omission of the verb is paralleled by *in mine ears [said] the LORD of hosts* (Isa. v. 9).

*and that in regard . . . God.* A particular reason is given for submission to the king. This is due from the subject, not merely as an act of prudence, but because it is obligatory in view of the oath in the name of God which is taken at the time of the coronation. For historical instances, cf. 2 Sam. v. 3; 2 Kings xi. 17.

3. *be not hasty . . . presence.* lit. 'be not hasty from his presence going forth.' Should the king do or say anything to cause you resentment, do not act impulsively and withdraw your allegiance, or, if you hold office under him, resign your appointment. Koheleth repeats this advice in x. 4.

out of his presence; stand not in an evil thing; for he doeth whatsoever pleaseth him. 4. Forasmuch as the king's word hath power; and who may say unto him: 'What doest thou?'

5 Whoso keepeth the commandment
shall know no evil thing;
And a wise man's heart discerneth
time and judgment.

6. For to every matter there is a time and judgment; for the evil of man is

תֵּלֵךְ אַל־תַּעֲמֹד בְּדָבָר רָע
כִּי כָּל־אֲשֶׁר יַחְפֹּץ יַעֲשֶׂה׃
4 בַּאֲשֶׁר דְּבַר־מֶלֶךְ שִׁלְטוֹן וּמִי
5 יֹאמַר־לוֹ מַה־תַּעֲשֶׂה׃ שׁוֹמֵר
מִצְוָה לֹא יֵדַע דָּבָר רָע וְעֵת
6 וּמִשְׁפָּט יֵדַע לֵב חָכָם׃ כִּי
לְכָל־חֵפֶץ יֵשׁ עֵת וּמִשְׁפָּט
כִּי־רָעַת הָאָדָם רַבָּה עָלָיו׃

*stand not in an evil thing.* A phrase of doubtful meaning. Ginsburg translates, 'do not even stand up because of an evil word,' i.e. do not make a sign of protest if the king expresses himself harshly. R.V. renders, 'persist not in an evil thing,' by which is probably meant a course of action which is frowned upon by the king. Many moderns understand the phrase: do not join in a conspiracy against him. The conclusion of the verse suits either the first or second interpretation, but not the third.

*for he doeth.* You may have right on your side, but the king wields autocratic power; therefore the wise course to follow is to submit to him even when he is unjust or unreasonable.

4. *hath power.* The Hebrew is more forceful, 'is power.'

*who may say . . . doest thou?* Almost identical with Job ix. 12, where the reference is to God. If Koheleth consciously quoted the phrase, he may have implied that, from the practical point of view, a king exercises an unquestioning authority comparable to God's.

5. The verse is a proverb, and the second clause somewhat enigmatic.

*the commandment.* i.e. the king's enactment even when it is despotic.

*shall know no evil thing.* Will not come to harm; whereas if he criticizes or revolts against *the commandment,* he will suffer the consequences of the king's anger.

*heart.* The seat of intelligence; equivalent of 'mind.'

*time and judgment.* Ginsburg takes the phrase to mean 'a time of judgment'; the reason which induces a wise man to submit to an unjust king is his conviction that a time of retribution will come. Such an interpretation is doubtful. *Time* is to be understood as 'right time' and *judgment* as 'right procedure.' What is here said is that if the law becomes too oppressive, the wise man will know how to bide his time and resort to appropriate measures for the purpose of escaping its harsh restrictions. To do this inopportunely and openly would be treated as rebellion and punished accordingly.

6. *for to every matter . . . judgment.* This clause is parenthetical in support of the assertion just made. Not only in that specific instance, but in all matters, there is need for the exercise of prudence in timing and method.

*for the evil of man . . . him.* The words are usually interpreted: the oppression of the tyrant is severe upon its victims.

great upon him. 7. For he knoweth not that which shall be; for even when it cometh to pass, who shall declare it unto him? 8. There is no man that hath power over the wind to retain the wind; neither hath he power over the day of death; and there is no discharge in war; neither shall wickedness deliver him that is given to it. 9. All this have I seen, even applied my heart thereto, whatever the work that is done under the sun; what time one man had power over another to his hurt.

7 כִּי־אֵינֶנּוּ יֹדֵעַ מַה־שֶּׁיִּהְיֶה כִּי
8 כַּאֲשֶׁר יִהְיֶה מִי יַגִּיד לוֹ׃ אֵין
אָדָם שַׁלִּיט בָּרוּחַ לִכְלוֹא
אֶת־הָרוּחַ וְאֵין שִׁלְטוֹן בְּיוֹם
הַמָּוֶת וְאֵין מִשְׁלַחַת בַּמִּלְחָמָה
וְלֹא־יְמַלֵּט רֶשַׁע אֶת־
9 בְּעָלָיו׃ אֶת־כָּל־זֶה רָאִיתִי
וְנָתוֹן אֶת־לִבִּי לְכָל־מַעֲשֶׂה
אֲשֶׁר נַעֲשָׂה תַּחַת הַשָּׁמֶשׁ עֵת
אֲשֶׁר שָׁלַט הָאָדָם בְּאָדָם לְרַע

But it is a strange way to refer to the king as 'the man' (so lit., and Ginsburg's explanation is unconvincing, viz. this generic term is evidently chosen because a despotic sovereign necessarily has a host of lawless and debased officials). A more literal interpretation is: a man has enough troubles without deliberately adding to them by open revolt against an intolerable ruler; consequently he should submit and bide his time.

7. *he knoweth not.* Some commentators take the king to be the subject of the verb: 'he goes on with infatuated blindness to the doom that lies ahead' (Plumptre). More naturally the verse suggests a further reason for the wise man's submission. He cannot foresee what event will occur which might end the tyrant's rule and bring him relief. Death comes to all, even to an autocrat; that is the thought which the wise man bears in mind and gives him strength to endure.

8. *wind.* Ginsburg agrees with Ibn Ezra in translating 'spirit'; but most moderns accept the rendering 'wind,' and the idea is the same as *who hath gathered the wind in his fists?* (Prov. xxx. 4). Such power is exercised only by God. The verse sets side by side two human impossibilities: to prevent the wind from blowing and to defer the day of death.

*retain.* Better, 'restrain,' hold it back.

*power over the day of death.* To postpone it when it has been willed by God.

*there is no discharge in war.* Two interpretations are given by the Midrash. The first takes the word in the sense of 'sending (another in one's place, substitution)': 'A man is unable to say (when the summons of death comes), Behold my son, or my slave, or one of my household instead of me.' Alternatively *mishlachath* is connected with *shelach* 'weapon' (cf. 2 Chron. xxxii. 5): 'A man cannot forge a weapon and deliver himself from the Angel of Death.' This latter explanation is accepted by Ehrlich who understands the phrase as 'there is no armed host (of defence) in the war (against death)'. A cognate Arabic noun means 'an armed party.'

*wickedness.* The probable intention is that no schemes, however wicked, can bring escape from death to him who devises them for that purpose.

9. *all this have I seen.* viz. the conditions which arise from tyranny and how men react to them.

*even applied . . . sun.* He had carefully

10. And so I saw the wicked buried and they entered into their rest; but they that had done right went away from the holy place, and were forgotten in the city; this also is vanity.

10 לוֹ׃ וּבְכֵן רָאִיתִי רְשָׁעִים
קְבֻרִים וָבָאוּ וּמִמְּקוֹם קָדוֹשׁ
יְהַלֵּכוּ וְיִשְׁתַּכְּחוּ בָעִיר אֲשֶׁר

studied all the different circumstances associated with autocratic power.

*what time . . . hurt.* When a ruler employs his unrestricted sovereignty not as a just judge but as a despot.

### 10-15 AN ANOMALY OF LIFE

In these verses Koheleth dwells again upon the problem created by the fate of the righteous and unrighteous (cf. vii. 15).

**10.** Ibn Ezra asserts that the verse had been misinterpreted by other commentators and devotes space to refuting their explanations. His own reading has been accepted by Ginsburg and is, on the whole, the most probable: 'I saw the wicked who rule over their fellow-men, and tyrannize over them, die without anguish, and they came into the world a second time (i.e. their children succeed to their places and perpetuate them); whilst those who departed from the holy place (i.e. the holy ones) die without issue, and are forgotten in the city where they were, and these are they who executed justice.'

*buried.* According to Ibn Ezra this is the equivalent of *there are no pangs at their death* (Ps. lxxiii. 4), said of the wicked. It is doubtful whether the term can denote 'honourable burial,' or 'died a natural death and were carried to the grave.' The contrast of the verse appears to indicate that these wicked men lived and died and were buried, but that was not the end of them. They had sons who continued their evil practices.

*and they entered into their rest.* The literal translation of the Hebrew is 'and they came,' and the verb has the same force as in i. 4, *another generation cometh.* They had successors.

*right.* Hebrew *ken* (cf. Num. xxvii. 7; 2 Kings vii. 9, *we do not well*).

*went away.* An intensive form of the verb used in *one generation passeth away* (i. 4); they perished completely in that they left no issue.

*from the holy place.* These men are obviously the opposite of *the wicked*, and the phrase may intend that they lived under the inspiration of the Temple. But it appears an unnatural way to describe pious men. If *the wicked* are the secular rulers who abused their authority and rebelled against the will of God, an excellent contrast is obtained if we understand the second clause as an allusion to the religious leaders of the community, the priests who served in *the holy place.* Some of these devoted servants of God, Koheleth noticed, died without sons to carry on their ministrations.

*were forgotten.* Their name was not preserved either through their offspring or in the minds of the members of the community as a pious memory.

*the city.* Jerusalem where their righteous lives had been spent.

*this also is vanity.* 'The recurrence of the refrain of the Book at this point is interesting. It is precisely the survey of the moral anomalies of the world that originates and sustains the feeling so expressed' (Plumptre).

11. Because sentence against an evil
work is not executed speedily, therefore the heart of the sons of men is
fully set in them to do evil; 12. because a sinner doeth evil a hundred
times, and prolongeth his days—
though yet I know that it shall be
well with them that fear God, that
fear before Him; 13. but it shall not
be well with the wicked, neither shall
he prolong his days, which are as a
shadow, because he feareth not
before God. 14. There is a vanity

11 כֵּן־עָשׂוּ גַּם־זֶה הָבֶל׃ אֲשֶׁר
אֵין־נַעֲשָׂה פִתְגָם מַעֲשֵׂה
הָרָעָה מְהֵרָה עַל־כֵּן מָלֵא
לֵב בְּנֵי־הָאָדָם בָּהֶם לַעֲשׂוֹת
12 רָע׃ אֲשֶׁר חֹטֶא עֹשֶׂה רָע
מְאַת וּמַאֲרִיךְ לוֹ כִּי גַּם־יוֹדֵעַ
אָנִי אֲשֶׁר יִהְיֶה־טּוֹב לְיִרְאֵי
13 הָאֱלֹהִים אֲשֶׁר יִירְאוּ מִלְּפָנָיו׃
וְטוֹב לֹא־יִהְיֶה לָרָשָׁע וְלֹא־
יַאֲרִיךְ יָמִים כַּצֵּל אֲשֶׁר אֵינֶנּוּ
14 יָרֵא מִלִּפְנֵי אֱלֹהִים׃ יֶשׁ־

11. The phenomenon described in the last verse has a disturbing effect upon the morals of the people. It induces in them the belief that they can sin with impunity.

*sentence.* This word, of Persian origin, is found again only in Esther I. 20 where it is used of a royal decree. Here it means the manifestation of Divine judgment.

*the heart . . . fully set in them.* lit. 'the heart . . . is full in them.' Their mind is completely occupied with the intention to do wrong without any place for the thought that God will hold them to account.

12. *because a sinner.* Koheleth comments on the fact that *sentence against an evil work is not executed speedily.*

*a hundred times.* lit. 'a hundred,' which stands for a large number (cf. Prov. xvii. 10). The Targum and Rashi supply 'years,' but Ibn Ezra prefers 'times.'

*I know.* As against *I saw* (verse 10). Faith is a necessary supplement to what one observes.

*that fear God, that fear before Him.* Ginsburg overcomes the apparent tautology by translating 'who truly fear before Him;' but, as Plumptre suggests, the term 'God-fearers' may have been the distinctive name of a religious class.

13. *neither . . . a shadow.* The Hebrew is literally 'neither shall he prolong days like the shadow (which does not prolong days).' There is an apparent contradiction between this assertion and *prolongeth his days* (verse 12). Martin points out that verses 12f. 'are in the form of a double paradox. "Though the life of the sinful man may be a long one, still it is in reality fleeting as a shadow, whereas the righteous, even with a short earthly life, has in it the promise of eternity." It is one of the strongest passages, therefore, in the Book in favour of the doctrine of a resurrection.'

14. *there is a vanity.* Despite his declaration of faith, Koheleth still holds that life presents an anomaly which confounds mankind, viz. there are righteous men to whom evil comes as though they had

which is done upon the earth: that there are righteous men, unto whom it happeneth according to the work of the wicked; again, there are wicked men, to whom it happeneth according to the work of the righteous—I said that this also is vanity. 15. So I commended mirth, that a man hath no better thing under the sun, than to eat, and to drink, and to be merry, and that this should accompany him in his labour all the days of his life which God hath given him under the sun.

16. When I applied my heart to

הֶבֶל אֲשֶׁר נַעֲשָׂה עַל־הָאָרֶץ
אֲשֶׁר ׀ יֵשׁ צַדִּיקִים אֲשֶׁר מַגִּיעַ
אֲלֵהֶם כְּמַעֲשֵׂה הָרְשָׁעִים וְיֵשׁ
רְשָׁעִים שֶׁמַּגִּיעַ אֲלֵהֶם
כְּמַעֲשֵׂה הַצַּדִּיקִים אָמַרְתִּי
15 שֶׁגַּם־זֶה הָבֶל׃ וְשִׁבַּחְתִּי אֲנִי
אֶת־הַשִּׂמְחָה אֲשֶׁר אֵין־טוֹב
לָאָדָם תַּחַת הַשֶּׁמֶשׁ כִּי אִם־
לֶאֱכֹל וְלִשְׁתּוֹת וְלִשְׂמוֹחַ וְהוּא
יִלְוֶנּוּ בַעֲמָלוֹ יְמֵי חַיָּיו אֲשֶׁר־
נָתַן־לוֹ הָאֱלֹהִים תַּחַת
16 הַשָּׁמֶשׁ׃ כַּאֲשֶׁר נָתַתִּי אֶת־

done the work of the wicked, and wicked men to whom good comes as though they had practised righteousness. Rashi quotes the interpretation of the Talmud: Happy are the *righteous men unto whom it happeneth* in this world *according to the work of the wicked* in the world to come (i.e. who suffer on earth as the unrighteous will suffer in the hereafter); woe to the *wicked men to whom it happeneth* in this world *according to the work of the righteous* in the world to come (who have well-being on earth as the righteous have in the hereafter, but will receive due punishment when their life is ended). Rashi then remarks that, in view of this interpretation, the statement of Koheleth, *I said that this also is vanity*, 'is not agreeable to me.'

**15.** *so I commended mirth.* As in iii. 12, 22, v. 17 Koheleth recommends escape from the insoluble riddles of life in a self-enjoyment which is tempered by reverence of God.

*to eat, and to drink.* 'Of what the Holy One, blessed be He, hath bestowed upon him and to rejoice in his portion' (Rashi). Conscious that God had provided him with the means of enjoyment, he will not degrade himself by his abuse of them.

*accompany him in his labour.* i.e. let him find at least this satisfaction from his toil and so give it meaning and purpose.

*life which God hath given him.* Since the span of life is given by God and He has provided the sources of physical pleasure, man fulfils His design by a judicious enjoyment of His bounty.

### 16-17 GOD'S ULTIMATE PURPOSE IS UNFATHOMABLE

So much of the Divine plan for the human being, mentioned in the last verse, is comprehensible, but His ultimate design in devising the scheme of life is beyond man's understanding.

know wisdom, and to see the business
that is done upon the earth—for
neither day nor night do men see
sleep with their eyes—17. then I beheld all the work of God, that man
cannot find out the work that is done
under the sun; because though a
man labour to seek it out, yet he
shall not find it; yea further, though
a wise man think to know it, yet
shall he not be able to find it.

לִבִּי לָדַעַת חָכְמָה וְלִרְאוֹת
אֶת־הָעִנְיָן אֲשֶׁר נַעֲשָׂה עַל־
הָאָרֶץ כִּי גַם בַּיּוֹם וּבַלַּיְלָה
שֵׁנָה בְּעֵינָיו אֵינֶנּוּ רֹאֶה׃
17 וְרָאִיתִי אֶת־כָּל־מַעֲשֵׂה
הָאֱלֹהִים כִּי לֹא יוּכַל הָאָדָם
לִמְצוֹא אֶת־הַמַּעֲשֶׂה אֲשֶׁר
נַעֲשָׂה תַחַת־הַשֶּׁמֶשׁ בְּשֶׁל
אֲשֶׁר יַעֲמֹל הָאָדָם לְבַקֵּשׁ
וְלֹא יִמְצָא וְגַם אִם־יֹאמַר
הֶחָכָם לָדַעַת לֹא יוּכַל
לִמְצֹא׃

**16.** *when I applied my heart.* Cf. i. 13.

*for neither day . . . eyes.* Moffatt paraphrases, 'he may labour in his efforts to attain it, in a sleepless quest for it by day and night.' Instead of *for* render 'though': however hard a man try even by denying himself sleep by day or night. The phrase 'to see sleep with the eyes' derives from the thought that the eyes are the organ with which sleep is most closely connected (cf. Gen. xxxi. 40; Ps. cxxxii. 4; Prov. vi. 4).

**17.** *all the work of God.* i.e. with respect to God's government of the universe.

*the work that is done.* See on i. 14.

*labour.* No amount of physical effort can bring one to the desired goal.

*think to know it.* lit. 'say to know'; no intellectual effort will enable one to attain the knowledge.

1. For all this I laid to my heart,
even to make clear all this: that
the righteous, and the wise, and their
works, are in the hand of God;
whether it be love or hatred, man
knoweth it not; all is before them.
2. All things come alike to all; there
is one event to the righteous and to
the wicked; to the good and to the

1 כִּי אֶת־כָּל־זֶה נָתַתִּי אֶל־
לִבִּי וְלָבוּר אֶת־כָּל־זֶה
אֲשֶׁר הַצַּדִּיקִים וְהַחֲכָמִים
וַעֲבָדֵיהֶם בְּיַד הָאֱלֹהִים גַּם־
אַהֲבָה גַם־שִׂנְאָה אֵין יוֹדֵעַ
2 הָאָדָם הַכֹּל לִפְנֵיהֶם׃ הַכֹּל
כַּאֲשֶׁר לַכֹּל מִקְרֶה אֶחָד
לַצַּדִּיק וְלָרָשָׁע לַטּוֹב

**1-6** PROVIDENCE IS INSCRUTABLE

THE fact that man's vicissitudes on earth, in their relationship to Divine Providence, baffle every effort at comprehension is repeated in this passage.

1. *all this.* viz. the problem of the prosperity of the wicked and the adversity of the righteous.

*to make clear.* Plumptre's translation, 'to dig through,' is erroneous. The root *bur* is a rare by-form of *barar*, 'to select, sift.'

*are in the hand of God.* They are subject to the Divine will, but in a manner which is unintelligible to the human mind.

*whether it be love or hatred.* It is unforeseeable whether the works of the pious and wise (i.e. morally good-living men) will gain for them God's *love* or *hatred.* These terms are sometimes employed in Hebrew to express nothing more than preference and its opposite (cf. of a man's two wives, *the one beloved and the other hated*, Deut. xxi. 15, which only means that one of them is his favourite; *I loved Jacob, but Esau I hated* Mal. i. 2f., i.e. God showed a preference for Jacob over Esau). So here the intention is, nobody can tell whether a righteous life will receive from God a manifestation of His approval in the form of prosperity.

*all is before them.* The sense is: either may happen to them; the righteous and wise may experience *love* or *hatred.*

2. *all things come alike to all.* lit. 'the all as to the all.' Plumptre defines the intention in concrete terms):'Earthquakes, pestilences, tempests make no discrimination between good and evil.' The same sentiment is forcibly expressed by Job, *He destroyeth the innocent and the wicked. If the scourge slay suddenly, He will mock at the calamity of the guiltless* (Job ix. 22f.).

*one event.* Cf. ii. 14. There it alludes to death; here to the unpleasant experiences of life.

*the righteous.* The man who fulfils his obligations to his fellows.

*to the good and to the clean.* Since *clean* and *unclean* are normally used to denote clean and to the unclean; to him that sacrificeth and to him that sacrificeth not; as is the good, so is the sinner, and he that sweareth, as he that feareth an oath. 3. This is an evil in all that is done under the sun, that there is one event unto all; yea also, the heart of the sons of men is full of evil, and madness is in their heart while they live, and after that they go to the dead.

4. For to him that is joined to all

וְלַטָּהוֹר וְלַטָּמֵא וְלַזֹּבֵחַ
וְלַאֲשֶׁר אֵינֶנּוּ זֹבֵחַ כַּטּוֹב
כַּחֹטֶא הַנִּשְׁבָּע כַּאֲשֶׁר שְׁבוּעָה
יָרֵא׃ זֶה ׀ רָע בְּכֹל אֲשֶׁר־ 3
נַעֲשָׂה תַּחַת הַשֶּׁמֶשׁ כִּי־מִקְרֶה
אֶחָד לַכֹּל וְגַם לֵב בְּנֵי־הָאָדָם
מָלֵא־רָע וְהוֹלֵלוֹת בִּלְבָבָם
בְּחַיֵּיהֶם וְאַחֲרָיו אֶל־
הַמֵּתִים׃ כִּי־מִי אֲשֶׁר יְבֻחַר 4

v. 4. יחבר ק׳

ritualistic purity or impurity, *to the good* is added for the purpose of making it clear that the morally good are meant.

*to him that sacrificeth.* Describing the man who is punctilious in his duties to the Temple.

*as is the good, so is the sinner.* As against the *righteous* and *wicked*, these terms may perhaps define the men who respectively discharge or disregard their obligations to God.

*he that sweareth.* Most commentators regard the verb as equal to 'sweareth rashly'; but since with the other pairs the good man is placed first, 'it would seem that the person who takes an oath, and loyally observes it, is set over against a man who, in a spirit of caution or cowardice, is afraid either to take the oath or to carry out its conditions when he has taken it' (Martin).

3. *this is an evil.* Best understood as the superlative: the fact that there is *one event* is an especial evil because it has a harmful effect upon the human temperament. Inasmuch as men see that there is no discrimination between the good and bad in a general calamity, they conclude that there is no advantage in being good.

*yea also.* Introduces the effect upon man's conduct produced by the absence of distinction between the two classes in their plight.

*madness.* 'Mad desires' (Moffatt).

*after that they go to the dead.* The Hebrew is briefer and more forceful: 'and after it (i.e. life) to the dead.' Alike in their common fate during life, the righteous and wicked proceed to the same goal—union with the dead.

4. The rendering of A.J. follows the *kerë* (*yechubbar*); the *kethib* (*yebuchar*) is adopted by R.V. margin, 'For who is exempted? with all the living there is hope.' The sense remains the same on either reading, viz. 'while there is life there is hope,' but even that consoling distinction does not apply to the righteous and wicked, since they both have to die. It is doubtful, however, whether *yebuchar*, lit. 'chosen,' can mean 'exempted.' The LXX supports the *kerë*, and on the alternative reading Martin observes,

the living there is hope; for a living
dog is better than a dead lion. 5. For
the living know that they shall die;
but the dead know not anything,
neither have they any more a reward; for the memory of them is
forgotten. 6. As well their love, as
their hatred and their envy, is long
ago perished; neither have they any
more a portion for ever in any thing
that is done under the sun.

אֶל כָּל־הַחַיִּים יֵשׁ בִּטָּחוֹן
כִּי־לְכֶלֶב חַי הוּא טוֹב מִן־
5 הָאַרְיֵה הַמֵּת׃ כִּי הַחַיִּים
יוֹדְעִים שֶׁיָּמֻתוּ וְהַמֵּתִים אֵינָם
יוֹדְעִים מְאוּמָה וְאֵין־עוֹד
לָהֶם שָׂכָר כִּי נִשְׁכַּח זִכְרָם׃
6 גַּם אַהֲבָתָם גַּם־שִׂנְאָתָם גַּם־
קִנְאָתָם כְּבָר אָבָדָה וְחֵלֶק
אֵין־לָהֶם עוֹד לְעוֹלָם בְּכֹל
אֲשֶׁר־נַעֲשָׂה תַּחַת הַשָּׁמֶשׁ׃

The Bible knows of no life or existence after this life. "Olam habaah" is a rabbinic concept. However, there is the sense that the nation lives on.

'there seems no purpose in the question and no advantage in the change.'

*all the living.* The word *all* 'seems to hint that the dead are not worth enumerating in comparison with the living' (Williams).

*dog . . . lion.* The former was the most despised of animals (cf. 1 Sam. xvii. 43; Prov. xxvi. 11) and the latter the *mightiest among beasts* (Prov. xxx. 30).

5. In this verse Koheleth gives the reason why he holds life, despite all its contradictions, preferable to death. While alive man at any rate possesses consciousness, if only the consciousness that he must sooner or later die, whereas in death all perception ceases.

*a reward.* He is not thinking of a reward in the hereafter. The reasoning is that during lifetime, man is able to earn something from his labour, but that possibility ends with death.

*the memory of them is forgotten.* That is the element in death which Koheleth feels so bitterly (see on i. 11). A living person is a somebody; a dead person is less than a nobody; he is not even a memory.

6. *love . . . hatred . . . envy.* These are the dominant passions which motive conduct. Active in life, they have no force in death.

*a portion.* While he is on earth, the human being participates in the scene around him and is an actor upon life's stage; with the advent of death his rôle comes to a complete end.

7 Go thy way, eat thy bread with joy,
And drink thy wine with a merry heart;
For God hath already accepted thy works.
8 Let thy garments be always white;
And let thy head lack no oil.

7 לֵךְ אֱכֹל בְּשִׂמְחָה לַחְמֶךָ
וּשֲׁתֵה בְלֶב־טוֹב יֵינֶךָ כִּי כְבָר
רָצָה הָאֱלֹהִים אֶת־מַעֲשֶׂיךָ׃
8 בְּכָל־עֵת יִהְיוּ בְגָדֶיךָ לְבָנִים
וְשֶׁמֶן עַל־רֹאשְׁךָ אַל־יֶחְסָר׃

**7-10** PRACTICAL ADVICE ON LIVING

Having asserted that there is some advantage in living as compared with death, Koheleth advises how the maximum cheerfulness may be derived from life notwithstanding its disturbing phenomena.

7. *go thy way.* lit. 'go'; be up and doing and stop worrying about problems which cannot be solved.

*eat . . . drink.* As in ii. 24. *Bread* and *wine* formed a large part of the popular diet (Gen. xxvii. 28; 1 Sam. xvi. 20). One should not partake of these products of nature just to maintain life, but with *joy* and *a merry heart.* An ascetic way of living would only intensify the gloom which arises from contemplation, but it may be dispelled by temperate pleasures.

*God hath already accepted thy works.* 'For these are the things that God wishes you to do' (Ibn Ezra) does not quite meet the point which is being made. Investigation proves that life is so constituted that the only satisfaction it yields is the happiness which man is able to experience; that being so, to extract this enjoyment cannot be wrong but must have the approval of the Creator.

8. The Targum, Midrash and Rashi interpreted the verse metaphorically to tone down the hedonistic view expounded in the preceding verse: the whiteness of the garments being a symbol of a sinless life and the *oil* of a good name (vii. 1). Ibn Ezra rejects this explanation and understands the advice to refer to physical comforts, and that is the interpretation now adopted.

*garments . . . white.* These were worn on festive occasions, and the exhortation advises men to embrace every opportunity to have a happy time.

*oil.* In the heat of the Orient oil was poured on the head to cool it and the effect was refreshing. A striking parallel to this passage has been found in the Babylonian Gilgamesh epic, dated about 2,000 B.C.E., part of which reads: 'O Gilgamesh, fill thy belly; day and night be joyful . . . let thy garments be bright; anoint thy head and purify thyself; with the children at thy side, enjoy the wife of thy bosom.' The resemblance does not necessarily indicate direct borrowing, and the two writers may independently have summarized the essential joys of life in identical terms.

9. Enjoy life with ~~the wife~~ a woman whom
thou lovest all the days of the life of
thy vanity, which He hath given thee
under the sun, all the days of thy
vanity; for that is thy portion in life,
and in thy labour wherein thou
labourest under the sun. 10. Whatsoever thy hand attaineth to do by
thy strength, that do; for there is no
work, nor device, nor knowledge, nor
wisdom, in the grave, whither thou
goest.

11. I returned, and saw under the

9 רְאֵה חַיִּים עִם־אִשָּׁה אֲשֶׁר־
אָהַבְתָּ כָּל־יְמֵי חַיֵּי הֶבְלֶךָ
אֲשֶׁר נָתַן־לְךָ תַּחַת הַשֶּׁמֶשׁ
כֹּל יְמֵי הֶבְלֶךָ כִּי הוּא חֶלְקְךָ
בַּחַיִּים וּבַעֲמָלְךָ אֲשֶׁר־אַתָּה
10 עָמֵל תַּחַת הַשָּׁמֶשׁ׃ כֹּל אֲשֶׁר
תִּמְצָא יָדְךָ לַעֲשׂוֹת בְּכֹחֲךָ
עֲשֵׂה כִּי אֵין מַעֲשֶׂה וְחֶשְׁבּוֹן
וְדַעַת וְחָכְמָה בִּשְׁאוֹל אֲשֶׁר
11 אַתָּה הֹלֵךְ שָׁמָּה׃ שַׁבְתִּי וְרָאֹה

**9.** *enjoy life.* lit. 'see life'; for the verb, see on ii. 1.

*the wife.* Hebrew has only one word for 'woman' and 'wife,' and the definite article is omitted here. Ginsburg agrees with Jerome in interpreting the word as woman in general, and Koheleth's advice as relating to free sexual indulgence. The more modern view is that matrimony is intended, and the sentiment is in harmony with the Rabbinic statement, 'A man who has no wife lives without joy, blessing and good.'

*the life of thy vanity.* See on vii. 15. Life is short and fleeting; it can best be enjoyed within a family circle.

*which He hath given thee.* Cf. viii. 15.

*that is thy portion in life.* Such happiness as here described is all that men can draw out of his term of existence and the toil on which he expends his strength (cf. iii. 22, v. 17).

**10.** *whatsoever . . . that do.* The familiar rendering of A.V. and R.V. *whatsoever thy hand findeth to do, do it with thy might,* follows the Targum but is incorrect. Rashi gives the true sense of *with thy might,* viz. while thou possessest the power; and Ibn Ezra rightly connects the verse with what precedes. The phrase *thy hand findeth* occurs in Judges ix. 33 where it is translated *as thou shalt be able* (cf. 1 Sam. x. 7). The meaning is: all the sources of happiness which have been mentioned should be utilized while man has power to do so during the brief time allotted to him on earth. With the arrival of death, all activity and planning come to an abrupt end.

*grave.* Hebrew *Sheol,* the abode of the dead, but also used for the grave. 'This verse is perhaps the strongest of Koheleth's statements about the absence of physical or mental toil or progress after death. But it is hardly enough to warrant us in saying that he expected annihilation or even mere semi-conscious existence after death. He may still be contrasting the evident silence of the grave with the activity of earth' (Williams).

### 11-12 UNCERTAINTY OF REWARD FOR SKILL

Another phase of the inscrutability of Providence is touched upon. In the same sun, that the race is not to the swift, nor the battle to the strong, neither yet bread to the wise, nor yet riches to men of understanding, nor yet favour to men of skill; but time and chance happeneth to them all.

12. For man also knoweth not his time; as the fishes that are taken in an evil net, and as the birds that are caught in the snare, even so are the sons of men snared in an evil time,

תַּחַת־הַשֶּׁמֶשׁ כִּי לֹא לַקַּלִּים
הַמֵּרוֹץ וְלֹא לַגִּבּוֹרִים
הַמִּלְחָמָה וְגַם לֹא לַחֲכָמִים
לֶחֶם וְגַם לֹא לַנְּבֹנִים עֹשֶׁר
וְגַם לֹא לַיֹּדְעִים חֵן כִּי־עֵת
12 וָפֶגַע יִקְרֶה אֶת־כֻּלָּם׃ כִּי גַּם
לֹא־יֵדַע הָאָדָם אֶת־עִתּוֹ
כַּדָּגִים שֶׁנֶּאֱחָזִים בִּמְצוֹדָה
רָעָה וְכַצִּפֳּרִים הָאֲחֻזוֹת בַּפָּח
כָּהֵם יוּקָשִׁים בְּנֵי הָאָדָם לְעֵת

manner that good fortune and misfortune are not apportioned to men according to their deserts, so success does not come to those who most merit it.

11. *I returned, and saw.* Cf. iv. 1.

*the race is not to the swift.* The fastest runner does not always reach the goal first.

*the battle.* i.e. victory in battle.

*bread to the wise.* Sometimes clever men fail to earn a living.

*favour.* The appreciation of their fellowmen. An illustration is given in verses 14f.

*to men of skill.* lit. 'to them who know.'

*time and chance.* Ginsburg construes the two nouns as 'the time of misfortune,' but this is unacceptable. *Time* seems to indicate that it is an element in deciding whether a person succeeds or fails in what he does. He may then be 'out of form' and unable to put forth his best effort. *Chance* only occurs again in 1 Kings v. 18, *evil occurrences*; a mishap may rob the better man of the prize which he deserves.

12. *his time.* Many expositors think of the time of death, but it is more feasible to give the word the same meaning as in the last verse. The thought which Koheleth brings out is that man is incapable of foreseeing what will be his 'form' at the critical moment when he is put to the test. He goes in for his venture and courts failure as blindly as fishes entangle themselves in nets and birds fly into the trap.

*an evil net.* If so rendered, it must denote a net which spells disaster for those caught in it. A Rabbi defined it as 'a fish-hook,' i.e. a painful method of being caught as compared with the painless net. Ehrlich understands the word as a 'container' in which fish are kept until required for use; and *evil* is added because the noun is also employed in a favourable sense of 'entrenchment' (Isa. xxix. 7).

*an evil time.* When a man is unable to

when it falleth suddenly upon them.

13. This also have I seen as wisdom under the sun, and it seemed great unto me: 14. there was a little city, and few men within it; and there came a great king against it, and besieged it, and built great bulwarks against it; 15. now there was found in it a man poor and wise, and he by his wisdom delivered the city; yet no man remembered that same poor man. 16. Then said I:

רָעָה כְּשֶׁתִּפּוֹל עֲלֵיהֶם
13 פִּתְאֹם׃ גַּם־זֹה רָאִיתִי חָכְמָה
תַּחַת הַשָּׁמֶשׁ וּגְדוֹלָה הִיא אֵלָי׃
14 עִיר קְטַנָּה וַאֲנָשִׁים בָּהּ מְעָט
וּבָא־אֵלֶיהָ מֶלֶךְ גָּדוֹל וְסָבַב
אֹתָהּ וּבָנָה עָלֶיהָ מְצוֹדִים
15 גְּדוֹלִים׃ וּמָצָא בָהּ אִישׁ מִסְכֵּן
חָכָם וּמִלַּט־הוּא אֶת־הָעִיר
בְּחָכְמָתוֹ וְאָדָם לֹא זָכַר אֶת־
16 הָאִישׁ הַמִּסְכֵּן הַהוּא׃ וְאָמַרְתִּי

exercise his superior attainments and reap their reward.

*suddenly.* He is therefore not able to prepare for the contingency.

13-16 WISDOM UNAPPRECIATED

An anecdote is included to substantiate the assertion made in verse 11. Many suggestions, of little probability, have been proposed to identify what is related with a historical incident. The circumstances correspond with the narrative of 2 Sam. xx. 15ff. which tells how the city of Abel of Beth-maacah, when besieged by Joab, was saved by the wit of one of its inhabitants; but so little was it appreciated that the name of the person has not been preserved. An important disparity is that it was a woman who was concerned in this episode. Most probably Koheleth just invented a situation to point his moral. 'The whole narrative, however, is sufficiently true to human experience to make it very telling' (Martin).

13. *as wisdom.* i.e. an instance of the application of wisdom which, however, received no recognition.

*it seemed great unto me.* lit. 'it (was) great unto me'; it made a deep impression upon me.

14. *a little city.* Its small size is mentioned to emphasize that normally it could easily have been stormed.

*few men.* The defending force was consequently small and should have been readily overcome.

*a great king.* With presumably a large and powerful army.

*against it.* Ibn Ezra prefers the translation 'over it,' and explains that the city was built on an incline so that it was easy to erect mounds overlooking it from which the besiegers could attack.

15. *now there was found.* Better, 'but he (the king) encountered.'

*poor and wise.* The Hebrew is 'poor wise,' i.e. poor though wise, in accordance with what was stated in verse 11. Although he had wisdom to save the city, it did not save him from poverty.

*remembered.* After he had brought salvation to the city; not, as Ibn Ezra explains, nobody gave him a thought before the crisis arose although he was so wise.

'Wisdom is better than strength; nevertheless the poor man's wisdom is despised, and his words are not heard.'

**17** The words of the wise spoken in quiet
Are more acceptable than the cry of a ruler among fools.

**18** Wisdom is better than weapons of war;
But one sinner destroyeth much good.

אָנִי טוֹבָה חָכְמָה מִגְּבוּרָה
וְחָכְמַת הַמִּסְכֵּן בְּזוּיָה וּדְבָרָיו
17 אֵינָם נִשְׁמָעִים: דִּבְרֵי חֲכָמִים
בְּנַחַת נִשְׁמָעִים מִזַּעֲקַת מוֹשֵׁל
18 בַּכְּסִילִים: טוֹבָה חָכְמָה
מִכְּלֵי קְרָב וְחוֹטֶא אֶחָד יְאַבֵּד
טוֹבָה הַרְבֵּה:

**16.** *wisdom is better than strength.* Cf. vii. 19.

*the poor man's wisdom is despised.* People take advantage of his sagacity and benefit from it; but if he is poor, he will gain neither recognition nor reward.

*his words are not heard.* As a rule he is ignored, and only in an extreme case do people pay attention to him. Another interpretation is: when he has rendered a service and asks for payment, no notice is taken of his words.

### 17-18 ON WISDOM

From verse 17 down to xii. 8 (with the exception of x. 3) is composed in poetical form, and resembles the Book of Proverbs in style and thought.

**17.** Translate: 'The words of the wise are heard (though spoken) in quiet more than the cry of a ruler over fools.' The quiet and dignified utterances of wise men are listened to rather than the noisy declamation of an arch-fool. This proverb is added here as an indication that what was said in verse 16 is not always true. Generally speaking, attention is paid to the words of the wise.

**18.** *better than weapons of war.* As a means of gaining victory, proved by the incident described in verses 14f. The word for *war* is poetical (cf. Ps. cxliv. 1).

*one sinner.* The contrast shows that a man who acts thoughtlessly is meant.

*destroyeth much good.* Cf. the story of Achan (Josh. vii. 1ff.).

1 Dead flies make the ointment of the perfumer fetid and putrid;
So doth a little folly outweigh wisdom and honour.

2 A wise man's understanding is at his right hand;
But a fool's understanding at his left.

3 Yea also, when a fool walketh by the way, his understanding faileth him, and he saith to every one that he is a fool.

1 זְבוּבֵי מָוֶת יַבְאִישׁ יַבִּיעַ שֶׁמֶן
רוֹקֵחַ יָקָר מֵחָכְמָה מִכָּבוֹד
2 סִכְלוּת מְעָט׃ לֵב חָכָם
לִימִינוֹ וְלֵב כְּסִיל לִשְׂמֹאלוֹ׃
3 וְגַם־בַּדֶּרֶךְ כְּשֶׁהַ*סָּכָל הֹלֵךְ
לִבּוֹ חָסֵר וְאָמַר לַכֹּל סָכָל

v. 3. יתיר ה'

1-3 FOLLY AND WISDOM

1. *dead flies.* lit. 'flies of death.' On the analogy of the phrase in I Sam. xx. 31, *for he deserveth to die* (lit. 'a son of death,' i.e. one whose death is imminent), the correct meaning is 'flies about to die.' 'In the winter-time, when flies have no strength and are near death, should one come into the ointment of the perfumer and be mingled with the scented ingredients, it makes it putrid. It is something insignificant, yet spoils a precious article. So a little folly may be more costly than wisdom and honour, for it outweighs them all. Take the case of a man equally balanced in his faults and virtues; should he commit one transgression, it inclines the scales to guilt' (Rashi).

*make . . . fetid and putrid.* The verbs are singular, indicating that one fly produces the harmful effect. The second verb means 'causeth to bubble,' creates fermentation.

*so doth . . . honour.* lit. 'more weighty than wisdom and honour is a little folly.' These high qualifications in a man correspond to the costly ingredients used by a perfumer; and as one dead fly can destroy the value of his preparation, so a single act of folly is sufficient to unmake a good reputation.

2. *understanding.* lit. 'heart'; a better translation is 'mind,' the directive of his thoughts and actions.

*at his right hand.* Ginsburg explains this as 'ready to guard and defend him from a thousand dangers', comparing Ps. xvi. 8, cx. 5. But a more exact translation is '(inclineth) to his right hand,' the right being considered the auspicious and favourable side and the left regarded as sinister (that is the sense of this word in Latin). The phrase accordingly indicates that a wise heart brings its possessor advantages: it warns him against a step which may prove disastrous and helps him to success.

3. *walketh by the way.* Cf. Deut. vi. 7 where it is the contrast of *when thou sittest in thy house,* i.e. when he is abroad mingling with other men.

*faileth him.* The Hebrew word can be a verb which is, however, intransitive and so precludes Ginsburg's translation 'he lacketh his mind,' or an adjective. The latter is preferable: 'his heart (mind) is lacking'; he displays a lack of intelligence in the way he behaves.

*he saith to every one that he is a fool.* The clause can be construed in two ways.

4 If the spirit of the ruler rise up against thee,
Leave not thy place;
For gentleness allayeth great offences.

5 There is an evil which I have seen under the sun,
Like an error which proceedeth from a ruler:

6 Folly is set on great heights,
And the rich sit in low place.

7 I have seen servants upon horses,
And princes walking as servants upon the earth.

הוּא׃ 4 אִם־רוּחַ הַמּוֹשֵׁל
תַּעֲלֶה עָלֶיךָ מְקוֹמְךָ אַל־
תַּנַּח כִּי מַרְפֵּא יַנִּיחַ חֲטָאִים
5 גְּדוֹלִים׃ יֵשׁ רָעָה רָאִיתִי תַּחַת
הַשָּׁמֶשׁ כִּשְׁגָגָה שֶׁיֹּצָא מִלִּפְנֵי
6 הַשַּׁלִּיט׃ נִתַּן הַסֶּכֶל
בַּמְּרוֹמִים רַבִּים וַעֲשִׁירִים
7 בַּשֵּׁפֶל יֵשֵׁבוּ׃ רָאִיתִי עֲבָדִים
עַל־סוּסִים וְשָׂרִים הֹלְכִים

By his stupid conduct he lets everybody know that he is a fool (Rashi, Ibn Ezra); or, he calls everybody a fool who disagrees with or corrects him. The latter is more probable.

### 4-7 THE CONDUCT OF AUTOCRATS

4. *if the spirit.* Should you arouse the ruler's anger.

*leave not thy place.* Cf. viii. 3. Here it is usually explained as 'do not resign thy office as one of his attendants.'

5. *an evil.* viz. what is stated in verses 6f. The phrase is repeated from vi. 1.

*like an error.* In spite of the seriousness of the appointments or dismissals to the persons concerned and the community, an autocrat treats them *like an error*, an inadvertent action, the noun *shegagah* signifying an unintentional wrong. 'Koheleth here exhibits some of the pacifying spirit which he has just advised. He does not excite the anger of a despot by suggesting that his errors are intentional. Underneath his expression we detect a deeper note; it is revealed in the word *evil.* One must bow to the despot, but the despot is not always right. This is a blot on the government of the world' (Barton).

*proceedeth.* The peculiar form of the Hebrew is intended as the feminine participle to agree with the gender of the noun.

*ruler.* A different word from that in verse 4 and better translated 'despot.'

6. *folly.* Ibn Ezra suggests that the noun is of the same form as *yeled* and signifies 'a fool'; but Rashi rightly understands it as the abstract noun employed in a concrete sense.

*on great heights.* i.e. are given high office in the state. Ginsburg renders 'in many high positions,' Barton 'in high positions often.'

*the rich.* Jastrow translates 'the choice spirits,' on the assumption that the noun is to be pointed, *asirim*, 'the tens,' i.e., the upper ten.' With greater probability Plumptre explains, 'The *rich* here are those who by birth and station are looked on as the natural rulers of mankind.'

7. *servants.* Better, 'slaves,' and similarly in the second clause.

*upon horses.* Commoners rode on mules and asses; only the highest in the land were allowed the use of horses (cf. Jer. xvii. 25; Esth. vi. 8f.). This verse repeats the point of the preceding.

*princes.* The Hebrew *sar* has a wider significance which includes 'chief official': e.g. *chief of the butlers* and *chief of the bakers* (Gen. xl. 2). Men holding high office are reduced to the status of slaves.

8 He that diggeth a pit shall fall into it;
And whoso breaketh through a fence, a serpent shall bite him.
9 Whoso quarrieth stones shall be hurt therewith;
And he that cleaveth wood is endangered thereby.
10 If the iron be blunt,
And one do not whet the edge,
Then must he put to more strength;
But wisdom is profitable to direct.
11 If the serpent bite before it is charmed,
Then the charmer hath no advantage.

8 כַּעֲבָדִים עַל־הָאָרֶץ׃ חֹפֵר
גּוּמָּץ בּוֹ יִפּוֹל וּפֹרֵץ גָּדֵר
9 יִשְּׁכֶנּוּ נָחָשׁ׃ מַסִּיעַ אֲבָנִים
יֵעָצֵב בָּהֶם בּוֹקֵעַ עֵצִים יִסָּכֶן
10 בָּם׃ אִם־קֵהָה הַבַּרְזֶל וְהוּא
לֹא־פָנִים קִלְקַל וַחֲיָלִים
יְגַבֵּר וְיִתְרוֹן הַכְשֵׁיר חָכְמָה׃
11 אִם־יִשֹּׁךְ הַנָּחָשׁ בְּלוֹא־לָחַשׁ
וְאֵין יִתְרוֹן לְבַעַל הַלָּשׁוֹן׃

master of the tongue (slanderer)

**8-11** SOME LESSONS OF WISDOM

In the opinion of some commentators, these verses are connected with the foregoing and are intended as warnings addressed to men in attendance upon a king. They may, on the other hand, follow the style of the Book of Proverbs and teach general rules of prudence.

**8.** The verse is made up of figures taken from other parts of the Bible.

*he that diggeth . . . into it.* Cf. Ps. vii. 16, lvii. 7; Prov. xxvi. 27. The teaching is either that a plotter against the king will come to harm, or one who conspires against his fellow-man will fall into his own trap.

*fence.* Better, 'a wall' (Prov. xxiv. 31) in the crevices of which a serpent may be lurking, and when disturbed by the breach in the wall is infuriated. One breaks through a wall to rob the field or house.

*a serpent shall bite him.* Cf. Amos v. 19.

**9.** *quarrieth stones.* This meaning appears to be established by 1 Kings v. 31 as against 'moveth stones (i.e. used as a landmark).' The dangerous character of this employment is the point of the remark, and similarly in the next clause.

*is endangered thereby.* He may injure himself with the axe, or its head may fly off killing a bystander (Deut. xix. 5) and his own life be placed in danger from the vengeance of the dead man's relatives.

**10.** *the iron.* The metal part of the hatchet.

*then must he . . . strength.* He is compelled to strike harder and more often to fell the tree. On the first mentioned interpretation of this section, this is an enigmatic piece of advice to would-be conspirators to see that all details of their scheme are carefully examined and prepared before attempting an insurrection.

*wisdom is profitable to direct. Wisdom* is here plain common sense. If the workman had prepared his tool properly, he would have accomplished his task more successfully.

**11.** The meaning of the verse is well expressed in the comment of Rashbam: If the serpent stings a man because the charmer failed to charm it, there is no advantage in knowing how to exercise a charm and not making use of it.

12 The words of a wise man's mouth
are gracious;
But the lips of a fool will swallow
up himself.

13 The beginning of the words of
his mouth is foolishness;
And the end of his talk is grievous madness.

14 A fool also multiplieth words;
Yet man knoweth not what shall
be;
And that which shall be after him,
Who can tell him?

15 The labour of fools wearieth
every one of them,
For he knoweth not how to go to
the city.

12 דִּבְרֵי פִי־חָכָם חֵן וְשִׂפְתוֹת
13 כְּסִיל תְּבַלְּעֶנּוּ׃ תְּחִלַּת
דִּבְרֵי־פִיהוּ סִכְלוּת וְאַחֲרִית
14 פִּיהוּ הוֹלֵלוּת רָעָה׃ וְהַסָּכָל
יַרְבֶּה דְבָרִים לֹא־יֵדַע
הָאָדָם מַה־שֶּׁיִּהְיֶה וַאֲשֶׁר
יִהְיֶה מֵאַחֲרָיו מִי יַגִּיד לוֹ׃
15 עֲמַל הַכְּסִילִים תְּיַגְּעֶנּוּ אֲשֶׁר
לֹא־יָדַע לָלֶכֶת אֶל־עִיר׃

*if the serpent.* This continues the figure at the end of verse 8.

*the charmer hath no advantage.* i.e. there is no advantage in being a snake-charmer (lit. 'master of the tongue').

### 12-15 WISE MEN AND FOOLS

**12.** *are gracious.* Or, 'are favour'; they meet with the approbation of those who hear them (Rashi).

*will swallow up himself.* Will be the cause of his own undoing.

**13.** *the beginning . . . and the end.* For this idiom denoting totality, see on iii. 11. Ibn Ezra correctly explains, 'There is no sense in his words from start to finish.' It does not mean 'progress from bad to worse' (Plumptre).

*grievous madness.* An extreme form of folly (cf. i. 17).

**14.** *multiplieth words.* 'The irony of this verse consists in the fact that a fool will talk glibly about all sorts of mysteries, while he ignores man's real ignorance of the destinies of human life' (Martin).

*what shall be . . . after him.* Or, 'after it.' Ginsburg renders: 'no man knoweth what shall be here nor what shall be hereafter.' A more literal translation would be: 'what shall be (in the immediate future) and what shall be after that, who can tell him?' For the wording, cf. viii. 7.

**15.** *wearieth every one of them.* lit. 'wearieth him,' i.e. each fool. He toils unceasingly until his strength is exhausted without his accomplishing anything.

*he knoweth . . . city.* Evidently a proverbial saying. There is always a well-marked road leading to a city and only an utter fool could miss it (cf. Isa. xxxv. 8). So there is a common-sense method of accomplishing a task which only a fool fails to see and spends his efforts to no avail.

16 Woe to thee, O land, when thy king is a boy,
And thy princes feast in the morning!
17 Happy art thou, O land, when thy king is a free man,
And thy princes eat in due season,
In strength, and not in drunkenness!
18 By slothfulness the rafters sink in;
And through idleness of the hands the house leaketh.
19 A feast is made for laughter,
And wine maketh glad the life;
And money answereth all things.

16 אִי־לָךְ אֶרֶץ שֶׁמַּלְכֵּךְ נָעַר
17 וְשָׂרַיִךְ בַּבֹּקֶר יֹאכֵלוּ׃ אַשְׁרֵיךְ
אֶרֶץ שֶׁמַּלְכֵּךְ בֶּן־חוֹרִים
וְשָׂרַיִךְ בָּעֵת יֹאכֵלוּ בִּגְבוּרָה
18 וְלֹא בַשְּׁתִי׃ בַּעֲצַלְתַּיִם יִמַּךְ
הַמְּקָרֶה וּבְשִׁפְלוּת יָדָיִם
19 יִדְלֹף הַבָּיִת׃ לִשְׂחוֹק עֹשִׂים
לֶחֶם וְיַיִן יְשַׂמַּח חַיִּים וְהַכֶּסֶף

**16-20** EFFECT OF GOVERNMENT UPON A LAND

The consequences of wisdom and folly in the life of the common people have a parallel in wise and foolish governorship.

**16.** *a boy.* The Hebrew means 'a young man.' It is a bad thing for a State when its king is young in years and inexperienced. Not only is he likely to make mistakes, but also to fall under the influence of unscrupulous advisers.

*princes.* Officials (see on verse 7).

*feast in the morning.* lit. 'eat in the morning.' The contrast in the next verse proves that the reference is not to feasting, but taking the heavy meal of the day at a time when work has to be done.

**17.** *a free man.* One who is able to act on his own judgment and is not the pawn of his councillors. A.V. and R.V. *the son of nobles* does not give the right contrast to *boy* in verse 16.

*eat in due season.* viz. in the evening when the day's work is done.

*in strength, and not in drunkenness.* Plumptre explains in *strength* as 'with the self-control of temperance.' *In drunkenness* then signifies excessive indulgence in wine which formed part of the meal (cf. *it is not for kings to drink wine*, Prov. xxxi. 4, and *woe unto them that are mighty to drink wine*, Isa. v. 22). A probable translation is 'with manliness and not with carousal,' i.e. 'although they have the appetite of strong and vigorous men, their interests do not lie in drinking bouts' (Williams).

**18.** This verse is a disconnected proverb inserted at this point because its application suited the subject which is treated. It tells of the ruinous effect which neglect has upon a building. As Ibn Ezra remarks, it is the same with a community when its affairs are neglected by the ruling powers.

*rafters.* The word is singular in a collective sense.

*idleness.* lit. 'lowliness,' letting down the hands when they should be working.

**19.** Various explanations have been given to the verse. If it is connected with verse 18, it draws a contrast between the effects of idleness and industry. With the money one earns a man is able to procure the means to a comfortable life. A better sense is obtained by construing verses 17f. as parenthetical and understanding this verse as the continuation of *thy princes feast in the morning*. Translate: 'for merriment they prepare (lit. make) food and wine (which) gladdeneth life and (acquire) the money (which)

20 Curse not the king, no, not in thy
thought,
And curse not the rich in thy bed-
chamber;
For a bird of the air shall carry
the voice,
And that which hath wings shall
tell the matter.

20 יַעֲנֶה אֶת־הַכֹּל׃ גַּם בְּמַדָּעֲךָ
מֶלֶךְ אַל־תְּקַלֵּל וּבְחַדְרֵי
מִשְׁכָּבְךָ אַל־תְּקַלֵּל עָשִׁיר כִּי
עוֹף הַשָּׁמַיִם יוֹלִיךְ אֶת־
הַקּוֹל וּבַעַל הַכְּנָפַיִם יַגֵּיד
דָּבָר׃

v. 20. יתיר ה'

providеth all the things.' Not only do the *princes* have their meal at the wrong time of the day, but they turn it into an occasion of revelry and spend the money they extort from the people on dissipation.

*feast.* lit. 'bread, food.'

*laughter.* i.e. merriment; see on ii. 2.

*wine maketh glad.* Cf. Ps. civ. 15. Both the words *wine* and *money* are objects of 'they make.'

*answereth.* For this verb, see on v. 19, and it is here in the causative mood (hiphil). Literally the clause means, 'and the money which is occupied with the task (of supplying) the all.'

**20.** The failings and extravagance of the ruling class naturally arouse criticism; but it is unwise to give voice to it or even to entertain it in one's thoughts, because one may inadvertently make a remark which will endanger his life. An autocrat spreads spies throughout the land to report on his subjects.

*thought.* lit. 'knowledge'; here it is 'the seat of knowledge,' the mind.

*the rich.* i.e. the wealthy families who govern the country.

*in thy bed-chamber.* In a remote part of the house when conversing with another person (cf. 2 Kings vi. 12).

*a bird of the air.* An idiom found in many languages (cf. the English expression, 'A little bird told me').

*the voice.* Better, 'the report,' as the word is translated in Genesis xlv. 16.

*shall tell the matter.* 'Because a wall has ears' (Midrash).

1 Cast thy bread upon the waters,
For thou shalt find it after many days.

2 Divide a portion into seven, yea, even into eight;
For thou knowest not what evil shall be upon the earth.

3 If the clouds be full of rain,
They empty themselves upon the earth;
And if a tree fall in the south, or in the north,

1 שַׁלַּח לַחְמְךָ עַל־פְּנֵי הַמָּיִם
כִּי־בְרֹב הַיָּמִים תִּמְצָאֶנּוּ׃
2 תֶּן־חֵלֶק לְשִׁבְעָה וְגַם
לִשְׁמוֹנָה כִּי לֹא תֵדַע מַה־
3 יִּהְיֶה רָעָה עַל־הָאָרֶץ׃ אִם־
יִמָּלְאוּ הֶעָבִים גֶּשֶׁם עַל־
הָאָרֶץ יָרִיקוּ וְאִם־יִפּוֹל עֵץ

It has been truly said, 'The Book, as it draws nearer to its close, becomes more and more enigmatic, and each single verse is as a parable and dark saying' (Plumptre).

**1-8 THE UNCERTAINTY OF LIFE**

1. *cast thy bread upon the waters.* For *cast* substitute 'send forth.' Jastrow, following Moses Mendelssohn and others, sees in the verse shrewd advice to take risks in business by trusting one's goods or ships that will after many days return with a profit, but not to commit all one's possessions to a single venture. As a proverbial saying this may have been its original intention. But the traditional Jewish interpretation is accepted by many moderns, that the exhortation is to practise goodness and kindness from which a reward may unexpectedly and after a long interval be reaped.

2. This verse continues the preceding and offers a similar divergence of interpretation. As a piece of advice in business, it warns against putting all one's eggs in one basket. As a moral maxim it counsels a man to practise his benevolence towards as many as possible, in order to make numerous friends. He is then more likely to receive help should bad times befall him.

*divide.* lit. 'give a portion (of *thy bread*) to seven and even to eight.' The last words are a Hebrew way of signifying an indefinite number.

*evil.* Misfortune.

3. The connection of ideas appears to be: a man should perform kindly acts although the future is hidden from him; in the same way, he should proceed with his daily work in spite of the impossibility of knowing whether it may not be spoilt by natural conditions which he cannot control.

*if the clouds be full of rain.* Koheleth draws upon a phenomenon of nature to teach his lesson. Rain is dependent upon the appearance of heavy clouds, and the farmer has to depend upon rain at the time of sowing.

*if a tree fall.* Uprooted in a gale. This is another illustration of man's helplessness in the face of the forces of nature, and 'we must take things as they are' (Williams).

In the place where the tree falleth,
there shall it be.

4 He that observeth the wind shall
not sow;
And he that regardeth the clouds
shall not reap.

5 As thou knowest not what is the
way of the wind,
Nor how the bones do grow in the
womb of her that is with child;
Even so thou knowest not the work
of God
Who doeth all things.

6 In the morning sow thy seed,
And in the evening withhold not
thy hand;
For thou knowest not which shall
prosper, whether this or that,

בַּדָּרוֹם וְאִם בַּצָּפוֹן מְקוֹם
4 שֶׁיִּפּוֹל הָעֵץ שָׁם יְהוּא׃ שֹׁמֵר
רוּחַ לֹא יִזְרָע וְרֹאֶה בֶעָבִים
5 לֹא יִקְצוֹר׃ כַּאֲשֶׁר אֵינְךָ יוֹדֵעַ
מַה־דֶּרֶךְ הָרוּחַ כַּעֲצָמִים
בְּבֶטֶן הַמְּלֵאָה כָּכָה לֹא תֵדַע
אֶת־מַעֲשֵׂה הָאֱלֹהִים אֲשֶׁר
6 יַעֲשֶׂה אֶת־הַכֹּל׃ בַּבֹּקֶר זְרַע
אֶת־זַרְעֶךָ וְלָעֶרֶב אַל־תַּנַּח
יָדֶךָ כִּי אֵינְךָ יוֹדֵעַ אֵי זֶה יִכְשָׁר
הֲזֶה אוֹ־זֶה וְאִם־שְׁנֵיהֶם

4. Another instance of 'chiasmus' (see on vii. 7). In the last verse we first have mention of *clouds* and then an implied reference to the wind; in this verse the order is reversed.

*observeth the wind.* If the farmer occupies his mind with the possibility of violent winds which will blow away the seed he sows, he will be reduced to inaction.

*regardeth the clouds.* Similarly if he wastes his time gazing at the clouds during harvest time, dreading lest rain falls and spoils the crops, he may be deterred from carrying on his work and the corn will be left uncut in the field.

5. *wind.* The Hebrew can also mean 'spirit,' the breath of life, and some commentators prefer this signification here: as one who is ignorant how life enters the embryo. But it is more natural to understand it as in the previous verse. Man's ignorance about the changes of the wind is as profound as about the formation of a child in the womb.

*nor how . . . child.* More literally, 'as (thou knowest not) the bones in a womb which is filled.' The mystery of procreation and birth impressed the Hebrew mind deeply (cf. Ps. cxxxix. 13ff.; Prov. xxx. 19).

*the work of God.* Cf. vii. 13, God's control of the universe.

6. *morning . . . evening.* These terms are understood by some in a figurative way: 'From youth till the evening of life, one is manfully to perform the full round of life's tasks, that he is not to hesitate because of the uncertainties which were set forth in verse 5, and that he is to take the losses which come in a philosophical spirit' (Barton). *Metsudath David*, on the other hand, interprets the verse literally to refer to the work of the farmer: In the morning sow thy field, and in the evening do not withhold thy hand from sowing; i.e. at all times sow thy field and wait not upon the wind. The context seems to favour the latter interpretation.

*this or that.* viz. sowing in the morning

Or whether they both shall be
alike good.

7 And the light is sweet,
And a pleasant thing it is for the
eyes to behold the sun.

8 For if a man live many years,
Let him rejoice in them all,
And remember the days of dark-
ness,
For they shall be many.
All that cometh is vanity.

9 Rejoice, O young man, in thy
youth;
And let thy heart cheer thee in
the days of thy youth,

7 כְּאֶחָד טוֹבִים׃ וּמָתוֹק הָאוֹר
וְטוֹב לַעֵינַיִם לִרְאוֹת אֶת־
8 הַשָּׁמֶשׁ׃ כִּי אִם־שָׁנִים הַרְבֵּה
יִחְיֶה הָאָדָם בְּכֻלָּם יִשְׂמָח
וְיִזְכֹּר אֶת־יְמֵי הַחֹשֶׁךְ כִּי־
הַרְבֵּה יִהְיוּ כָּל־שֶׁבָּא הָבֶל׃
9 שְׂמַח בָּחוּר בְּיַלְדוּתֶךָ וִיטִיבְךָ

or evening. The moral is, when there is work to be done, perform it diligently and exhaustively, and do not concern yourself with the factors which are beyond your understanding.

7. *and the light is sweet.* Better, 'then sweet is the light.' By following the advice given, viz. to act benevolently and work diligently, life will be found worth living notwithstanding its uncertainties. The hopeful, optimistic mood has returned, in striking contrast to such dark moments as called forth ii. 17, iv. 2.

*to behold the sun.* To be alive. 'The *light* and the *sun* are designedly used for "life," in harmony with the *clouds, wind* and especially the *day* spoken of in the foregoing verses' (Ginsburg).

8. *the days of darkness.* Practically all commentators, ancient and modern, have explained the phrase as an allusion to death. Parallels have been found in the practice among the Egyptians, as recorded by Herodotus, and the Babylonians of carrying a coffin into a banqueting hall to remind the guests 'Drink and be merry, because it will be impossible when you are dead.' Very attractive is Ehrlich's suggestion that the words denote 'the evening of life,' and the admonition is to enjoy that period of existence when enjoyment is possible.

*all that cometh*, viz. the years of decrepit old age, *is vanity*, in that the faculties have lost their power. This explanation accords with the section which follows where that thought is elaborated.

### 9-10 EXHORTATION TO YOUTH

9. 'The Rabbis sought to suppress the Book of Koheleth because they discovered therein words which tend towards heresy. They declared, "This is the wisdom of Solomon that he said, *Rejoice, O young man, in thy youth!* Now Moses said, *That ye go not about after your own heart* (Num. xv. 39), whereas Solomon said, *Walk in the ways of thy heart!* Is restraint to be abolished? Is there no judgment and no Judge?" But since he continued, *But know thou, that for all these things God will bring thee into judgment*, they exclaimed, "Well has Solomon spoken"' (Midrash).

*youth.* Two different Hebrew terms are used which may be distinguished in English by 'youth' and 'adolescence.'

And walk in the ways of thy heart,
And in the sight of thine eyes;
But know thou, that for all these things
God will bring thee into judgment.
10 Therefore remove vexation from thy heart,
And put away evil from thy flesh;
For childhood and youth are vanity.

לִבְּךָ֙ בִּימֵ֣י בְחוּרוֹתֶ֔יךָ וְהַלֵּךְ֙
בְּדַרְכֵ֣י לִבְּךָ֔ וּבְמַרְאֵ֖י* עֵינֶ֑יךָ
וְדָ֕ע כִּ֥י עַל־כָּל־אֵ֖לֶּה יְבִיאֲךָ֥
10 הָאֱלֹהִ֖ים בַּמִּשְׁפָּֽט׃ וְהָסֵ֤ר
כַּ֙עַס֙ מִלִּבֶּ֔ךָ וְהַעֲבֵ֥ר רָעָ֖ה
מִבְּשָׂרֶ֑ךָ כִּֽי־הַיַּלְד֥וּת
וְהַשַּׁחֲר֖וּת הָֽבֶל׃

v. 9. ובמראה ק׳

*walk in the ways of thy heart.* i.e. satisfy thy longings.

*the sight of thine eyes.* See on vi. 9.

*God will bring thee into judgment.* This is the sobering reminder to curb excess and unlawful indulgence.

**10.** The usual explanation is, that to secure the happiness which is recommended, it is necessary to banish worry and unpleasant physical experiences. It seems preferable to construe *but know thou . . . thy flesh* as a parenthesis. The meaning would then be: Bear in mind that thou art answerable to God for the way thou employest the powers and opportunities of youth, 'and so remove vexation from thy heart and make harm to pass away from thy flesh.' By avoiding abuse, a young man will escape the consequences of debauchery to mind and body.

*for childhood and youth are vanity.* Better, 'for youth and manhood are vanity,' and the words are to be connected with *rejoice, O young man . . . sight of thine eyes.* *Childhood* (*yalduth*) is the same word as *in thy youth* (verse 9). The second term *youth* (*shacharuth*) is by some associated with *shachar* 'dawn,' but the 'dawn of life' is infancy when the opportunities of enjoyment, as here implied, are not yet available. Preference must, therefore, be given to the derivation from *shachor* 'black.' It denotes 'blackness of the hair,' i.e. manhood as against *sebah* 'white hair,' the indication of old age. *Vanity* here signifies 'fleeting,' as in vii. 15, ix. 9.

1 Remember then thy Creator in the days of thy youth,
Before the evil days come,
And the years draw nigh, when thou shalt say:
'I have no pleasure in them';

2 Before the sun, and the light, and the moon,
And the stars, are darkened,
And the clouds return after the rain;

1 וּזְכֹר אֶת־בּוֹרְאֶיךָ בִּימֵי
בְּחוּרֹתֶיךָ עַד אֲשֶׁר לֹא־יָבֹאוּ
יְמֵי הָרָעָה וְהִגִּיעוּ שָׁנִים אֲשֶׁר
תֹּאמַר אֵין־לִי בָהֶם חֵפֶץ׃
2 עַד אֲשֶׁר לֹא־תֶחְשַׁךְ הַשֶּׁמֶשׁ
וְהָאוֹר וְהַיָּרֵחַ וְהַכּוֹכָבִים
וְשָׁבוּ הֶעָבִים אַחַר הַגָּשֶׁם׃

### 1-8 THE DECLINE OF LIFE

In this section we have a graphic account of *the days of darkness* (xi. 8) which succeed the period of 'youth and manhood' (xi. 10). It has been referred to as 'one of the most famous passages in all literature' (Martin).

1. *remember then.* Better, 'and remember,' which brings out the sequence of ideas and the close connection with what precedes. Although a new chapter begins here, there is no division of subject and the verse is the continuation of xi. 10. The admonition to *remember* is parallel to *know thou* in xi. 9.

*Creator.* If the noun is construed as plural, it is the 'plural of majesty.' 'This designation of God was chosen as laying stress on Him as the ultimate cause and designer of our bodily frame, of which the inherent weakness and transitoriness are emphasized. It suggests that the clay must not find fault with the potter, and that He ought to be the object of our regard whatever comes' (Williams).

*youth.* This is the word defined as 'adolescence' in the note on xi. 9.

*the evil days.* In contrast to the happy days of life's prime when man is full of vitality; 'the days of old age and feebleness' (Rashi). At the time when the passions of youth have subsided, there is less urgency to be mindful of man's accountability to his Creator.

2ff. The imagery under which the oncoming of age is figured has called forth a variety of interpretations. Only two need be mentioned as being most favoured: (*a*) Koheleth describes the waning powers of the organs of the body, employing symbolic terms for them. (*b*) The blotting out of the light of life by advancing years is likened to a gathering storm and its effects. The Talmud (Shabbath 152a) favours (*a*) and includes an anecdote to show how the phraseology had passed into current speech: In answer to a question put to him, a Rabbi pleaded old age in these words, 'The mountain is snow, it is surrounded by ice, the dog does not bark and the grinders do not grind.' The verses will be commented upon in agreement with both theories.

2. (*a*) *The sun, and the light* denote the forehead and the nose, *the moon*, the soul, *the stars* the cheeks, *the clouds*

3 In the day when the keepers of the house shall tremble,
And the strong men shall bow themselves,
And the grinders cease because they are few,
And those that look out shall be darkened in the windows,
4 And the doors shall be shut in the street,
When the sound of the grinding is low;
And one shall start up at the voice of a bird,

3 בַּיּוֹם שֶׁיָּזֻעוּ שֹׁמְרֵי הַבַּיִת
וְהִתְעַוְּתוּ אַנְשֵׁי הֶחָיִל וּבָטְלוּ
הַטֹּחֲנוֹת כִּי מִעֵטוּ וְחָשְׁכוּ
4 הָרֹאוֹת בָּאֲרֻבּוֹת׃ וְסֻגְּרוּ
דְלָתַיִם בַּשּׁוּק בִּשְׁפַל קוֹל
הַטַּחֲנָה וְיָקוּם לְקוֹל הַצִּפּוֹר

*after the rain* the eyesight which is enfeebled by weeping due to trouble and sickness (Talmud). (*b*) The clouds gather and obscure the sun during the day, and the moon and stars during the night. The rain pours down heavily; but as soon as it stops, the clouds return for another downpour. Thus there is no check to the creeping on of old age, 'which cannot look forward to a renewal of youth and sunshine, but only to inactivity and final darkness' (Jastrow).

3. (*a*) *The keepers of the house* are the flanks and ribs, *the strong men* the legs which support the body but grow bent in old age, *the grinders* the teeth, *those that look out* the eyes (Talmud). Ibn Ezra and others see in *the keepers of the house* a reference to the arms and hands. (*b*) The verse presents a picture of the terrifying effect produced upon the members of the household by the storm. *The keepers of the house* are the staff of servants and *the strong men* those appointed to guard the building against robbers. Plumptre understands the phrase as 'men of might,' the wealthy and noble who reside in the mansion. The *grinders* (the word is feminine) are the women employed upon providing the daily supply of flour required for baking. 'A stoppage of the mills, occasioned by a storm as described in the text, would be as terrible as a cessation of business in our towns under similar circumstances' (Ginsburg). *Those that look out* (also feminine) alludes to the ladies of the house who were not at liberty to walk abroad, and so gazed through the lattice windows to see what went on outside (cf. Judg. v. 28; 2 Sam. vi. 16).

4. (*a*) *The doors shall be shut* alludes to the apertures of the body; *the sound of grinding is low* is the failing power of the stomach to digest food; *one shall start up at the voice of a bird*—even a bird will awake him from sleep; *the daughters of music*—even the voices of male and female singers sound to him like a whisper because of deafness (cf. 2 Sam. xix. 36) (Talmud). Possibly *the doors* are the ears which grow hard of hearing. Some render the Hebrew of *and shall start . . . a bird* as 'and he shall rise to the voice of a bird,' i.e. his voice becomes high pitched and tremulous like a bird's. Another explanation is that an old man has little sleep at night and awakens as soon as the birds begin to sing. *The daughters of music* is probably an idiomatic expression for 'musical notes' which are *brought low*, i.e. sound softer than they really are to an old person with impaired hearing. (*b*) Because of the storm the doors are closed since nobody ventures forth in the

And all the daughters of music
shall be brought low;
5 Also when they shall be afraid of
that which is high,
And terrors shall be in the way;
And the almond-tree shall blossom,
And the grasshopper shall drag
itself along,
And the caperberry shall fail;
Because man goeth to his long
home,
And the mourners go about the
streets;
6 Before the silver cord is snapped
asunder,

5 וְיִשַּׁחוּ כָּל־בְּנוֹת הַשִּׁיר׃ גַּם
מִגָּבֹהַּ יִרָאוּ וְחַתְחַתִּים בַּדֶּרֶךְ
וְיָנֵאץ הַשָּׁקֵד וְיִסְתַּבֵּל הֶחָגָב
וְתָפֵר הָאֲבִיּוֹנָה כִּי־הֹלֵךְ
הָאָדָם אֶל־בֵּית עֹלָמוֹ וְסָבְבוּ
6 בַשּׁוּק הַסֹּפְדִים׃ עַד אֲשֶׁר
לֹא־יֵרָחֵק* חֶבֶל הַכֶּסֶף וְתָרֻץ

v. 6. ירתק ק'

streets, the noise of milling stops, 'the swallow shall rise to shriek (lit. to a voice) and all the singing birds shall retire.' This is Ginsburg's translation, and he comments: 'The portentous swallows, in anticipation of the storm, quit their nests with shrieks to fly about; whilst the singing birds, which mount the air with their warbling songs, for the same reason descend and retire.'

5. (*a*) *They shall be afraid of that which is high*—even a small knoll looks to each old man like the highest of mountains when he has to walk up it; *terrors shall be in the way*—when he walks on a road his heart is filled with fears because his legs are unsteady; *the almond tree*, i.e. the coccyx (the lowest end of the vertebræ); *shall blossom* means shall protrude and be moved from its place; *the grasshopper*, i.e. the rump; *the caperberry shall fail*—this is a fruit which excites sensual passion, but it will produce no effect (Talmud). Many explain *the almond trees* as depicting the whiteness of the hair; but its blossom is pinkish in colour. Therefore Tristram suggests that 'the better interpretation seems to be that as the almond blossom ushers in the spring, so do the signs referred to in the context indicate the hastening of old age and death.' (*b*) *That which is high* is the heavens black with the threatening clouds which portend 'terrors on the way.' For *the almond tree shall blossom* Ginsburg substitutes 'the almond shall be despised' and remarks, 'It is well known that the delicious almond is a highly prized fruit, and great indeed must be the consternation of an Oriental which makes him disgusted with this delicacy.' Instead of *the grasshopper shall fail* Ginsburg translates, 'and the locust shall be loathed.' These were permitted as food (Lev. xi. 22), 'and still are to the present day very agreeable, wholesome, and nutritious food both in the East and in other countries.' As for the *caperberry*, it was used, he says, as a condiment to stimulate the palate. 'The mention of the caperberry is exceedingly striking. Having stated that all desire for food, however tempting, shall vanish in this awful scene, Koheleth says that even the caperberry, with all its provocative properties, will fail to excite appetite' (Ginsburg).

*his long home.* Or, 'his eternal home,' the grave. Jews still use the phrase *Beth Olam* for a cemetery. According to (*b*), the storm arouses fears of death which destroy the desire for food.

*the mourners go about the streets.* Professional mourners were hired to wail at funerals (cf. Jer. ix. 16f.). With the smell of death in the air, they do not wait to be summoned, but wander about in the expectation of being called upon to render their services.

6. (*a*) *The silver cord* is the spinal cord; *the golden bowl* is the skull; *the pitcher* is the stomach which has a similar shape

And the golden bowl is shattered,
And the pitcher is broken at the fountain,
And the wheel falleth shattered into the pit;

7 And the dust returneth to the earth as it was,
And the spirit returneth unto God who gave it.

8 Vanity of vanities, saith Koheleth;
All is vanity.

9. And besides that Koheleth was wise, he also taught the people

גֻּלַּת הַזָּהָב וְתִשָּׁבֶר כַּד עַל־
הַמַּבּוּעַ וְנָרֹץ הַגַּלְגַּל אֶל־
7 הַבּוֹר׃ וְיָשֹׁב הֶעָפָר עַל־
הָאָרֶץ כְּשֶׁהָיָה וְהָרוּחַ תָּשׁוּב
אֶל־הָאֱלֹהִים אֲשֶׁר נְתָנָהּ׃
8 הֲבֵל הֲבָלִים אָמַר הַקּוֹהֶלֶת
9 הַכֹּל הָבֶל׃ וְיֹתֵר שֶׁהָיָה
קֹהֶלֶת חָכָם עוֹד לִמַּד־דַּעַת

(Midrash). Ibn Ezra, who explains *the golden bowl* as the brain, identifies *the fountain* with the liver and *the wheel* with the skull. (*b*) This verse is not part of the storm allegory which ended with verse 5. On either theory, we have presented in highly figurative language a description of the body's dissolution.

*the silver cord.* Hanging from the ceiling to which the lamp is attached.

*snapped.* The *kerë* is an unusual verb. It occurs once again in Nahum iii. 10 and in later Hebrew with the meaning 'to be chained.' Ibn Ezra therefore renders 'before the cord is tied,' but the parallelism requires the translation of A.J. although its derivation has not yet been traced. The *kethib* means 'is far, parted.'

*the golden bowl.* Which contains the oil that feeds the flame (cf. Zech. iv. 2). Death severs the cord, the golden bowl falls, the oil is lost and the light extinguished.

*the pitcher . . . fountain.* The Psalmist spoke of *the fountain of life* (xxxvi. 10) although he employed a different word. The connection of life and water is an obvious one to an Oriental who knew from experience how the first was dependent upon the other. With the pitcher broken and the consequent impossibility of drawing the vital supply, death ensues from thirst. The *wheel* is an indispensable part of the machinery; the cord tied to the pitcher runs round it and enables one to pull up the bucket without spilling the water. If the wheel broke away and collapsed into the well, the water would be unobtainable. In like manner, the machinery of the body wears out with age and its owner is incapable of drawing sustenance from the reservoir of life.

7. *the dust returneth.* See on iii. 20.

*the spirit.* Cf. Gen. ii. 7, defined as 'that which remains of man after his death and is not subject to destruction' (Maimonides).

*returneth unto God.* 'Death is the great "return," the great liberation from the merely earthly and limiting; earth vanishes and eternity receives' (Baeck).

8. *vanity of vanities.* Once again, as at the beginning of this amazingly contradictory Book, which moves between the poles of scepticism and piety, we hear the melancholy note of life's shadowy illusion. Ginsburg argues that the verse is the introduction to the Epilogue, but in the opinion of Cheyne 'between verse 8 and that which follows there is no inner

knowledge; yea, he pondered, and
sought out, and set in order many
proverbs. 10. Koheleth sought to
find out words of delight, and that
which was written uprightly, even
words of truth.

11. The words of the wise are as
goads, and as nails well fastened are

אֶת־הָעָם וְאִזֵּן וְחִקֵּר תִּקֵּן
10 מְשָׁלִים הַרְבֵּה׃ בִּקֵּשׁ קֹהֶלֶת
לִמְצֹא דִּבְרֵי־חֵפֶץ וְכָתוּב
11 יֹשֶׁר דִּבְרֵי אֱמֶת׃ דִּבְרֵי
חֲכָמִים כַּדָּרְבֹנוֹת וּכְמַשְׂמְרוֹת

connection.' It would well accord with Koheleth's mentality for him to conclude his argument with the same statement as at the beginning. He commenced by remarking that all things in nature move in a circle; he concludes by implying that the same is true of human reasoning. It ends where it started.

*Koheleth.* The Hebrew is 'the Koheleth.' 'The object of the article is perhaps to suggest that Koheleth is not really a proper name' (Cheyne).

### 9-14 THE EPILOGUE

Modern scholars are divided on the authenticity of this section as an original part of the Book. Some consider it an editorial addition by a scribe who sought to defend the worth of Koheleth's writing at a time when the question was the subject of debate. On the other side Delitzsch has written, 'The spirit and tone of the Book and Epilogue are one. The Epilogue only seals the distinction between the pessimism of the Book and the modern pessimism which is without God and without a future.' He is supported by Driver who asserts, 'There does not appear to be any sufficient reason for doubting that xii. 9-12 is by the author of the Book . . . and the author himself may have appended the two closing verses with the same purpose in view as his supposed editor.'

9. *and besides that.* A statement is added to stress the high intellectual qualifications possessed by Koheleth for the task undertaken in this Book. Cheyne translates, 'and moreover (it should be said) that.' Perhaps the most exact rendering would be, 'and it remains (to be said) that.'

*wise.* i.e. one skilled in moral philosophy.

*he also taught.* He not only meditated upon the intricate problems of life, but also imparted instruction in popular form.

*pondered.* Better, 'weighed, tested.' He made an examination of the large number of proverbial sayings which had been composed and tested their truth and worth, to select those which he considered deserving of circulation among the people.

*sought out.* Rather, 'he searched, investigated,' to ascertain their moral and application.

*set in order.* Either 'compiled a collection of,' or 'composed.' As Ibn Ezra suggests, these words allude to the statement that Solomon *spoke three thousand proverbs* (1 Kings v. 12).

*proverbs.* *Mashal* has a wider connotation than the word 'proverb,' and includes allegory, aphorism and ethical discourse.

10. *to find out words of delight.* i.e. to search for subjects which would give his readers pleasure and interest them. Barton explains, 'he tried to give his composition a pleasant or elegant form.'

*and that which was written . . . truth.* Better, 'and that which is properly written (by him) is words of truth.'

11. *goads.* Used by shepherds to prod the animals and induce them to move forward. A similar effect is produced by *the words of the wise*; they stimulate thought and make for ethical progress.

*nails well fastened.* As these are fixed and difficult to remove, so the doctrines those that are composed in collections; they are given from one shepherd. 12. And furthermore, my son, be admonished: of making many books there is no end; and much study is a weariness of the flesh.

13. The end of the matter, all

נְטוּעִים בַּעֲלֵי אֲסֻפּוֹת נִתְּנוּ
מֵרֹעֶה אֶחָד׃ וְיֹתֵר מֵהֵמָּה 12
בְּנִי הִזָּהֵר עֲשׂוֹת סְפָרִים
הַרְבֵּה אֵין קֵץ וְלַהַג הַרְבֵּה
יְגִעַת בָּשָׂר׃ סוֹף דָּבָר הַכֹּל 13

ס׳ רבתי v. 13.

taught are well established and not easily overthrown.

*are those that are composed in collections.* lit. '(are) the words of the masters of assemblies,' and the word 'masters' can only refer to persons. The allusion is evidently to schools of wise men from which teaching was issued to the people.

*one shepherd.* This word is no doubt selected because of the mention of *goads*. It is interpreted either of a teacher, i.e. although the sources are numerous and varied, they pass to the reader through the medium of one teacher, viz. the author of this Book; or as a reference to God Who is often designated 'Shepherd' (cf. Ps. xxiii. 1), and He 'alone imparts these different lessons of heavenly wisdom to His inspired servants' (Ginsburg). The latter explanation is perhaps preferable.

12. *and furthermore . . . be admonished.* Translate: 'and of more than these beware.' Koheleth utters a warning against going beyond what is taught in *the words of the wise* and by 'the masters of assemblies.' There are other sources of instruction, but their teachings are unwholesome and even dangerous to faith.

*my son.* A term of endearment used by a teacher to his disciple, common in the Book of Proverbs (e.g. ii. 1, iii. 1).

*of making . . . no end.* 'If the words had force then, they have undoubtedly much more force to-day, when we are easily tempted to dissipate our energies in either the reading or writing of useless books, and when we might with profit lay to heart not only this counsel, but that of the Stoic emperor [Marcus Aurelius] that we should free ourselves from the thirst for books' (Martin).

*much study.* The writer does not deprecate the devotion of much time and energy to study of the sources he recommends, but the waste of effort in reading the many books outside those prescribed.

13. *the end of the matter.* This is the final summing up of the whole argument of the Book, after taking all matters into consideration.

*fear God.* Cf. v. 6, vii. 18. 'The philosophy of Ecclesiastes may thus be ostensibly stamped with scepticism; but in a truer analysis it turns out to embody the traditional maxim of Hebrew teaching, to rejoice in the statutes of God and delight in His commandments. The Book, indeed, could scarcely have approved itself to Hebrew tradition, or have won its way into the sacred canon of writings, unless some such religious purport had been felt to constitute its claim. The return of the rebel to Faith is its real refrain' (Levine).

having been heard: fear God, and keep His commandments; for this is the whole man. 14. For God shall bring every work into the judgment concerning every hidden thing, whether it be good or whether it be evil.

נִשְׁמָע אֶת־הָאֱלֹהִים יְרָא
וְאֶת־מִצְוֺתָיו שְׁמוֹר כִּי־זֶה
כָּל־הָאָדָם׃ כִּי אֶת־כָּל־ 14
מַעֲשֶׂה הָאֱלֹהִים יָבִא בְמִשְׁפָּט
עַל כָּל־נֶעְלָם אִם־טוֹב
וְאִם־רָע׃

The end of the matter, all having been heard: fear God, and keep His commandments; for this is the whole man.

סוף דבר הכל נשמע את האלהים ירא ואת מצותיו שמור כי זה כל האדם׃

*this is the whole man.* Other renderings are: 'this is every man's duty,' 'this (concerns) every man.' 'What is meant is that this is the only true answer to that quest of the chief good in which the thinker had been engaged' (Plumptre).

**14.** This concluding verse expresses a characteristically Hebraic point of view. Man has to give a reckoning to God for all his deeds, even those which are known only to himself and hidden from his fellows. The true philosophy of life must consequently have relationship to conduct, and so direct it that it can bear the Divine scrutiny. Such, then, is the reason for the summing-up in the preceding verse.

Not to conclude the Book with the ominous word *evil*, M.T. repeats verse 13. A similar arrangement is found at the end of Isaiah, Malachi and Lamentations.

This happens in
Isaiah
Malachi
Kohelet
Lamentations

(dirge) קִינוֹת

# אסתר

# ESTHER

INTRODUCTION AND COMMENTARY

*by*

REV. DR. S. GOLDMAN, M.A., D.PHIL.

# INTRODUCTION

## POSITION IN THE CANON

THE Book of Esther, in the Hebrew Bible, is the last of the five Megilloth; last, because the scrolls are arranged in the order in which they are read in Synagogue throughout the year. Although one of the five, it is universally known as *the* Megillah, not because it is the most important of the five, but due to its immense popularity, the prominence which is given to its public reading, and the fact that it is the only one which is still generally read from a parchment scroll. At one time it was normal for every Jewish household to possess a Megillah, and much time and skill were devoted to the production of beautifully illuminated texts and elaborately worked cases.

## ITS POPULARITY

*Esther* is, among the generality of Jews, the best known of all the Books of the Bible. Many circumstances have combined to make it so: its simple, popular, yet dramatic and even exciting story, its clearly drawn heroine, hero and villain, the jollity and liveliness of the feast of Purim at which it is read, but above all, what might be called the perennial truth of its narrative. Haman has become the prototype of all the many persecutors of the Jewish people, and his plot the standard of all schemes devised against the Jews; and the drama of his downfall has been in all ages a hope and refuge for the unfortunate people of suffering. It is a Book which exemplifies, vividly and concisely, the eternal miracle of Jewish survival.

## AUTHORSHIP

The authorship of *Esther* is unknown. There are variant views on the subject even in Jewish tradition, the Talmud ascribing it to the men of the Great Synagogue (B.B. 15a), and Rashi and others, on the basis of ix. 20 and 32, to Mordecai himself. All that can be asserted on this subject is that, most likely, the author was a Persian Jew. He displays a most intimate and accurate knowledge of the Persian court; so much so that the Book of Esther is recognized to be a valuable source of information, filling many gaps in the accounts of classical historians.

## ITS LITERARY MERIT

It is a work of considerable literary merit. The characters are distinctly portrayed, the descriptions graphic ; the language is clear, concise and adequate, with very few obscurities. A remarkable amount of action and description is crowded into its few chapters. Above all one must admire the author's ability as a narrator. He has a keen sense of situation and contrast, and manages his timing and entrances with the skill of a consummate dramatist. The Hebrew is post-exilic, and therefore occasional harsh syntactical constructions, a freer use of foreign and especially Persian words, and a rhythm less smooth than that of the classical period of the Hebrew language, are to be expected and are found; but at its best, it is still as capable as the Hebrew of earlier writers of expressing the highest sentiments of nobility and pathos.

## LITERATURE ON THE BOOK

The Book of Esther has been so popular among Jews that, in spite of the clarity and simplicity of its narrative, a vast body of Midrashic amplification, commentary and exposition has grown up round it. There are the Apocryphal additions to the Book; Josephus in his *Antiquities* gives a largely elaborated account of the story; the Talmud in tractate *Megillah* devotes many pages to a haggadic interpretation and elaboration of its narrative. The two main Targums are much more than translations: each is a Midrash in itself. There is a series of Midrashim on the Book which, for number and extent, are without parallel for any other Book of the Bible. In addition to the standard Hebrew commentaries, there is a host of special commentaries on *Esther* alone. And the non-Jewish commentaries and studies on the Book are legion. In a commentary of this nature, which is intended for the general reader, much of this literature cannot be taken into account; but the reader who wishes to pursue his investigations further is referred to the volume on *Esther* in the International Critical Commentary, a work of immense, if at times pedantic, scholarship, from which hardly anything has been omitted.

### OMISSION OF THE DIVINE NAME

A remarkable and unique feature of the Book of Esther is the complete absence of the name of God, and indeed, apart from the mention of fasting, of any direct reference to Divine Providence and Judaism. It is almost universally agreed that this omission must have been intentional. The author seems at times even to go out of his way to avoid mention of the Divine Name (e.g. iv. 14). The reason for the omission can only be surmised. Perhaps, since the Megillah was to be read at the annual merry-making of Purim, when considerable licence was permitted, the author feared that the Divine Name might be profaned, if it occurred in the reading. Perhaps he feared that the Book might be profanely treated by Gentiles, because of its story of the triumph of the Jews over their enemies. But whatever the reason for the omission of the Name of God, the sense of Divine Providence pervades the Book. The statement of Mordecai in iv. 14 shows unfailing trust in God's providential care for His people, and *He that keepeth Israel doth neither slumber nor sleep* (Ps. cxxi. 4) might well be the motto of the narrative.

# ESTHER

## 1 CHAPTER I א

[1]Now it came to pass in the days of
Ahasuerus—this is Ahasuerus who
reigned, from India even unto Ethiopia, over a hundred and seven and
twenty provinces—[2]that in those
days, when the king Ahasuerus sat
on the throne of his kingdom, which

1 וַיְהִי בִּימֵי אֲחַשְׁוֵרוֹשׁ הוּא
אֲחַשְׁוֵרוֹשׁ הַמֹּלֵךְ מֵהֹדּוּ וְעַד־
כּוּשׁ שֶׁבַע וְעֶשְׂרִים וּמֵאָה
2 מְדִינָה׃ בַּיָּמִים הָהֵם כְּשֶׁבֶת ׀
הַמֶּלֶךְ אֲחַשְׁוֵרוֹשׁ עַל כִּסֵּא

### 1-8 AHASUERUS' FEASTS

1. *Ahasuerus.* It is now generally recognized that he is identical with Xerxes I (485-464 B.C.E.). The Hebrew *Achashwerosh* is an attempt to represent the Persian *Khshayarsha*, whence was derived the Greek name Xerxes; and the description which Herodotus gives of Xerxes, a vain, foolish, capricious and hot-tempered king, agrees well with his portrayal in this Book. The Ahasuerus of *Esther* is therefore to be distinguished from his namesake in Ezra iv. and Daniel ix, where probably Cambyses, Cyrus' successor, is intended; but the older Jewish commentators, identifying the two, treat the Ahasuerus of *Esther* as Cyrus' successor.

*this is Ahasuerus.* A parenthetical note to distinguish this king from others of the same name.

*India.* The Hebrew *Hoddu*, is really 'Indus,' and refers to the north-western portion of the Indian peninsula which was drained by the Indus. This territory was added to the Persian Empire by Darius.

*Ethiopia.* Conquered by Cambyses, king of Persia (529-522 B.C.E.).

*a hundred and seven and twenty provinces.* The Persian Empire was divided into satrapies, which in turn were subdivided into *provinces* (cf. iii. 12). According to Dan. vi. 2 Darius *set over the kingdom a hundred and twenty satraps.*

2. *when the king sat.* The Hebrew suggests 'when he took his seat.' Such a phrase seems unsuitable in a description of events in the third year of his reign, and the Talmud and the older Jewish commentators hold the view that he was a usurper, and take the phrase to mean 'when he was established,' i.e. after a period of political disturbances. More probably the meaning is 'when he took up residence in Susa.' The Medo-Persian Empire had three capitals: Susa, Ecbatana and Babylon, and the king held court in each in turn.

*Shushan the castle.* Better, 'the fortress.' This was the palace quarter, which was surrounded by the less strongly fortified city of Susa. The fortress contained the homes of humble citizens, as well as of the king, his wives and royal officials. Mordecai lived there (ii. 5); and 500 of its inhabitants were killed in the later fighting (ix. 12). Susa was the capital of ancient Elam as early as the third millennium B.C.E. It was doubtless the residence of Chedorlaomer (Gen. xiv). About 596 B.C.E. it was incorporated into the Medo-Persian Empire, and when the Persians under Cyrus and his successors became the senior partner in the Empire, Susa was the chief capital. The city ceased to be inhabited some time in the

was in Shushan the castle, [3]in the
third year of his reign, he made a
feast unto all his princes and his
servants; the army of Persia and
Media, the nobles and princes of the
provinces, being before him; [4]when
he showed the riches of his glorious
kingdom and the honour of his
excellent majesty, many days, even
a hundred and fourscore days. [5]And
when these days were fulfilled, the
king made a feast unto all the people
that were present in Shushan the

מַלְכוּתוֹ אֲשֶׁר בְּשׁוּשַׁן הַבִּירָה׃
3 בִּשְׁנַת שָׁלוֹשׁ לְמָלְכוֹ עָשָׂה
מִשְׁתֶּה לְכָל־שָׂרָיו וַעֲבָדָיו
חֵיל ׀ פָּרַס וּמָדַי הַפַּרְתְּמִים
וְשָׂרֵי הַמְּדִינוֹת לְפָנָיו׃
4 בְּהַרְאֹתוֹ אֶת־עֹשֶׁר כְּבוֹד
מַלְכוּתוֹ וְאֶת־יְקָר תִּפְאֶרֶת
גְּדוּלָּתוֹ יָמִים רַבִּים שְׁמוֹנִים
5 וּמְאַת יוֹם׃ וּבִמְלוֹאת ׀ הַיָּמִים
הָאֵלֶּה עָשָׂה הַמֶּלֶךְ לְכָל־
הָעָם הַנִּמְצְאִים בְּשׁוּשַׁן

v. 3. ב״א ר׳ בקמץ v. 5. ובמלאות ק׳

Middle Ages, but excavations in the mounds which mark its site have revealed evidences of its former glory. The main city had a circumference of six to seven miles, and the fortress occupied an elevated site enclosed by a massive wall two and a half miles in length, and crowned by the royal palace. Benjamin of Tudela, the Spanish-Jewish traveller of the twelfth century, mentions visiting the ruins of Xerxes' palace, adding that even at that time, 7,000 Jews lived in Susa.

3. *in the third year.* Herodotus tells of a great gathering of satraps in Susa in Xerxes' third year to make arrangements for the attack on Greece two years later.

*feast.* lit. 'a drinking,' because that was its principal feature.

*princes.* Better, 'officials.' Princes would be members of the royal family.

*servants.* i.e. members of the royal household, courtiers.

*army.* Obviously not the whole army, but chosen representatives.

*Persia and Media.* The Medes and Persians were two peoples of the same racial origin, who jointly established a vast empire. At first Media was the stronger kingdom, and Median kings held sway over Persia; but from the time when Cyrus the Persian seized the throne (549), the Persians held the hegemony, and the empire became Perso-Median, instead of Medo-Persian. Hence Persia is here named first.

4. *honour of his excellent majesty.* Better, 'costliness of his kingly apparel,' i.e. his regalia (Paton). The wealth and splendour of Persian kings are celebrated by classical writers.

*a hundred and fourscore days.* This may mean a series of entertainments to successive relays of guests (Rawlinson). It is unlikely that the king's officials could have stayed away from their posts for all this period.

5. *all the people.* Referring to the men; the women were invited to a separate feast (verse 9).

*that were present.* The words imply that visitors as well as the inhabitants were included.

castle, both great and small, seven days, in the court of the garden of the king's palace; [6]there were hangings of white, fine cotton, and blue, bordered with cords of fine linen and purple, upon silver rods and pillars of marble; the couches were of gold and silver, upon a pavement of green, and white, and shell, and onyx marble. [7]And they gave them drink in vessels of gold—the vessels being diverse one from another—and royal wine in abundance, according to the bounty of the king. [8]And the drinking was according to the law; none did compel; for so the king had appointed to all the officers of his house, that they should do according to every man's pleasure.

[9]Also Vashti the queen made a feast for the women in the royal

הַבִּירָה לְמִגָּדוֹל וְעַד־קָטָן
מִשְׁתֶּה שִׁבְעַת יָמִים בַּחֲצַר
6 גִּנַּת בִּיתַן הַמֶּלֶךְ׃ חוּר ׀
כַּרְפַּס וּתְכֵלֶת אָחוּז בְּחַבְלֵי־
בוּץ וְאַרְגָּמָן עַל־גְּלִילֵי כֶסֶף
וְעַמּוּדֵי שֵׁשׁ מִטּוֹת ׀ זָהָב וָכֶסֶף
עַל רִצְפַת בַּהַט־וָשֵׁשׁ וְדַר
7 וְסֹחָרֶת׃ וְהַשְׁקוֹת בִּכְלֵי זָהָב
וְכֵלִים מִכֵּלִים שׁוֹנִים וְיֵין
מַלְכוּת רָב כְּיַד הַמֶּלֶךְ׃
8 וְהַשְּׁתִיָּה כַדָּת אֵין אֹנֵס כִּי־
כֵן ׀ יִסַּד הַמֶּלֶךְ עַל כָּל־רַב
בֵּיתוֹ לַעֲשׂוֹת כִּרְצוֹן אִישׁ־
9 וָאִישׁ׃ גַּם וַשְׁתִּי הַמַּלְכָּה
עָשְׂתָה מִשְׁתֵּה נָשִׁים בֵּית

ח׳ רבתי v. 6.

6. The magnificence of the appointments of the feast is not an exaggeration. Persian feasts were proverbial in antiquity for their extravagance.

*couches.* Divans; reclining at table was a Persian custom.

7. *bounty.* lit. 'hand,' i.e. the king's boundless means.

8. *none did compel.* Ordinarily, guests drank together at a word of command from the toastmaster, but this time they were allowed to drink as they pleased. The Persians were great drinkers, and Xenophon said of them, 'They drink so much that they cannot stand upright on their feet, and must be carried out.'

### 9-12 VASHTI'S REFUSAL OF THE KING'S SUMMONS

9. *feast for the women.* There is no evidence that Persian custom demanded that women feast separately from men (we see later that Esther invited Haman to a feast); and therefore we have to assume that the number of guests necessitated dividing the two companies.

house which belonged to king Ahasuerus. 10 On the seventh day, when the heart of the king was merry with wine, he commanded Mehuman, Bizzetha, Harbona, Bigtha, and Abagtha, Zethar, and Carcas, the seven chamberlains that ministered in the presence of Ahasuerus the king, 11 to bring Vashti the queen before the king with the crown royal, to show the peoples and the princes her beauty; for she was fair to look on. 12 But the queen Vashti refused to come at the king's commandment by the chamberlains; therefore was the king very wroth, and his anger burned in him.

13 Then the king said to the wise men, who knew the times—for so

הַמַּלְכוּת אֲשֶׁר לַמֶּלֶךְ
10 אֲחַשְׁוֵרוֹשׁ׃ בַּיּוֹם הַשְּׁבִיעִי
כְּטוֹב לֵב־הַמֶּלֶךְ בַּיָּיִן אָמַר
לִמְהוּמָן בִּזְּתָא חַרְבוֹנָא בִּגְתָא
וַאֲבַגְתָא זֵתַר וְכַרְכַּס שִׁבְעַת
הַסָּרִיסִים הַמְשָׁרְתִים אֶת־
פְּנֵי הַמֶּלֶךְ אֲחַשְׁוֵרוֹשׁ׃
11 לְהָבִיא אֶת־וַשְׁתִּי הַמַּלְכָּה
לִפְנֵי הַמֶּלֶךְ בְּכֶתֶר מַלְכוּת
לְהַרְאוֹת הָעַמִּים וְהַשָּׂרִים
אֶת־יָפְיָהּ כִּי־טוֹבַת מַרְאֶה
12 הִיא׃ וַתְּמָאֵן הַמַּלְכָּה וַשְׁתִּי
לָבוֹא בִּדְבַר הַמֶּלֶךְ אֲשֶׁר
בְּיַד הַסָּרִיסִים וַיִּקְצֹף הַמֶּלֶךְ
מְאֹד וַחֲמָתוֹ בָּעֲרָה בוֹ׃
13 וַיֹּאמֶר הַמֶּלֶךְ לַחֲכָמִים יֹדְעֵי
הָעִתִּים כִּי־כֵן דְּבַר הַמֶּלֶךְ

**10.** The names of the chamberlains here and in verse 14 are Persian, but the Rabbis attempted to give Hebrew meanings to them.

**11.** The Talmud and Jewish commentators understand the command to be 'only with the royal crown,' i.e. naked. The king's heart was *merry with wine* at the time; he was intoxicated and not responsible for his actions.

**12.** It is unlikely that the reason for Vashti's refusal is that suggested by Josephus and later writers, viz. that it was a law of the Persians that wives should not show their faces to strangers. The reason can only be guessed at. Perhaps Vashti objected to being exhibited to a host of drunken commoners. Vashti, too, may have drunk too much and thereby have been fortified in her refusal.

**13-22 THE DEPOSITION OF VASHTI**

**13.** *who knew the times.* The Talmud understands this as 'astrologers.' But the phrase is parallel with *all that knew law and judgment*, and probably means 'those who were familiar with historical precedents, having the power of law' (Paton).

was the king's manner toward all that
knew law and judgment; [14]and the
next unto him was Carshena, Shethar, Admatha, Tarshish, Meres,
Marsena, and Memucan, the seven
princes of Persia and Media, who
saw the king's face, and sat first in
the kingdom: [15]'What shall we do
unto the queen Vashti according to
law, forasmuch as she hath not done
the bidding of the king Ahasuerus
by the chamberlains?'

[16]And Memucan answered before
the king and the princes: 'Vashti
the queen hath not done wrong to
the king only, but also to all the
princes, and to all the peoples, that
are in all the provinces of the king
Ahasuerus. [17]For this deed of the

לִפְנֵי כָּל־יֹדְעֵי דָּת וָדִין׃
14 וְהַקָּרֹב אֵלָיו כַּרְשְׁנָא שֵׁתָר
אַדְמָתָא תַרְשִׁישׁ מֶרֶס מַרְסְנָא
מְמוּכָן שִׁבְעַת שָׂרֵי ׀ פָּרַס
וּמָדַי רֹאֵי פְּנֵי הַמֶּלֶךְ הַיֹּשְׁבִים
15 רִאשֹׁנָה בַּמַּלְכוּת׃ כְּדָת מַה־
לַּעֲשׂוֹת בַּמַּלְכָּה וַשְׁתִּי עַל ׀
אֲשֶׁר לֹא־עָשְׂתָה אֶת־מַאֲמַר
הַמֶּלֶךְ אֲחַשְׁוֵרוֹשׁ בְּיַד
16 הַסָּרִיסִים׃ וַיֹּאמֶר מוֹמֻכָן
לִפְנֵי הַמֶּלֶךְ וְהַשָּׂרִים לֹא עַל־
הַמֶּלֶךְ לְבַדּוֹ עָוְתָה וַשְׁתִּי
הַמַּלְכָּה כִּי עַל־כָּל־
הַשָּׂרִים וְעַל־כָּל־הָעַמִּים
אֲשֶׁר בְּכָל־מְדִינוֹת הַמֶּלֶךְ
17 אֲחַשְׁוֵרוֹשׁ׃ כִּי־יֵצֵא דְבַר־

ממוכן ק' v. 16.

*manner toward.* Better, 'procedure (to bring all such matters) before.'

14. The existence of a king's council of seven is confirmed by Ezra vii. 14, Herodotus and Josephus. These councillors had access to the king at all times (*saw the king's face*), except when he was in the company of one of his wives.

*sat first in the kingdom.* Took precedence next to the king.

15. *according to law.* The king wishes to give a semblance of law to the punishment which his rage compels him to inflict upon Vashti.

16. Memucan probably realized that it was the king's wish to condemn Vashti, and gave advice which would suggest that her punishment was a matter of public policy and the welfare of the state, and not merely the gratification of a personal grudge. Perhaps the courtiers were glad of an opportunity to intrigue against the influence of the queen.

queen will come abroad unto all women, to make their husbands contemptible in their eyes, when it will be said: The king Ahasuerus commanded Vashti the queen to be brought in before him, but she came not. [18]And this day will the princesses of Persia and Media who have heard of the deed of the queen say the like unto all the king's princes. So will there arise enough contempt and wrath. [19]If it please the king, let there go forth a royal commandment from him, and let it be written among the laws of the Persians and the Medes, that it be not altered, that Vashti come no more before king Ahasuerus, and that the king give her royal estate unto another that is better than she. [20]And when the king's decree which he shall make shall be published throughout all his kingdom, great though it be, all the wives will give to their husbands

הַמַּלְכָּה עַל־כָּל־הַנָּשִׁים
לְהַבְזוֹת בַּעְלֵיהֶן בְּעֵינֵיהֶן
בְּאָמְרָם הַמֶּלֶךְ אֲחַשְׁוֵרוֹשׁ
אָמַר לְהָבִיא אֶת־וַשְׁתִּי
הַמַּלְכָּה לְפָנָיו וְלֹא־בָאָה׃
18 וְהַיּוֹם הַזֶּה תֹּאמַרְנָה ׀ שָׂרוֹת
פָּרַס־וּמָדַי אֲשֶׁר שָׁמְעוּ אֶת־
דְּבַר הַמַּלְכָּה לְכֹל שָׂרֵי
הַמֶּלֶךְ וּכְדַי בִּזָּיוֹן וָקָצֶף׃
19 אִם־עַל־הַמֶּלֶךְ טוֹב יֵצֵא
דְבַר־מַלְכוּת מִלְּפָנָיו וְיִכָּתֵב
בְּדָתֵי פָרַס־וּמָדַי וְלֹא יַעֲבוֹר
אֲשֶׁר לֹא־תָבוֹא וַשְׁתִּי לִפְנֵי
הַמֶּלֶךְ אֲחַשְׁוֵרוֹשׁ וּמַלְכוּתָהּ
יִתֵּן הַמֶּלֶךְ לִרְעוּתָהּ הַטּוֹבָה
20 מִמֶּנָּה׃ וְנִשְׁמַע פִּתְגָם הַמֶּלֶךְ
אֲשֶׁר־יַעֲשֶׂה בְּכָל־מַלְכוּתוֹ
כִּי רַבָּה הִיא וְכָל־הַנָּשִׁים

17f. Their reasoning will be, 'The queen did not obey, therefore we need not obey.'

18. *enough contempt and wrath.* An ironical understatement. He means 'too much.'

19. *royal commandment.* i.e. an edict which, although directed against an individual, should be registered as a public ordinance, and thereby be unalterable (Streane). Memucan would have good cause to fear the vengeance of Vashti, if she should regain the throne.

*that it be not altered.* Apparently, the laws of the Medo-Persian Empire were unalterable (cf. viii. 8; Dan. vi. 9, 13, 16). To retract or alter a decree, and thereby to suggest that it was an unwise one or in other respects faulty, would be a reproach on the king's wisdom.

*and that the king give her royal estate.* Better, 'and let the king give.' This was not part of the decree, but a further suggestion (Paton).

honour, both to great and small.'
21 And the word pleased the king and
the princes; and the king did according to the word of Memucan; 22 for
he sent letters into all the king's provinces, into every province according to the writing thereof, and to every people after their language, that every man should bear rule in his own house, and speak according to the language of his people.

יִתְּנוּ יְקָר לְבַעְלֵיהֶן לְמִגָּדוֹל
21 וְעַד־קָטָן׃ וַיִּיטַב הַדָּבָר
בְּעֵינֵי הַמֶּלֶךְ וְהַשָּׂרִים וַיַּעַשׂ
22 הַמֶּלֶךְ כִּדְבַר מְמוּכָן׃ וַיִּשְׁלַח
סְפָרִים אֶל־כָּל־מְדִינוֹת
הַמֶּלֶךְ אֶל־מְדִינָה וּמְדִינָה
כִּכְתָבָהּ וְאֶל־עַם וָעָם
כִּלְשׁוֹנוֹ לִהְיוֹת כָּל־אִישׁ שֹׂרֵר
בְּבֵיתוֹ וּמְדַבֵּר כִּלְשׁוֹן עַמּוֹ׃

## 2 CHAPTER II ב

1 After these things, when the wrath
of king Ahasuerus was assuaged, he remembered Vashti, and what she had done, and what was decreed
against her. 2 Then said the king's servants that ministered unto him: 'Let there be sought for the king

1 אַחַר הַדְּבָרִים הָאֵלֶּה כְּשֹׁךְ
חֲמַת הַמֶּלֶךְ אֲחַשְׁוֵרוֹשׁ זָכַר
אֶת־וַשְׁתִּי וְאֵת אֲשֶׁר־
עָשָׂתָה וְאֵת אֲשֶׁר־נִגְזַר
2 עָלֶיהָ׃ וַיֹּאמְרוּ נַעֲרֵי־הַמֶּלֶךְ

20. *great and small.* The nobility and mass of the people.

22. *that every man . . . house.* R. Huna said, 'Ahasuerus was utterly devoid of sense in so decreeing,' and R. Phineas added, 'Nay more, he made himself a laughing-stock' (Midrash).

*speak according to the language of his people.* The relevance of this second part of the decree is hard to see. A vast number of languages were spoken in the Persian Empire in the time of Xerxes, and the Midrash and Jewish commentators take the phrase to mean that, if a husband and wife were of different race and language, he was to compel her to speak his tongue. Cassel translates, 'should command in his own language.' We are not told what happened to Vashti. The Rabbis held that she was executed, and judging from the fate of so many deposed queens in the East, they were probably right.

## CHAPTER II

### 1-4 AHASUERUS SEEKS A QUEEN

1. *after these things.* Probably not very long after, certainly less than two years, since Xerxes departed for Greece in the fifth year of his reign.

*remembered Vashti.* With remorse. He

young virgins fair to look on; [3]and let the king appoint officers in all the provinces of his kingdom, that they may gather together all the fair young virgins unto Shushan the castle, to the house of the women, unto the custody of [a]Hegai the king's chamberlain, keeper of the women; and let their ointments be given them; [4]and let the maiden that pleaseth the king be queen instead of Vashti.' And the thing pleased the king; and he did so.

[5]There was a certain Jew in Shushan the castle, whose name was Mordecai the son of Jair the son of Shimei the son of Kish, a Benjamite,

[a]Heb. Hege.

מְשָׁרְתָיו יְבַקְשׁוּ לַמֶּלֶךְ נְעָרוֹת
בְּתוּלוֹת טוֹבוֹת מַרְאֶה׃
3 וְיַפְקֵד הַמֶּלֶךְ פְּקִידִים בְּכָל־
מְדִינוֹת מַלְכוּתוֹ וְיִקְבְּצוּ אֶת־
כָּל־נַעֲרָה־בְתוּלָה טוֹבַת
מַרְאֶה אֶל־שׁוּשַׁן הַבִּירָה
אֶל־בֵּית הַנָּשִׁים אֶל־יַד הֵגֶא
סְרִיס הַמֶּלֶךְ שֹׁמֵר הַנָּשִׁים
4 וְנָתוֹן תַּמְרוּקֵיהֶן׃ וְהַנַּעֲרָה
אֲשֶׁר תִּיטַב בְּעֵינֵי הַמֶּלֶךְ
תִּמְלֹךְ תַּחַת וַשְׁתִּי וַיִּיטַב
הַדָּבָר בְּעֵינֵי הַמֶּלֶךְ וַיַּעַשׂ כֵּן׃
5 אִישׁ יְהוּדִי הָיָה בְּשׁוּשַׁן הַבִּירָה
וּשְׁמוֹ מָרְדֳּכַי בֶּן יָאִיר בֶּן־
שִׁמְעִי בֶּן־קִישׁ אִישׁ יְמִינִי׃

v. 5. סגול בלא מקף

realized that she had acted properly in refusing to display herself. His counsellors might well fear the effects on themselves, if the king were allowed to brood on Vashti's fate; and so they hasten to suggest an alternative occupation for the king's thoughts, and one which would prove a pleasant diversion.

3. *house of the women.* The harem which excavations revealed to have been situated in the north-west of the palace buildings.

### 5-7 MORDECAI AND ESTHER

5. This verse and viii. 15, 16, ix. 7, 8, 9 and x. 3 are, in the reading of the Megillah in Synagogue, recited aloud by the congregation in advance of the Precentor to enhance their importance.

*Jew.* The Hebrew *Yehudi* originally meant 'a man of the kingdom of Judah,' and after the Babylonian captivity it came to be a generic term for all Israelites.

*Shimei . . . Kish.* Jewish tradition, and many non-Jewish scholars, hold that these are remote ancestors of Mordecai, Kish being Saul's father, and Shimei the one mentioned in 2 Sam. xvi. 5; and that they are named here to show the noble origin of Mordecai (but it is not suggested that he was a descendant of king Saul: in that case Saul would certainly be mentioned in the genealogy). Some commentators, however, have maintained that they are Mordecai's immediate ancestors, his grandfather and great-grandfather respectively.

6 who had been carried away from
Jerusalem with the captives that had
been carried away with Jeconiah king
of Judah, whom Nebuchadnezzar
the king of Babylon had carried away.
7 And he brought up Hadassah, that
is, Esther, his uncle's daughter; for
she had neither father nor mother,
and the maiden was of beautiful form
and fair to look on; and when her
father and mother were dead, Mordecai took her for his own daughter.

6 אֲשֶׁר הָגְלָה מִירוּשָׁלַיִם עִם־
הַגֹּלָה אֲשֶׁר הָגְלְתָה עִם יְכָנְיָה
מֶלֶךְ־יְהוּדָה אֲשֶׁר הֶגְלָה
7 נְבוּכַדְנֶאצַּר מֶלֶךְ בָּבֶל׃ וַיְהִי
אֹמֵן אֶת־הֲדַסָּה הִיא אֶסְתֵּר
בַּת־דֹּדוֹ כִּי אֵין לָהּ אָב וָאֵם
וְהַנַּעֲרָה יְפַת־תֹּאַר וְטוֹבַת
מַרְאֶה וּבְמוֹת אָבִיהָ וְאִמָּהּ
לְקָחָהּ מָרְדֳּכַי לוֹ לְבַת׃

He is her cousin.

6. *who had been carried away.* To whom does the relative pronoun refer, to Mordecai or to Kish? This is one of the most controversial questions in the Book of Esther. Hebrew usage seems to demand that it refer to Mordecai, but then Mordecai's age becomes a difficulty. If he had been carried into captivity, even as an infant, with Jeconiah (Jehoiachin) in 596 B.C.E., he would be 122 years of age when he became prime minister in the twelfth year of Xerxes' reign (474); and he apparently enjoys office for a considerable time afterwards (x. 2f.). This difficulty has led many to identify Ahasuerus with Cambyses, Darius or one of the earlier kings of Persia; and others to refer the relative pronoun to Kish, who would then be an immediate ancestor of Mordecai (his great-grandfather, and not the Kish of the Book of Samuel). Many commentators think that *carried away* means only that his ancestors were exiled by Nebuchadnezzar, i.e. that he lived in captivity because of the Exile. Mordecai is not a Hebrew name (it is generally derived from Marduk, the name of the Babylonian god), and would most naturally be given to one born in captivity.

7. *and he brought up.* The Rabbis apply the verse, *Happy are they . . . that do righteousness at all times* (Ps. cvi. 3), to a person who brings up an orphan in his house.

*Hadassah, that is, Esther.* Probably Hadassah was her Hebrew name, and Esther a Persian name, perhaps given to her when she became queen. Hadassah is derived from the Hebrew word for 'myrtle'; and Esther is variously derived from the Persian *stara*, i.e. star, or from the name of the Babylonian goddess Ishtar (Hebrew *Ashtoreth*). Astarte

*and when her father and mother were dead.* The Talmud, from the double phrasing *she had neither father nor mother* and *when her father and mother were dead,* derives the opinion that her father died before she was born and her mother at her birth.

8 So it came to pass, when the
king's commandment and his decree
was published, and when many maidens were gathered together unto
Shushan the castle, to the custody of
Hegai, that Esther was taken into
the king's house, to the custody of
Hegai, keeper of the women. 9 And
the maiden pleased him, and she
obtained kindness of him; and he
speedily gave her her ointments, with
her portions, and the seven maidens,
who were meet to be given her out
of the king's house; and he advanced
her and her maidens to the best place
in the house of the women. 10 Esther
had not made known her people nor
her kindred; for Mordecai had

8 וַיְהִי בְּהִשָּׁמַע דְּבַר־הַמֶּלֶךְ
וְדָתוֹ וּבְהִקָּבֵץ נְעָרוֹת רַבּוֹת
אֶל־שׁוּשַׁן הַבִּירָה אֶל־יַד הֵגָי
וַתִּלָּקַח אֶסְתֵּר אֶל־בֵּית
הַמֶּלֶךְ אֶל־יַד הֵגַי שֹׁמֵר
9 הַנָּשִׁים׃ וַתִּיטַב הַנַּעֲרָה
בְעֵינָיו וַתִּשָּׂא חֶסֶד לְפָנָיו
וַיְבַהֵל אֶת־תַּמְרוּקֶיהָ וְאֶת־
מְנוֹתֶיהָ לָתֵת לָהּ וְאֵת שֶׁבַע
הַנְּעָרוֹת הָרְאֻיוֹת לָתֶת־לָהּ
מִבֵּית הַמֶּלֶךְ וַיְשַׁנֶּהָ וְאֶת־
נַעֲרוֹתֶיהָ לְטוֹב בֵּית הַנָּשִׁים׃
10 לֹא־הִגִּידָה אֶסְתֵּר אֶת־עַמָּהּ
וְאֶת־מוֹלַדְתָּהּ כִּי מָרְדֳּכַי

**8-18 THE CHOICE OF ESTHER**

8. *Esther was taken.* The Rabbis read into this phrase that she was taken by force. In the second Targum there is a story that Mordecai attempted to conceal her from the king's officers.

9. *speedily gave her.* As a mark of favour he lost no time in beginning the necessary preparations.

*portions.* Not cosmetics, but special foods which were part of the preparations (cf. Dan. i. 5). The Hebrew word is the same as that for *portions* (of food) in ix. 19, 22.

*seven maidens, who were meet.* Each candidate had the right to be given seven women attendants. Esther was given maidens suitable to her exceptional charms.

10. *for Mordecai . . . not tell it.* Mordecai must have reasoned something like this: If Esther is chosen queen, it can only be because God desires to make her the instrument of His purpose. If then she reveals the fact that she is a Jewess, and therefore a member of a subject people, she will prejudice her choice, and thereby the possibility of becoming God's instrument. This interpretation is suggested in the Midrash: 'He thought to himself: How is it possible that this righteous maiden should be married to a non-Israelite? It must be because some great calamity is going to befall Israel who will be delivered through her.' This concealment has been so often condemned, that it would be well to quote some of the many other explanations of it. Rashi comments, 'She did not declare her *royal* origin (i.e. that she was descended

צִוָּה עָלֶיהָ אֲשֶׁר לֹא־תַגִּיד׃
11 וּבְכָל־יוֹם וָיוֹם מָרְדֳּכַי
מִתְהַלֵּךְ לִפְנֵי חֲצַר בֵּית־
הַנָּשִׁים לָדַעַת אֶת־שְׁלוֹם
אֶסְתֵּר וּמַה־יֵּעָשֶׂה בָּהּ׃
12 וּבְהַגִּיעַ תֹּר נַעֲרָה וְנַעֲרָה
לָבוֹא ׀ אֶל־הַמֶּלֶךְ אֲחַשְׁוֵרוֹשׁ
מִקֵּץ הֱיוֹת לָהּ כְּדָת הַנָּשִׁים
שְׁנֵים עָשָׂר חֹדֶשׁ כִּי כֵּן יִמְלְאוּ
יְמֵי מְרוּקֵיהֶן שִׁשָּׁה חֳדָשִׁים
בְּשֶׁמֶן הַמֹּר וְשִׁשָּׁה חֳדָשִׁים
בַּבְּשָׂמִים וּבְתַמְרוּקֵי הַנָּשִׁים׃
13 וּבָזֶה הַנַּעֲרָה בָּאָה אֶל־
הַמֶּלֶךְ אֵת כָּל־אֲשֶׁר תֹּאמַר
יִנָּתֵן לָהּ לָבוֹא עִמָּהּ מִבֵּית
הַנָּשִׁים עַד־בֵּית הַמֶּלֶךְ׃

charged her that she should not tell
it. 11 And Mordecai walked every
day before the court of the women's house, to know how Esther did, and what would become of her.

12 Now when the turn of every maiden was come to go in to king Ahasuerus, after that it had been done to her according to the law for the women, twelve months—for so were the days of their anointing accomplished, to wit, six months with oil of myrrh, and six months with sweet odours, and with other ointments of the women—
13 when
then the maiden came unto the king, whatsoever she desired was given her to go with her out of the house of the women unto the king's house.

from the family of king Saul), so that the king might think that she was of humble origin and send her away.' Ibn Ezra remarked, 'So that she might observe her religious obligations secretly. If she declared her faith, she would be forced to transgress.' The Yalkut ascribes the concealment to Mordecai's modesty; he feared the advancement and publicity which would come to him if his relationship to the queen were known—an explanation well in keeping with Mordecai's self-effacing disposition.

**11.** The verse does not tell that Mordecai had immediate and personal access to Esther. The access of outsiders to the women of the harem would not have been allowed.

**12.** *according to the law for the women.* i.e. in the manner prescribed for the women, as defined later in the sentence.

**13.** *whatsoever she desired was given her.* Each maiden was given the opportunity of creating the best possible impression, and therefore was allowed to select anything in the way of dress or jewellery which might enhance her beauty.

14 בָּעֶ֣רֶב ׀ הִ֣יא בָאָ֗ה וּ֠בַבֹּקֶר
הִ֣יא שָׁבָ֞ה אֶל־בֵּ֤ית הַנָּשִׁים֙
שֵׁנִ֔י אֶל־יַ֛ד שַֽׁעַשְׁגַ֥ז סְרִ֥יס
הַמֶּ֖לֶךְ שֹׁמֵ֣ר הַפִּֽילַגְשִׁ֑ים לֹֽא־
תָב֥וֹא עוֹד֙ אֶל־הַמֶּ֔לֶךְ כִּ֣י
אִם־חָפֵ֥ץ בָּ֛הּ הַמֶּ֖לֶךְ וְנִקְרְאָ֥ה
15 בְשֵֽׁם׃ וּבְהַגִּ֣יעַ תֹּר־אֶסְתֵּ֣ר
בַּת־אֲבִיחַ֣יִל ׀ דֹּ֣ד מָרְדֳּכַ֡י
אֲשֶׁר֩ לָֽקַֽח־ל֨וֹ לְבַ֜ת לָב֣וֹא
אֶל־הַמֶּ֗לֶךְ לֹ֤א בִקְשָׁה֙ דָּבָ֔ר
כִּ֠י אִ֣ם אֶת־אֲשֶׁ֥ר יֹאמַ֛ר הֵגַ֥י
סְרִיס־הַמֶּ֖לֶךְ שֹׁמֵ֣ר הַנָּשִׁ֑ים
וַתְּהִ֤י אֶסְתֵּר֙ נֹשֵׂ֣את חֵ֔ן בְּעֵינֵ֖י
16 כָּל־רֹאֶֽיהָ׃ וַתִּלָּקַ֨ח אֶסְתֵּ֜ר
אֶל־הַמֶּ֤לֶךְ אֲחַשְׁוֵרוֹשׁ֙ אֶל־
בֵּ֣ית מַלְכוּת֔וֹ בַּחֹ֥דֶשׁ הָעֲשִׂירִ֖י
הוּא־חֹ֣דֶשׁ טֵבֵ֑ת בִּשְׁנַת־שֶׁ֖בַע
17 לְמַלְכוּתֽוֹ׃ וַיֶּאֱהַ֨ב הַמֶּ֤לֶךְ
אֶת־אֶסְתֵּר֙ מִכָּל־הַנָּשִׁ֔ים

[14]In the evening she went, and on the
morrow she returned into the second
house of the women, to the custody
of Shaashgaz, the king's chamberlain, who kept the concubines; she
came in unto the king no more,
except the king delighted in her, and
she were called by name.

[15]Now when the turn of Esther,
the daughter of Abihail the uncle of
Mordecai, who had taken her for his
daughter, was come to go in unto the
king, she required nothing but what
Hegai the king's chamberlain, the
keeper of the women, appointed.
And Esther obtained favour in the
sight of all them that looked upon
her. [16]So Esther was taken unto king
Ahasuerus into his house royal in
the tenth month, which is the month
Tebeth, in the seventh year of his
reign. [17]And the king loved Esther
above all the women, and she ob-

**14.** *second house of the women.* Where they would remain for the rest of their lives in practical widowhood. They would not be permitted to go into the world and marry, after consorting with the king.

**15.** *she required nothing.* Either because of her modesty, or because she did not care to be chosen as queen.

**16.** *Tebeth.* The names of the months in the Book of Esther are those adopted by the Jews in Babylonia and still in use.

*seventh year.* Shortly after his ignominious return from his defeat in the Greek war.

**17.** *the women.* The Rabbis deduced that married women were also taken to the king. But ii. 2f. explicitly states that only virgins were to be collected. Perhaps the phrase means 'better than the wives he already had.'

tained grace and favour in his sight
more than all the virgins; so that he
set the royal crown upon her head,
and made her queen instead of
Vashti. 18Then the king made a
great feast unto all his princes and
his servants, even Esther's feast;
and he made a release to the provinces, and gave gifts, according to
the bounty of the king.

19And when the virgins were gathered together the second time, and
Mordecai sat in the king's gate—
20Esther had not yet made known
her kindred nor her people; as Mordecai had charged her; for Esther
did the commandment of Mordecai,

וַתִּשָּׂא־חֵן וָחֶסֶד לְפָנָיו מִכָּל־
הַבְּתוּלֹת וַיָּשֶׂם כֶּתֶר־
מַלְכוּת בְּרֹאשָׁהּ וַיַּמְלִיכֶהָ
18 תַּחַת וַשְׁתִּי׃ וַיַּעַשׂ הַמֶּלֶךְ
מִשְׁתֶּה גָדוֹל לְכָל־שָׂרָיו
וַעֲבָדָיו אֵת מִשְׁתֵּה אֶסְתֵּר
וַהֲנָחָה לַמְּדִינוֹת עָשָׂה וַיִּתֵּן
19 מַשְׂאֵת כְּיַד הַמֶּלֶךְ׃ וּבְהִקָּבֵץ
בְּתוּלוֹת שֵׁנִית וּמָרְדֳּכַי יֹשֵׁב
20 בְּשַׁעַר־הַמֶּלֶךְ׃ אֵין אֶסְתֵּר
מַגֶּדֶת מוֹלַדְתָּהּ וְאֶת־עַמָּהּ
כַּאֲשֶׁר צִוָּה עָלֶיהָ מָרְדֳּכָי

**18.** *even Esther's feast.* In later years, when people recalled this feast, they would call it by this name.

*release.* Variously explained as from tribute, from forced labour, from prison, from military service—an amnesty of some sort.

**19-23** MORDECAI SAVES THE KING'S LIFE

**19.** *the second time.* This is one of the phrases in the Book which are really difficult to understand. Why should there have been a second gathering of virgins? According to Rabbinic interpretation, its purpose was to rouse Esther's jealousy, and thereby induce her to declare her kindred and origin. Some have suggested that these were the maidens who arrived late from the distant provinces of the empire. Others, that the king, even though he loved Esther, retained his desire for fresh women gathered from all over his empire. Many other explanations have been offered, none of which is completely satisfying.

*sat in the king's gate.* The large fortified entrance to the palace enclosure. Such gates have always been used in the East as courts of justice and meeting places for discussion and the exchange of news. They were the 'village-pumps' of the Orient. The phrase does not necessarily mean, as some have assumed, that Mordecai had entered the king's service; the reason for his sitting there was probably that he wished to obtain news of Esther.

**20.** *Esther had not yet made known her kindred.* The purpose of the parenthetical statement in this place is to make it clear that Mordecai was not known to be a relative of the queen, and therefore

וְאֶת־מַאֲמַר מָרְדֳּכַי אֶסְתֵּר
עֹשָׂה כַּאֲשֶׁר הָיְתָה בְאָמְנָה
21 אִתּוֹ׃ בַּיָּמִים הָהֵם וּמָרְדֳּכַי
יֹשֵׁב בְּשַׁעַר־הַמֶּלֶךְ קָצַף
בִּגְתָן וָתֶרֶשׁ שְׁנֵי־סָרִיסֵי
הַמֶּלֶךְ מִשֹּׁמְרֵי הַסַּף וַיְבַקְשׁוּ
לִשְׁלֹחַ יָד בַּמֶּלֶךְ אֲחַשְׁוֵרֹשׁ׃
22 וַיִּוָּדַע הַדָּבָר לְמָרְדֳּכַי וַיַּגֵּד
לְאֶסְתֵּר הַמַּלְכָּה וַתֹּאמֶר
אֶסְתֵּר לַמֶּלֶךְ בְּשֵׁם מָרְדֳּכָי׃
23 וַיְבֻקַּשׁ הַדָּבָר וַיִּמָּצֵא וַיִּתָּלוּ
שְׁנֵיהֶם עַל־עֵץ וַיִּכָּתֵב בְּסֵפֶר
דִּבְרֵי הַיָּמִים לִפְנֵי הַמֶּלֶךְ׃

like as when she was brought up
with him—[21]in those days, while
Mordecai sat in the king's gate, two
of the king's chamberlains, Bigthan
and Teresh, of those that kept the
door, were wroth, and sought to lay
hands on the king Ahasuerus. [22]And
the thing became known to Mordecai, who told it unto Esther the
queen; and Esther told the king
thereof in Mordecai's name. [23]And
when inquisition was made of the
matter, and it was found to be so,
they were both hanged on a tree;
and it was written in the book of the
chronicles before the king.

conspirators were not likely to be on their guard against him.

*Esther did the commandment of Mordecai.* This is a very pleasant note on Esther's character. She remained unspoiled by the riches and splendour of her new position, and retained her filial piety.

21. *kept the door.* Guarded the door of the king's private apartments. They were consequently his most trusted servants, and at the same time those with easiest access to the king's person. Xerxes actually met his end by such a conspiracy.

*were wroth.* According to the Targum, they plotted to poison his wine; but the cause of their anger is not stated.

22. *became known to Mordecai.* We are not told how. The Rabbis say that it was through his knowledge of foreign tongues that he overheard their conversation in a foreign language. Josephus attributes it to information obtained from a Jewish slave of the conspirators, but this can hardly be more than a guess on his part.

*in Mordecai's name.* The sentence is quoted in the *Ethics of the Fathers* to support the maxim, 'Whoever repeats a thing in the name of him that said it brings deliverance to the world.'

23. *book of the chronicles.* lit. 'book of the acts of the day.' This was in the nature of a royal diary. Such annals were kept by the ancient kings of Babylonia and Assyria and by the Hebrew kings as well. This record played a vital part in the sequel (vi. 1ff.).

*before the king.* Indicating that it was kept in his apartment, so that anything important might be recorded at once. This is confirmed by Herodotus.

[1]After these things did king Ahasuerus promote Haman the son of Hammedatha the Agagite, and advanced him, and set his seat above all the princes that were with him. [2]And all the king's servants, that were in the king's gate, bowed down, and prostrated themselves before Haman; for the king had so commanded concerning him. But Mordecai bowed not down, nor prostrated himself before him. [3]Then the king's servants, that were in the king's gate, said unto Mordecai: 'Why transgressest thou the king's commandment?' [4]Now it came to pass, when

1 אַחַר ׀ הַדְּבָרִים הָאֵלֶּה גִּדַּל
הַמֶּלֶךְ אֲחַשְׁוֵרוֹשׁ אֶת־הָמָן
בֶּן־הַמְּדָתָא הָאֲגָגִי וַיְנַשְּׂאֵהוּ
וַיָּשֶׂם אֶת־כִּסְאוֹ מֵעַל כָּל־
2 הַשָּׂרִים אֲשֶׁר אִתּוֹ׃ וְכָל־
עַבְדֵי הַמֶּלֶךְ אֲשֶׁר־בְּשַׁעַר
הַמֶּלֶךְ כֹּרְעִים וּמִשְׁתַּחֲוִים
לְהָמָן כִּי־כֵן צִוָּה־לוֹ הַמֶּלֶךְ
וּמָרְדֳּכַי לֹא יִכְרַע וְלֹא
3 יִשְׁתַּחֲוֶה׃ וַיֹּאמְרוּ עַבְדֵי
הַמֶּלֶךְ אֲשֶׁר־בְּשַׁעַר הַמֶּלֶךְ
לְמָרְדֳּכָי מַדּוּעַ אַתָּה עוֹבֵר
4 אֵת מִצְוַת הַמֶּלֶךְ׃ וַיְהִי

**1-5 THE ADVANCEMENT OF HAMAN**

1. *after these things.* Between the seventh (ii. 16) and twelfth (verse 7 below) years of Xerxes' reign.

*promote.* Made him grand vizier, with powers in an autocracy greater than those of a modern prime minister.

*Agagite.* A descendant of Agag, king of Amalek (1 Sam. xv. 9). If, then, the Kish of Mordecai's genealogy is Saul's father, Mordecai and Haman were, so to speak, traditional enemies.

*set his seat.* Gave him an office.

2. *prostrated themselves.* Prostration before high officials was a universal custom in the Orient.

*for the king . . . concerning him.* Since prostration before a superior was such a general rule, it is strange that a special order should have been necessary to enforce it in the case of Haman. It has been well suggested that the reason was that Haman was of low origin and small deserts, a man before whom the established nobility were loth to bow. Haman's overweaning vanity is that of an upstart.

*Mordecai bowed not down.* The oldest, and probably the best, explanation of Mordecai's refusal to bow is that Haman claimed divine honours for himself. The Midrash adds that he wore an image of an idol on his clothing. Mordecai, in his refusal to bow, displayed not only religious conscientiousness, but also a daring independence of spirit.

they spoke daily unto him, and he hearkened not unto them, that they told Haman, to see whether Mordecai's words would stand; for he had told them that he was a Jew. [5]And when Haman saw that Mordecai bowed not down, nor prostrated himself before him, then was Haman full of wrath. [6]But it seemed contemptible in his eyes to lay hands on Mordecai alone; for they had made known to him the people of Mordecai; wherefore Haman sought to destroy all the Jews that were throughout the whole kingdom of Ahasuerus, even the people of Mordecai. [7]In the first month, which is the month Nisan, in

בְּאָמְרָם אֵלָיו יוֹם וָיוֹם וְלֹא
שָׁמַע אֲלֵיהֶם וַיַּגִּידוּ לְהָמָן
לִרְאוֹת הֲיַעַמְדוּ דִּבְרֵי
מָרְדֳּכַי כִּי־הִגִּיד לָהֶם
5 אֲשֶׁר־הוּא יְהוּדִי׃ וַיַּרְא
הָמָן כִּי־אֵין מָרְדֳּכַי כֹּרֵעַ
וּמִשְׁתַּחֲוֶה לוֹ וַיִּמָּלֵא הָמָן
6 חֵמָה׃ וַיִּבֶז בְּעֵינָיו לִשְׁלֹחַ יָד
בְּמָרְדֳּכַי לְבַדּוֹ כִּי־הִגִּידוּ לוֹ
אֶת־עַם מָרְדֳּכָי וַיְבַקֵּשׁ הָמָן
לְהַשְׁמִיד אֶת־כָּל־הַיְּהוּדִים
אֲשֶׁר בְּכָל־מַלְכוּת אֲחַשְׁוֵרוֹשׁ
7 עַם מָרְדֳּכָי׃ בַּחֹדֶשׁ הָרִאשׁוֹן
הוּא־חֹדֶשׁ נִיסָן בִּשְׁנַת שְׁתֵּים

v. 4. כאמרם ק׳

4. *words would stand.* Whether his explanation would be accepted.

*that he was a Jew.* And therefore could not pay Haman divine honour.

5. *when Haman saw.* Apparently Haman did not notice Mordecai's behaviour until it was pointed out to him. Mordecai would have passed unnoticed in the busy gate-way. Now Haman makes a point of looking for the offence.

*then was Haman full of wrath.* Haman is so puffed up with vanity that the refusal of a humble and inconspicuous Jew to bow before him is sufficient to fill him with inordinate rage. A less vain man would have ignored the offence as beneath his notice.

**6-15 HAMAN PLANS EXTERMINATION OF THE JEWS**

6. The insight into the psychology of Jew-hatred in this verse is remarkable. How often is a personal grievance or grudge (imagined or real) against a single Jew the occasion of attacks against the whole Jewish people!

7. *in the first month.* It is an interesting coincidence that the plotting of the destruction of the Jews should have been in the month of their deliverance from Egypt.

the twelfth year of king Ahasuerus, they cast pur, that is, the lot, before Haman from day to day, and from month to month, to the twelfth month, which is the month Adar.

[8]And Haman said unto king Ahasuerus: 'There is a certain people scattered abroad and dispersed among the peoples in all the provinces of thy kingdom; and their laws are diverse from those of every people; neither keep they the king's laws; therefore it profiteth not the king to suffer them. [9]If it please

עֶשְׂרֵה לַמֶּלֶךְ אֲחַשְׁוֵרוֹשׁ
הִפִּיל פּוּר הוּא הַגּוֹרָל לִפְנֵי
הָמָן מִיּוֹם ׀ לְיוֹם וּמֵחֹדֶשׁ
לְחֹדֶשׁ שְׁנֵים־עָשָׂר הוּא־
8 חֹדֶשׁ אֲדָר׃ וַיֹּאמֶר הָמָן
לַמֶּלֶךְ אֲחַשְׁוֵרוֹשׁ יֶשְׁנוֹ עַם־
אֶחָד מְפֻזָּר וּמְפֹרָד בֵּין
הָעַמִּים בְּכֹל מְדִינוֹת
מַלְכוּתֶךָ וְדָתֵיהֶם שֹׁנוֹת
מִכָּל־עָם וְאֶת־דָּתֵי הַמֶּלֶךְ
אֵינָם עֹשִׂים וְלַמֶּלֶךְ אֵין־שֹׁוֶה
9 לְהַנִּיחָם׃ אִם־עַל־הַמֶּלֶךְ

*they cast pur.* To find an auspicious month and day. *They* might refer either to his slaves or to diviners.

*pur.* No such word for 'lot' has been traced in Persian, but Streane's conjecture, that it is the same word as the Assyrian *puru*, 'a stone,' has been proved correct by the discovery in a tablet of the word *puru* in the phrase 'he cast lots.'

*from day . . . to month.* Haman seems to have gone through the process of trying each day of the successive months.

*Adar.* Haman rejoiced: My lot has fallen in the month in which Moses died. But he did not know that Moses was also born in Adar (Talmud).

8. *there is a certain people.* Haman rationalizes his personal hatred of Mordecai into a political theory directed against all the Jews: a familiar device of the Jew-hater. The Talmud says of Haman that no one knew better than he how to slander.

*scattered abroad.* Living among other nationalities and therefore a menace to the Persians.

*their laws are diverse.* 'They do not eat with us, nor drink with us, nor intermarry with us' (Talmud). Haman's charge is true, but no argument for the destruction of the Jews. Professor Witton Davies has well remarked: 'When due to religious principles the separateness of the Jew is to his credit rather than the reverse. No people on the face of the earth have paid or pay more dearly for their religion than the Jews.'

*neither keep they the king's laws.* This charge was, of course, invented. Jeremiah's instruction to the exiles, *Seek the peace of the city whither I have caused you to be carried away captive, and pray* the king, let it be written that they be destroyed; and I will pay ten thousand talents of silver into the hands of those that have the charge of the king's business, to bring it into the king's treasuries.' [10]And the king took his ring from his hand, and gave it unto Haman the son of Hammedatha the Agagite, the Jews' enemy. [11]And the king said unto Haman: 'The silver is given to thee, the people also, to do with them as it seemeth good to thee.'

טוֹב יִכָּתֵב לְאַבְּדָם וַעֲשֶׂרֶת
אֲלָפִים כִּכַּר־כֶּסֶף אֶשְׁקוֹל
עַל־יְדֵי עֹשֵׂי הַמְּלָאכָה
לְהָבִיא אֶל־גִּנְזֵי הַמֶּלֶךְ׃
10 וַיָּסַר הַמֶּלֶךְ אֶת־טַבַּעְתּוֹ
מֵעַל יָדוֹ וַיִּתְּנָהּ לְהָמָן בֶּן־
הַמְּדָתָא הָאֲגָגִי צֹרֵר
11 הַיְּהוּדִים׃ וַיֹּאמֶר הַמֶּלֶךְ
לְהָמָן הַכֶּסֶף נָתוּן לָךְ וְהָעָם
לַעֲשׂוֹת בּוֹ כַּטּוֹב בְּעֵינֶיךָ׃

*unto the LORD for it; for in the peace thereof shall ye have peace* (Jer. xxix. 7), became the law for the Jews in captivity and was faithfully observed. In Rabbinic law it became the principle, 'The law of the country in which you live is binding.'

**9.** *that they be destroyed.* 'With what can the wicked Haman be compared? With a bird which made its nest on the seashore and the sea swept away its nest, whereupon it said, "I will not move from here until I turn the dry land into sea and the sea into dry land." What did it do? It took water from the sea in its mouth and poured it on the dry land, and it took dust from the dry land and cast it in the sea. Its companions came and stood by it and said, "Luckless unfortunate, with all your labour what will you effect?" ' (Midrash).

*and I will pay.* The startling proposition that a whole people be destroyed is followed immediately by the tempting offer of a huge bribe.

*ten thousand talents of silver.* A sum of about £3,600,000, many times more in value than it is to-day, owing to the much greater purchasing power of money. This sum was equal to the annual revenue in silver of the whole Persian Empire (Herodotus). Ahasuerus' resources may have been so exhausted by the war with Greece that Haman's offer was a tempting means of replenishing the treasury (Streane).

**10.** *ring.* His signet ring, the possession of which gave Haman full authority to act on the king's behalf (cf. viii. 2).

**11.** The ease with which the king is persuaded by Haman is typical of the Oriental despot's confidence in, and dependence on, his favourite of the moment.

*the silver is given to thee.* It has been noted that in Hebrew the numerical value of *the silver* is equal to that of *the gallows*, viz. 165. At first sight, it would seem that the king declined Haman's bribe and gave him free leave to massacre the Jews. But Mordecai's information suggests that Haman's offer of money was accepted (iv. 7). Perhaps the king agreed that the promised payment should be made out of the spoils, instead of Haman's private fortune.

[12]Then were the king's scribes called in the first month, on the thirteenth day thereof, and there was written, according to all that Haman commanded, unto the king's satraps, and to the governors that were over every province, and to the princes of every people; to every province according to the writing thereof, and to every people after their language; in the name of king Ahasuerus was it written, and it was sealed with the king's ring. [13]And letters were sent by posts into all the king's provinces, to destroy, to slay, and to cause to perish, all Jews, both young and old, little children and women, in one day, even upon the thirteenth day of the

12 וַיִּקָּרְאוּ סֹפְרֵי הַמֶּלֶךְ בַּחֹדֶשׁ
הָרִאשׁוֹן בִּשְׁלוֹשָׁה עָשָׂר יוֹם
בּוֹ וַיִּכָּתֵב כְּכָל־אֲשֶׁר־צִוָּה
הָמָן אֶל אֲחַשְׁדַּרְפְּנֵי־הַמֶּלֶךְ
וְאֶל־הַפַּחוֹת אֲשֶׁר | עַל־
מְדִינָה וּמְדִינָה וְאֶל־שָׂרֵי עַם
וָעָם מְדִינָה וּמְדִינָה כִּכְתָבָהּ
וְעַם וָעָם כִּלְשׁוֹנוֹ בְּשֵׁם הַמֶּלֶךְ
אֲחַשְׁוֵרֹשׁ נִכְתָּב וְנֶחְתָּם
13 בְּטַבַּעַת הַמֶּלֶךְ׃ וְנִשְׁלוֹחַ
סְפָרִים בְּיַד הָרָצִים אֶל־
כָּל־מְדִינוֹת הַמֶּלֶךְ לְהַשְׁמִיד
לַהֲרֹג וּלְאַבֵּד אֶת־כָּל־
הַיְּהוּדִים מִנַּעַר וְעַד־זָקֵן טַף
וְנָשִׁים בְּיוֹם אֶחָד בִּשְׁלוֹשָׁה

13. *posts.* The Hebrew means literally 'runners.' There was an excellent system of posts in Persia which, according to Herodotus, was in full working order by the time of Xerxes. Stations were established at convenient distances apart, supplying relays of horses and men.

*to destroy, to slay, and to cause to perish, all Jews.* The accumulation of verbs suggests the phraseology of a legal enactment. Some critics have thought it so improbable that such a decree of wholesale slaughter should be issued that they have cast doubts on the genuineness of the Book. Defenders of its authenticity have quoted from history examples of similar massacres. The example of Mithridates of Pontus (quoted by Cassel from Appian) is remarkable in its similarity, even as to language: 'He sent secret order to all the satraps and the mayors of cities that they should within the space of thirty days fall upon the resident Romans and Italians, upon their wives and children and upon all the freemen of Italian origin, and kill them . . . and take their goods as possessions . . . When the appointed day came, there was wailing and lamentation in the whole of Asia.' To-day we need not go to ancient history for parallels. In our own time we have seen decrees for the extermination of whole Jewish populations not only passed, but put into effect.

עָשָׂר לְחֹדֶשׁ שְׁנֵים־עָשָׂר
הוּא־חֹדֶשׁ אֲדָר וּשְׁלָלָם
14 לָבוֹז׃ פַּתְשֶׁגֶן הַכְּתָב לְהִנָּתֵן
דָּת בְּכָל־מְדִינָה וּמְדִינָה גָּלוּי
לְכָל־הָעַמִּים לִהְיוֹת עֲתִידִים
15 לַיּוֹם הַזֶּה׃ הָרָצִים יָצְאוּ
דְחוּפִים בִּדְבַר הַמֶּלֶךְ וְהַדָּת
נִתְּנָה בְּשׁוּשַׁן הַבִּירָה וְהַמֶּלֶךְ
וְהָמָן יָשְׁבוּ לִשְׁתּוֹת וְהָעִיר
שׁוּשָׁן נָבוֹכָה׃

twelfth month, which is the month Adar, and to take the spoil of them for a prey. [14]The copy of the writing, to be given out for a decree in every province, was to be published unto all the peoples, that they should be ready against that day. [15]The posts went forth in haste by the king's commandment, and the decree was given out in Shushan the castle; and the king and Haman sat down to drink; but the city of Shushan was perplexed.

## 4 CHAPTER IV ד

1 וּמָרְדֳּכַי יָדַע אֶת־כָּל־אֲשֶׁר
נַעֲשָׂה וַיִּקְרַע מָרְדֳּכַי אֶת־
בְּגָדָיו וַיִּלְבַּשׁ שַׂק וָאֵפֶר וַיֵּצֵא
בְּתוֹךְ הָעִיר וַיִּזְעַק זְעָקָה
2 גְדוֹלָה וּמָרָה׃ וַיָּבוֹא עַד לִפְנֵי
שַׁעַר־הַמֶּלֶךְ כִּי אֵין לָבוֹא
אֶל־שַׁעַר הַמֶּלֶךְ בִּלְבוּשׁ שָׂק׃

[1]Now when Mordecai knew all that was done, Mordecai rent his clothes, and put on sackcloth with ashes, and went out into the midst of the city, and cried with a loud and a bitter cry; [2]and he came even before the king's gate; for none might enter within the king's gate clothed with

15. *the king and Haman sat down to drink.* This is a most effective piece of literary contrast. Orders had been issued to destroy tens of thousands of human beings, but the king and his chief vizier callously enjoy a banquet.

*was perplexed.* As decent and thinking citizens would be at so outrageous and unaccountable an edict.

## CHAPTER IV

MORDECAI ASKS ESTHER TO INTERCEDE

1. *rent his clothes.* A manifestation of grief (cf. Gen. xxxvii. 34).

*sackcloth with ashes.* The outward signs, not only of mourning, but of repentance and contrition (cf. Jonah iii. 6).

2. *none might enter.* This rule of the

sackcloth. 3And in every province, whithersoever the king's commandment and his decree came, there was great mourning among the Jews, and fasting, and weeping, and wailing; and many lay in sackcloth and ashes.

4And Esther's maidens and her chamberlains came and told it her; and the queen was exceedingly pained; and she sent raiment to clothe Mordecai, and to take his sackcloth from off him; but he accepted it not. 5Then called Esther for Hathach, one of the king's chamberlains, whom he had appointed to attend upon her, and charged him to go to Mordecai, to know what this was, and why it was. 6So Hathach went forth to Mordecai unto the broad place of the city, which was

3 וּבְכָל־מְדִינָה וּמְדִינָה מְקוֹם
אֲשֶׁר דְּבַר־הַמֶּלֶךְ וְדָתוֹ מַגִּיעַ
אֵבֶל גָּדוֹל לַיְּהוּדִים וְצוֹם
וּבְכִי וּמִסְפֵּד שַׂק וָאֵפֶר יֻצַּע
4 לָֽרַבִּים׃ וַתָּבוֹאינָה נַעֲרוֹת
אֶסְתֵּר וְסָרִיסֶיהָ וַיַּגִּידוּ לָהּ
וַתִּתְחַלְחַל הַמַּלְכָּה מְאֹד
וַתִּשְׁלַח בְּגָדִים לְהַלְבִּישׁ אֶת־
מָרְדֳּכַי וּלְהָסִיר שַׂקּוֹ מֵעָלָיו
5 וְלֹא קִבֵּל׃ וַתִּקְרָא אֶסְתֵּר
לַהֲתָךְ מִסָּרִיסֵי הַמֶּלֶךְ אֲשֶׁר
הֶעֱמִיד לְפָנֶיהָ וַתְּצַוֵּהוּ עַל־
מָרְדֳּכַי לָדַעַת מַה־זֶּה וְעַל־
6 מַה־זֶּה׃ וַיֵּצֵא הֲתָךְ אֶל־
מָרְדֳּכַי אֶל־רְחוֹב הָעִיר
אֲשֶׁר לִפְנֵי שַׁעַר־הַמֶּלֶךְ׃

v. 4. יתיר י׳

Persian court is confirmed from other sources.

3. *fasting.* Probably, public fast days.

*many lay in sackcloth and ashes.* lit. 'sackcloth and ashes were spread out under the many.' Cassel prefers the translation 'most prominent' for that of *many*, i.e. the rich and Persianized Jews shared the danger with their poorer and more pious brethren.

4. *told it her.* That Mordecai was in sackcloth and ashes. They knew that Mordecai was interested in Esther (he had enquired about her welfare), even if they did not know of the blood relationship between them.

*pained.* Esther could not have thought that Mordecai had suffered a personal bereavement. If that had been so, he would not have appeared in public. She must have realized immediately that he was bewailing a public calamity.

*sent raiment.* So that Mordecai might enter within the king's gate and communicate with her.

6. *broad place of the city.* The city square, the open space outside the gates of Oriental cities, which is used as the market place.

before the king's gate. [7]And Mordecai told him of all that had happened unto him, and the exact sum of the money that Haman had promised to pay to the king's treasuries for the Jews, to destroy them. [8]Also he gave him the copy of the writing of the decree that was given out in Shushan to destroy them, to show it unto Esther, and to declare it unto her; and to charge her that she should go in unto the king, to make supplication unto him, and to make request before him, for her people.

[9]And Hathach came and told Esther the words of Mordecai. [10]Then Esther spoke unto Hathach, and gave him a message unto Mordecai: [11]'All the king's servants, and

7 וַיַּגֶּד־ל֣וֹ מָרְדֳּכַ֔י אֵ֖ת כָּל־
אֲשֶׁ֣ר קָרָ֑הוּ וְאֵ֣ת ׀ פָּרָשַׁ֣ת
הַכֶּ֗סֶף אֲשֶׁ֨ר אָמַ֤ר הָמָן֙ לִשְׁק֔וֹל
עַל־גִּנְזֵ֥י הַמֶּ֛לֶךְ בַּיְּהוּדִ֖יים
8 לְאַבְּדָֽם׃ וְאֶת־פַּתְשֶׁ֣גֶן כְּתָב־
הַדָּ֡ת אֲשֶׁר־נִתַּ֨ן בְּשׁוּשָׁ֤ן
לְהַשְׁמִידָם֙ נָ֣תַן ל֔וֹ לְהַרְא֥וֹת
אֶת־אֶסְתֵּ֖ר וּלְהַגִּ֣יד לָ֑הּ
וּלְצַוּ֣וֹת עָלֶ֗יהָ לָב֨וֹא אֶל־
הַמֶּ֧לֶךְ לְהִֽתְחַנֶּן־ל֛וֹ וּלְבַקֵּ֥שׁ
9 מִלְּפָנָ֖יו עַל־עַמָּֽהּ׃ וַיָּב֖וֹא
הֲתָ֑ךְ וַיַּגֵּ֣ד לְאֶסְתֵּ֔ר אֵ֖ת דִּבְרֵ֥י
10 מָרְדֳּכָֽי׃ וַתֹּ֤אמֶר אֶסְתֵּר֙
לַהֲתָ֔ךְ וַתְּצַוֵּ֖הוּ אֶל־מָרְדֳּכָֽי׃
11 כָּל־עַבְדֵ֣י הַ֠מֶּלֶךְ וְעַם

v. 7. יתיר י'

7. *all that had happened unto him.* How his refusal to bow before Haman had had such wide and tragic repercussions. The first part of this sentence answers Esther's question *why it was*? and the second half the question *what this was*?

8. *to declare it unto her.* We may perhaps infer from the need to explain the document that Esther could not read Persian (Paton).

*to charge her . . . the king.* Mordecai had summed up the situation quickly. Action had to be taken immediately if the Jews were to be saved, and there were only two people in a position to help the threatened community: Esther as queen, and he himself as the queen's cousin. He recognized the responsibility for his people which his special position placed upon him, and his first duty was to rouse Esther to an equal sense of her responsibility. There is a distinct tone of urgency in Mordecai's message.

*make request before him, for her people.* It was now necessary for Esther to declare her nationality; and, just as Mordecai had advised her to conceal it, he now advises her to reveal it.

the people of the king's provinces, do know, that whosoever, whether man or woman, shall come unto the king into the inner court, who is not called, there is one law for him, that he be put to death, except such to whom the king shall hold out the golden sceptre, that he may live; but I have not been called to come in unto the king these thirty days.'
12 And they told to Mordecai Esther's words.

13 Then Mordecai bade them return answer unto Esther: 'Think not with thyself that thou shalt escape in the king's house, more than all the Jews.
14 For if thou altogether holdest thy peace at this time, then will relief and deliverance arise to the Jews from another place, but thou and thy father's house will perish; and who knoweth whether thou art not come to royal estate for such a

מְדִינוֹת הַמֶּלֶךְ יוֹדְעִים אֲשֶׁר
כָּל־אִישׁ וְאִשָּׁה אֲשֶׁר־יָבוֹא
אֶל־הַמֶּלֶךְ אֶל־הֶחָצֵר
הַפְּנִימִית אֲשֶׁר לֹא־יִקָּרֵא
אַחַת דָּתוֹ לְהָמִית לְבַד מֵאֲשֶׁר
יוֹשִׁיט־לוֹ הַמֶּלֶךְ אֶת־
שַׁרְבִיט הַזָּהָב וְחָיָה וַאֲנִי לֹא
נִקְרֵאתִי לָבוֹא אֶל־הַמֶּלֶךְ
12 זֶה שְׁלוֹשִׁים יוֹם׃ וַיַּגִּידוּ
לְמָרְדֳּכָי אֵת דִּבְרֵי אֶסְתֵּר׃
13 וַיֹּאמֶר מָרְדֳּכַי לְהָשִׁיב אֶל־
אֶסְתֵּר אַל־תְּדַמִּי בְנַפְשֵׁךְ
לְהִמָּלֵט בֵּית־הַמֶּלֶךְ
14 מִכָּל־הַיְּהוּדִים׃ כִּי אִם־
הַחֲרֵשׁ תַּחֲרִישִׁי בָּעֵת הַזֹּאת
רֶוַח וְהַצָּלָה יַעֲמוֹד לַיְּהוּדִים
מִמָּקוֹם אַחֵר וְאַתְּ וּבֵית־
אָבִיךְ תֹּאבֵדוּ וּמִי יוֹדֵעַ אִם־
לְעֵת כָּזֹאת הִגַּעַתְּ לַמַּלְכוּת׃

11. *who is not called.* The purpose of this law must have been to protect the king from attempts at assassination.

13. Mordecai's rebuke is stern and uncompromising. In face of the calamity which threatened the whole Jewish population of the empire, there was no place for considerations of personal safety.

14. *from another place.* Mordecai is obviously referring to Divine help, but the author deliberately avoids the use of God's name (see Introduction).

*will perish.* By Divine judgment, for the neglect of duty.

*for such a time as this.* Mordecai had realized the Divine purpose of Esther's choice as queen (see on ii. 10), and Esther too understands that her special position entails a corresponding obligation.

time as this?' 15 Then Esther bade
them return answer unto Mordecai:
16 'Go, gather together all the Jews
that are present in Shushan, and fast
ye for me, and neither eat nor drink
three days, night or day; I also and
my maidens will fast in like manner;
and so will I go in unto the king,
which is not according to the law;
and if I perish, I perish.' 17 So Mordecai went his way, and did according to all that Esther had commanded
him.

15 וַתֹּאמֶר אֶסְתֵּר לְהָשִׁיב אֶל־
16 מָרְדֳּכָי׃ לֵךְ כְּנוֹס אֶת־כָּל־
הַיְּהוּדִים הַנִּמְצְאִים בְּשׁוּשָׁן
וְצוּמוּ עָלַי וְאַל־תֹּאכְלוּ
וְאַל־תִּשְׁתּוּ שְׁלֹשֶׁת יָמִים
לַיְלָה וָיוֹם גַּם־אֲנִי וְנַעֲרֹתַי
אָצוּם כֵּן וּבְכֵן אָבוֹא אֶל־
הַמֶּלֶךְ אֲשֶׁר לֹא־כַדָּת
וְכַאֲשֶׁר אָבַדְתִּי אָבָדְתִּי׃
17 וַיַּעֲבֹר מָרְדֳּכָי וַיַּעַשׂ כְּכֹל
אֲשֶׁר־צִוְּתָה עָלָיו אֶסְתֵּר׃

**16.** *fast ye for me.* Prayer must have accompanied the fasting, but again the author avoids any language which might necessitate the mention of God.

*three days, night or day.* It need not have been a continuous fast for three days. The Midrash asserts that food was taken at the sunset of each day.

*if I perish, I perish.* A simple, but sublime and courageous statement of resignation to God's will (cf. Jacob's exclamation, *If I be bereaved, I am bereaved,* Gen. xliii. 14).

**17.** *went his way.* The Hebrew word can mean either 'crossed over' or 'transgressed.' In the Talmud, (Rabbi) Samuel adopts the first interpretation, and Rab the second. Samuel interprets 'crossed the water,' and it is a fact that the palace of Susa was separated by the river Choaspes from the city. This is probably what is meant. Rab takes the meaning to be 'transgressed the Passover law by fasting on a Festival day.' He held that the three fast days included the first day of Passover. (The decree was issued on the 13th of Nisan (iii. 12), and the Rabbinical view is that the fast days followed immediately. According to the Midrash they were the 13th, 14th and 15th; according to Rashi the 14th, 15th and 16th of Nisan.) The Midrash represents Mordecai as protesting to Esther, 'But these three days include the first day of Passover!' and Esther as replying, 'If there is no Israel, how can there be a Passover!'

1Now it came to pass on the third day, that Esther put on her royal apparel, and stood in the inner court of the king's house, over against the king's house; and the king sat upon his royal throne in the royal house, over against the entrance of the house. 2And it was so, when the king saw Esther the queen standing in the court, that she obtained favour in his sight; and the king held out to Esther the golden sceptre that was in his hand. So Esther drew near, and touched the top of the sceptre. 3Then said the king unto her: 'What wilt thou, queen Esther? for whatever thy request, even to the half of the kingdom, it shall be given thee.' 4And Esther said: 'If it seem good

1 וַיְהִי | בַּיּוֹם הַשְּׁלִישִׁי וַתִּלְבַּשׁ
אֶסְתֵּר מַלְכוּת וַתַּעֲמֹד בַּחֲצַר
בֵּית־הַמֶּלֶךְ הַפְּנִימִית נֹכַח
בֵּית הַמֶּלֶךְ וְהַמֶּלֶךְ יוֹשֵׁב עַל־
כִּסֵּא מַלְכוּתוֹ בְּבֵית הַמַּלְכוּת
2 נֹכַח פֶּתַח הַבָּיִת׃ וַיְהִי כִרְאוֹת
הַמֶּלֶךְ אֶת־אֶסְתֵּר הַמַּלְכָּה
עֹמֶדֶת בֶּחָצֵר נָשְׂאָה חֵן בְּעֵינָיו
וַיּוֹשֶׁט הַמֶּלֶךְ לְאֶסְתֵּר אֶת־
שַׁרְבִיט הַזָּהָב אֲשֶׁר בְּיָדוֹ
וַתִּקְרַב אֶסְתֵּר וַתִּגַּע בְּרֹאשׁ
3 הַשַּׁרְבִיט׃ וַיֹּאמֶר לָהּ הַמֶּלֶךְ
מַה־לָּךְ אֶסְתֵּר הַמַּלְכָּה
וּמַה־בַּקָּשָׁתֵךְ עַד־חֲצִי
4 הַמַּלְכוּת וְיִנָּתֵן לָךְ׃ וַתֹּאמֶר
אֶסְתֵּר אִם־עַל־הַמֶּלֶךְ טוֹב

**1-4 ESTHER GOES TO THE KING**

1. *on the third day.* Counting the day on which she gave Mordecai her promise as the first day.

*put on her royal apparel.* Probably, while fasting, she had worn mourning garb.

*inner court.* From this court it was possible to see the king sitting on his throne.

*over against the entrance.* This is the normal situation of the throne in the throne-room of an Oriental palace—opposite an open doorway leading into the inner court.

3. *what wilt thou, queen Esther?* The king realized immediately that Esther's appearance unsummoned must mean that she had an urgent request to make of him.

*even to the half of the kingdom.* A grandiose complimentary gesture, not intended to be taken seriously.

unto the king, let the king and Haman come this day unto the banquet that I have prepared for him.' 5 Then the king said: 'Cause Haman to make haste, that it may be done as Esther hath said.' So the king and Haman came to the banquet that Esther had prepared. 6 And the king said unto Esther at the banquet of wine: 'Whatever thy petition, it shall be granted thee; and whatever thy request, even to the half of the kingdom, it shall be performed.' 7 Then answered Esther, and said: 'My petition and my request is— 8 if I have found favour in the sight of the king, and if it please the king to grant my petition, and to perform my request—let the king and Haman come to the banquet that I shall prepare for them, and I will do to-morrow as the king hath said.'

יָב֨וֹא הַמֶּ֤לֶךְ וְהָמָן֙ הַיּ֔וֹם אֶל־
הַמִּשְׁתֶּ֖ה אֲשֶׁר־עָשִׂ֥יתִי לֽוֹ׃
5 וַיֹּ֣אמֶר הַמֶּ֔לֶךְ מַהֲרוּ֙ אֶת־הָמָ֔ן
לַעֲשׂ֖וֹת אֶת־דְּבַ֣ר אֶסְתֵּ֑ר
וַיָּבֹ֤א הַמֶּ֙לֶךְ֙ וְהָמָ֔ן אֶל־
הַמִּשְׁתֶּ֖ה אֲשֶׁר־עָשְׂתָ֥ה
6 אֶסְתֵּֽר׃ וַיֹּ֨אמֶר הַמֶּ֤לֶךְ
לְאֶסְתֵּר֙ בְּמִשְׁתֵּ֣ה הַיַּ֔יִן מַה־
שְּׁאֵלָתֵ֖ךְ וְיִנָּ֣תֵֽן לָ֑ךְ וּמַה־
בַּקָּשָׁתֵ֛ךְ עַד־חֲצִ֥י הַמַּלְכ֖וּת
7 וְתֵעָֽשׂ׃ * וַתַּ֥עַן אֶסְתֵּ֖ר וַתֹּאמַ֑ר
8 שְׁאֵלָתִ֖י וּבַקָּשָׁתִֽי׃ אִם־
מָצָ֨אתִי חֵ֜ן בְּעֵינֵ֣י הַמֶּ֗לֶךְ וְאִם־
עַל־הַמֶּ֙לֶךְ֙ ט֔וֹב לָתֵת֙ אֶת־
שְׁאֵ֣לָתִ֔י וְלַעֲשׂ֖וֹת אֶת־בַּקָּשָׁתִ֑י
יָב֣וֹא הַמֶּ֤לֶךְ וְהָמָן֙ אֶל־
הַמִּשְׁתֶּה֙ אֲשֶׁ֣ר אֶֽעֱשֶׂ֣ה לָהֶ֔ם
וּמָחָ֥ר אֶֽעֱשֶׂ֖ה כִּדְבַ֥ר הַמֶּֽלֶךְ׃

v. 7. חצי הספר בפסוקים

4. *let the king and Haman come.* Esther had some good reason for wishing Haman present when she petitioned the king. Twelve surmises at the reason are advanced by the Rabbis in the Talmud. Perhaps the best are (1) that Esther was purposely showing a great interest in Haman, to arouse the king's jealousy and to disarm Haman; (2) that Esther wished to expose Haman in the king's presence so that he might not have an opportunity to prepare excuses or persuade the king against relenting.

**5-8** THE FIRST BANQUET

6. The king understood that Esther had not risked her life merely to come and invite him to a banquet. He therefore repeated his enquiry into the real nature of Esther's wish.

7. *my petition and my request is.* Esther begins as if she is about to reveal her request, but either decides that the time is not ripe, or else cleverly holds the king in suspense. The more curious the king was as to the nature of Esther's

[9]Then went Haman forth that day
joyful and glad of heart; but when
Haman saw Mordecai in the king's
gate, that he stood not up nor moved
for him, Haman was filled with wrath
against Mordecai. [10]Nevertheless
Haman refrained himself, and went
home; and he sent and fetched his
friends and Zeresh his wife. [11]And
Haman recounted unto them the
glory of his riches, and the multitude
of his children, and everything as to
how the king had promoted him, and
how he had advanced him above the
princes and servants of the king.
[12]Haman said moreover: 'Yea, Esther
the queen did let no man come in
with the king unto the banquet that
she had prepared but myself; and
to-morrow also am I invited by her

9 וַיֵּצֵא הָמָן בַּיּוֹם הַהוּא שָׂמֵחַ
וְטוֹב לֵב וְכִרְאוֹת הָמָן אֶת־
מָרְדֳּכַי בְּשַׁעַר הַמֶּלֶךְ וְלֹא־
קָם וְלֹא־זָע מִמֶּנּוּ וַיִּמָּלֵא הָמָן
10 עַל־מָרְדֳּכַי חֵמָה׃ וַיִּתְאַפַּק
הָמָן וַיָּבוֹא אֶל־בֵּיתוֹ וַיִּשְׁלַח
וַיָּבֵא אֶת־אֹהֲבָיו וְאֶת־זֶרֶשׁ
11 אִשְׁתּוֹ׃ וַיְסַפֵּר לָהֶם הָמָן אֶת־
כְּבוֹד עָשְׁרוֹ וְרֹב בָּנָיו וְאֵת
כָּל־אֲשֶׁר גִּדְּלוֹ הַמֶּלֶךְ וְאֵת
אֲשֶׁר נִשְּׂאוֹ עַל־הַשָּׂרִים
12 וְעַבְדֵי הַמֶּלֶךְ׃ וַיֹּאמֶר הָמָן
אַף לֹא־הֵבִיאָה אֶסְתֵּר
הַמַּלְכָּה עִם־הַמֶּלֶךְ אֶל־
הַמִּשְׁתֶּה אֲשֶׁר־עָשָׂתָה כִּי
אִם־אוֹתִי וְגַם־לְמָחָר אֲנִי
קְרוּא־לָהּ עִם־הַמֶּלֶךְ׃

request, the more anxious he was likely to become to fulfil it.

**9-14 HAMAN DECIDES TO ASK FOR MORDECAI'S LIFE**

**9.** *joyful and glad of heart.* He had not only received one mark of special favour from the queen, but was to receive a second on the morrow.

*in the king's gate.* Mordecai must have put off his mourning apparel now that hope had dawned.

**10.** *refrained himself.* From taking precipitate action against Mordecai.

*fetched his friends.* To boast to them of the special favour which had been shown to him by the queen.

**11.** *the multitude of his children.* According to Herodotus, those Persians were held in highest honour who had the largest number of sons. Haman had ten sons (ix. 7ff.).

together with the king. [13]Yet all this
availeth me nothing, so long as I see
Mordecai the Jew sitting at the king's
gate.' [14]Then said Zeresh his wife
and all his friends unto him: 'Let
a gallows be made of fifty cubits high,
and in the morning speak thou unto
the king that Mordecai may be
hanged thereon; then go thou in
merrily with the king unto the
banquet.' And the thing pleased
Haman; and he caused the gallows to
be made.

13 וְכָל־זֶה אֵינֶנּוּ שֹׁוֶה לִי בְּכָל־
עֵת אֲשֶׁר אֲנִי רֹאֶה אֶת־
מָרְדֳּכַי הַיְּהוּדִי יוֹשֵׁב בְּשַׁעַר
14 הַמֶּלֶךְ׃ וַתֹּאמֶר לוֹ זֶרֶשׁ אִשְׁתּוֹ
וְכָל־אֹהֲבָיו יַעֲשׂוּ־עֵץ גָּבֹהַּ
חֲמִשִּׁים אַמָּה וּבַבֹּקֶר ׀ אֱמֹר
לַמֶּלֶךְ וְיִתְלוּ אֶת־מָרְדֳּכַי
עָלָיו וּבֹא עִם־הַמֶּלֶךְ אֶל־
הַמִּשְׁתֶּה שָׂמֵחַ וַיִּיטַב הַדָּבָר
לִפְנֵי הָמָן וַיַּעַשׂ הָעֵץ׃

## 6 CHAPTER VI ו

[1]On that night could not the king
sleep; and he commanded to bring
the book of records of the chronicles,
and they were read before the king.

1 בַּלַּיְלָה הַהוּא נָדְדָה שְׁנַת
הַמֶּלֶךְ וַיֹּאמֶר לְהָבִיא אֶת־
סֵפֶר הַזִּכְרֹנוֹת דִּבְרֵי הַיָּמִים
וַיִּהְיוּ נִקְרָאִים לִפְנֵי הַמֶּלֶךְ׃

13. *availeth me nothing.* Better, 'fails to satisfy me.' The literal meaning of the Hebrew is 'is not adequate for me.' It is usual in the excessively vain, that the smallest slight or reflection is so exaggerated and brooded on that all the enjoyment of power, position and honour is lost.

14. *speak thou unto the king.* According to Persian law, power over life and death rested with the king alone.

*that Mordecai may be hanged thereon.* Neither Zeresh nor his friends nor Haman himself had any doubt that the king would grant the life of an insignificant Jew to his favourite minister, especially after he had granted him the lives of a whole people.

*hanged.* Impalement is probably meant, since hanging was not a Persian method of capital punishment.

## CHAPTER VI

### 1-9 THE KING REMINDED OF MORDECAI'S SERVICE

1. *could not the king sleep.* It would be profitless to speculate on the cause of the king's insomnia; but that sleep should fail him just on that night was, to the Rabbis, not a mere coincidence, but evidence of God's intervention. It may be noted again how the author seems

[2]And it was found written, that Mordecai had told of Bigthana and Teresh, two of the king's chamberlains, of those that kept the door, who had sought to lay hands on the king Ahasuerus. [3]And the king said: 'What honour and dignity hath been done to Mordecai for this?' Then said the king's servants that ministered unto him: 'There is nothing done for him.' [4]And the king said: 'Who is in the court?'—Now Haman was come into the outer court of the king's house, to speak unto the king to hang Mordecai on the gallows that he had prepared for him.—[5]And the king's servants said unto him: 'Be-

2 וַיִּמָּצֵא כָתוּב אֲשֶׁר הִגִּיד
מָרְדֳּכַי עַל־בִּגְתָנָא וָתֶרֶשׁ שְׁנֵי
סָרִיסֵי הַמֶּלֶךְ מִשֹּׁמְרֵי הַסַּף
אֲשֶׁר בִּקְשׁוּ לִשְׁלֹחַ יָד בַּמֶּלֶךְ
3 אֲחַשְׁוֵרוֹשׁ׃ וַיֹּאמֶר הַמֶּלֶךְ
מַה־נַּעֲשָׂה יְקָר וּגְדוּלָּה
לְמָרְדֳּכַי עַל־זֶה וַיֹּאמְרוּ
נַעֲרֵי הַמֶּלֶךְ מְשָׁרְתָיו לֹא־
4 נַעֲשָׂה עִמּוֹ דָּבָר׃ וַיֹּאמֶר
הַמֶּלֶךְ מִי בֶחָצֵר וְהָמָן בָּא
לַחֲצַר בֵּית־הַמֶּלֶךְ הַחִיצוֹנָה
לֵאמֹר לַמֶּלֶךְ לִתְלוֹת אֶת־
מָרְדֳּכַי עַל־הָעֵץ אֲשֶׁר־
5 הֵכִין לוֹ׃ וַיֹּאמְרוּ נַעֲרֵי הַמֶּלֶךְ

carefully to refrain from mentioning the Deity. From any other Biblical author we should expect some such phrase as 'The Lord took away the king's sleep.'

*they were read.* The Hebrew verb is more than a simple past tense, and a better rendering would be 'they kept on reading them.'

2. As related in ii. 21ff.

4. *who is in the court?* Not that the king had seen or heard someone arrive, but probably there were always one or two courtiers in attendance in the court, and the king asks in effect, 'Who is in attendance who might at once rectify this omission?' The servants, seeing Haman there, would naturally mention him as the most important person in waiting.

*now Haman was come.* Haman is so obsessed with his plan to hang Mordecai that he cannot wait until his next audience with the king, but comes during the night, or in the early hours of the morning, to ask the king's permission. This is the beginning of his undoing, because his very eagerness brings him to the king at the most inopportune time for him, at that moment when the king is concerned about rewarding Mordecai.

*outer court.* He dared not come into the inner court without a summons from the king.

hold, Haman standeth in the
court.' And the king said: 'Let
him come in.' [6]So Haman came in.
And the king said unto him: 'What
shall be done unto the man whom
the king delighteth to honour?'—
Now Haman said in his heart:
'Whom would the king delight to
honour besides myself?'—[7]And
Haman said unto the king: 'For the
man whom the king delighteth to
honour, [8]let royal apparel be brought
which the king useth to wear, and
the horse that the king rideth upon,
and on whose head a crown royal is
set; [9]and let the apparel and the horse
be delivered to the hand of one of
the king's most noble princes, that
they may array the man therewith

אֵלָיו הִנֵּה הָמָן עֹמֵד בֶּחָצֵר
6 וַיֹּאמֶר הַמֶּלֶךְ יָבוֹא׃ וַיָּבוֹא
הָמָן וַיֹּאמֶר לוֹ הַמֶּלֶךְ מַה־
לַעֲשׂוֹת בָּאִישׁ אֲשֶׁר הַמֶּלֶךְ
חָפֵץ בִּיקָרוֹ וַיֹּאמֶר הָמָן בְּלִבּוֹ
לְמִי יַחְפֹּץ הַמֶּלֶךְ לַעֲשׂוֹת
7 יְקָר יוֹתֵר מִמֶּנִּי׃ וַיֹּאמֶר הָמָן
אֶל־הַמֶּלֶךְ אִישׁ אֲשֶׁר הַמֶּלֶךְ
8 חָפֵץ בִּיקָרוֹ׃ יָבִיאוּ לְבוּשׁ
מַלְכוּת אֲשֶׁר לָבַשׁ־בּוֹ הַמֶּלֶךְ
וְסוּס אֲשֶׁר רָכַב עָלָיו הַמֶּלֶךְ
וַאֲשֶׁר נִתַּן כֶּתֶר מַלְכוּת
9 בְּרֹאשׁוֹ׃ וְנָתוֹן הַלְּבוּשׁ וְהַסּוּס
עַל־יַד־אִישׁ מִשָּׂרֵי הַמֶּלֶךְ
הַפַּרְתְּמִים וְהִלְבִּשׁוּ אֶת־

v. 9. ב״א והלבישו

5. *let him come in.* i.e. to the king's bed-chamber.

6. *and the king said unto him.* The king's mind is so full with the thought of rewarding Mordecai that he does not ask Haman what had brought him at so early an hour.

*said in his heart.* The Talmud argues that since the writer of the Book knew what was in Haman's heart, he must have been inspired.

8. *let royal apparel be brought.* The signal honour which Haman suggests is not without parallel. Plutarch tells that 'when Xerxes allowed Demaratus the Spartan frankly to ask what he wanted, he requested to have the king's crown placed on his head and to be led through the city in the same manner as the king was.'

*on whose head a crown royal is set.* The head of the horse is meant. Assyrian reliefs depict kings' horses with tall, pointed ornaments like royal turbans on their heads.

whom the king delighteth to honour,
and cause him to ride on horseback
through the street of the city, and
proclaim before him: Thus shall it be
done to the man whom the king delighteth to honour.' [10]Then the king
said to Haman: 'Make haste, and
take the apparel and the horse, as
thou hast said, and do even so to
Mordecai the Jew, that sitteth at the
king's gate; let nothing fail of all that
thou hast spoken.' [11]Then took
Haman the apparel and the horse,
and arrayed Mordecai, and caused
him to ride through the street of
the city, and proclaimed before him:
'Thus shall it be done unto the man
whom the king delighteth to honour.'

[12]And Mordecai returned to the
king's gate. But Haman hastened to
his house, mourning and having his
head covered. [13]And Haman recounted unto Zeresh his wife and all

הָאִישׁ אֲשֶׁר הַמֶּלֶךְ חָפֵץ
בִּיקָרוֹ וְהִרְכִּיבֻהוּ עַל־הַסּוּס
בִּרְחוֹב הָעִיר וְקָרְאוּ לְפָנָיו
כָּכָה יֵעָשֶׂה לָאִישׁ אֲשֶׁר הַמֶּלֶךְ
10 חָפֵץ בִּיקָרוֹ׃ וַיֹּאמֶר הַמֶּלֶךְ
לְהָמָן מַהֵר קַח אֶת־הַלְּבוּשׁ
וְאֶת־הַסּוּס כַּאֲשֶׁר דִּבַּרְתָּ
וַעֲשֵׂה־כֵן לְמָרְדֳּכַי הַיְּהוּדִי
הַיּוֹשֵׁב בְּשַׁעַר הַמֶּלֶךְ אַל־
תַּפֵּל דָּבָר מִכֹּל אֲשֶׁר דִּבַּרְתָּ׃
11 וַיִּקַּח הָמָן אֶת־הַלְּבוּשׁ וְאֶת־
הַסּוּס וַיַּלְבֵּשׁ אֶת־מָרְדֳּכָי
וַיַּרְכִּיבֵהוּ בִּרְחוֹב הָעִיר
וַיִּקְרָא לְפָנָיו כָּכָה יֵעָשֶׂה
לָאִישׁ אֲשֶׁר הַמֶּלֶךְ חָפֵץ
12 בִּיקָרוֹ׃ וַיָּשָׁב מָרְדֳּכַי אֶל־
שַׁעַר הַמֶּלֶךְ וְהָמָן נִדְחַף אֶל־
בֵּיתוֹ אָבֵל וַחֲפוּי רֹאשׁ׃
13 וַיְסַפֵּר הָמָן לְזֶרֶשׁ אִשְׁתּוֹ
וּלְכָל־אֹהֲבָיו אֵת כָּל־אֲשֶׁר

**10-14 HAMAN'S HUMILIATION**

**10.** *do even so to Mordecai the Jew.* The tables are turned with poetic justice, and for all to see. The courtiers would know of Haman's hatred of Mordecai. 'He was compelled, through the irony of fate, to carry out to the letter in his enemy's case the proposals which he had made on his own behalf' (Streane).

**12.** *head covered.* A sign of mourning (cf. 2 Sam. xv. 30).

his friends every thing that had befallen him. Then said his wise men and Zeresh his wife unto him: 'If Mordecai, before whom thou hast begun to fall, be of the seed of the Jews, thou shalt not prevail against him, but shalt surely fall before him.'
14 While they were yet talking with him, came the king's chamberlains, and hastened to bring Haman unto the banquet that Esther had prepared.

קָרָהוּ וַיֹּאמְרוּ לוֹ חֲכָמָיו
וְזֶרֶשׁ אִשְׁתּוֹ אִם מִזֶּרַע
הַיְּהוּדִים מָרְדֳּכַי אֲשֶׁר
הַחִלּוֹתָ לִנְפֹּל לְפָנָיו לֹא־
תוּכַל לוֹ כִּי־נָפוֹל תִּפּוֹל
14 לְפָנָיו׃ עוֹדָם מְדַבְּרִים עִמּוֹ
וְסָרִיסֵי הַמֶּלֶךְ הִגִּיעוּ וַיַּבְהִלוּ
לְהָבִיא אֶת־הָמָן אֶל־
הַמִּשְׁתֶּה אֲשֶׁר־עָשְׂתָה
אֶסְתֵּר׃

## 7 CHAPTER VII ז

1 So the king and Haman came to banquet with Esther the queen.
2 And the king said again unto Esther on the second day at the banquet

1 וַיָּבֹא הַמֶּלֶךְ וְהָמָן לִשְׁתּוֹת
2 עִם־אֶסְתֵּר הַמַּלְכָּה׃ וַיֹּאמֶר
הַמֶּלֶךְ לְאֶסְתֵּר גַּם בַּיּוֹם הַשֵּׁנִי
בְּמִשְׁתֵּה הַיַּיִן מַה־שְּׁאֵלָתֵךְ

13. *wise men.* These are his friends of the previous sentence. Perhaps the use of the word is an intentional irony: they were wise after the event. Haman had already told them that Mordecai was a Jew (v. 13); but instead of advising caution and restraint, they it was who suggested the gallows. But now, conveniently forgetting that Haman's humiliation was largely the fault of their suggestion, they heap coals on his head and, perhaps deriving some malicious satisfaction from his miserable predicament, warn him that this is the beginning of his end.

*but shalt surely fall before him.* A reference to God's promises to Israel that none shall prevail against them.

14. *hastened to bring Haman.* This does not necessarily mean that Haman in his grief had forgotten about Esther's invitation, or that he was afraid to go and had to be sent for. It was the custom to send servants to escort guests. But how different must Haman's feelings have been from those he had anticipated (v. 14)! This is another instance of the author's skilful use of dramatic contrast

of wine: 'Whatever thy petition, queen Esther, it shall be granted thee; and whatever thy request, even to the half of the kingdom, it shall be performed.' [3]Then Esther the queen answered and said: 'If I have found favour in thy sight, O king, and if it please the king, let my life be given me at my petition, and my people at my request; [4]for we are sold, I and my people, to be destroyed, to be slain, and to perish. But if we had been sold for bondmen and bondwomen, I had held my peace, for the adversary is not worthy that the king be endamaged.'

[5]Then spoke the king Ahasuerus and said unto Esther the queen: 'Who is he, and where is he, that

אֶסְתֵּר הַמַּלְכָּה וְתִנָּתֵן לָךְ
וּמַה־בַּקָּשָׁתֵךְ עַד־חֲצִי
3 הַמַּלְכוּת וְתֵעָשׂ׃ וַתַּעַן אֶסְתֵּר
הַמַּלְכָּה וַתֹּאמַר אִם־
מָצָאתִי חֵן בְּעֵינֶיךָ הַמֶּלֶךְ
וְאִם־עַל־הַמֶּלֶךְ טוֹב תִּנָּתֶן
לִי נַפְשִׁי בִּשְׁאֵלָתִי וְעַמִּי
4 בְּבַקָּשָׁתִי׃ כִּי נִמְכַּרְנוּ אֲנִי
וְעַמִּי לְהַשְׁמִיד לַהֲרוֹג וּלְאַבֵּד
וְאִלּוּ לַעֲבָדִים וְלִשְׁפָחוֹת
נִמְכַּרְנוּ הֶחֱרַשְׁתִּי כִּי אֵין הַצָּר
5 שֹׁוֶה בְּנֵזֶק הַמֶּלֶךְ׃ וַיֹּאמֶר
הַמֶּלֶךְ אֲחַשְׁוֵרוֹשׁ וַיֹּאמֶר
לְאֶסְתֵּר הַמַּלְכָּה מִי הוּא זֶה
וְאֵי־זֶה הוּא אֲשֶׁר־מְלָאוֹ לִבּוֹ

## CHAPTER VII.

**1-6** THE SECOND BANQUET: ESTHER PRESENTS HER PETITION

3. *my life . . . at my request.* In the Hebrew there are only four words; but they are words which have a specially poignant appeal to the Jew who is conscious of the interdependence of the fate of the individual Jew and the fate of the Jewish people. The words have supplied a haunting refrain for two of the loveliest Pizmonim (liturgical poems) in the Selichoth (penitential prayers). Esther showed great tact in placing the plea for her own life first. This opening at once roused the king. Who would dare lay hands on my favourite wife? (Adeney).

4. *for the adversary . . . endamaged.* Another difficult and obscure phrase in the Hebrew which has been variously translated and interpreted. Perhaps the meaning is: If the Jews had been sold as slaves, the king would have derived a considerable revenue from the sale; and if Esther had intervened, her intervention would have resulted in the loss of this revenue to the king. The downfall of the enemy Haman would not then have been sufficient compensation for the loss to the king; and Esther in that case would have kept silence, rather than that the king should suffer damage, i.e. loss. If Haman's plan had been to sell the Jews into slavery, at least their lives would not have been in danger.

5. *who is he, and where is he?* Not that the king had forgotten his grant to

durst presume in his heart to do so?' [6]And Esther said: 'An adversary and an enemy, even this wicked Haman.' Then Haman was terrified before the king and the queen. [7]And the king arose in his wrath from the banquet of wine and went into the palace garden; but Haman remained to make request for his life to Esther the queen; for he saw that there was evil determined against him by the king. [8]Then the king returned out of the palace garden into the place of the banquet of wine; and Haman was fallen upon the couch whereon Esther was. Then said the king: 'Will he even force the queen before me in the house?' As the word went

6 לַעֲשׂ֥וֹת כֵּֽן׃ וַתֹּ֣אמֶר אֶסְתֵּ֔ר
אִ֚ישׁ צַ֣ר וְאוֹיֵ֔ב הָמָ֥ן הָרָ֖ע הַזֶּ֑ה
וְהָמָ֣ן נִבְעָ֔ת מִלִּפְנֵ֥י הַמֶּ֖לֶךְ
7 וְהַמַּלְכָּֽה׃ וְהַמֶּ֜לֶךְ קָ֤ם
בַּחֲמָתוֹ֙ מִמִּשְׁתֵּ֣ה הַיַּ֔יִן אֶל־גִּנַּ֖ת
הַבִּיתָ֑ן וְהָמָ֣ן עָמַ֗ד לְבַקֵּ֤שׁ עַל־
נַפְשׁוֹ֙ מֵאֶסְתֵּ֣ר הַמַּלְכָּ֔ה כִּ֣י
רָאָ֔ה כִּֽי־כָלְתָ֥ה אֵלָ֛יו הָרָעָ֖ה
8 מֵאֵ֥ת הַמֶּֽלֶךְ׃ וְהַמֶּ֡לֶךְ שָׁ֠ב
מִגִּנַּ֨ת הַבִּיתָ֜ן אֶל־בֵּ֣ית ׀ מִשְׁתֵּ֣ה
הַיַּ֗יִן וְהָמָן֙ נֹפֵ֔ל עַל־הַמִּטָּה֙
אֲשֶׁ֣ר אֶסְתֵּ֣ר עָלֶ֔יהָ וַיֹּ֣אמֶר
הַמֶּ֔לֶךְ הֲ֠גַם לִכְבּ֧וֹשׁ אֶת־
הַמַּלְכָּ֛ה עִמִּ֖י בַּבָּ֑יִת הַדָּבָ֗ר

Haman; but since he was unaware that Esther was a Jewess, he did not know to what she referred.

6. *an adversary . . . Haman.* Either the king and Haman, when Esther denounces Haman as the author of the plot to exterminate her people, immediately realize that she is referring to the edict against the Jews and deduce that Esther is a Jewess; or Esther said more than the author tells us. In this dialogue, she does not directly reveal that she is a Jewess.

### 7-10 DOWNFALL AND EXECUTION OF HAMAN

7. *went into the palace garden.* Not for any special purpose, but because his anger made him restless and unable to stay in one place.

*there was evil determined against him.* Haman knew the king well enough to be able to interpret his expressions and his moods.

8. *Haman was fallen.* Prostrating himself to beg for his life. The arrogant bully became, as usually in the face of disaster, a whining coward.

*couch.* On which Esther was reclining during the feast.

*force the queen.* In his blind rage, the king completely misinterprets Haman's posture as one of assault; or perhaps he deliberately misinterprets it, to add to Haman's misery.

*the word.* i.e. the words preceding, from which it was clear to the servants, without any more specific utterance, that Haman was doomed to death.

out of the king's mouth, they covered Haman's face. [9]Then said Harbonah, one of the chamberlains that were before the king: 'Behold also the gallows fifty cubits high, which Haman hath made for Mordecai, who spoke good for the king, standeth in the house of Haman.' And the king said: 'Hang him thereon.' [10]So they hanged Haman on the gallows that he had prepared for Mordecai. Then was the king's wrath assuaged.

יָצָא מִפִּי הַמֶּלֶךְ וּפְנֵי הָמָן
9 חָפוּ׃ וַיֹּאמֶר חַרְבוֹנָה אֶחָד
מִן־הַסָּרִיסִים לִפְנֵי הַמֶּלֶךְ
גַּם הִנֵּה־הָעֵץ אֲשֶׁר־עָשָׂה
הָמָן לְמָרְדֳּכַי אֲשֶׁר דִּבֶּר־
טוֹב עַל־הַמֶּלֶךְ עֹמֵד בְּבֵית
הָמָן גָּבֹהַּ חֲמִשִּׁים אַמָּה וַיֹּאמֶר
10 הַמֶּלֶךְ תְּלֻהוּ עָלָיו׃ וַיִּתְלוּ
אֶת־הָמָן עַל־הָעֵץ אֲשֶׁר־
הֵכִין לְמָרְדֳּכָי וַחֲמַת הַמֶּלֶךְ
שָׁכָכָה׃

## 8 CHAPTER VIII ח

[1]On that day did the king Ahasuerus give the house of Haman the Jews' enemy unto Esther the queen. And Mordecai came before the king;

1 בַּיּוֹם הַהוּא נָתַן הַמֶּלֶךְ
אֲחַשְׁוֵרוֹשׁ לְאֶסְתֵּר הַמַּלְכָּה
אֶת־בֵּית הָמָן צֹרֵר הַיְּהוּדִיִּים
וּמָרְדֳּכַי בָּא לִפְנֵי הַמֶּלֶךְ כִּי־

v. 1. יתיר י׳

*they covered Haman's face.* In token of the sentence of death. This was the practice among the Greeks and the Romans, but it is not elsewhere mentioned of the Persians.

10. *on the gallows . . . for Mordecai.* This is in truth 'measure for measure.'

## CHAPTER VIII

**1-2** MORDECAI MADE FIRST MINISTER

1. *house of Haman. House* here means not only dwelling-place, but all Haman's property. The property of criminals was forfeited to the state.

*came before the king.* Was raised to the rank of high officials *who saw the king's face* (i. 14).

2. The giving of the ring meant the transfer to Mordecai of the power to act in the king's name which had previously belonged to Haman (cf. iii. 10).

for Esther had told what he was unto
her. [2]And the king took off his ring,
which he had taken from Haman, and
gave it unto Mordecai. And Esther
set Mordecai over the house of
Haman.

[3]And Esther spoke yet again before
the king, and fell down at his feet,
and besought him with tears to put
away the mischief of Haman the
Agagite, and his device that he had
devised against the Jews. [4]Then
the king held out to Esther the
golden sceptre. So Esther arose,
and stood before the king. [5]And she
said: 'If it please the king, and if I
have found favour in his sight, and
the thing seem right before the king,
and I be pleasing in his eyes, let it
be written to reverse the letters
devised by Haman the son of Hammedatha the Agagite, which he wrote

הִגִּידָה אֶסְתֵּר מַה הוּא־לָהּ׃
2 וַיָּסַר הַמֶּלֶךְ אֶת־טַבַּעְתּוֹ
אֲשֶׁר הֶעֱבִיר מֵהָמָן וַיִּתְּנָהּ
לְמָרְדֳּכָי וַתָּשֶׂם אֶסְתֵּר אֶת־
מָרְדֳּכַי עַל־בֵּית הָמָן׃
3 וַתּוֹסֶף אֶסְתֵּר וַתְּדַבֵּר לִפְנֵי
הַמֶּלֶךְ וַתִּפֹּל לִפְנֵי רַגְלָיו
וַתֵּבְךְּ וַתִּתְחַנֶּן־לוֹ לְהַעֲבִיר
אֶת־רָעַת הָמָן הָאֲגָגִי וְאֵת
מַחֲשַׁבְתּוֹ אֲשֶׁר חָשַׁב עַל־
4 הַיְּהוּדִים׃ וַיּוֹשֶׁט הַמֶּלֶךְ
לְאֶסְתֵּר אֵת שַׁרְבִט הַזָּהָב
וַתָּקָם אֶסְתֵּר וַתַּעֲמֹד לִפְנֵי
5 הַמֶּלֶךְ׃ וַתֹּאמֶר אִם־עַל־
הַמֶּלֶךְ טוֹב וְאִם־מָצָאתִי חֵן
לְפָנָיו וְכָשֵׁר הַדָּבָר לִפְנֵי
הַמֶּלֶךְ וְטוֹבָה אֲנִי בְּעֵינָיו
יִכָּתֵב לְהָשִׁיב אֶת־הַסְּפָרִים
מַחֲשֶׁבֶת הָמָן בֶּן־הַמְּדָתָא
הָאֲגָגִי אֲשֶׁר כָּתַב לְאַבֵּד אֶת־

**3-7 ESTHER ASKS FOR REVOCATION OF THE DECREE**

3. *mischief of Haman.* Although Haman was dead, his decree against the Jews was still law.

4. *held out . . . sceptre.* It would appear that Esther once more risked her life by going to the king unsummoned. Although Mordecai is now Grand Vizier, it is Esther who makes this further intercession because her influence with the king had been proved, whereas Mordecai's is untested.

5. *to reverse.* Better, 'to revoke.'

*letters devised by Haman.* Esther tactfully tries to represent it as the work of Haman, not of the king. She wishes at the same time to suggest that, as the work of Haman, the decree is revocable.

to destroy the Jews that are in all the
king's provinces; 6for how can I
endure to see the evil that shall come
unto my people? or how can I endure
to see the destruction of my kindred?'

7Then the king Ahasuerus said
unto Esther the queen and to Mordecai the Jew: 'Behold, I have given
Esther the house of Haman, and him
they have hanged upon the gallows,
because he laid his hand upon the
Jews. 8Write ye also concerning the
Jews, as it liketh you, in the king's
name, and seal it with the king's ring;
for the writing which is written in
the king's name, and sealed with the
king's ring, may no man reverse.'
9Then were the king's scribes called

הַיְּהוּדִים אֲשֶׁר בְּכָל־מְדִינוֹת
הַמֶּלֶךְ׃ כִּי אֵיכָכָה אוּכַל 6
וְרָאִיתִי בָּרָעָה אֲשֶׁר־יִמְצָא
אֶת־עַמִּי וְאֵיכָכָה אוּכַל
וְרָאִיתִי בְּאָבְדַן מוֹלַדְתִּי׃
וַיֹּאמֶר הַמֶּלֶךְ אֲחַשְׁוֵרֹשׁ 7
לְאֶסְתֵּר הַמַּלְכָּה וּלְמָרְדֳּכַי
הַיְּהוּדִי הִנֵּה בֵית־הָמָן נָתַתִּי
לְאֶסְתֵּר וְאֹתוֹ תָּלוּ עַל־הָעֵץ
עַל אֲשֶׁר־שָׁלַח יָדוֹ
בַּיְּהוּדִיים׃ וְאַתֶּם כִּתְבוּ עַל־ 8
הַיְּהוּדִים כַּטּוֹב בְּעֵינֵיכֶם
בְּשֵׁם הַמֶּלֶךְ וְחִתְמוּ בְּטַבַּעַת
הַמֶּלֶךְ כִּי־כְתָב אֲשֶׁר־נִכְתָּב
בְּשֵׁם־הַמֶּלֶךְ וְנַחְתּוֹם בְּטַבַּעַת
הַמֶּלֶךְ אֵין לְהָשִׁיב׃ וַיִּקָּרְאוּ 9
סֹפְרֵי־הַמֶּלֶךְ בָּעֵת־הַהִיא

v. 7. יתיר י׳

6. *my people . . . my kindred.* Now that the king knows that Esther is a Jewess, her life is no longer in danger, nor is Mordecai's. Her plea is now only for her *people*, who were her *kindred*.

7. *behold, I have given Esther.* This sentence should be understood, not in the sense of 'I have given you all this: is it not enough for you?' but, 'You see by what I have already done that I am well-disposed to you and ready to grant any request that I can fulfil.'

### 8-14 THE COUNTER-DECREE

8. *also.* i.e. as Haman had written in the king's name.

*may no man reverse.* The king is forced to reject the argument of verse 5 and replies, 'It is impossible to grant your request that the previous decree be revoked, since the king's decrees are irrevocable, and Haman's decree was in my name. But you may devise methods of counteracting and neutralizing it.'

9. This, in the Hebrew, is the longest

at that time, in the third month, which is the month Sivan, on the three and twentieth day thereof; and it was written according to all that Mordecai commanded concerning the Jews, even to the satraps, and the governors and princes of the provinces which are from India unto Ethiopia, a hundred twenty and seven provinces, unto every province according to the writing thereof, and unto every people after their language, and to the Jews according to their writing, and according to their language. [10]And they wrote in the name of king Ahasuerus, and sealed it with the king's ring, and sent letters by posts on horseback, riding on swift steeds that were used in the king's service, bred of the stud; [11]that the king had granted the Jews that were in every city to gather themselves together, and to stand for their life, to destroy, and to slay,

בַּחֹדֶשׁ הַשְּׁלִישִׁי הוּא־חֹדֶשׁ
סִיוָן בִּשְׁלוֹשָׁה וְעֶשְׂרִים בּוֹ
וַיִּכָּתֵב כְּכָל־אֲשֶׁר־צִוָּה
מָרְדֳּכַי אֶל־הַיְּהוּדִים וְאֶל
הָאֲחַשְׁדַּרְפְּנִים וְהַפַּחוֹת וְשָׂרֵי
הַמְּדִינוֹת אֲשֶׁר ׀ מֵהֹדּוּ וְעַד־
כּוּשׁ שֶׁבַע וְעֶשְׂרִים וּמֵאָה
מְדִינָה מְדִינָה וּמְדִינָה
כִּכְתָבָהּ וְעַם וָעָם כִּלְשֹׁנוֹ
וְאֶל־הַיְּהוּדִים כִּכְתָבָם
10 וְכִלְשׁוֹנָם׃ וַיִּכְתֹּב בְּשֵׁם
הַמֶּלֶךְ אֲחַשְׁוֵרֹשׁ וַיַּחְתֹּם
בְּטַבַּעַת הַמֶּלֶךְ וַיִּשְׁלַח
סְפָרִים בְּיַד הָרָצִים בַּסּוּסִים
רֹכְבֵי הָרֶכֶשׁ הָאֲחַשְׁתְּרָנִים
11 בְּנֵי הָרַמָּכִים׃ אֲשֶׁר נָתַן
הַמֶּלֶךְ לַיְּהוּדִים ׀ אֲשֶׁר בְּכָל־
עִיר־וָעִיר לְהִקָּהֵל וְלַעֲמֹד
עַל־נַפְשָׁם לְהַשְׁמִיד לַהֲרֹג

sentence in the Hagiographa, the third section of the Bible.

*and to the Jews.* Naturally, these words are not to be found in the parallel account of the dispatch of Haman's decree. There the Jews, as the victims, were not addressed.

**11.** *that the king had granted the Jews.* The new decree granted the Jews the right of organized self-defence, whereas the previous decree had suggested, at least by implication, that they should submit quietly to slaughter. The knowledge that the king favoured them would strengthen them and weaken the attacks of their enemies. It is to be noted that the right of attack is not granted, only that of defence against *the forces that would assault them.*

and to cause to perish, all the forces of the people and province that would assault them, their little ones and women, and to take the spoil of them for a prey, [12]upon one day in all the provinces of king Ahasuerus, namely, upon the thirteenth day of the twelfth month, which is the month Adar. [13]The copy of the writing, to be given out for a decree in every province, was to be published unto all the peoples, and that the Jews should be ready against that day to avenge themselves on their enemies. [14]So the posts that rode upon swift steeds that were used in the king's service went out, being hastened and pressed on by the king's commandment; and the decree was given out in Shushan the castle.

[15]And Mordecai went forth from the presence of the king in royal apparel of blue and white, and with a great crown of gold, and with a robe of fine linen and purple; and the city of Shushan shouted and was glad. [16]The Jews had light and gladness,

וּלְאַבֵּד אֶת־כָּל־חֵיל עַם
וּמְדִינָה הַצָּרִים אֹתָם טַף
12 וְנָשִׁים וּשְׁלָלָם לָבוֹז׃ בְּיוֹם
אֶחָד בְּכָל־מְדִינוֹת הַמֶּלֶךְ
אֲחַשְׁוֵרוֹשׁ בִּשְׁלוֹשָׁה עָשָׂר
לְחֹדֶשׁ שְׁנֵים־עָשָׂר הוּא־
13 חֹדֶשׁ אֲדָר׃ פַּתְשֶׁגֶן הַכְּתָב
לְהִנָּתֵן דָּת בְּכָל־מְדִינָה
וּמְדִינָה גָּלוּי לְכָל־הָעַמִּים
וְלִהְיוֹת הַיְּהוּדִיִּים עֲתוֹדִים
לַיּוֹם הַזֶּה לְהִנָּקֵם מֵאֹיְבֵיהֶם׃
14 הָרָצִים רֹכְבֵי הָרֶכֶשׁ
הָאֲחַשְׁתְּרָנִים יָצְאוּ מְבֹהָלִים
וּדְחוּפִים בִּדְבַר הַמֶּלֶךְ וְהַדָּת
נִתְּנָה בְּשׁוּשַׁן הַבִּירָה׃
15 וּמָרְדֳּכַי יָצָא | מִלִּפְנֵי הַמֶּלֶךְ
בִּלְבוּשׁ מַלְכוּת תְּכֵלֶת וָחוּר
וַעֲטֶרֶת זָהָב גְּדוֹלָה וְתַכְרִיךְ
בּוּץ וְאַרְגָּמָן וְהָעִיר שׁוּשָׁן
16 צָהֲלָה וְשָׂמֵחָה׃ לַיְּהוּדִים
הָיְתָה אוֹרָה וְשִׂמְחָה וְשָׂשֹׂן

v. 13. יתיר י׳ v. 13. עתידים ק׳

15-17 RELIEF OF THE JEWS

15. *and the city of Shushan shouted and was glad.* This can hardly be, as it may seem at first sight, the converse of *but the city of Shushan was perplexed* (iii. 15). Nor is the intention that the inhabitants of Susa shouted with joy because the Jews were saved. More probably the reference is to the shoutings which greeted Mordecai as he left the palace as Grand Vizier.

16. *the Jews had . . . honour.* These words are included in the home service

and joy and honour. [17]And in every province, and in every city, whithersoever the king's commandment and his decree came, the Jews had gladness and joy, a feast and a good day. And many from among the peoples of the land became Jews; for the fear of the Jews was fallen upon them.

17 וִיקָר׃ וּבְכָל־מְדִינָה וּמְדִינָה
וּבְכָל־עִיר וָעִיר מְקוֹם אֲשֶׁר
דְּבַר־הַמֶּלֶךְ וְדָתוֹ מַגִּיעַ
שִׂמְחָה וְשָׂשׂוֹן לַיְּהוּדִים מִשְׁתֶּה
וְיוֹם טוֹב וְרַבִּים מֵעַמֵּי הָאָרֶץ
מִתְיַהֲדִים כִּי־נָפַל פַּחַד־
הַיְּהוּדִים עֲלֵיהֶם׃

## 9 CHAPTER IX ט

[1]Now in the twelfth month, which is the month Adar, on the thirteenth day of the same, when the king's commandment and his decree drew near to be put in execution, in the day that the enemies of the Jews hoped to have rule over them; whereas it was turned to the contrary, that the Jews had rule over them that hated them; [2]the Jews gathered themselves together in their cities throughout all the provinces

1 וּבִשְׁנֵים עָשָׂר חֹדֶשׁ הוּא־חֹדֶשׁ
אֲדָר בִּשְׁלוֹשָׁה עָשָׂר יוֹם בּוֹ
אֲשֶׁר הִגִּיעַ דְּבַר־הַמֶּלֶךְ וְדָתוֹ
לְהֵעָשׂוֹת בַּיּוֹם אֲשֶׁר שִׂבְּרוּ
אֹיְבֵי הַיְּהוּדִים לִשְׁלוֹט בָּהֶם
וְנַהֲפוֹךְ הוּא אֲשֶׁר יִשְׁלְטוּ
הַיְּהוּדִים הֵמָּה בְּשֹׂנְאֵיהֶם׃
2 נִקְהֲלוּ הַיְּהוּדִים בְּעָרֵיהֶם

at the termination of the Sabbath, with the addition of 'So be it with us' (*P.B.*, p. 216).

**17.** *good day*. The Hebrew *yom tov* is not to be taken in the post-Biblical sense of Holy Day or Festival, but in its literal sense of good or happy day. May it be that this is the source of the phrase *yom tov* as now used? Apart from this Book, the words are found in the Bible only in 1 Sam. xxv. 8.

*became Jews*. The Hebrew verb is a denominative from *Yehudi*, 'Jew.' Since nowhere else, either in the Bible or in Rabbinic Hebrew, is this verb used to denote proselytization, it may be argued with some reason that a better translation is 'took the part of the Jews.'

## CHAPTER IX

**1-10** THE JEWS SLAY THEIR ENEMIES

**2.** *in their cities*. The cities in which Jews lived.

**3.** *helped the Jews*. Mordecai, as Grand Vizier, would have the power of dismissing and even punishing any of the king's officers who did otherwise.

of the king Ahasuerus, to lay hand
on such as sought their hurt; and
no man could withstand them; for
the fear of them was fallen upon all
the peoples. 3And all the princes of
the provinces, and the satraps, and
the governors, and they that did the
king's business, helped the Jews;
because the fear of Mordecai was
fallen upon them. 4For Mordecai
was great in the king's house, and
his fame went forth throughout all
the provinces; for the man Mordecai
waxed greater and greater. 5And
the Jews smote all their enemies with
the stroke of the sword, and with
slaughter and destruction, and did
what they would unto them that
hated them. 6And in Shushan the
castle the Jews slew and destroyed

בְּכָל־מְדִינוֹת הַמֶּלֶךְ
אֲחַשְׁוֵרוֹשׁ לִשְׁלֹחַ יָד בִּמְבַקְשֵׁי
רָעָתָם וְאִישׁ לֹא־עָמַד
בִּפְנֵיהֶם כִּי־נָפַל פַּחְדָּם
3 עַל־כָּל־הָעַמִּים׃ וְכָל־
שָׂרֵי הַמְּדִינוֹת וְהָאֲחַשְׁדַּרְפְּנִים
וְהַפַּחוֹת וְעֹשֵׂי הַמְּלָאכָה אֲשֶׁר
לַמֶּלֶךְ מְנַשְּׂאִים אֶת־
הַיְּהוּדִים כִּי־נָפַל פַּחַד־
4 מָרְדֳּכַי עֲלֵיהֶם׃ כִּי־גָדוֹל
מָרְדֳּכַי בְּבֵית הַמֶּלֶךְ וְשָׁמְעוֹ
הוֹלֵךְ בְּכָל־הַמְּדִינוֹת כִּי־
הָאִישׁ מָרְדֳּכַי הוֹלֵךְ וְגָדוֹל׃
5 וַיַּכּוּ הַיְּהוּדִים בְּכָל־אֹיְבֵיהֶם
מַכַּת־חֶרֶב וְהֶרֶג וְאַבְדָן
וַיַּעֲשׂוּ בְשֹׂנְאֵיהֶם כִּרְצוֹנָם׃
6 וּבְשׁוּשַׁן הַבִּירָה הָרְגוּ
הַיְּהוּדִים וְאַבֵּד חֲמֵשׁ מֵאוֹת
אִישׁ׃

6. *five hundred men.* Probably the Jews of Shushan concentrated on such enemies as were to be found in the fortress, as being the most dangerous; or perhaps the known enemies of the Jews sought to protect themselves in the fortress, thinking that in the palace quarter they would be safe.

five hundred men. [7]And Parshan-
datha, and Dalphon, and Aspatha,
[8]and Poratha, and Adalia, and
Aridatha, [9]and Parmashta, and
Arisai, and Aridai, and Vaizatha,
[10]the ten sons of Haman the son of
Hammedatha, the Jews' enemy, slew
they; but on the spoil they laid not
their hand.

[11]On that day the number of those
that were slain in Shushan the castle
was brought before the king. [12]And
the king said unto Esther the queen:
'The Jews have slain and destroyed
five hundred men in Shushan the

וְאֵ֣ת ׀ 7
פַּרְשַׁנְדָּ֑תָא וְאֵ֣ת ׀
דַּלְפ֖וֹן וְאֵ֥ת ׀
אַסְפָּֽתָא׃ וְאֵ֣ת ׀ 8
פּוֹרָ֑תָא וְאֵ֥ת ׀
אֲדַלְיָ֖א וְאֵ֥ת ׀
אֲרִידָֽתָא׃ וְאֵ֣ת ׀ 9
פַּרְמַשְׁתָּ֑א וְאֵ֣ת ׀
אֲרִיסַ֔י וְאֵ֥ת ׀
אֲרִידַ֖י וְאֵ֥ת ׀
וַיְזָֽתָא׃ עֲ֠שֶׂרֶת 10
בְּנֵ֨י הָמָ֧ן בֶּֽן־הַמְּדָ֛תָא צֹרֵ֥ר
הַיְּהוּדִ֖ים הָרָ֑גוּ וּבַּבִּזָּ֕ה לֹ֥א
שָֽׁלְח֖וּ אֶת־יָדָֽם׃ בַּיּ֣וֹם הַה֗וּא 11
בָּ֣א מִסְפַּ֧ר הַהֲרוּגִ֛ים בְּשׁוּשַׁ֥ן
הַבִּירָ֖ה לִפְנֵ֥י הַמֶּֽלֶךְ׃ וַיֹּ֨אמֶר 12
הַמֶּ֜לֶךְ לְאֶסְתֵּ֣ר הַמַּלְכָּ֗ה
בְּשׁוּשַׁ֣ן הַבִּירָ֡ה הָרְגוּ֩ הַיְּהוּדִ֨ים

v. 7. ס"א ש' זעירא ת' זעירא v. 9. ס"א ר' זעירא ש' ות' זעירא v. 9. ו' רבתי v. 9. ז' זעירא

**7-9.** The Massorah prescribes that the names of the ten sons of Haman be written in a perpendicular column on the right-hand side of the page, with the *vav*, i.e. *and*, on the left-hand side. This is probably derived from the tradition that the ten sons were hanged on a tall gallows, one above the other. It is also customary in the reading of the Megillah on Purim, to read the names of the ten sons and the word *ten* in one breath, 'because they all died together' (Talmud).

**10.** *on the spoil they laid not their hand,* The Jews had but one thought, viz. self-protection and this piece of information stresses the fact.

### 11-17 A SECOND DAY GRANTED TO THE JEWS OF SUSA

**11.** *the number.* There must have been quite a highly developed system of civic organization in Susa for the number of casualties to be known on the same day.

castle, and the ten sons of Haman; what then have they done in the rest of the king's provinces! Now whatever thy petition, it shall be granted thee; and whatever thy request further, it shall be done.'
13 Then said Esther: 'If it please the king, let it be granted to the Jews that are in Shushan to do to-morrow also according unto this day's decree, and let Haman's ten sons be hanged upon the gallows.'
14 And the king commanded it so to be done; and a decree was given out in Shushan; and they hanged Haman's ten sons.
15 And the Jews that were in Shushan gathered themselves together on the fourteenth day also of the month Adar, and slew three hundred men in Shushan; but on the spoil they laid not their hand.

16 And the other Jews that were in the king's provinces gathered themselves together, and stood for their

וְאַבֵּ֗ד חֲמֵ֤שׁ מֵאוֹת֙ אִ֔ישׁ וְאֵת֙
עֲשֶׂ֣רֶת בְּנֵי־הָמָ֔ן בִּשְׁאָ֛ר
מְדִינ֥וֹת הַמֶּ֖לֶךְ מֶ֣ה עָשׂ֑וּ וּמַה־
שְּׁאֵלָתֵךְ֙ וְיִנָּ֣תֵֽן לָ֔ךְ וּמַה־
13 בַּקָּשָׁתֵ֥ךְ ע֖וֹד וְתֵעָֽשׂ׃ וַתֹּ֤אמֶר
אֶסְתֵּר֙ אִם־עַל־הַמֶּ֣לֶךְ ט֔וֹב
יִנָּתֵ֣ן גַּם־מָחָ֗ר לַיְּהוּדִים֙ אֲשֶׁ֣ר
בְּשׁוּשָׁ֔ן לַעֲשׂ֖וֹת כְּדָ֣ת הַיּ֑וֹם
וְאֵ֛ת עֲשֶׂ֥רֶת בְּנֵי־הָמָ֖ן יִתְל֥וּ
14 עַל־הָעֵֽץ׃ וַיֹּ֤אמֶר הַמֶּ֙לֶךְ֙
לְהֵעָשׂ֣וֹת כֵּ֔ן וַתִּנָּתֵ֥ן דָּ֖ת בְּשׁוּשָׁ֑ן
וְאֵ֛ת עֲשֶׂ֥רֶת בְּנֵי־הָמָ֖ן תָּלֽוּ׃
15 וַיִּקָּהֲל֞וּ הַיְּהוּדִ֣יים* אֲשֶׁר־
בְּשׁוּשָׁ֗ן גַּ֠ם בְּי֨וֹם אַרְבָּעָ֤ה עָשָׂר֙
לְחֹ֣דֶשׁ אֲדָ֔ר וַיַּֽהַרְג֣וּ בְשׁוּשָׁ֔ן
שְׁלֹ֥שׁ מֵא֖וֹת אִ֑ישׁ וּבַ֨בִּזָּ֔ה לֹ֥א
16 שָׁלְח֖וּ אֶת־יָדָֽם׃ וּשְׁאָ֣ר
הַיְּהוּדִ֡ים אֲשֶׁר֩ בִּמְדִינ֨וֹת
הַמֶּ֜לֶךְ נִקְהֲל֣וּ ׀ וְעָמֹ֣ד עַל־

v. 15. יתיר י׳

**13.** *according unto this day's decree.* To avenge themselves on their enemies. A second day may have been necessary in Susa, which, as the chief capital, was probably the centre of anti-Jewish feeling, for the Jews to free themselves from all danger of further persecution.

*be hanged.* Impalement (see on v. 14) after death was a great degradation.

**15.** *three hundred men.* This number, for the whole city of Susa, is small compared with the 500 killed in the fortress alone on the first day. It proves further that the Jews did not kill indiscriminately, but only those known to be hostile.

**16.** *gathered themselves together, and stood.* Better, 'had gathered themselves together and had stood.' These verses are not a continuation of the narrative, but a supplementary statement.

lives, and had rest from their
enemies, and slew of them that
hated them seventy and five thousand—but on the spoil they laid not
their hand—[17]on the thirteenth day
of the month Adar, and on the fourteenth day of the same they rested,
and made it a day of feasting and
gladness. [18]But the Jews that were
in Shushan assembled together on
the thirteenth day thereof, and on
the fourteenth thereof; and on the
fifteenth day of the same they rested,
and made it a day of feasting and
gladness. [19]Therefore do the Jews
of the villages, that dwell in the un-
walled towns, make the fourteenth
day of the month Adar a day of
gladness and feasting, and a good day,
and of sending portions one to
another.

[20]And Mordecai wrote these things,
and sent letters unto all the Jews that

נַפְשָׁם וְנוֹחַ מֵאֹיְבֵיהֶם וְהָרוֹג
בְּשֹׂנְאֵיהֶם חֲמִשָּׁה וְשִׁבְעִים
אָלֶף וּבַבִּזָּה לֹא שָׁלְחוּ אֶת־
17 יָדָם׃ בְּיוֹם־שְׁלוֹשָׁה עָשָׂר
לְחֹדֶשׁ אֲדָר וְנוֹחַ בְּאַרְבָּעָה
עָשָׂר בּוֹ וְעָשֹׂה אֹתוֹ יוֹם מִשְׁתֶּה
18 וְשִׂמְחָה׃ וְהַיְּהוּדִיים אֲשֶׁר־
בְּשׁוּשָׁן נִקְהֲלוּ בִּשְׁלוֹשָׁה עָשָׂר
בּוֹ וּבְאַרְבָּעָה עָשָׂר בּוֹ וְנוֹחַ
בַּחֲמִשָּׁה עָשָׂר בּוֹ וְעָשֹׂה אֹתוֹ
19 יוֹם מִשְׁתֶּה וְשִׂמְחָה׃ עַל־כֵּן
הַיְּהוּדִים הַפְּרוֹזִים הַיֹּשְׁבִים
בְּעָרֵי הַפְּרָזוֹת עֹשִׂים אֵת יוֹם
אַרְבָּעָה עָשָׂר לְחֹדֶשׁ אֲדָר
שִׂמְחָה וּמִשְׁתֶּה וְיוֹם טוֹב
וּמִשְׁלֹחַ מָנוֹת אִישׁ לְרֵעֵהוּ׃
20 וַיִּכְתֹּב מָרְדֳּכַי אֶת־הַדְּבָרִים
הָאֵלֶּה וַיִּשְׁלַח סְפָרִים אֶל־
כָּל־הַיְּהוּדִים אֲשֶׁר בְּכָל־

v. 18. יתיר י׳ v. 19. יתיר ו׳

**18-19** FIRST MENTION OF THE FEAST OF PURIM

**19.** After this verse we would expect another verse giving the law of 'Shushan Purim,' that those who dwell in walled cities keep the 15th of Adar. The law of Shushan Purim is not explicitly stated in the Megillah, but is implied in verses 19 and 21. The Rabbis determined that cities walled since the days of Joshua were under the obligation to observe Purim on the 15th of Adar.

*portions.* Gifts of foodstuffs. At least two kinds of foodstuffs should constitute the gift (Talmud).

were in all the provinces of the king
Ahasuerus, both nigh and far, 21to
enjoin them that they should keep
the fourteenth day of the month
Adar, and the fifteenth day of the
same, yearly, 22the days wherein the
Jews had rest from their enemies,
and the month which was turned
unto them from sorrow to gladness,
and from mourning into a good day;
that they should make them days of
feasting and gladness, and of sending
portions one to another, and gifts to
the poor. 23And the Jews took upon
them to do as they had begun, and
as Mordecai had written unto them;
24because Haman the son of Hammedatha, the Agagite, the enemy of
all the Jews, had devised against the
Jews to destroy them, and had cast

מְדִינוֹת הַמֶּלֶךְ אֲחַשְׁוֵרוֹשׁ
21 הַקְּרוֹבִים וְהָרְחוֹקִים׃ לְקַיֵּם
עֲלֵיהֶם לִהְיוֹת עֹשִׂים אֵת יוֹם
אַרְבָּעָה עָשָׂר לְחֹדֶשׁ אֲדָר
וְאֵת יוֹם־חֲמִשָּׁה עָשָׂר בּוֹ
22 בְּכָל־שָׁנָה וְשָׁנָה׃ כַּיָּמִים
אֲשֶׁר־נָחוּ בָהֶם הַיְּהוּדִים
מֵאֹיְבֵיהֶם וְהַחֹדֶשׁ אֲשֶׁר נֶהְפַּךְ
לָהֶם מִיָּגוֹן לְשִׂמְחָה וּמֵאֵבֶל
לְיוֹם טוֹב לַעֲשׂוֹת אוֹתָם יְמֵי
מִשְׁתֶּה וְשִׂמְחָה וּמִשְׁלוֹחַ מָנוֹת
אִישׁ לְרֵעֵהוּ וּמַתָּנוֹת
23 לָאֶבְיוֹנִים׃ וְקִבֵּל הַיְּהוּדִים
אֵת אֲשֶׁר־הֵחֵלּוּ לַעֲשׂוֹת וְאֵת
אֲשֶׁר־כָּתַב מָרְדֳּכַי אֲלֵיהֶם׃
24 כִּי הָמָן בֶּן־הַמְּדָתָא הָאֲגָגִי
צֹרֵר כָּל־הַיְּהוּדִים חָשַׁב
עַל־הַיְּהוּדִים לְאַבְּדָם וְהִפִּל

**20-23 MORDECAI'S LETTER INSTITUTING THE TWO DAYS OF PURIM**

**20.** *these things.* Rashi understands the phrase as referring to the whole Book, and considers Mordecai to have been the author of *Esther*. But the words need not have this meaning, and a better translation is 'the following words.'

**22.** *gifts to the poor.* This feature of the celebration of Purim is the sole addition which Mordecai prescribed to the spontaneous celebration which the Jews observed in the year of their salvation (verse 19). It is a characteristically Jewish addition; a thought for the needy has to accompany every occasion of rejoicing. Gifts should be given to at least two poor persons (Talmud).

**23.** *as they had begun.* Spontaneously in the year of their deliverance.

pur, that is, the lot, to discomfit them, and to destroy them; [25]but when [a]she came before the king, he commanded by letters that his wicked device, which he had devised against the Jews, should return upon his own head; and that he and his sons should be hanged on the gallows. [26]Wherefore they called these days Purim, after the name of pur. Therefore because of all the words of this letter, and of that which they had seen concerning this matter, and that which had come unto them, [27]the Jews ordained, and took upon them, and upon their seed, and upon all such as joined themselves unto them, so as it should not fail, that they would keep these two days according to the writing thereof, and according to the appointed

[a]That is, Esther.

פּוּר הוּא הַגּוֹרָל לְהֻמָּם
25 וּלְאַבְּדָם׃ וּבְבֹאָהּ לִפְנֵי
הַמֶּלֶךְ אָמַר עִם־הַסֵּפֶר יָשׁוּב
מַחֲשַׁבְתּוֹ הָרָעָה אֲשֶׁר־חָשַׁב
עַל־הַיְּהוּדִים עַל־רֹאשׁוֹ
וְתָלוּ אֹתוֹ וְאֶת־בָּנָיו עַל־
26 הָעֵץ׃ עַל־כֵּן קָרְאוּ לַיָּמִים
הָאֵלֶּה פוּרִים עַל־שֵׁם הַפּוּר
עַל־כֵּן עַל־כָּל־דִּבְרֵי
הָאִגֶּרֶת הַזֹּאת וּמָה־רָאוּ עַל־
כָּכָה וּמָה הִגִּיעַ אֲלֵיהֶם׃
27 קִיְּמוּ וְקִבְּלֻ* הַיְּהוּדִים ׀
עֲלֵיהֶם ׀ וְעַל־זַרְעָם וְעַל
כָּל־הַנִּלְוִים עֲלֵיהֶם וְלֹא
יַעֲבוֹר לִהְיוֹת עֹשִׂים אֶת־שְׁנֵי
הַיָּמִים הָאֵלֶּה כִּכְתָבָם
וְכִזְמַנָּם בְּכָל־שָׁנָה וְשָׁנָה׃

v. 27. וקבלו ק׳

**24-28** A BRIEF SUMMARY OF THE EPISODE

**25.** *that he and his sons should be hanged.* The story is, as it were, telescoped. The words are not to be taken to mean that Haman and his sons were hanged at the same time.

**26.** *that which they had seen.* Their personal experience of being saved, as much as Mordecai's injunction, made them anxious to accept Purim as a permanent feast. The personal experience of persecution has given added significance to Purim to many of those who have escaped from Europe in our days. To the oppressed it brings a message of hope.

**27.** *joined themselves.* As proselytes.

*according to the writing thereof.* A better sense is obtained by translating 'in accordance with the letter that prescribed them.' In addition to the feasting and gladness, sending of portions and gifts to the poor, which are prescribed in the Megillah, the following observances are obligatory on Purim: the reading of the Megillah, evening and morning, with its accompanying blessings and hymns (women are obliged to attend the reading, since it was through a woman that the deliverance was accomplished), and one festive meal towards the evening of the

time thereof, every year; 28and that
these days should be remembered
and kept throughout every generation, every family, every province,
and every city; and that these days
of Purim should not fail from among
the Jews, nor the memorial of them
perish from their seed.

29Then Esther the queen, the
daughter of Abihail, and Mordecai
the Jew, wrote down all the acts of
power, to confirm this second letter
of Purim. 30And he sent letters unto

28 וְהַיָּמִים הָאֵלֶּה נִזְכָּרִים
וְנַעֲשִׂים בְּכָל־דּוֹר וָדוֹר
מִשְׁפָּחָה וּמִשְׁפָּחָה מְדִינָה
וּמְדִינָה וְעִיר וָעִיר וִימֵי
הַפּוּרִים הָאֵלֶּה לֹא יַעַבְרוּ
מִתּוֹךְ הַיְּהוּדִים וְזִכְרָם לֹא־
29 יָסוּף מִזַּרְעָם׃ וַתִּכְתֹּב
אֶסְתֵּר הַמַּלְכָּה בַת־אֲבִיחַיִל
וּמָרְדֳּכַי הַיְּהוּדִי אֶת־כָּל־
תֹּקֶף לְקַיֵּם אֶת־אִגֶּרֶת
30 הַפֻּרִים הַזֹּאת הַשֵּׁנִית׃ וַיִּשְׁלַח

v. 29. ת רבתי

fourteenth (*Se'udath Purim*). The Megillah is read with a traditional chant which is distinct from that used in reading the Pentateuch or the Haphtarah. In the course of the centuries, as well, many more observances became customary, e.g. special cakes (Hamantaschen), masquerading, Purim plays, hissing, stamping and rattling (with the 'gregar,' Purim rattle) at the mention of the name of Haman during the reading of the Megillah, the burning of Haman in effigy and all kinds of merry-making, often verging on frivolity—so that among the masses it became almost a general rule that 'on Purim everything is allowed.' (For a more detailed account of these customs, see the Jewish Encyclopædia, under 'Purim.')

28. *remembered.* By reading the Megillah (Rashi).

*kept.* With feast, gladness, portions and gifts (Rashi).

*should not fail.* 'Even if all the Festivals should be annulled, Purim will never be annulled' (Midrash).

*nor the memorial of them perish.* 'We learn from this that the Book of Esther will never be abolished' (Palestinian Talmud).

### 29-32 ESTHER ADDS HER AUTHORITY TO MORDECAI'S

29. *wrote down all the acts of power.* Better, 'wrote with all power,' meaning either, with all emphasis, or, with all the authority of their position.

*this second letter.* The contents of which are given in verse 31. Apparently, a second message instituting Purim was sent out, this time Esther associating herself with it and confirming it. Rashi suggests that the second letter was a reminder sent out in the following year.

*letter.* Therefore it has become customary to unroll the whole Megillah before reading it, to give the appearance of a letter.

all the Jews, to the hundred twenty and seven provinces of the kingdom of Ahasuerus, with words of peace and truth, [31]to confirm these days of Purim in their appointed times, according as Mordecai the Jew and Esther the queen had enjoined them, and as they had ordained for themselves and for their seed, the matters of the fastings and their cry. [32]And the commandment of Esther confirmed these matters of Purim; and it was written in the book.

סְפָרִ֜ים אֶל־כָּל־הַיְּהוּדִ֗ים
אֶל־שֶׁ֨בַע וְעֶשְׂרִ֤ים וּמֵאָה֙
מְדִינָ֔ה מַלְכ֖וּת אֲחַשְׁוֵר֑וֹשׁ
31 דִּבְרֵ֥י שָׁל֖וֹם וֶאֱמֶֽת׃ לְקַיֵּ֡ם
אֶת־יְמֵי֩ הַפֻּרִ֨ים הָאֵ֜לֶּה
בִּזְמַנֵּיהֶ֗ם כַּאֲשֶׁר֩ קִיַּ֨ם עֲלֵיהֶ֜ם
מָרְדֳּכַ֤י הַיְּהוּדִי֙ וְאֶסְתֵּ֣ר
הַמַּלְכָּ֔ה וְכַאֲשֶׁ֛ר קִיְּמ֥וּ עַל־
נַפְשָׁ֖ם וְעַל־זַרְעָ֑ם דִּבְרֵ֥י
32 הַצּוֹמ֖וֹת וְזַעֲקָתָֽם׃ וּמַאֲמַ֣ר
אֶסְתֵּ֔ר קִיַּ֕ם דִּבְרֵ֥י הַפֻּרִ֖ים
הָאֵ֑לֶּה וְנִכְתָּ֖ב בַּסֵּֽפֶר׃

## 10 CHAPTER X י

[1]And the king Ahasuerus laid a tribute upon the land, and upon the isles of the sea. [2]And all the acts of

1 וַיָּשֶׂם֩ הַמֶּ֨לֶךְ אֲחַשְׁרֹ֥שׁ ׀ מַ֛ס
2 עַל־הָאָ֖רֶץ וְאִיֵּ֥י הַיָּֽם׃ וְכָל־

v. 1. אחשורוש ק׳

**30.** *with words of peace and truth.* i.e. with a message of sincere greeting.

**31.** *the fastings.* Cf. iv. 16.

*their cry.* Cf. iv. 3.

**32.** *it was written in the book.* Some Jewish commentators take this to refer to the Book of Esther. But probably the phrase means no more than 'it was committed to writing.'

## CHAPTER X

GREATNESS OF AHASUERUS AND MORDECAI

This chapter is an appendix or postscript to the Book, emphasizing the power of Ahasuerus and the glory which was thereby reflected on Mordecai as his first minister. The thought is: Ahasuerus, whose prime minister Mordecai was, could command the service of the continent of Asia and the coast of the Mediterranean (Streane).

his power and of his might, and the
full account of the greatness of Mordecai, how the king advanced him,
are they not written in the book of
the chronicles of the kings of Media
and Persia? 3 For Mordecai the Jew
was next unto king Ahasuerus, and
great among the Jews, and accepted
of the multitude of his brethren;
seeking the good of his people and
speaking peace to all his seed.

מַעֲשֵׂה תָקְפּוֹ וּגְבוּרָתוֹ וּפָרָשַׁת
גְּדֻלַּת מָרְדֳּכַי אֲשֶׁר גִּדְּלוֹ
הַמֶּלֶךְ הֲלוֹא־הֵם כְּתוּבִים
עַל־סֵפֶר דִּבְרֵי הַיָּמִים
3 לְמַלְכֵי מָדַי וּפָרָס׃ כִּי ׀
מָרְדֳּכַי הַיְּהוּדִי מִשְׁנֶה לַמֶּלֶךְ
אֲחַשְׁוֵרוֹשׁ וְגָדוֹל לַיְּהוּדִים
וְרָצוּי לְרֹב אֶחָיו דֹּרֵשׁ טוֹב
לְעַמּוֹ וְדֹבֵר שָׁלוֹם לְכָל־
זַרְעוֹ׃

1. *tribute.* Since the Hebrew word everywhere else means 'forced labour,' a better translation is 'imposed forced labour.'

*isles of the sea.* The coast-lands of the eastern Mediterranean, with their adjacent islands.

2. *book of the chronicles.* This is not necessarily identical with the royal diary mentioned in ii. 23 and vi. 1. Some history of the Medo-Persian kings is apparently meant, of a similar nature to the *books of the chronicles* of the kings of Israel and Judah, which are so frequently referred to in Kings and Chronicles.

3. *for Mordecai the Jew was next.* This is the reason why so much is said about him in the *book of the chronicles.*

*seeking the good of his people.* In his high position, he did not forget his kinsmen, but constantly laboured for their good.

*speaking peace.* A Hebrew idiom with the meaning, 'caring for the welfare of' (Ps. lxxxv. 9). Thus the Book closes with a pleasant picture of the happiness and prosperity of the Jews under the beneficent rule of their co-religionist (Paton).

*Authorities quoted*

*Terms and Abbreviations*

*Index*

## AUTHORITIES QUOTED

Aboth—*Pirke Aboth, Sayings of the Fathers:* Mishnaic tractate.

Adeney, W. F. (Christian Hebraist), *Lamentations* (The Expositor's Bible), *Jeremiah and Lamentations* (The Pulpit Commentary), *Esther* (The Expositor's Bible).

Alshich, Moses (Bible Commentator and Preacher, second half of the 16th century).

Baeck, L. (Jewish Theologian), *The Essence of Judaism.*

Barton, G. A. (Christian Hebraist), *The Book of Ecclesiastes* (International Critical Commentary).

Benjamin of Tudela (Jewish Traveller, 12th century).

Bertheau, E. (Christian Hebraist), *Das Buch der Richter und Ruth.*

Breuer, R. (Jewish Commentator), *Die fünf Megilloth.*

Cassell, P. (Christian Hebraist), *An Explanatory Commentary on Ruth.*

Cheyne, T. K. (Christian Hebraist), *Job and Solomon.*

Cook, F. C. (Christian Hebraist), *The Holy Bible with Commentary.*

Davies, T. Witton (Christian Hebraist), *Esther* (The Century Bible).

Delitzsch, Franz (Christian Hebraist), *Commentary on Ecclesiastes.*

Devine, M. (Christian Theologian), *Ecclesiastes, or The Confessions of an Adventurous Soul.*

Driver, S. R. (Christian Hebraist), *An Introduction to the Literature of the Old Testament.*

Ehrlich, A. B. (Bible Exegete), *Randglossen zur hebräischen Bibel.*

Eisenstadt, J. D. (Jewish Encyclopædist), *Otsar Yisrael.*

Eitan, I. (Jewish Orientalist), *A Contribution to Biblical Lexicography.*

Gesenius, W. (Christian Grammarian and Lexicographer).

Ginsburg, C. D. (Christian Hebraist), *Commentary on the Song of Songs, Commentary on Ecclesiastes.*

Grätz, H. (Jewish Historian and Exegete).

Harper, A. (Christian Hebraist), *The Song of Songs* (The Cambridge Bible).

Hastings, J. (Christian Bible Scholar), *The Greater Men and Women of the Bible.*

Herder, J. G. (German Authority on Literature).

Herodotus (Greek Historian, 5th century B.C.E.)

How, J. C. H. (Christian Hebraist), *Esther* in Gore's *New Commentary on the Holy Scriptures.*

Ibn Ezra, Abraham (1092-1167, Bible Commentator).

Ibn Gabirol, Solomon (1022-1069, Poet and Ethicist), *Choice of Pearls.*

Ibn Yachya, Joseph ben David (1494-1539, Bible Commentator).

Jastrow, M. (Jewish Orientalist), *A Gentle Cynic.*

Jehudah Halevi (1085-1142, Poet and Philosopher).

Josephus, Flavius (Jewish Historian, 1st century C.E.).

Keil, K. F. (Christian Hebraist), *Commentar über den alten Testament.*
Kimchi, David (1160-1235, Bible Commentator).
Klausner, J. (Jewish Historian).

Levine, I. (Anglo-Jewish Philosopher), *Faithful Rebels.*

Maclaren, A. (Christian Exegete), *Expositions of Holy Scripture.*
Maimonides, Moses (1135-1204, Jewish Philosopher), *Guide for the Perplexed.*
Malbim, M. L. (1809-1879, Jewish Commentator).
Martin, G. C. (Christian Hebraist), *Ecclesiastes* (The Century Bible).
Metsudath David ('Tower of David'), Hebrew Commentary on Books of the Bible by David Altschul (17th century).
Midrash—Rabbinic Homilies on the Pentateuch, etc.
Moffatt, J. (Christian Bible Translator), *The Old Testament: A New Translation.*

Nowack, W. (Christian Hebraist), *Handkommentar zum alten Testament.*

Paton, L. B. (Christian Hebraist), *Esther* (International Critical Commentary).
Plumptre, E. H. (Christian Hebraist), *Ecclesiastes* (The Cambridge Bible).

Ralbag (Rabbi Levi ben Gershon, 1288-1344, Bible Commentator and Philosopher).
Rashbam (Rabbi Samuel ben Meir, 12th-century Bible Commentator).
Rashi (Rabbi Solomon ben Isaac, 1040-1105, Bible Commentator).
Rawlinson, G. (Christian Hebraist), *Esther* (The Pulpit Commentary).
Renan, E. (French Orientalist).
Robinson, E. (Bible Scholar and Traveller in the East), *Biblical Researches.*

Saadia (882-942, Bible Exegete and Philosopher).
Samuel ibn Tibbon (1160-1230, Jewish Philosopher).
Schechter, S. (Jewish Theologian), *Studies in Judaism.*
Septuagint—Greek Translation of the Bible, begun in the 3rd century B.C.E.
Sforno, Obadiah (1475-1550, Bible Commentator).
Streane, A. W. (Christian Hebraist), *Jeremiah and Lamentations* (The Cambridge Bible), *Esther* (The Cambridge Bible).

Talmud—Corpus of Jewish Law and Thought (compiled at the end of the 5th century C.E.).
Targum—Aramaic Translation of the Bible (1st and 2nd centuries C.E.).
Thatcher, G. W. (Christian Hebraist), *Ruth* (The Century Bible).
Tristram, H. B. (Natural Scientist), *The Natural History of the Bible.*

Vulgate—Latin Translation of the Bible by Jerome (4th century C.E.).

Watson, R. A. (Christian Hebraist), *Ruth* (The Expositor's Bible).
Williams, A. Lukyn (Christian Hebraist), *Ecclesiastes* (The Cambridge Bible, revised edition).
Wright, C. H. H. (Christian Hebraist), *Ruth.*

Yahuda, A. S. (Jewish Orientalist).
Yavets, Isaac (Bible Commentator and Preacher, second half of the 16th century), *Torath Chesed.*

## TERMS AND ABBREVIATIONS

A.J. American-Jewish translation of the Scriptures.

A.V. Authorized Version.

B.B. *Baba Bathra*, Talmudical tractate.

B.C.E. Before the Christian era.

C.E. Common era.

cf. Compare, refer to.

ch. chapter.

Ecclus. Apocryphal Book of Ecclesiasticus.

e.g. For example.

f. Following verse or chapter (plural ff.).

fem. Feminine.

i.e. That is.

*kerë*. The Hebrew as it is to be read according to the Masoretes.

*kethib*. The Hebrew as it is written according to tradition.

lit. Literally.

LXX. Septuagint (see Authorities Quoted).

masc. Masculine.

MS. Manuscript (plural MSS.).

M.T. Masoretic text.

*P.B.* Authorized Daily Prayer Book.

R.V. Revised Version.

sing. Singular.

viz. Namely.

# INDEX

## I. Names and Subjects

# INDEX

## II. Hebrew Words

# INDEX